RED LETTER NIGHTS

RED LETTER NIGHTS

*A Survey of the Post-Elizabethan Drama
in Actual Performance on the London
Stage, 1921-1943*

by

JAMES AGATE

BENJAMIN BLOM  New York/London

First Published 1944
Reissued 1969 by
Benjamin Blom, Inc., Bronx, New York 10452
and 56 Doughty Street, London, W.C. 1

Library of Congress Catalog Card Number 71-91886

Printed in United States of America
at Westbrook Lithographers, Inc.
Westbury, New York

CONTENTS

5

CONTENTS

CONTENTS

CONTENTS

CONTENTS

9

CONTENTS

CONTENTS

CONTENTS

CONTENTS

CONTENTS

CONTENTS

CONTENTS

CONTENTS

CONTENTS

ACKNOWLEDGMENTS

My thanks are due to the proprietors of the *Sunday Times*, in whose columns all the matter of this book with the exception of one article originally appeared, for their courteous permission to reproduce that matter here.

Also to Messrs. Chapman and Hall (*The Contemporary Theatre, 1924, 1925 and 1926*), Victor Gollancz Ltd. (*More First Nights*), and George G. Harrap & Co. Ltd. (*The Amazing Theatre*).

DEDICATORY LETTER

ALAN DENT

MY DEAR ALAN,

I am not a believer in doing things by halves. The present volume is the complement to *Brief Chronicles*, and I offer it to you as I did the earlier book. It is made out of my notices of plays other than Elizabethan seen by me in actual performance on the London stage between the years 1921 and 1943. I have divided it into five sections — Restoration Comedy, Ibsen, Foreign Plays — whether in the original language or in translation — our own New Plays, and the pieces which have come to us from America.

Some readers, looking to find what was said about their favourite play and not finding it, will be disappointed. Not everybody will realize that in twenty-two years I have seen between four and five thousand plays. Or perceive that since this book is limited to one hundred notices, the method of compilation must have been one of dipping. In this I have tried to combine generosity with discrimination. There is some account of every Restoration comedy the London scene has retrieved during the period. There is an almost complete record of Ibsen, nearly all of whose plays have been produced in my time, in one way or another, in this hole or that corner. I believe the Foreign and American sections to be reasonably representative, and in the matter of the new English plays I have sought to choose the best. Nevertheless the reader may be worried by certain omissions. Some of these are accounted for by the fact that when the plays were first produced I was on holiday and did not write about them. Though I made it my business to see them at some later date I have not thought fit to invent a later opinion. Others because the notices are not worth reproduction. *Journey's End*? The plain truth is that I broadcast twice about Sherriff's tragic anecdote before writing in the *Sunday Times* about it. Which means that I had said over the air all I had to say, and more.

G.B.S. once declared that he could detect in Jane Austen the point at which she indulged in a cup of tea. You were my pupil during fourteen out of the twenty-two years covered by this book, and I feel I must leave it to some pedant of the German school to decide in which of these old notices the immense and highly critical stimulus of your presence first declared itself. Please see in this book a tribute to what I have sensed of your scholarship, perceptiveness, wit and love of the theatre.

JAMES AGATE

London.
November 10, 1943

RESTORATION PLAYS

THE COUNTRY WIFE
BY WILLIAM WYCHERLEY
(Phœnix)

BALIOL HOLLOWAY, ISABEL JEANS

THIS is the play to have kept old Polonius awake. Few writers have been more studious of grossness in thought and expression than its author. Conduct is notoriously three parts of life; misconduct is the whole of this outspoken comedy, which, until this week, had not been performed for nearly two hundred years. The characteristics of Wycherley are not in dispute; the point is whether we are to range ourselves with the censors or against them.

Considering first the dramatist's friends, we remember that Lamb took out a special licence legalizing the monstrous quality of this entertainment — the pretence that it was all a fairy tale happening in a land innocent of right and wrong. But that was only Elia's way, and I have never believed that he was really sincere in all that pleading for an airing beyond the diocese of the strict conscience. Lamb consented that Wycherley should divide the world into betrayers and betrayed with the same light-heartedness with which later critics permitted the creator of *Iolanthe* to apportion it between Liberals and Conservatives. But whereas politics may provide excellent fun, marriage is no joke, not even a poor one. To treat the sanctity of the hearth flippantly is to make enemies in both camps — among the serious-minded, who raise the moral question, and among the lax, who say that where morality is not regarded immorality loses its savour. On the whole, one takes Lamb's defence to be

23

thoroughly unsound. Leigh Hunt and Hazlitt were better champions, since they boggled at nothing and enjoyed their author straightforwardly and for all he was worth, which, after all, was the manlier way. There is something un-English about sneaking regard, and this, if you take away the fine writing, is all that Elia's essay amounts to.

Macaulay, of course, is the Big Noise among Wycherley's enemies. He rails against the man's immunity from criticism, and declares him safe since he is 'too filthy to handle and too noisome even to approach'. But perhaps we need not bother our heads too much about a critic who could deem Boswell a fool. When Macaulay, discussing Wycherley's old age, says that he can conceive nothing more miserable than the figure made by 'this ribald old man' among those rising poets, Addison, Philips, and Rowe, we realize that he is talking the purest and earliest Victorian nonsense. A later Victorian was still echoing Macaulay when he described Wycherley's dialogue as possessing the 'miasmatic radiance of a foul ditch shimmering in the sun'. Yet not even the bitterest detractors of the playwright have been able to deny him the possession of talents of a brilliant order. Even Macaulay concedes ingenuity, observation, and patience in the work of polishing. What about the dramatist himself? There can be little doubt, I think, that he posed as a satirist and reformer of manners. All that we know of Wycherley points to a man almost grotesquely covetous of literary fame. He had no feeling for poetry and was a versifier of mean calibre. He was devoid of sentiment. From the expression of his countenance, 'suggestive of a poet who had married a dowager countess and awakened to the situation', we divine that he snatched at the mantle of the satirist, and used it to cover his relish for the low. It was in this garb alone that he could hope to capture the town.

The Phœnix Society's performance, following upon the heels of the Congreve revival, brought up these old judgments for fresh examination. Let us agree that Wycherley's wit is to Congreve's as a taper to the sun. This is not to say that wit was not in the older writer. Lady Fidget's rebuke to Mrs. Dainty: 'Fy, fy, fy, for shame, sister! whither shall we ramble?' — is, on the stage, and given the context, as witty as anything in Congreve. The author of *The Way of the World* has the air of a *grand seigneur* who has dropped a diamond in a rubbish heap and would recover it at the point of his cane. Whereas Wycherley is one with his rubbishy world. He enjoys the rough-and-tumble, and is at home in it. He has ten times Congreve's gusto, though he lacks his good taste, and owns a superiority in vigour, naturalness, and the art of telling a story which make up, or very nearly, for the inferiority in style. Strip Millamant of her satins and laces and she ceases to exist; reduce Mrs. Pinchwife to her native woollens, and she is unchanged. There is nothing in *The Way of the World* to equal the letter-writing scene in fun, plausibility, and theatrical effectiveness.

Wycherley's coarseness of language is neither here nor there — even Macaulay was not troubled about a matter of fashion. But the coarseness of mind is more difficult to overlook. There is hardly any pretence that the satirist does not enjoy the state of things satirized; indeed, it is obvious that he revels in it. Congreve saved our faces with some polite pretence as to passion; there is none in Wycherley, whose characters are given up to uncontrolled appetite. No moral laws are broken in this play, not because it takes place in fairyland, but because its author has no conception of morality. His domain is the slope leading to that chaos in which even the polite world must perish. Yet one has to be extraordinarily careful in bringing accusations of a wilful attempt to debase the public mind. We remember what happened to Flaubert, and what stupid people thought and said of Ibsen. The same charges which have always been brought against Wycherley were levelled at Choderlos de Laclos, who, one hundred years later, in *Les Liaisons Dangeureuses*, drew an equally candid and unflattering portrait of French society. 'A barrack-room Satyricon!' said Nodier of the book of which Baudelaire was to declare that if it burned, it burned with the fire of ice. Yet this can never be Wycherley's quality, and one will boldly continue to deny him any moral impulse, and say rather that his talent lay in lighting a bonfire in St. James's Park. At this he warmed his hands, rejoicing in the glare which it cast upon the fashionable promenaders. There are people who divine a thesis behind this comedy — that if husbands were not tyrants wives would not be faithless — who suggest that the piece is a forerunner of *A Doll's House*. Do not believe it. The thing is a guffaw, and a rude one. If virtue is not made a mock of in this play, care is taken that the virtuous people shall all be fools; the rogues are rated according to their success in roguery, and the fops blamed because they have not wit enough to be knaves. To sum up, we may pardon the verbal grossness of Wycherley, but not his ethics, or the lack of them. The framework and the subject of his picture are unpardonable, yet we cannot deny that the brush is that of a master.

Mr. Baliol Holloway once more proved how good an actor he is when he has an author and a part to stand up to. Horner's machinations make up a muddy sea, to be ridden boldly or not at all, and the actor ploughed through them with a will, and in the grand manner. We shall never know how Quin came to do such wonders with Pinchwife, unless we conceive him to have played it as Mr. Cellier and Mr. Randle Ayrton play Ford. The part proved an uphill one for Mr. Howard Rose. Possibly Mr. Stanley Lathbury did not get the full measure of humour out of Sir Jasper Fidget. Something richer seemed indicated, since the comicality of unfaithfulness must lie, not in the deceiver, but in the deceived. Contrariwise, Mr. Thesiger got more meaning out of Sparkish than was there. Miss Athene Seyler dealt adequately with Mrs. Pritchard's great rôle of Lady Fidget. But the feat of the evening was the Margery Pinchwife of Miss Isabel Jeans. This character has been exploited by all the great comic actresses of the past — Mrs. Knep, Mrs. Clive, Mrs. Pritchard, and, in the version called *The Country Girl*, by Mrs. Jordan, whose immediate success in it raised her weekly salary from four pounds to eight, and then twelve. But I find it hard to think that any of them can have bettered Miss Jeans, who got absolutely into Margery's skin, or have improved upon that look which stole into her face when she first glimpsed the possibilities of lying. I have not seen sufficient of this actress to make any definite estimate of her capabilities. It may be that as Lady Macbeth she would say, 'Give me the daggers, sweet bud', with the same air of roguish innocence. Even so, I vow I should be enraptured.

February 24, 1924

THE OLD BACHELOR
BY WILLIAM CONGREVE
(Lyric, Hammersmith)

O. B. CLARENCE, EDITH EVANS

How all the other passions fleet to air in the presence of acting like that which at Hammersmith embellishes this play's core! And also, let it be said, in the presence of such playwriting! Macaulay is right only as to this comedy's husk when he tells us that 'the plot is equally destitute of interest and of probability. The characters are either not distinguishable, or are distinguished only by peculiarities of the most glaring kind'. In all that concerns Mr. and Mrs. Fondlewife, Congreve copied Nature, except that like a good artist he made her wittier. No banker of the eighteenth or any other century has been vexed by the ugly passion of jealousy to such handsome expression of it as 'apocryphal elder!' and 'dissembling vermin!' What writing all through this scene for a boy of twenty! This part of the intrigue might stand by itself and is an understandable whole, in contradistinction to the rest of the plot, which nobody has ever unravelled or, succeeding, has deemed worthy of the task.

There is a moment in this scene in which Letitia throws herself in counterfeit dismay into Fondlewife's arms and accuses of lion-like audacity that harmless sheep Wittol, tumbled in horror upon a chair. Here, you say to yourself, is something that Zoffany ought to have painted, only to find that in all likelihood he did.

27

Then comes Bellmour's confession, and you wonder whether even Garrick could have had Mr. Clarence's sere and gentle pathos, probably to discover when you get home that not Garrick but King or somebody else was the better man in the part. Perfection should be rarely claimed, but whoso asked for anything lovelier than Mr. Clarence's playing here would be a too exorbitant counsellor. Then what shall I say of Miss Evans, playing with a roguery, an abandon, a zest, a fertility of gesture and expression, and a happy suiting of Millamant's great air to the more approachable class next below? Simply perhaps that she with Mr. Clarence and Mr. Eric Portman as Bellmour threw everything else int he play into the shade.

Except that Mr. Miles Malleson declined to be eclipsed. Was there ever so full, so rich, so varied, so blessed an inanity? This actor's Wittol proves that he must be the next great Aguecheek, and incidentally the character shows that Congreve had no silly scruples about borrowing, and like a good borrower could do it with a grace. But surely 'dear knight' was a trifle unblushing? Space is wanting to refer the excellences of a brilliant cast each to its respective character. I shall have to be content with the bare statement that Mr. Hay Petrie was an imp of joy, though a composer of acrostics might claim that 'imp' has been beheaded. But all the play's pimps, panders, go-betweens, and, by your leave, lovers did well, and one would pay a graceful if an omnibus compliment to Mesdames Diana Wynyard, Marda Vanne, Grace Wilson, Betty Baxendale, and Dorothy Dunkels, and to Messieurs Henry Hewitt, Roland Culver and Harvey Braban. As the old bachelor who vainly pretends to be the play's centre Mr. James Dale had a lonely furrow to plough, but he stuck to it manfully.

September 18, 1931

LOVE FOR LOVE

BY WILLIAM CONGREVE

(Sadler's Wells)

SAM LIVESEY, ROGER LIVESEY, BARRIE LIVESEY,
CHARLES LAUGHTON, MORLAND GRAHAM, JAMES
MASON, ATHENE SEYLER, FLORA ROBSON, ELSA
LANCHESTER

How stupid it is to apply moral standards to any work of art!
How ten times more stupid is it to apply to any work of art the
moral standards of an age other than that to which it belongs!
In our own time Mr. Maugham's *Our Betters*, Mr. Coward's *The
Vortex*, and Mr. Waugh's *Vile Bodies* seem to us, or did so seem a few
years ago, reasonable and faithful transcripts of life as it is, or was,
lived by a considerable number of people in these islands. It would
be interesting if we could know what would be the attitude to
these plays of critics a hundred years hence, wearing not our
white waistcoats, but Nasty Shirts or Commonest Blouses. Will
they continue in the nonsense of excusing us on the grounds that
we were allowing ourselves a breather 'from the burthen of a
perpetual moral questioning'? Or will they straightforwardly say
that we knew these plays to be both true and amusing, and had
the common decency to say so?

Perhaps this is to postulate the end of cant? Perhaps the age of
cant is already behind us? Perhaps we have ceased putting a
dramatist's characters to the moral test and no longer 'screw
everything up to that'? I am inclined to think that taste has
veered in the opposite direction, and that a play which does not
pass the improper test is in danger of having the lid screwed down
on it. Victorian mentality put the English in a woeful difficulty
with regard to Restoration drama. Wit, or the taste for wit, never
went with whiskers, so that the Dundrearys could only put Congreve beyond the pale, while not even English hypocrisy was equal

to muffling the legs of its pianos and then sallying forth to snigger over Wycherley. Last week's reception of *The Country Wife* and this week's acclamation of *Love for Love* suggest that we are at last coming round to the view that moral judgments have no place in art, and that plays, like people, are either charming or tedious.

The present coincidence enables us to put to the test a famous judgment of Hazlitt's: 'It may be said of Congreve that the workmanship overlays the materials: in Wycherley, the casting of the parts and the fable are alone sufficient to ensure success. We forget Congreve's characters, and only remember what they say: we remember Wycherley's characters, and the incidents they meet with, just as if they were· real, and forget what they say, comparatively speaking.' In a great measure one agrees, while jibbing a little at 'We forget Congreve's characters'. Would it not have been better to say that Wycherley, having found his characters in Nature, invented something memorable for them to do, whereas Congreve, taking Nature as his basis, elaborated his characters to the point of fantastication without finding anything coherent for them to perform? Perhaps Hazlitt was feeling his way to this when he said of Congreve's best play: 'It is in essence almost too fine; and the sense of pleasure evaporates in an aspiration after something that seems too exquisite ever to have been realized.'

So in a way it is with *Love for Love*. Valentine and Ben, old Foresight and Sir Sampson, Scandal and Tattle, even the ladies — all these seem perfectly realized while, even as you watch them, vanishing into the air of their author's exquisite prose. Thus the evening has little to do with the unfolding of a story, but resolves itself into a series of fleeting impressions. One moment you have the illusion of seeing the stage as though some painter had grouped it; the next minute it is your ear which is being enchanted with the miraculous orchestration of Congreve's dialogue. In retrospect, then, what one sees is never quite a play, but some other devising of Beauty for which it is worth sacrificing the excitements of human action and motive.

The performance at Sadler's Wells has an all-round excellence which makes it difficult to know whom to lead off with. Valentine, the hero, is the play's worst part, being no more than a peg for the actor's personal airs and graces; Mr. Barrie Livesey provides these in abundance. Ben is the very broth of a part, negativing failure, but to which few actors can have brought Mr. Roger Livesey's happy naïveté; he is the young salt to perfection and looks like a drawing by Morland. A colleague's 'pig-headed splendour' is so good for Mr. Sam Livesey's Sir Sampson Legend that the wind is quite out of my sails; this ogre looms large and round and over-red, like the sun through fog. Mr. Laughton makes Tattle a delicious figure of fun and under-breeding, a mixture of wiggery and waggery, at once coy and servile, male yet mincing. This Tattle is a Roi Soleil about whom still hangs the barber's shop of his probable upbringing. Mr. Morland Graham's Foresight is a saga of senility almost dazzlingly ludicrous, and there is a clever performance of the servant Jeremy by Mr. James Mason. That Mesdames Seyler and Robson cannot make more of Mrs. Frail and Mrs. Foresight merely proves that the play is by Congreve and not Wycherley, and if I fault Miss Lanchester's highly amusing Miss Prue it is only because her hoydenism seems to me urban rather than rustic; such a chit has climbed more steps of areas than trunks of trees.

The grandeur of the evening as both enterprise and entertainment need hardly be stressed. It was graceful of Mr. Laughton to come forward at the close and demand our applause for the three Liveseys, and it was a legendary moment when Sir Sampson took a son in each hand and led them to the footlights.

March 6, 1934

THE WAY OF THE WORLD
BY WILLIAM CONGREVE
(Lyric, Hammersmith)

ROBERT LORAINE, EDITH EVANS

CHARLES LAMB did a world of mischief when he put before his most famous essay the title *On the Artificial Comedy of the Last Century*. Sitting at this performance of the greatest prose comedy in the English language, I could not, for the life of me, see anything artificial in the personages beyond their inessentials — dress, speech, and polite notions. Manners change, but not the man who wears them. If Lady Wishfort is artificial, then so, too, is Falstaff. I see equally little reason why Congreve's hot-handed widow should be so superfluous to demand the time of day, except for the causes assigned to that other gormandizer. Wishfort is all appetite, and as real as any canvas of old Hogarth or modern page of Zola. One of her kind attends dinner parties to this day, less her candour and wit.

Millamant, too, could go into any novel of Meredith, *mutatis mutandis*, and having regard to the topics which a more generous age has conceded to the sex. Wit of Millamant's order is imperishable, for the simple reason that her creator gave her a mind. Lamb's celebrated excuse for compunctionless laughter is that these creatures never were. The truth is that they are, and always will be. 'The effect of Congreve's plays', says Hazlitt, 'is prodigious *on the well-informed spectator*.' It is easy to pronounce as artificial a world of which you are ignorant; in the Hebrides *Our Betters* would doubtless be dubbed fantastic. There are more Wishforts and Millamants about town to-day than there are Hedda Gablers. Mirabell is a poseur, but he does not date one-tenth as much as Wilde's Lord Henry Wotton. And as for Sir Wilfull Witwould, one of his kidney sold me a horse no later than Wednesday last. Congreve, in a word, was the well from which Sheridan, Wilde, and our own Somerset Maugham have drawn their 'natural table-waters'. Without, I venture to think, quite so much naturalness.

How is the piece played at Hammersmith? For all it is worth, is the answer; and perhaps just a teeny-weeny bit popularized; we could do without that business with the chandelier and the be-wigged orchestra. The play is keyed up to the highest pitch known to classic comedy. It may be that Mr. Playfair was afraid to trust us with the pure distillation of the Comic Spirit; it is much more probable that he recognized that in Miss Margaret Yarde he had a Wishfort who must prove a moral and physical eruption in — to use Prince Hal's phrase — flame-coloured taffeta. It was a first-class performance, striking alike to eye and ear. There was cut-and-come-again, you felt, in the way of grotesque, unbridled fancy.

But what of Millamant? Almost everything, is our answer this time. Never can actress have spoken the epilogue with less belief in its aptness:

> There are some critics so with spleen diseased,
> They scarcely come inclining to be pleased.

This was not true of those who on Thursday came to see, not only the old piece, but the speaker of the epilogue fulfil prophecy. Let me not mince matters. Miss Edith Evans is the most accomplished of living and practising English actresses. Leaving tragedy to Miss Thorndike, she has a wider range than any other artist before the public, and is unrivalled alike in sentimental and brittle comedy. A year or two ago there were to be seen at intervals upon the London stage elderly spinsters with white hair purring the fire out in vacuity. These tabbies were all Miss Evans. Her *dévote* in *Les Trois Filles de M. Dupont* and her housemaid in *I Serve* showed a quality of pathos which, one thought, had left the scene with Mrs. Kendal. This actress's Cleopatra in *All for Love* might, though tragedy is not her *forte*, have hung without discrepancy among the Lelys at Hampton Court. Her performances in *Heartbreak House* and *Back to Methuselah* are too glitteringly new to need recalling. Her Mistress Page was the quintessence of gaiety.

I am tired of recounting all this, but the thing has got to be per-sisted in. Miss Evans has simply to be dinned into the most insensitive of auricular appendages — the ear of the West End manager. They say that, by the tape-measure, this actress has not the fashionable type of feature, for all the world as though her business were to grin before a camera. Bluntly and frankly, I will agree that if I wanted to hire a chit to carry a banner in a panto-mime I should not engage this artist. But if she does not possess rare beauty in the highest sense, then I know not that quality. This countenance is replete, as was said of Congreve's style, 'with sense and satire, conveyed in the most pointed and polished terms'. This acting is 'a shower of brilliant conceits, a new triumph of wit, *a new conquest over dullness*'. You could hang any one of this player's portraits on the sky, and challenge the Zodiac.

And why?

Her Millamant is impertinent without being pert, graceless without being ill-graced. She has only two scenes, but what scenes they are of unending subtlety and finesse! Never can that astonishing 'Ah! idle creature, get up when you will' have taken on greater delicacy, nor 'I may by degrees *dwindle* into a wife' a more delicious mockery. '*Adieu*, my morning thoughts, agreeable wakings, indolent slumbers, all ye *douceurs*, ye *sommeils du matin, adieu*' — all this was breathed out as though it were early Ronsard or du Bellay. And 'I nauseate walking', and 'Natural, easy Suck-ling!' bespoke the very genius of humour. There is a pout of the lips, a jutting forward of the chin to greet the conceit, and a smile of happy deliverance when it is uttered, which defy the chronicler. This face, at such moments, is like a city in illumination, and when it is withdrawn leaves a glow behind. One fault I find, and one only. Millamant's first entry bears out Mirabell's announcement: 'Here she comes, i'faith, full sail, with her fan spread and her streamers out.' The actress made her appearance something lap-wing fashion, a trifle too close to the ground. It is possible, too, that Mrs. Abington gave the whole character a bigger sweep. Miss Evans conceived her as a rogue in porcelain, and kept her within that conception. Walpole, one feels sure, would have had civil things to say of this performance, of which the perfect enunciation was one of the minor marvels.

The Mirabell of Mr. Robert Loraine was a trifle on the sober side, but showed distinction if a trifle too much heart. The part was beautifully spoken, and the actor used only the suavest and most gentle notes in his voice. He listened exquisitely. Miss Dorothy Green made great music of her lines, and Messrs. Playfair and Norman enjoyed themselves hugely.

February 10, 1924

THE PROVOKED WIFE
BY SIR JOHN VANBRUGH
(Embassy)

MERVYN JOHNS, JULIA CRAWLEY, MARDA VANNE

IN a little-known anthology entitled *The English Dramatic Critics*, I find this passage, culled from the *London Chronicle* of October 7, 1758:

It is amazing to me that Mr. Garrick will *attempt* the part of Sir John Brute; a part which he not only apparently *mistakes*, but in which he is absolutely prejudicial to the morals of his countrymen. Quin made him a Brute indeed, an ill-natured, surly swine of a fellow; and I dare swear everybody most heartily despised and detested him: But with Garrick it is quite a different case; the knight is the greatest favourite in the play; such a joyous agreeable wicked dog, that we never think we can have enough of his company; and when he drinks confusion to all order, there is scarce a man in the house, I believe, who is not for that moment a reprobate in his heart. In truth he is so very much the entertainment of the audience, that, to speak in a phrase which Sir John Brute might be supposed to make use of himself, whenever he goes off the stage, we are like so many people sitting round a table

35

after the wine and glasses are removed, till he comes on again.

Carefully avoiding the temptation to declare that Mr. Johns, whom one is seeing for the first time, is another Garrick, I say without hesitation that what the dramatic critic of the *London Chronicle* wrote of the great actor's performance in this part applies also to Mr. Johns, though we should have to see the two performances together in order to judge to which it applies the more. This is not so foolish as it sounds, for I guess that the stage is emptier when Mr. Johns leaves it than when Garrick did. This for the reason that Garrick left behind him Mrs. Cibber and Mrs. Clive as Lady Brute and Lady Fanciful. Whereas Mr. Johns leaves on the stage two actresses, one of whom, in my opinion, has not sufficient of the particular talent required, while the other, though a very talented actress, is entirely miscast. Even Mrs. Cibber, acknowledged to be a grand actress in the right part, was alleged to want a trifle of spirit in the character of Lady Brute. But I can find no justification for Miss Julia Crawley's whole-hearted melancholy. Nobody admires more than I do Miss Marda Vanne's genius for representing the sturdy, commonsensical woman of to-day. But to suggest that this is right for Lady Fanciful is like casting Mrs. Siddons for Mrs. Dombey. One of the Embassy actresses has no manner at all; the other lays it on so thick that we see through it. As a flibbertigibbet Miss Vanne puts the old play in the cart, from which Mr. Johns marvellously extricates it at each and every appearance. This is a magnificent performance which would have warmed the heart-cockles of the old playgoers. 'Can any man wonder like him?' asked Lamb about Munden. It is certain that no actor of to-day can stare like Mr. Johns. Many things help this player. He is Garrick's size and looks like a Zoffany come to life. But I think he is chiefly helped by his talent, which is up to every demand made upon it by this magnificent part. In this actor's hands Sir John is a brute indeed, not a puling mooncalf but a roaring bull. But there is more to it than that. Mr. Johns lets us see the pleasure he is taking in the fellow's

brutish gusto. There are actors who could make the man as unbearable to an audience as he was to his own circle. If Quin did
this he was wrong, and Mr. Johns, by lifting a corner of the
brute's mind to show us his own, is right with Garrick. The
Embassy production of this delightful play contains one other
good performance, Mr. Christopher Steele's most amusing thumb-
nail sketch of the Justice.

October 8, 1936

THE CONSTANT COUPLE

BY GEORGE FARQUHAR

(Arts)

ALEC CLUNES, AVICE LANDONE

IF one were lecturing on George Farquhar's *The Constant Couple* to
a class of school children, I imagine one would say something like
this: 'Dear boys and girls, this is not a nice play. Why? Because it
is about people who are not nice. You all know that we are sent
into this world to behave ourselves, and if we don't we are
punished. When you children misbehave you have to go and
stand in the corner. But Farquhar does not make his grown-up
people stand in the corner. Indeed, he thinks they are very
amusing grown-ups, and his play about them invites us to condone
the wickedness which makes them amusing. A great poet called
Tennyson advised all young men "To love one maiden only, cleave
to her, And worship her by years of noble deeds". But Farquhar's
characters are sadly lacking in the Tennysonian spirit. They
have no notion of cleaving; indeed they think it dull. Still
less did this most reprehensible playwright agree with that great
living novelist who recently told us that the object of love is to
create a "hypostasis more beautiful, vital, and lasting than ourselves". Whereas naughty, earth-minded Farquhar asks us to
accept the passion of love as understood by Sir Harry Wildair and
Lady Lurewell — names of horrid significance — as "a sterile

37

pleasure and no more". Stop fidgeting, children! What is it, Tommy? You don't know the meaning of "hypostasis"? I'm ashamed of you. It is a Greek word meaning a concept or mental entity conceived or treated as an existing being or thing. That will do for to-day.'

Addressing older students, one might run through some of the nonsense uttered on this subject by Macaulay. One would, perhaps, go on to point out that even so great a critic as Hazlitt could fall headlong into the old trap of confounding art with morality. That in the matter of Jonson's *Volpone* he denies its author gusto because he doesn't like the things the gusto is about. He desires that comedy shall make him think better of mankind, whereas reasonable persons will demand of comedy only that it shall make them think. *Volpone* he calls 'cross-grained', 'prolix', 'improbable', 'repulsive', and even 'revolting'. Yet he cannot help saying that the play 'is written *con amore*'. This sentence clinches my argument. Substitute *The Constant Couple* for Jonson's masterpiece, and every word of the foregoing applies.

The old habit of confounding dies hard. Many modern critics have complained of what they have called the 'absurd' and 'unnatural' scene between Sir Harry Wildair and Angelica. They have only to turn to Maupassant's delicious story, *Une Soirée*, to find the exact counterpart enacted in modern times in a small town in Brittany! The more respectable half of the plot is concerned with the belated coming together of Colonel Standard and Lady Lurewell. Of the Colonel, our old friend Archer says that he is a 'bluff, honest soldier, not a saint, but still less a black-guard . . . Gives clear evidence of an innate decency of feeling denied to other playwrights of the time . . . The character is not very vividly drawn'. What Archer is trying to say is that he is a bore. By the way, whenever he could forget that he was a Scot and a confessed puritan the critic of the *World* was capable of great perception; he was the first to make out a case for Farquhar as a better *dramatist* than Congreve, Wycherley, or Vanbrugh. He points out that when Congreve strayed into the country he took his London cast with him and made a house-party of them, whereas Farquhar made a play out of the people he found at Shrewsbury and Lichfield. But fuller consideration of Farquhar's standing must be left to the time when criticism is not written on a postage stamp.

Mr. Alec Clunes does not pretend that the hero is one of Congreve's wits, but gives him all of his author's good humour and sincerity, which the other neither dreamed of nor aimed at. After fifteen bumpers of burgundy his Sir Harry is still a gentleman. Lurewell is nicely played by Miss Avice Landone, though I think she should put a deadlier poison in her venom. Mr. Billy Shine is extremely amusing as the 'prentice turned beau. It is given to this character to speak a passage which puts in a nutshell all I think about Restoration Comedy: 'Sir, I admire the mode of your shoulder-knot; methinks it hangs very emphatically, and carries an air of travel in it; your sword-knot too is most ornamentally modish, and bears a foreign mien.' When I hear English like this, morals can go hang.

August 1, 1943

THE BEAUX' STRATAGEM

BY GEORGE FARQUHAR
(Lyric, Hammersmith)

NIGEL PLAYFAIR, EDITH EVANS

'IT is my ambition', said Mr. Playfair, as the curtain fell on this brilliant revival, 'to restore the old English comedies to the place to which they rightly belong, the English theatre.' Those were fair words, and the audience cheered them. But it takes two to realize an ambition of this sort; in addition to the restorer there must be a public to connive at the restoration. Mr. Playfair will forgive me if I say that in this matter he is very much in the position of the auctioneer at a horse-sale who, pointing to some noble beast curvetting and caracoling in the straw, can do no

more than say: 'Gentlemen, I leave the animal in your hands.'
The revival of this famous piece is something more than an
occasion for adding to your collector's bag. Farquhar's comedy
is no mere curio. You may get greater zest from it if you are
fortunate enough to have some instruction in literary genealogy.
You may conjecture that if Congreve was Sheridan's father,
Farquhar counts Goldsmith among his immediate issue. You
may hazard that in the scene in which he dissolves the marriage
between the Sullens Farquhar shows an understanding of that tie
which is two hundred years before his time. You may reflect upon
the foolish sayings of the wise, and recall Pope's 'What pert, low
dialogue has Farquhar writ!' It may entertain you to remember
Taine's misunderstanding: 'On a passé une heure, et violà tout;
le divertissement vous laisse vide, et n'est bon que pour occuper
les soirées de coquettes et de fats.' The point is that you may
journey to Hammersmith unencumbered by any of this academic
baggage, and be sure of a delightful play which demands nothing
for its appreciation except your own untrammelled mind. Mr.
Playfair would be well advised not to confuse the public with the
restoration issue. Let him announce simply: 'The best show in
London.'

The last production of *The Beaux' Stratagem* on the grand scale
was in 1879, at which period English playwrights seem to have
been considerably exercised as to the propriety of revivals. Thus
we find Boucicault writing: 'I no more desire to see the defunct
dramatist occupying the stage than I wish to see my grandfather
rise out of his respected tomb and reclaim my inheritance.' To
which a critic of the period retorted that not everyone was in a
position to regard the public stage as his own private property.
This particular revival appears to have been a low-spirited affair,
largely marred by the fact that the part of Mrs. Sullen was entrusted to a soubrette instead of an actress possessed of the grand
manner. The part was originally played by Mrs. Oldfield, and
I found myself wondering on Thursday evening whether an
actress living and playing in the first years of the eighteenth century could have had her successor's exquisite period-sense. The

answer, surely, must be in the negative. To Oldfield 1707 was
not a period but the time of day, and Mrs. Sullen was to be seen
in any box at Covent Garden. Given that the older actress's
emotional, intellectual, and aesthetic equipment was equal to that
of her successor, to what extent can the two performances be
identical? For Miss Evans brings to the part more than faithfulness; she brings also a knowledge of that which only a very few years
ago it was fashionable to call emancipation, and an implication
of the altered relationship between the sexes. No actor, though he
be steeped in Pirandello to the very lips, can make Aimwell and
Archer other than the high-spirited sparks of Farquhar's imagining. Is it fancy, reason, or the intoxication of the delighted sense
which, as we gaze at the new Mrs. Sullen, makes one see her
double? Does not Miss Evans set beside her literal presentation
something which we might call a critical estimate, a revision of
the character as seen through modern eyes? Does she not bring
to the modish ornament a delicacy and perception which were no
part of the feminine equipment of Farquhar's day? Take her
first words. Dorinda says: 'Morrow, my dear sister; are you for
church this morning?' I find it hard to believe that Oldfield's
'Anywhere to pray' can have had behind it an impertinence, a
malice, and a scorn which would not have been out of place in
the mouth of Clara Middleton or any other six-foot of Meredithian
womanhood legging it healthily to her devotions over six miles of
hill and dale. Must not the eighteenth-century actress have filled
with a sense of present injury the passage beginning: 'O, sister,
sister! If ever you marry, beware of a sullen, silent sot,' instead
of informing it, as Miss Evans does, with the amused recollection
of a chatteldom that is past? These may be vain imaginings; but
one reflects that the beauty of an exquisite performance is far-
reaching, and may open more avenues than the artist suspects.
The love-scene with Archer was played with the last refinement
of wit and spirit, and it was a pin-still house which marvelled as
the actress breathed out the closing passage: 'Look ye, sister, I
have no supernatural gifts — I can't swear I could resist temptation; though I can safely promise to avoid it; and that's as much

as the best of us can do.' I will vouch for it that here was an emotion which the dramatist never glimpsed. Yet to this modern quality was added one older than Farquhar: the actress having divested herself of her hoop, the bosom upon which she sighed became Celia's, and round about them rose up the Forest of Arden. Great playing has this merit, that it makes the mind free of time and space, and sends the imagination of the spectator blowing where it listeth.

There was a moment of something resembling pathos when Miss Evans recited the epilogue in which the dying playwright pleaded for his play. Sir Edmund Gosse has told us that Farquhar was half actor and quarter poet, to which one would add that in the practical business of living he was one hundred per cent failure. He knew the value of money to a farthing and expired in a garret without one. In spite of seven plays, all of which were reasonably successful, he died at the age of twenty-nine 'leaving nothing to perpetuate my memory but two helpless girls'. The playwright was as wrong in his estimate of his genius as about everything else. As an actor he could not pretend to kill a fellow-player without wounding him so badly that he had to give up the stage. As a wife-hunter he could not marry a rich woman without finding out after marriage that she hadn't a penny. As a soldier he could not sell out of one regiment on a ducal promise of a captaincy in another without hitting upon a duke who did not keep his promises. And he left two comedies, not knowing them to be immortal.

Nothing being duller than undiluted panegyric, let me say that it was unkind of Mr. Playfair to cast introspective Mr. James Whale for that pure blockhead and dolt, Squire Sullen, and still unkinder to entrust the part of Dorinda to an actress of insufficient experience, thus leaving Miss Evans high and dry without anybody to play to. In compensation Mr. Playfair himself delighted inordinately, and had the co-operation of Messrs. George Hayes, Scott Russell, and Miles Malleson, while Mesdames Winifred Evans and Dorothy Hope were perfectly agreeable.

January 20, 1927

MARRIAGE À LA MODE

MARRIAGE À LA MODE

BY JOHN DRYDEN

(Lyric, Hammersmith)

GEORGE HAYES, ANGELA BADDELEY

NOBODY is going to risk saying that Dryden is a dull dog. But what he might do is to shelter himself behind Professor Saintsbury, who says with appropriate solemnity: 'Dryden's want of lightness on the comic side does not seem to me more fatal than his want of pathos on the tragic. That he shares this to some extent with Corneille is true: but this is no exoneration. A tragedy of the highest class without "the pity of it" is almost inconceivable.' Is it impious to suggest that a comedy of the highest class without the fun of it is equally inconceivable? Take away Melantha, the affected French-speaking moppet, and what is there left in this comedy to entertain? If it be argued that one has no right to suppose such an act of butchery, my defence would be that if you took away Dogberry or Touchstone or Sir Toby a good deal would remain. Without Melantha, Dryden's *Marriage à la Mode* would not, I venture to suggest, begin to stand the strain of stage-performance to-day. But Heaven be thanked she is there, and played by Miss Athene Seyler, and the pair make a riotous three hours out of a matter we should otherwise be glad to commend and have done with at the end of some fifty minutes. If that is too personal a view I apologize for it. But is anybody really interested in what actually happens to the philanderers, or amused by the fact of their philandering? Here, surely, one falls back upon the wit and the reflection that the piece must originally have had the bite of current satire. Is anybody moved by the story of the preposterous foundlings and their more than tedious progenitor? Here one falls back upon the stately, stilted lines, the decorum of the diction, the wiggery and haberdashery adorning the actors, and the reflection that instead of listening to Dryden you might have had to listen to one of his forbears.

43

Professor Saintsbury writes: 'I am not myself fond of the theatre, but I should like to see one of these [Dryden's] plays acted.' I claim to be as fond of the theatre as any man may be who must go to all of it, and hope Sir Nigel in his sudden enthusiasm for Dryden's plays is not going to give us the lot. 'Undoubtedly, however, the curse of the musical drama is a curse never fully escaped by anybody.' Here again I join issue. This play, in my uneducated view, could not have been too greatly overloaded with all those trappings, musical and scenic, for indulgence in which Sir Nigel is occasionally teased. Scenically Sir Nigel has put himself and us on the shortest possible commons. In the matter of music he has engaged Mr. Alfred Reynolds to decorate the piece with an occasional chord, and as to this, I can only say what the French dramatic critic said on the occasion of an early performance of Goethe's *Egmont*: '*Musique de Beethoven. Hélas, pourquoi y en a-t-il si peu?*' May it be pleaded once more that the emission of whoops of joy on any and every occasion is an exhausting business, and that to express moderate delight is no sign of discourtesy to project or players? An hour of this piece was enchanting; after that honesty compels me to say that I should have preferred to look at something else. 'That will do, child; you have delighted us sufficiently,' applies to other entertainers besides Mr. Bennet's daughter. Even the Professor seems to doubt the effectiveness of Dryden in the modern theatre, since he says: 'If, especially in his plays, he is to be liked, it can only be by persons who love literature for itself, who can see and can taste good work wherever it exists, on whatever subject and in whatever fashion it presents itself.' Nobody is going to deny that Dryden was a literary swell or that for anybody with a *tendre*, as Melantha would say, for the seventeenth century this production is the perfect banquet.

The piece had the finest possible polish put on it by the players. Mr. George Hayes discovered a fine superbity in Palamede, which was perfectly matched by the insolence of Mr. Anthony Ireland's Rhodophil. Mr. Herbert Waring as Polydamas, Usurper of Sicily, presided majestically over the tragic revels, and in blue doublet and puce hose came near to shedding purple tears. As the envious Argaleon Mr. Richard Caldicott contrived to be agreeably nasty; as Hermogenes Mr. Scott Russell did everything expected of foster-fathers in classic dilemma; and perhaps in some other play we shall see Mr. Glen Byam Shaw fulfilling his early promise. As Palmyra Miss Angela Baddeley nicely parcelled out her emotion and spoke beautifully. As Doralice, Miss Adèle Dixon was good, and a similar encomium shall be passed upon Miss Kathleen Boutall for her Philotis. A quintet of other ladies merited bouquets for their respective and fragrant minutes. Of Miss Seyler's Melantha, coiffed in magenta and caparisoned *à outrance*, it is only necessary to say that she played the tripping fool to the top of her delicious bent. One word of criticism: one actress described somebody as being 'a law*r* to me', while another said: 'The Princess Amalthea*r* is at hand', and another: 'O Melantha*r*, I can tell you!' This habit of introducing an *r* between two vowels and in other unnecessary places is a vile one, so much so that upon one occasion even the Dalmatian dogs, who formed part of the Usurper's retinue, barked.

October 9, 1930

THE SOLDIER'S FORTUNE

BY THOMAS OTWAY

(Ambassadors)

BALIOL HOLLOWAY, HUNTLEY WRIGHT, LESLEY WAREING, ATHENE SEYLER

'Wot 'ave you got there, mate?' asked one Tommy of another carrying a sandbag. And received the reply: ' 'Arf of effing France, and 'ad to walk the other 'arf to fetch it!' In the matter of these Restoration comedies half the cant in the world has to be cleared away, even if we have to walk the other half to find a place in which to dump it. Anybody who should think he had rendered this bawdy old comedy inoffensive to modern ears would be deceiving himself. 'Have you heard the argument? Is there no offence in't?' asked Claudius of Hamlet. To which that young man returned his famous reply about the galled jade. Of course there is offence in *The Soldier's Fortune*, and it is alike in conveying that offence and enjoying its conveyance that the skill of this play's actors and of its audience lies. For not to offend would be to miss its whole point, while not to revel in the offence would be clumsy playgoing! There is an old theatrical chestnut about a street tout offering to Lady Gorgius Midas the synopsis of Dumas's *Dam o' Cameleers* and being repulsed with the words: 'We have come to see the acting. We have no desire to understand the play!' It would be the height of playgoing hypocrisy to pretend that one went to the theatre to enjoy Otway's wit and not the subject of it. Otway was no near-knuckler; he dealt in the knuckle itself. One understands that a well-known farinaceous sweet, according to the suburb in which it is encountered, is dubbed blanc-mange, mould, or even shape. The English language has scores of periphrases for the one name which Desdemona would not speak, and which Othello had called her. But Otway does not go round about, and we are to suppose that his Sir Jolly Jumble would hardly know what you meant by such refinements as 'courtesan' or even 'harlot'. One word resounds throughout this piece, which might be described as a fanfare on Otway's trumpet.

The plot is of an intricacy which suggests that Restoration audiences must have attended more intently than modern ones. The kernel of it is this. Sir Davy Dunce, a snuffy, elderly husband, is allowed to think that he has caused his wife's lover to be murdered, and that his only chance of evading the consequences is to put the body, in which there is faint hope of life, into his wife's bed, draw the curtains, and leave it to the lady's ministrations. The whole imbroglio has been devised by Sir Jolly Jumble, a Peeping Tom whose heart, like that of *Lear's* old lecher, is a small spark, all the rest on's body cold. It should be said straight away that the revival is justified and saved by Mr. Roy Byford's Jumble.

There is a gusto about this actor for which Lamb would have claimed, as he did for Munden, the quality of ennoblement. As with the older actor's tub of butter, so Lady Dunce's four-poster, contemplated by Mr. Byford, amounts to a Platonic idea. But it would be wrong to imagine that Otway's fun is wholly indecent. Take that scene in which Fourbin, the valet, primes a footpad called Bloody-Bones in the matter of the pretended murder. Fourbin begins:

> War, friend and shining honour has been our province, till rusty peace reduced us to this base obscurity. Ah, Bloody-Bones! ah, when thou and I commanded that party at the siege of Philipsburg, where, in the face of the army, we took the impenetrable half-moon.

The playgoer of that day would know what was meant by 'half-moon', a military phrase to be made familiar later on in the mouths of My Uncle Toby and Corporal Trim. But Bloody-Bones does not know his cue and replies: 'Half-moon, sir! by your favour 'twas a whole moon!' Fourbin then asks Sir Davy if he thinks his rival Beaugard has a heart. Sir Davy has the reply: 'Oh, like a lion! he fears neither God, man, nor devil.' Whereupon Bloody-Bones, bettering instruction, says: 'I'll bring it to you for your breakfast to-morrow. Did you never eat a man's heart, sir?' To produce its proper effect this should be uttered in the tone in which the driver of the coach turned to little David Copperfield and asked him whether he was a breeder of Suffolk punches. The dialogue continues:

> SIR DAVY Eat a man's heart, friend?
>
> FOURBIN Ay, ay, a man's heart, sir; it makes absolutely the best ragout in the world: I have eaten forty of 'em in my time without bread.
>
> SIR DAVY O Lord, a man's heart! my humble service to you both, gentlemen.
>
> BLOODY-BONES Why, your Algerine pirates eat nothing else at sea; they have them always potted up like venison: your well-

grown Dutchman's heart makes an excellent dish with oil and pepper.

SIR DAVY O Lord, O Lord! friend, friend, a word with you: how much must you and your companion have to do this business?

FOURBIN What, and bring you the heart home to your house?

SIR DAVY No, no, keeping the heart for your own eating.

What great fun it all is! Sir Davy is asked two hundred pounds, and replies: 'Two hundred pounds! why, I'll have a physician shall kill a whole family for half the money!'

But the whole piece is full of permissible joking as well as impermissible. There is many a good phrase like Sir Davy's determination to 'crack the frame of nature and sally out like Tamberlane upon the Trojan horse'. And here and there a well-placed word like Lady Dunce's 'I tell thee, Sylvia, I was never married to that *engine* we have been talking of'. There is one little matter to intrigue the pedants. 'Curse on my fatal beauty!' says Lady Dunce, and the two points which arise are whether this is the first time the figure was used, and whether, when he made Archibald Grosvenor say, 'A curse on my fatal beauty, for I am sick of conquests!' Gilbert was consciously cribbing. The play is very well put on at the Ambassadors. Indeed, I am not sure whether with regard to one character the dressing is not a little too sumptuous, Courtine's clothes being much too tidy for his own description of them, and Mr. Anthony Quayle being too well in flesh for one of whom his mistress says: 'Considering he eats but once a week, the man is well enough.' Mr. Baliol Holloway as Beaugard sets the piece in the right key from his first words and keeps it there throughout the evening. Mr. Lawrence Baskcomb and Mr. Franklyn Kelsey extract all possible fun out of Fourbin and Bloody-Bones. And, as it is unnecessary again to praise Mr. Byford's Sir Jolly, this brings me to Mr. Huntley Wright's Sir Davy Dunce. In many ways this is a first-class performance, animated and ludicrous, and full of the sting of cuckoldry. But there are odd phrases which suggest that Otway did not intend the old man to be pure butt, and at moments we thought that Mr. Wright was going to treat the part as Mr. O. B. Clarence would treat it, though whether this would run the play out of gear cannot be determined unless one saw it. As for the ladies, Miss Lesley Wareing as Sylvia does very prettily, and Miss Athene Seyler is exactly the actress for Lady Dunce. She revels in the salacious salad and invariably chooses the right word to roll on the tongue. Miss Seyler keeps it up to the end, and informs the whole character with a perfect sense of its profound enormity.

October 6, 1935

IBSEN

THE VIKINGS AT HELGELAND
(Old Vic)

ESMÉ CHURCH

WHAT seeds, if any, of Ibsen's later genius has *The Vikings*? 'Embryos', said Samuel Butler, 'think with each stage of their development that they have now reached the only condition which really suits them.' Is this a general truth, or is there no rule in the matter? Corot did not become the Corot most of us know until he was seventy, and one doubts very much whether the Corot who for fifty years had devoted himself to absolute definition had any inkling of the feathery masterpieces to come. Did the thin trickle of early Verdi grow consciously into that mighty sap, or did it suffer miraculous change? Did the early genius of these two die and another kind of genius take its place? Or are we, as Butler points out, merely giving the name of death to a change so great that it destroys our power to recognize resemblances? So it is the natural thing to ask what promise *The Vikings* holds of the staider glories to come. In what berserk utterance shall we find the forerunner of, say, 'Mark my words, Mr. Hovstad, the baths will become the focus of our municipal life!'

At first sight the promise held out by Ibsen's early play was that the author was about to re-write the whole of Shakespeare's works. Ornulf's speech to his son is Polonius's advice all over again. Hjördis's 'Kill Sigurd!' is Beatrice's 'Kill Claudio!' all over again. An old man, being told that his son received his hurts before, replies: 'That is an honourable place!' and his refusal to mourn is an obvious echo of Siward's: 'He's worth no more!' The old fellow's threat of dread intention: 'I do not know what I shall do; but it will be enough to set men talking, far and wide', is Lear's:

> I will do such things —
> What they are, yet I know not, but they shall be
> The terrors of the earth.

And we feel that the only thing which prevents him from entering with his child in his arms is that he has just buried the brat. Actually another enters *to* the old boy carrying another dead child. Finally, there is Hjördis, who is another Lady Macbeth, the ambitious help-meet steeping her woman's breasts in gall and resolved to crown her thane. 'Erik is King of Norway. Pit yourself against him, and never rest until you are seated on the King's throne.' Yes, there can be no doubt that Ibsen at thirty had absorbed his Shakespeare. Alas that his regurgitation was that of the journeyman rather than the poet!

Or can it be the translation? Remembering the American's definition of Matthew Arnold, 'Nowhere to go for a laugh', one might define Archer as Nowhere to go for poetry. The use of 'hight' and 'wist' and a general conformity to the 'nathless-and-yclept' atmosphere are not poetry. *The Vikings* is always spoken of as a 'poetic romance'. Perhaps it is, in the original.

One finds, however, a graver fault than diction, which is that the play has no total significance. It is just a long, rambling, and rather tedious tale springing from two fountain-heads, which we might call (*a*) feminine imbecility and (*b*) masculine idiocy. Hjördis, in the third act, is a terrific creature who says: 'Mine is not the light love of a weak woman; happiness is worth some great deed to win it.' Yet we are asked to believe that, loving passionately one of two suitors, she left it to the chances of a fantastical combat with a white bear which should have her. The men are even sillier. Gunnar says he doesn't like white bears; whereupon Sigurd, who loves Hjördis with passion equal to Gunnar's, slays the animal and tells Gunnar he can have skin, credit, and woman all together. Was ever woman in such humour lost? The only trace of the old Ibsen that I find in the young one is that Sigurd's sacrifice is shown to be idiotic. The end of the play must always be irresistibly comic. Hjördis shoots Sigurd, after which and prior to jumping into the sea and riding to Valhalla across a rainbow, she informs him that now at last they belong to each other. 'Not so,' says Sigurd, and, with his last breath, tells the young woman that whilst he was over in England King Athelstan converted him to another faith. Here, in the young man, one sees the old boy of the later plays grinning at the inability of ultra-heroic people to manage even their tragedies sensibly. These too passionate lovers have made a mess of it, after all!

The Old Vic company put itself to great expense of purpose. Hjördis calls for an actress of what one might call outdoor scope, one who can put up an exhibition of black rage while the heavens lower; Miss Esmé Church is obviously a player of great ability, but one who would be better suited with an indoor rôle. Miss Iris Baker, though pretty and charming, was about a thousand years too modern. Her Dagny looked and spoke like one whose address might be The Icebergs, Floe Road. The gentlemen of the company shall be described as 'werry fierce'. Throughout, the play reminded one of a Wagnerian music-drama without the music. Which did not prevent the audience from punctuating each act with respectful applause.

October 1, 1928

THE PRETENDERS
(O.U.D.S.)

IBSEN's *The Pretenders* is his sternest, grimmest glorification of that hard condition, twin-born with greatness, which has irked so many self-centred rulers to no more than a gentle melancholy. The English Henry's 'What infinite heart's-ease must kings neglect, that private men enjoy!' is a purely selfish lament. 'Every one must go who is too dear to the King!' cries Haakon, banishing in a single sumptuary swoop both mother and mistress. Here, in a nutshell, is the philosophy of kingship. Kings are to consider not how jolly a thing it is 'to sit three steps above the floor', but how best they may fulfil their trusteeship and serve the kinghood which is in their meanest subjects. In this play Ibsen blares this nineteenth-century thought through a thirteenth-century trumpet. Harald the Fairhaired conceived it better for King Harald that Norway should have one ruler in place of a hundred. Haakon sees that it is better for Norway that she should be a 'nation' instead of a 'kingdom'. It is the people who exist by divine right and not their kings. Ibsen makes immense play with the idea that a country which is only a kingdom is 'a church which has not been consecrated'. Earl Skule, who would have Haakon's place, owes his defeat to his failure to rise to the heights of the 'great kingly thought' which he would usurp. His son, believing in the authenticity of Skule's thought, breaks open the church and violates the shrine that his father may be crowned king. This misfeasance works the wrong way; the superstitious soldiery defect. Whereupon Skule, in all humility, gives up the ghost. 'A man may die for the sake of the life-work of another; but if he is to live, he must live for his own.' And Haakon, who can trample the pride of rule under foot, goes forward to unwilling personal victory. 'His body blocks my path.' *Dagfinn*: 'If Haakon is to go forward, it must be over Skule's body!' *Haakon*: 'In God's name, then!'

It is not to be imagined that this *leit-motif* is easily detached. Even at this early date Ibsen was busy at his baffling game of keeping two plots going, a ground-floor of bricks and mortar, and a symbolical superstructure. Fail to get the hang of the upper story and you may well think yourself in the basement of a lunatic asylum. Rosmer inviting Rebecca to throw herself into the mill-race 'to show her confidence', Hedda handing Lövborg the pistol, Solness toppling off his steeple with Hilda crying 'Bravo!' — people really don't do such things, and it takes all Ibsen's mature genius to persuade us that given an extra spiritual dimension this may be sanity. But at thirty-five he was not very clever at the game. The ground-floor of *The Pretenders*, with its story of changelings and intercepted letters, is as complicated as a play by Sardou or Scribe. It is also a great deal less lucid, with the result that in fumbling for the symbolical staircase you bark your shins against a good deal of downstairs mahogany. To make confusion worse confounded add the overpowering figure of Bishop Nicholas. In the early acts this character has all the darkling imagination and inveterate horror of old-fashioned melodrama; it is only at the end of his tremendous death-scene that you in any way connect him with the play's philosophical basis. Only at the very end are you allowed to see that his malignancy springs from innate disability to grasp that kind of power which Haakon despises and Skule cannot leave behind. This materially towering character pulls all the play's strings; it is only at the last that you perceive him to have a finger in the philosophic pie. All this makes the play very difficult to act. There is hardly any 'furniture' in the later and avowedly symbolical dramas. Rosmer has a hat and stick, Hilda Wangel a kit-bag, and so on, but these are obvious imponderabilia. Whereas *The Pretenders* makes enormous parade with trials by ordeal, armies in rout, the paraphernalia of prelacy, and panoplied death-beds such as actors love. The dying of Bishop Nicholas is a collector's piece in the way of virtuosity. Unfortunately, it occurs in the middle of the play, with the result that no great actor will look at it; if only the bishop could have been kept going to the end, it is conceivable that old Irving would have had a shot at him.

Ibsen, we are told, used the historical struggle between Haakon and Skule to mirror his own unwilling jealousy of his successful rival Björnson. We need not labour this theory too much. It fits, but then these things always fit. Skule has the uneasy consciousness that the other's triumph is at once easy and deserved. Haakon possesses, as Bishop Nicholas puts it, *ingenium*, or the quality which Lord Beaverbrook and Mr. Selfridge insist upon as the true foundation of success. Haakon is the favourite of fortune, the born leader, begetting thought greater than he understands, following a path of which he cannot see the end. Skule's jealousy does not prevent him from recognizing his rival's great merits; it is in fact he who is their chief exponent and, as Ibsen's mouthpiece, does the bulk of the talking. In this great wilderness of a play much, perforce, must be cut, but it is a pity, surely, to cut the essential clues, as was done at the performance by the O.U.D.S. Obviously Haakon must have the 'great kingly thought' before Skule can be jealous of it. Unfortunately his sacrifice of mother and mistress was cut, and his reluctance from a personal victory minimized. Some of the critics, writing of the performance under their eyes, described Haakon as a man of physical courage only. This, it seems to me, is entirely to misunderstand the character. 'Am I to think that the king is made of different stuff from me?' wails Skule. Of course he is; of different and better stuff. That's the whole point. Haakon is inclined to talk a bit tall, through his spiritual hat, as it were. Like all Ibsen's great men he is a bit of a braggart. His spiritual bragging cut, Mr. E. L. Bush (Trin.) could perhaps do no other than play him like some stalwart, boasting for the *dedans* in the Oxford tennis-court. This it probably was which misled the critics. Earl Skule was much nearer the Ibsen spirit. I do not know what Mr. A. H. Howland (Worc.) thought of the part, but he looked hot and bothered, which was exactly right. Mr. G. G. Edwards (Oriel) gave a finely modulated, subtle performance of the most grateful part ever devised for an actor, except, of course, for the deep damnation of its cutting off in the middle of the evening.

February 25, 1922

PEER GYNT
(O.U.D.S.)

ROBERT SPEAIGHT

It must be a fine thing to be young and at Oxford, to wear pull-overs more gorgeous than the necks of pheasants, to proclaim flaming hopes of a Theatre of Ideas in which the world's master-pieces shall be constantly revived. Let me not dash youth's ardour by suggesting that this country knows no such theatre.

After all, the peculiar virtue of hope lies in the hoping, not in the realization.

Writing in 1896 of the performance of Ibsen's philosophic poem at the Théâtre de L'Œuvre, Mr. Shaw predicted an English vogue round about 1920. He was more or less right about the date, and more or less wrong about the vogue. Rapture at the 'Old Vic' spells something very different across the river. To affirm that the Boyg, the Button-Moulder, and the Strange Passenger would in our time — or, indeed, in any time — become as familiar to the English people as Shakespeare's Witches or Goethe's Mephistopheles — this was just Mr. Shaw's youthful fun. Your average English playgoer takes to the Witches in *Macbeth* because he is not compelled to think about them, and can simply accept them as part of the scenery, like the battlements at Elsinore; and it may be doubted whether he knows sufficient of Goethe's Mephistopheles to climb into the saddle of cogitation, Gounod's familiar personage being a horse of an entirely different colour. But the whole point about Ibsen's queer fish is that you *must* think about them. In the way of concrete, self-sufficing drama, standing tub-like on its own bottom — such drama as Hamlet's stabbing of the arras and his cry, 'Is it the King?' — these rum folk don't bear thinking about. Or, put it the other way round, and say that it is only by thinking about them that they can be made bearable. Now, thinking in the theatre may be fairly good meat for the Norwegians; it is still, whatever Mr. Shaw may say, pretty average poison for audiences assembling nor'-nor'-west of Waterloo.

The truth of the matter is that *Peer Gynt*, like *Faust*, falls into two parts, the second of which can never be intelligible unless it is acted in its entirety. The first half is as mother's milk — none can be so poor of imagination as not to behold his own boyhood in this shaggy Norwegian Hamlet. Ase's death is one of the most grandly inspired things in all romantic drama. The boy astride his chair, driving his mother hell-for-leather to the gates of Heaven, and all to the honour and glory of his wild, poetic, impossibly romantic self — this is a conception not above, nor below, but beside Shakespeare.

How great a poet Ibsen is in his own language I have no means of knowing, but even in translation the closing passage of this scene attains to marvellous beauty. Peer, his frenzy over, and closing his mother's eyes, has this requiem:

> For all of your days I thank you,
> For beatings and lullabys!

In its place, on the stage, there is nothing in all Shakespeare to shame 'beatings and lullabys'.

And since comparisons are going, then

> Saint Peter! you're in for it now!
> Have done with these jack-in-office airs, sir!

might be likened to the voice of Browning.

Up to Ase's death there is nothing which the most intrepid producer can cut, except, perhaps, about half of everything everybody has to say, and all the queer political allusions. No bulk excisions are possible. But two hours have passed, and less than two remain for all those diffuse yet reinforcing experiences of Peer's later life. Forty years of greed, vanity, egotism, braggadocio, heartlessness, sentimentality, courage, cowardice — each quality a facet of Gyntism, a way of 'being oneself' — if Ibsen could not get this into two hours it is certain that his abbreviators can't. What, then, is the proper thing to do? The obvious thing, one says hastily, is to cut all such irrelevances as gibes at the King of Sweden, and the note-mongering habit of Norwegian and Swedish officials. But the matter isn't as easy as all that. The scene in the mad-house, in which these apparent excrescences occur, is one of the most exciting in the whole play. The Fellah with the mummy on his back, the Pen which insists upon cutting itself, Peer's terror, his collapse and ironic coronation — all this is great drama to the eye, though it is not until Begriffenfeldt gives the shout 'Long Life to Self-hood's Kaiser!' that we can 'connect' with the central self-realization *motif*.

All honour to Mr. Reginald Denham that he retained this mad-house scene. Incidentally, the staging and grouping here were both expressionist and admirable. (Perhaps Huhu, who is no more than a skit on language-reformers, might have been omitted.) All honour to Mr. Denham, and his advisers, if any, that he retained the exquisite speech of the Pastor speaking beside the grave. Perhaps there was not quite enough insistence on Peer's smug reflection that he, too, is just such another simple hero as the dead man, who was, in fact, precisely his opposite in character. But amends were made in the Onion Scene, showing man to be all layers and no core—'Nature is so witty'. We were not to have the 'pig' speech, but we got most of the boat. Among the lost treasures was the scene in the water after the shipwreck, where Peer half-drowns the Cook and then holds him up by the hair so that he may mumble the, at that moment, irrelevant petition for daily bread. But we had the Strange Passenger's second appearance, and the whole meaning of the play was driven home by a full-length presentation of the Button-Moulder.

I am not sure that any producer, however skilful, can prevent the audience from interpreting Solveig's last consolatory appearance as the conventional Lyceum apotheosis of Redemption by Love. This is Peer's view of the situation which Ibsen is at such pains to deny. Demolition ought to come in the Button-Moulder's cackling threat that they will meet again at the last cross-road, 'and *then* we'll see whether . . .' His voice trails away. What is to be seen at the last cross-road is whether a good woman's love can redeem a weak man's paltriness. But that is in the future, whereas what the audience sees is Peer preparing to take his flight into Abraham's bosom *via* that of Solveig. And this ending is too comfortable and too little disconcerting not to be eagerly accepted by the sentimental.

At Oxford all the armoury of intelligence was used to keep this second part together. And yet the attempt failed, as it always must. One felt as if one were at the heart of meaning though unpossessed of its easier, more negotiable fringe. Thus a voyager lost in the bowels of a ship among the engines, and anxious to get his head above deck with a chance of asking the captain where he is making for. But Ibsen was never your man for a plain answer to a plain question, though he delighted in making a pet point some dozen or score of times. How tired we got at Oxford of those repeated expositions of the true meaning of 'being oneself'! And perhaps we didn't very greatly care how soon the middle-aged Peer ceased to be himself or anybody else! Peer in tattered shirt and with tousled hair is one thing: Peer in a caftan and, later, an abominable plaid deer-stalker, ear-flaps and all, is another. His tragedy is spiritual and profound, but it isn't visually too entertaining, and perhaps Mr. Kipling put it all rather more amusingly in *Tomlinson*. And the Button-Moulder, what a bore! Vital though he is, and the most important person in the piece after Peer, he becomes an intolerable nuisance round about half-past eleven. How he harps on the same worn string! How he must chop infantile logic with himself so that it sounds like an imaginary conversation between the authors of *Donovan* and *Robert Elsmere*. If there is any more tedious character in the play I should plump for Peer himself in his salacious moods. A clammy, cold mist has been declared by one great critic to enwrap Ibsen's sensuousness. 'The people cry up the roses and raptures of Swinburnian ethics in tones that would freeze a faun and send a Bacchante to the nearest Methodist chapel in search of doctrine less shiversome.' I agree. Peer as a middle-aged roué is unutterably depressing. *Read* Peer's tragedy, and you still see the fascinating boy in the maundering, mouthing compromise for a man. But see him on the stage fingering a greying beard, shaking the ponderous flaps of that awful deer-stalker, and leaning heavily on his umbrella, and you reflect first that the eyes of the mind and the eyes of the body are two different things, and second that the early caricaturists and parodists of Ibsen were not very wide of the mark.

Mr. R. W. Speaight gave an excellent performance of the youthful Peer. The impetuosity, the vanity, the adventure, the *excitement* of living were all admirably suggested. The prating boy's imagination was on fire, and that of the audience was soon sympathetically alight. The young actor's voice and gestures were extremely good; there was subtlety and modulation in both. If there was a fault here it was that Peer was too lovable. He lacked the uncouth husk, the gnarled ferocity which made him disliked of all his world. In the later scenes, which demanded the momentum of a much older player, Mr. Speaight was not very successful, and indeed could not hope to be. He was obviously a boy who had surrendered cranium and chin to the artifices of the admirable Mr. Willie Clarkson. But there is more than wiggery in the elder Peer. Mr. A. Tandy gave the Parson's long speech most beautifully, and if Mr. Gyles Isham (last year's Hamlet) thought he could cloak his fine delivery under a pseudonym and the mask of the Strange Passenger he was mistaken. Messrs. A. E. Franklin, J. H. James, J. Maud, L. Nye, and particularly H. Grisewood (the Button-Moulder) must be singled out for special praise. Miss Clare Greet was very moving throughout Ase's dying, and, realizing that the scene is really Peer's, she was content like the great artist she is to subordinate her share. Miss Joan Maude as Solveig looked and spoke prettily, and Miss Eva Albanesi's Anitra was pleasant. A large orchestra acquitted itself nobly under Dr. W. H. Harris, and the occasion was a great one, even for Oxford.

Let me end by repeating my admiration for Mr. Denham's producing. The lighting throughout was admirable, and so was the drilling. You could not have guessed that the cast were nearly all amateurs.

February 10, 1925

A DOLL'S HOUSE
(Duke of York's)

AUSTIN TREVOR, LUCIE MANNHEIM

THE fact that Ibsen's *A Doll's House* — I entirely decline to call the play *Nora!* — is being revived this week suggests that we should make up our minds once and for all where we stand in the matter of plays dating. There is a school which holds that with the emancipation of women this great play has lost much of its sting and tang. I do not agree, if only for the reason that the burning agitation over Women's Rights never, so far as I was concerned, gave this play any of its sting or tang! I am of the school which holds that there is a very good case to be made for Helmer, that Nora is a born dunce, a natural liar, and an incorrigible cheat, and that the world is no place for canaries to gad about in. That, in short, the proper place for a song-bird is its cage.

But it would be monstrously uncritical if dissension from everything Ibsen preached in this play should prevent one from realizing that it is, among prose dramas, the entire and perfect chrysolite. Being perfect in its day, it cannot date now. I am much more worried about another matter which concerns the nineteen-thirties, and moreover this particular year and this particular month. It has been maintained until one is blue in the face that the saving of the theatre in this country lies with the people who can afford only the cheaper seats. There are over a hundred pit-seats at the Duke of York's, and on Friday night only four of these were occupied. This is disgraceful. I am ashamed of and for our pittites. It is useless for the elderly and middle-aged to plead that they have had their fill of *A Doll's House*; they ought to want to see a new Nora, just as concert-goers ought and do want to hear a new reading of a symphony which they know by heart. As for the juniors, I just do not believe that every young person in London, excepting four, has seen this masterpiece. They cannot have done so because it is fourteen years since it was put on for a run.

It is not as though this production were frowsty, routine, hugger-mugger, dull, and just yet one more perfunctory effort of some notoriously tired and effete management. This is a *new* management horribly let down at its first venture. Mr. Marius Goring has produced, in my view, excitingly. There are some things to disagree with, beginning with the amazing architecture of Torvald's summer palace, which appears to be on the ground floor of Park Lane's latest and most luxurious block of flats. I think Mr. Austin Trevor's Torvald looms too large and makes too much noise; Torvald may be a windbag, but he should be a windbag of charm. I think that Miss Lucie Mannheim's Nora should not be allowed to let off shrieks and whistles which suggest a railway-engine in hysteria. I think the lighting at the end is wrong, that Nora should turn up the gas before having it out with Torvald, who should not be left standing in a reddish glare like the hero in a drama by Hall Caine.

But there objections end. What an extremely clever actress Miss Mannheim is when she does not act too much! And how great is her variety! She does not sit about, as English actresses do, waiting for something to happen; she is always making something happen. A great deal of her Nora is exceedingly touching, and the end of the second act is very nearly the best I have seen. Which is some compensation for the end of the third act, which is very nearly the worst. How refreshing it is to see Mr. Trevor away from Balkan inanity and pursuing his avocation as an actor! How good are Miss Marian Spencer's Mrs. Linden and Mr. Harold Scott's Krogstad! It has been suggested that the author ought to have written a play on what happened to Nora afterwards. But Ibsen was a wily old bird. He probably realized that such a play must include the Linden-Krogstad nuptials, and that before the spectacle of that joylessness even he must draw the line! Dr. Rank is an actor-proof part, which does not mean that any actor must necessarily be so good as Mr. John Abbott. We shall probably never be told to whom in this production should be given the credit for Rank's final and astonishing exit. The man is a little drunk. He has lit his last cigar. He is going to an undeserved death. And he stands in that doorway with his back to the audience, in gala costume, with confetti on his shoulders, and on his forehead a mask to which is attached a balloon, baleful and ridiculous. It is as though Ibsen, foreseeing Strindberg and wishful to take the wind out of his sails, had thrown in an entire Strindberg play as a mere decoration.

February 3, 1939

AN ENEMY OF THE PEOPLE
(Old Vic)

ROGER LIVESEY

EVEN to the faithful Ibsen's play was always minor and unexciting. It was precious little use telling us, as in the early years of this century we sat shivering in unwarmed provincial theatres, that the first thing to note about this Public Baths drama was its place in the canon. What did it help us to know that the next play was *The Wild Duck*, which nobody had seen, and that the previous one had been *Ghosts*, which again none of us had seen?

Unless, of course, our provincial town was Manchester, when, with luck, we might have been present ten years earlier at one of those historic five performances given in the lecture theatre at the Athenaeum in Princess Street. A young man engaged in peddling calico at a salary of thirty shillings a week, less sixpence laid out on the *Saturday Review*, was so greatly excited by some articles signed G.B.S. on the plays of one Ibsen that he determined to do something about it. He made inquiries, and discovered the existence of a troupe of Ibsenite players, headed by Charles Charrington, Janet Achurch, and Courtenay Thorpe, which was in the habit of traipsing the country with baggage consisting of a single dress-basket and Helmer's front-door, complete with letter-box. Our young man decided to intercept the company, which had slithered from a mission-hall in Darlington to a drill-hall in Dover, and was hoisting itself up to Dingwall at the invitation of the Institute for Deep Sea Fishermen. They were met at some hole in the Midlands, the young man having collected £90, in cash, *not* promises, from the wealthy German Jews to whom he sold his calico, *no Aryan contributing a penny*. The result was that performance of which Montague wrote: 'Tragedy burned up the lamp that had held it, and flamed like a star, unconditioned and absolute.'

Now *An Enemy of the People*, the panjandrums said, was conditioned and relative. But relative to what? In 1882 that which lay behind this play was Ibsen's quarrel over *Ghosts*. What lies behind it in 1939? Why, Democracy's quarrel with Dictatorship, or, rather, Dictatorship's low opinion of Democracy. 'Democracy is the right of imbeciles to govern themselves,' said a speaker at a recent debate at the Oxford Union. And, so saying, unwittingly condensed the whole of Dr. Stockman's great speech in Act IV. Yes, this play, and its revival, are miraculously apt to the times, and I fancy that not only Nazis and Communists, but famished tigers and pet lambs will have to do a lot of lying down together amicably before it is seen for what it is — a rather dreary parable about a lot of pump water. In the meantime it makes an intensely exciting evening.

The Old Vic company acts it very well. The Doctor is the difficulty, and Mr. Roger Livesey gets out of it by steering a middle course between the adroit and lavish insincerities of Beerbohm Tree and the muddled grandeurs of Henry Austin. The part is one for a great actor who is careful not to let any of his great acting show. Mr. Livesey does not carry quite enough guns, though he is correct in keeping the waterproof covers on such guns as he does carry. Stockman is a cruiser cruising, and not a battleship giving battle. Mr. Edward Chapman's Peter Stockman is a brilliant and most amusing bit of character-drawing. Mr. Jonathan Field as the young man in the printer's office knocks up something out of nothing. Mr. Frederick Bennett wittily makes up Morten Kiil to look like Ibsen himself in the mood to rout the entire hedge-crawling brood. For this was the period when the old porcupine's bristles were at their prickliest. Or if you prefer the badger simile, the period when he did not wait to be drawn, but adjusted his glasses, sharpened his nose, bared his teeth, and came out into the open uninvited.

February 24, 1939

THE WILD DUCK
(St. James's)

ION SWINLEY, MILTON ROSMER, ANGELA
BADDELEY

THIS play, if only you leave the wild duck out of it, is a good deal plainer than any pikestaff I have ever seen. It is as plain as the nose on anybody else's face, only you must not shut your eyes to it. You must not say: 'I do not like snub noses. All plays about snub noses are bad plays. This play is about a nose that is distinctly *retroussé*. Therefore, this play is a bad play.'

How it would have warmed the cockles of Ibsen's heart — presuming that frigid organ to have had any cockles — to have been present on Wednesday night at the St. James's Theatre and note how every thrust and sally went home to an ordinary, middle-brow audience! Why, one asks oneself, should there ever have been doubt as to the drift of the play's extraordinarily lucid argument, or the meaning of its total gesture? What, apart from the duck herself, can the bogy have been? Let us admit that that fearful wild-fowl and eponymous heroine has always been something of a difficulty, and remains so still. Who is it, besides herself, that in this play dives down into the ocean-depths and bites fast hold of the weed, wrack, and all the rubbish down there? Gregers, we know, tries to fasten the symbol upon Hjalmar Ekdal, likening himself to the clever dog who goes down after the wounded bird and rescues her. But there is nothing of the wild duck about the photographer, who is nothing but the most ordinary domestic gander, mistaking himself for one of life's swans. Is she Hedvig, the child who sacrifices herself for her father? Or the old sportsman Ekdal? Or is the poor fowl not anybody at all but the spirit of Truth, Sacrifice, or any other of the abstract Virtues?

All sorts of theories have been held about this piece. The older critics, from Brandes to William Archer, held that in it Ibsen, disappointed at the reception of *Ghosts*, turned and rent his own

65

ideals like the man who bites his finger to allay a hurt elsewhere. Or, again, Ibsen might possibly be deemed to turn upon his public with some such savage cry as: 'I tried to show you how much good facing the facts about marriage would have done the Alvings. You wouldn't have that. Here I show you how much harm came to the Ekdals by having the facts about their marriage thrust upon them by a meddlesome idealist. Let's see if you like that any better.'

But is not the play quite easy if we disregard the petty, spiteful consideration, and look squarely upon it as standing by itself, isolated, yet a link in the chain of Ibsen's thought like a peak in a mountain range? Is it not possible that, for once in a way, the vaunted symbolism just did not come off? Leave the duck out of it, close that garret door, and the piece is perfectly plain. The whole point is obviously the mischief wrought not by truth, but by the indiscreet use of truth. Gregers, by his gluttony for an idealism which he can only half digest, shows us first that one of the effects of thrusting your finger into a pie may be to ruin it, and second, that the proper people to conduct that operation are the owners of the pie. No attack is made upon the sanctity of marriage: wrath and ridicule are poured upon the husband, whose mind is so entirely eaten away by false pretence, folly, and indulgence in sham sentiment that it simply cannot entertain a sane thought about anything in the world, sacred or profane. This play is bound up with all the others in this — that the beneficence of an ideal depends not upon the ideal, but upon the fitness to receive it of the person upon whom it is thrust. Is he ready for it? If so, then the thrust may be expected to come from within. The play is really an attack upon meddlers.

It is not to be thought that the acted drama is anything like as serious as the analysis of it must be. The whole of the action is centred in the preposterous carryings-on of the farcical photographer. He is glorious fun, and the audience at the St. James's laughed long and loud enough to make nervous wrecks of themselves for weeks. Mr. Milton Rosmer, made up to look like young Beethoven, poured out Ekdal like a glass of beer, toasted our sense of fun, and blew the froth in our faces. It was a capital, racy performance. Possibly there might have been a trifle more exaltation about the Gregers Werle of Mr. Ion Swinley, made up to look like young Matthew Arnold, but also looking and talking rather like one of those ineffectual tub-thumpers whose audience has dwindled to two ragged little girls and a baby in arms. But within the limitations of personality the performance was good, and there was no gainsaying its intelligence.

As Old Ekdal, Mr. Brember Wills put on the full armour of Ibsenite senility, and, attired in the panoply of his old shako, and somebody else's stable jacket, presented the kind of figure whom William Blake would have asked to tea. Anything more terrifying than the jut of that right brow overhanging that cavernous right eye, while the left interrogated the heavens with the despondent glare of a moulting vulture — anything fuller of awe than this I do not remember. As Hedvig Miss Angela Baddeley acted astonishingly well, breaking down in one place only when, after one of the most lacerating storms of childish weeping I ever remember, she lifted her head from the horsehair sofa and revealed a countenance innocent of all emotion. It may be that the films and the geyser-like Gish family have vitiated taste to the extent of making us demand real tears. I leave this to the actress, but somehow or other she must get agony into her countenance commensurate with her weeping. But the rest of the part was played in an entirely lovely manner. Gina was acted cosily and comfortably by Miss Sybil Arundale, and the rest of the cast was quite good. The setting and dresses of 1884 were admirable.

July 15, 1925

IBSEN

ROSMERSHOLM
(Kingsway)

CHARLES CARSON, EDITH EVANS

SHALL it be confessed that one went to *Rosmersholm*, that very rare Ibsenite bird, with something of trepidation? Would the play seem the same magnificent, confused masterpiece that one remembered from a quarter of a century ago, or would the might have left it and only the muddle remain? One half-expected to see the stalls filled with the devotees of the late 'nineties and early nineteen-hundreds shaking a few sad, last, grey, spectral hairs. But on Friday night, at the second performance, one saw none such. The theatre was full of the people of Mr. Noel Coward's generation, frankly carried away by what, to make no foolish bones about it, always was, and always must be, a stupendous work.

I am not going to pretend that *Rosmersholm* is not absurdly difficult. As usual, the old man began at the end, telling you nothing about the real motives for the first wife's suicide until the second act, and withholding the essential facts about the character of Beata's supplanter until the third act. Yet what you might call the lay-out of the piece is magnificent; as a feat of exposition it is equalled only by *The Wild Duck*. Compared with Ibsen the technician, the Gallic exponents of the well-made drama are children playing in a nursery. *Rosmersholm* shows Ibsen to have been a master of thematic material in the Wagnerian sense. The play's primal theme is the one which always took first place in Ibsenite denunciation — the imposition of ideals upon other people. This is split up into two subsidiary themes — the superstition of expiation by sacrifice, and that attitude towards life which may possibly mean purification, but certainly kills joy. These two themes come together again in Ulrik Brendel's last-act pronouncement: 'All the wisdom of the world consists in being capable of living one's life without ideals.' Then add all those

68

minor themes which make up the texture of this play — the connivance of Rosmer's world at what it believed to be his secret sins
because of the damage resulting to the Party from an injury to
the figure-head, the silence of the Opposition because it hoped to
bring Rosmer over, the storm of personal rancour which was
raised by Rosmer's defection in the abstract matters of religion
and politics. Properly speaking, these are incidents, but their
significance raises them to the dignity of themes.

Add again the great figure of Rebecca. Rebecca begins as a
mere adventuress, who is shaken first by the new breeze of feminine
emancipation, and second by the old wind of sexual passion, both
of which die down to give place to the settled calm of the higher
love. This is the point which so much perplexed the critics of the
early performances of this play. They did not deny the possibility of spiritual love which, nevertheless, they knew better when
it was called settled affection. They did not, for example, boggle
at Beata's possession of that quality; what they found difficult to
swallow was the subjugation by Rebecca of her all-conquering
egotism. Certainly the printed page has never made one quite
believe in the possibility of this, and it required the very finest art
of Miss Edith Evans to achieve the complete triumph. This
superb artist — and I use the word deliberately, accepting all the
challenges it implies — had already in the second act given us one
great moment, that of the rejection of Rosmer's love. In the third
act she really did convince us of the translation of clay into spirit.
Here the play took on some of the simplicity of the great prophetic
truths, and to ask oneself whether people in real life would behave
like this seemed beside the point and meaningless. The fourth act
was not so good, but then it never can be. Rosmer and Rebecca
drop from the status of figures in a vision to that of diseased and
monstrous egotism. Doubtless Ibsen intended them to take the
highest flight of all, the flight into pure tragedy. But what Ibsen
proposed and what the common sense of an audience is disposed
to accord are two different things.

I shall say no more of Miss Evans's performance except that,
in my humble opinion, it is the best thing she has done, full of

the most subtle gradations of feeling and of an intellectuality which is not astonishing only because one expects it. The part of Rosmer is unactable except for a happy fluke in the way of personality, and that good actor Mr. Charles Carson will forgive me if I think that he was not well suited. What was wanted was an *exalté* of the sort Mr. William Stack presents so well. Mr. Carson worked very hard, and obviously knew all about Rosmer. But he has the round, contented face of the man who prefers pottering round the links to morbid introspection. It would not have surprised me if, at any moment, he had taken up his hat and said: 'My dear Rebecca and brother-in-law Kroll, you bore me to tears. I am off for a day's fishing.' Incidentally, Mr. Rupert Harvey played the very ungrateful part of the schoolmaster exceedingly well. Mr. Robert Farquharson acted Ulrik Brendel with his usual happy mixture of amateurishness and genius. I thought his first scene exaggerated and ineffective, and his make-up a Christmas-party imitation of Walt Whitman, but deemed his second scene magnificent, not to be improved upon by any actor that I know. Miss Muriel Aked's Mrs. Helseth was so good that I hold it not to have been acting at all. The old lady was obviously brought from Norway in the 'eighties, and had been kept in pickle ever since. Mr. Farquharson Sharp has made an excellent version, giving the names an English and pronounceable twist. I recommend everybody to see this play, and to spend the previous evening with the printed score and a wet towel.

October 1, 1926

THE LADY FROM THE SEA and GHOSTS
(New Oxford)

ELEONORA DUSE

TELL me not in mournful numbers that Ellida Wangel is a young woman and Duse an old. There is no age for those whose art is of the spirit, challenging Time. Duse asks for no quarter; and if there are allowances to be made it is she and not we who must make them. To have no more Italian than suffices to cope with a prima donna is an obvious handicap; hot from the text, I still could not be quite sure where, exactly, the actors were. Yet the bigger the play and the player, the less the disadvantage. You may not catch the drift of Arnholm's 'He explained his circumstances to me clearly', but it doesn't matter. The fellow is lying anyhow; nobody in this play ever really explains anything, in spite of a habit of exposition which amounts almost to mania.

Ibsen plunges at once into the middle of his favourite mess — a second marriage. What a lot they are! The elder daughter by the first marriage accepts her former tutor whom she does not love, rather than that life should pass her by; the younger wants to be engaged to a consumptive artist for the sheer fascination of wearing mourning, 'all black, up to the throat'. Queer fish? You may well say that! as Ibsen's people are always remarking. Ellida herself, in cold print, is as mad as a hatter. Before her marriage she was 'promised' to a seafaring man, who besides being a murderer has the power to haunt a woman and to give her husband's child fishlike eyes. Ellida is virtually an amphibian, and divides her waking hours between her bathing-van and the sea. Is the Stranger's power hypnotic, mystical, occult? We never know. As usual, Ibsen builds his play like a house of two storeys. Above stairs, where symbolism reigns, everything is as clear as day; down below, where the characters are actually living and taking meals, all is dark and you bark your shins horribly. These people are mad on the ground-floor only.

This play is a godsend to a great artist whose *forte* is not so much doing as suffering that which Fate has done to her. With Duse, speech is silver and silence golden. It is not so much that she 'acts' when she is silent, as that your mind has leisure to take in the accumulated wealth of all that has been said with voice and face and hands. The voice seemed to me to be just as exquisite as ever; the arms, with their grave dance, eked out the old insufficiency of words; the face, in moments of emotion, lit up from within as though a lime had been thrown upon it. There was the old, ineffable grace, the childish importunacy, the raising of human dignity to a power undreamt of. The long second act was a symphony for the voice, but to me the scene of greatest marvel was the third act. In this Duse scaled incredible heights. There was one moment when, drawn by every fibre of her being to the unknown irresistible of the Stranger and the sea, she blotted herself behind her husband and took comfort and courage from his hand. Here terror and ecstasy sweep over her face with that curious effect which this actress alone knows — as though this were not present stress, but havoc remembered of past time. Her features have the placidity of long grief; so many storms have broken over them that nothing can disturb again this sea of calm distress. If there be in acting such a thing as pure passion divorced from the body yet expressed in terms of the body, it is here. Now and again in this strange play Duse will seem to pass beyond our ken, and where she has been there is only a fragrance and a sound in our ears like water flowing under the stars. The end of the play sees her definitely on earth again, reinforcing the old man's moral that freedom means responsibility. Wangel gives Ellida her choice, and she renounces the sea.

I thought all the acting excellent, particularly the Doctor Wangel and the Lyngstrand. To the eye the young girls looked more like startled fawns or *ingénues* from Meilhac and Halévy than Ibsen's scarifying young women; but the fault, I am sure, lay in my insufficient apprehension of what they were saying. There was not the smallest pretence that anybody was Norwegian; Como was stamped over them all. They are a rum lot, these Northerners. One found oneself wishing now and again that the Wangels would do as Mrs. Crupp advised, and 'take to skittles, which is healthy, and so divert the mind'.

The history of Ibsen's *Ghosts* should prove that whatever else may be wrong, conservatism cannot possibly be right. Some twenty or twenty-five years ago the keepers of our play-going consciences decreed that if we in Manchester were so perverse as to want to abet the Norwegian's attack upon morality and the purity of the home, we must confine our eccentricity to a concert hall and pretend to be the actors' guests. Well, we did so pretend. Who that was present at that great assault upon his conscience by Janet Achurch and Courtenay Thorpe could have believed it possible that in his lifetime this 'odious' play would be chosen by the most distinguished living actress for presentation before a fashionable West End audience, and at the same time fill the bill in a people's theatre in the East End? Surely conservatism would be hard pressed to explain this transition from the scandalous to the exemplary! I have not seen the production at the Pavilion Theatre, Whitechapel. A dramatic critic's lot is not too happy as it is; to submit twice in one week to so emotional a gruelling is to take an exorbitant view of one's duties.

Ghosts is one of the most complicated of the Ibsen dramas. It bristles with challenge, provoking one to ask the old impertinent 'What does it mean?' Impatiently one brushes aside the old inhibition against what has always been, after all, a very natural question. The whole bite of tragedy is the warning lest by like folly the spectator bring like disaster upon himself. But what warning can teach the spectator's father to have behaved himself? And if the play be no more than a warning to the onlooker to see to his hygienic p's and q's, is it distinguishable from a tract? Surely there's more here than that? Why should all the characters so persistently hymn the song of living, if the upshot of the whole thing is repression?

There are some uprooting things in the play. When Mrs. Alving warns Regina that she is going to her ruin, the girl replies, 'Oh, stuff! Good-bye.' And you know that she is going to work out her own destiny, and incidentally do very well for herself. The play is hemmed in with ideas as precipitous as the mountains sloping to the fiord, and one wonders whether, in the same way that the melancholy of the Irish may be traced to their soil, so these Norwegian aspirations may not be a reflection in the mind of natural escarpments. As that awful night wears on, so the tragedy thickens to complete hopelessness. Dawn comes, and we see the sun rise over the distant hills. There is something baleful

73

and uncannily significant in the actual presence of that red disc. Oswald asks for it to be given him, and repeats tonelessly, 'The sun, the sun.' There is more here than a pretty touch in madness. But what?

Eleonora Duse presents Mrs. Alving as though that character were a ghost hallowed by memory and time. This weeping, tender lady, bending over Oswald like some sad willow, is not the woman whom Ibsen drew, gazing speechless upon her stricken son and twining her hands among horrific hairs. This exquisite creature, moving from grief to grief in some grey saraband of woe, was not Ibsen's still rebellious woman whose egotism, hardly baulked, breaks out again in bitter mockery of Pastor Manders. There is a moment when Mrs. Alving recognizes that the root of the tragedy is in herself, in a joylessness so austere that her husband was fain to pass his life between lying at home on the sofa reading an old Court Guide, and the lowest dissipation. It needs a woman of big bone to stand up to such a slap in the face as Ibsen here administers; Duse was not to be offended so. When the fire breaks out, the Pastor has some sententious nonsense about a 'judgment upon this house of sin'. 'Yes, of course,' replies Mrs. Alving with withering scorn; the man is such a fool that he cannot be argued with. Duse delivered this as though it were a benediction. Her performance was instinct with resignation, whereas Ibsen's character battled it to the end.

And in the beginning, too. One could not help feeling that this Mrs. Alving was as little likely to have read those books which so shocked the Pastor as Manders himself. It was incredible that she could ever have clinked glasses with her drunken husband. She blames her 'cowardice' that she has not openly encouraged her son to marry his half-sister. Duse utters the words, but we do not believe that she would have given the thought entrance to her mind. As well credit ribaldry in the mouth of a Madonna. Far truer, in my opinion, was the Mrs. Alving of Janet Achurch. This was Ibsen's heroine, a mountain of fierce egotism, of warped, twisted self-assertiveness. Janet was ungainly, and had none of Duse's exquisiteness. To see the Italian actress move, draped as she always is like a queen, is a whole folio in ecstasy, her play of hands about face and robe a revelation. Janet waddled; she hitched and thrust at her dress like a washerwoman; she was impatient of every kind of beauty. Yet she was alive, human, and warm, full of mockery, of revolt, and at the end, of horror. Ibsen meant the end of this play to be horrible, and would have resented any refining into Aristotelian suavity. He meant to shock, and to shock prosaically and provincially. The tragedy takes place in a little country town as *borné* as Balham; that this is dumped down by the side of a fiord makes no difference.

Janet Achurch sailed no blue and gold apartment, the doors of which would have fitted a palace; you could not have carved her tenderness upon a frieze as you could Duse's; she did not soothe you into accepting grief as a part of human heritage to be expressed in beauty. She brought you face to face with unendurable shock.

Signor Memo Benassi gave this impression of the purely unbearable. True that he did not present a pathological study of the same fidelity as Mr. Courtenay Thorpe's; there was no growing terror, since no more obviously healthy young man ever stepped. Signor Benassi strode the stage like Mr. Cyril Tolley after a 69 at St. Andrews. But when the first of his two great outbursts came, what a flood it was! Great and noble artist that she is, Duse gave the young actor the whole stage and effaced herself completely. There is no mawkish reticence about an Italian player in an agony, and it was a relief to hear someone make a noise. If only Duse would break that deadly, still monotony, even at the cost of something harsh and ugly! Lowness of tone is not the whole of acting. I do not want to be misunderstood. Duse is a very great artist who, nevertheless, gives one the impression of scorning to be an actress. She has nothing of what the Germans call *Humor*, and only the aftermath of passion. One feels that she would play Lady Macbeth like a wounded dove. She is always herself, her fastidious, beautiful self. So, you say, was Bernhardt. But Bernhardt had a hundred different ways of being the same person. She could shake Heaven and Hell; Duse breathes only a sigh. Sarah, in the mind, still flames and glows; Duse lingers like some exquisite, faint regret.

June 10 and 17, 1923

HEDDA GABLER
(Everyman)

MRS. PATRICK CAMPBELL

Hedda Gabler is a tremendous play in any but the strict sense of the word. It contains nothing of awe or terror, nothing to make us fearful lest our own *exaltées* should take to pistol-practice in the garden. Yet what a vogue was Hedda's in that heyday of long ago! Her lure was largely that of the incomprehensible. Who could read her? 'Kennen Sie Ibsen?' 'Nein, wie macht man das?' was a current joke. But 'How should Hedda be played?' persisted. Mr. Archer declared her to be the victim of hyperaesthesia; Mr. Beerbohm plumped for a woman under-sexed and under-vitalized. Mr. Shaw made some unforgettable pronouncement which I have forgotten; Mr. Grant Allen pretended that he was sent in to dinner with her every evening. All of which made one envious of that moral courage which could insist that the king in the fairy-story was without clothes. These clever persons seemed to me to be labelling something which was not there. Hedda, as she existed in real life before Ibsen's flaming genius transfigured her, was an earlier sister of the wood-carving young woman in *Kipps*. She was lymphatic, and a nuisance to any normally constituted society. But she was not dangerous, as was the Hedda of the play.

Some women do some of the things which Ibsen's heroine does, but no woman perpetrates them all. Let me admit that Hedda was bored, oh exquisitely bored, with Tesman, his slippers, his aunts, his aunts' illnesses and dyings and bonnets and midwifely pleasantries, Tesman's researches into the domestic industries of Brabant, his lack of talent, his spinelessness. Let me take into

76

account the atmosphere of yesterday's cold mutton which pervades these provincials at heart, the insufferable tedium of even the capital in a country of stoves and goloshes. Let me remember that Hedda was 'ninety-ish' in a society which saw not the modish possibilities. All this explains why she should marry — Tesman, in the worst event — philander with Brack, and ache to have a finger in the Lövborg pie. Fastidious yet curious, repelled by life yet attracted, she was the descendant of the patrician who, aloof from the arena, was sufficiently interested to turn down her thumb. Hedda has been called 'mesquine'. It is just that pinchbeck quality which leads her to steal Lövborg from Mrs. Elvsted, to provoke his befuddlement and to destroy his masterpiece. But that she would have put the pistol into his hand or used its fellow against herself I do not believe, nor will all the courtier-like worshippers of Ibsen make me believe it. There is no symbolism in *Hedda Gabler* upon which we can ride off into the clouds. When Hilda Wangel claps her hands at Solness's fall and acclaims it as a magnificent achievement, we know that she is speaking a language to which common sense holds no key. But there is nothing undecipherable about the present play. Put to the touchstone of rationality, it leaves a doubtful streak. Hedda, conceivably, would have urged Lövborg to the precipice; she gives no sign of the courage needful for that ultimate push. Nor yet for her own desperate leap. Brack's 'People don't do such things' is Ibsen's effort to prevent criticism, just as a playwright will sometimes strive to get behind verisimilitude by putting into the mouth of a character some such phrase as 'If we were people in a play...'

Not in the least like Ibsen's Hedda, Mrs. Patrick Campbell gives us a magnificent portrait of somebody else. Consider Ibsen's stage-directions and then look upon this actress's physical qualifications. Hedda's hair is of a 'medium brown, not particularly abundant'. Mrs. Campbell wears her black mane as it were a thunder-cloud. Hedda's eyes are 'steel-grey, expressive of cold, unruffled repose'. Mrs. Campbell's are twin-craters, presaging disaster. One actress, and one only, could be less Hedda, and that is Sarah. Duse got out of the necessity for interpretation by playing the part as though she were half-asleep, 'a somnolent guardian-angel' someone called her. Mrs. Campbell's Hedda of the first act is curiously becalmed, her dead-white face the sail riding the sullen sea of existence and awaiting the gathering storm. A wave of petty provocation strikes her and she shivers as a boat will shiver. The actress loads the vessel with the utmost of tragic beauty. Ever, to change the metaphor, more the antique Roman than the Norsewoman of the cold gaze and impoverished chignon, Mrs. Campbell fills the eye which Ibsen left empty. She gives the old haunting quest for beauty, the imperious line, the importunate sweep of the throat. Once more we hear the liquid utterance, fluent yet staccato, the old, exquisite phrasing. With what cruel delight does she torture her commonplace, successful rival, silly Mrs. Elvsted! What abyss of egoism is opened beneath our feet when, to the fretting Tesman hasting to Aunt Rina's death-bed, she throws that mocking 'Oh, if you run — !' Yet I cannot help feeling that Mrs. Campbell's very magnificence makes nonsense of the play. She makes it impossible for us to believe that she would ever have married Tesman. 'There is a world elsewhere' we feel she would have cried, turning her back upon Christiania. This is more Stella Gabler than Hedda, a creature whose bearing, outline, and colour suggest triumphant traipsing at the heels of fame. With her hand on extravagant hip, her mannered pose, her geranium-coloured shawl, the actress recalled the canvases of Goya. Hedda, really, should look like one of Miss Jean Cadell's old maids startled out of her virginity. It is in the last act that Mrs. Campbell is nearest to Ibsen. Here she delivers her challenge to life as though she were turned into stone; the throat has lost its line of luxury, is marble now.

May 27, 1922

THE MASTER BUILDER
(Westminster)

DONALD WOLFIT, ROSALIND IDEN

A dramatist has a perfect right to produce a great poem even in the guise of a prose play. — WILLIAM ARCHER.

IBSEN'S *Master Builder* is like a two-storey house whose inhabitants should eat, drink and sleep on the ground floor while doing their thinking upstairs. What inhabitants? Small-town doctors, bank managers, schoolmasters, photographers, married to humdrum wives and the willing prey of any hussy calling herself a house-keeper. And how do these people think? Like seers, philosophers, statesmen, poets. Ostensibly this play is all about an elderly architect who climbs to the top of a tower because a vital young woman has dared him to and offered herself as a reward. He knows he has no head for heights, risks it, and is killed. Where-upon the young woman waves her shawl and yawps her delight. On the ground floor this is lunacy.

But this is where we go upstairs and, leaving the suburban parlour, enter a cathedral vaster and more mysterious than any built of stone. You, reader, with your sharply realistic sense, say that you can't put a cathedral on the top of a parlour. Pre-cisely, and the whole of Ibsen's obscurity comes from the fact that his two storeys don't fit and his grim insistence that they must, shall and do. Let us admit that this play is obscure, that, set down in black and white, what happens in it doesn't make sense. But are we sure that Ibsen is thinking in terms of black and white? Or that our sense is his? One thing alone is clear. This is that Halvard Solness is an unhappy man. But why is he unhappy? What, in our modern vulgar parlance, is biting him?

The prospect of death? Other men have died from time to time, and worms have eaten them. His decreasing powers? That, too, is in nature. The parleyings with God, the result of which has been the taking away from him of, first, his joy in building churches, and second, his satisfaction in building homes for human beings? The burden of sin? But Solness believes he is in thrall to a troll, which enthralment must halve responsibility. The fear of madness? But there is no evidence that he is 'dreadfully attended'. His sinister gift of hypnotism? He has not misused it. His illicit traffic with 'helpers and servers'? The fact that he was morally responsible for the burning down of the house whereby his wife lost her two children? But that was twelve years ago, and Ibsen knows better than anybody that in twelve years one gets over anything from pitch-and-toss to infanticide. And then Solness doesn't care a fig for moral responsibility — he has a boyish wish to resemble the Vikings who sailed to foreign lands, plundered and burned, and killed men and carried off women. Why can't he have a robust conscience like them? And now, perhaps, we are getting near? 'La débauche veut des âmes fortes', wrote Balzac. Is Solness's unhappiness due to the recognition that he is a super-egoist without the courage of his egoism? Professor Herford suggested that in this play Ibsen 'was seeking to place one more crown, under the eyes of expectant Europe, upon the towering fabric of his finished work'. If so, then are Solness's churches Ibsen's poetic dramas? Are the homes for human beings his purely domestic pieces? Are the castles in the air the three or four plays he felt he still had it in him to write? Endless and fascinating speculation! Agreed that we must allow, as usual, for the old man's taste for perversity. One of Ibsen's kinks was to make things more difficult than they need be. Why not allow the fire to break out in Solness's hopefully neglected flue? Why insist that it started in a different part of the house? Because he knew it would tease. So Meredith, taunted with being obscure. Of one thing we are in no sort of doubt. This is that every line of this great poem proclaims dramatic genius of the highest order. The duet in the second act is the greatest colloquy in drama since Hamlet had that pow-wow with his mother.

Mr. Wolfit, who is a master of make-up, had contrived something suggesting in turns an amiable gorilla, a seaside phrenologist, and the late lamented Dr. Pritchard. Quickly overcoming this handicap, he proceeded to make out a brilliantly argued, immensely cogent case for Solness. 'Look, whether he has not tears in's eyes,' one found oneself murmuring. And he got as good as he gave, Miss Rosalind Iden putting up a great fight as the Nietzschean Hilda, a being, in Archer's words, 'radiantly, unscrupulously, immorally sane'. What! Have we got to the point where a dour, matter-of-fact Scot like Archer can call young women encouraging old men to break their necks sane? Yes, we have. And I suggest that a play which can bring about this feat must be getting on for a masterpiece. Is Miss Iden's reach a good deal beyond her grasp? Not a bad fault. At least she knew what the part was about and let us know she knew. Which is better than the blithe miscomprehension of some more practised ninny. I thought Miss Christine Silver not quite glum enough for Mrs. Solness, about whom there should be a good deal of Mrs. Gummidge. Halvard's duty-sodden spouse is the dankest tank among all Ibsen's woeful cisterns, and one should not feel that a cup of tea would work wonders. In other words, Miss Silver was too ready to cheer up. The house remained pin-still throughout.

July 4, 1943

LITTLE EYOLF
(Arts)

ERNEST MILTON, JEAN FORBES-ROBERTSON

THE proper study of mankind is monster. Such appears to have been the maxim of this frock-coated ogre retiring behind palisade of whisker and portcullis of upper-lip to demonstrate that the goodliest-looking apples are rottenest at the core. Now it may be said of naughty ogres as of naughty children that one shouldn't encourage them, and though in the far-away 'nineties those critics who had no glimmer of what the new drama was up to reproved

Ibsen amply, those who understood 'the movement' outvied each other in petting and fussing its chief exponent. Of *Little Eyolf* Archer doubted whether 'its soul-searching be not too terrible for human endurance in the theatre', the truth about this play being that it has a masterly first act followed by two others which, as Archer incautiously let out later, are 'sheer analysis, poignant and pathetic, *but the reverse of enlivening*'. The italics are mine. Now that Ibsen has been definitely and finally hoisted into place there can be no harm in saying that nowhere else throughout the great works is dullness so rampant as it is in the last half of this play, the chasm between its two tortured souls finding its image in the spectator's yawn.

While Archer was thus whirling in ecstasy in the daily Press, Mr. Shaw was doing a similar dance in the weekly. Ibsen's disconcerting discoveries about the nature of marriage and parenthood, and his digs at the people who contract both liabilities, are nòt, said Mr. Shaw, particular to introspectives living morosely on the margins of fjords. 'If you ask me where you can find the Helmer household, the Allmers household, the Solness household, the Rosmer household, and all the other Ibsen households, I reply: "Jump out of a train anywhere between Wimbledon and Haslemere; walk into the first villa you come to; and there you are".' Let us recall what happens in Allmers's dank villa — Ibsen insists three times upon his sister's umbrella — alleged to be indistinguishable from any in Godalming. Allmers, a schoolmaster, marries for her money Rita, a rich young woman of an amorous disposition, who looks upon her husband as greedily as a schoolgirl looks upon chocolates. Throwing up his job, this prig spends the next ten years between Rita's boudoir and the study in which he is writing his great work on, if you please, Human Responsibility. They have a baby who, during a moment of parental transport, falls off the table and is crippled for life. The father's recompense to his offspring takes the form of a priggish moulding of the boy's character to the end, forsooth, that when he is grown up he shall finish his father's book! All this time Rita has honeyed and made love to Allmers till he can stand it no longer. So the enervated fellow goes for a holiday into the mountains, and comes back resolved that, in the future, home is going to be less of a seraglio and more of a home, a decision received by Rita with asperity. When the play opens we see the wife disgruntled with everything that comes between her and possession of her husband, with the book on Responsibility, with the boy Eyolf, with Asta, Allmers's half-sister, yet another of Ibsen's spinsters, selfless and sad in the pastry sense, with the wide open spaces and narrow mountain tops, and with her husband for being attracted by them. She wishes Eyolf unborn, and in answer the Rat Wife rids her of him. The rest is the parents' recriminations.

This, then, is the play which Mr. Shaw declared to be 'as actual and near to us as the Brighton and South Coast Railway'. How far is it still 'the mercilessly heart-searching sermon, touching all of us somewhere, and some of us everywhere'? How many withers reclining patiently against the Arts Theatre Club fauteuils felt themselves to be wrung? In my view considerations of time and space, in other words dates and geography, have to be reckoned with. In the time case *A Doll's House* has no modern application because the modern Nora would simply tell Helmer to stop being daft, while in the matter of topography I have always doubted whether what is truth abroad is necessarily truth at home, whether human nature is inevitably the same among steppes and fjords, Spanish sierras and Surrey suburbs. I still doubt the applicability of Ibsen's clammy cogitations to a country in which the sexes settle their differences by the method of mixed foursomes on the golf-links at Sunningdale. Ibsen's humour is the grimmest vestige, and only less shuddersome than his conception of passion. He deems the egotistical, vapouring Allmers resisting his predatory spouse to be the normal husband, whereas we should take the Hindhead stockbroker feverishly climbing the Hog's Back in pursuit of what Archibald Grosvenor called 'the usual half-holiday' to be a very unusual husband indeed.

Other times, other manners, and we should make the same claim for other countries. A great French critic asking himself what he would feel if, by some fantastical trick of fate, he suddenly

discovered that he was the murderer of his father, the husband of
his mother, the son of his wife, the brother of his children, and the
grandson of his father-in-law, confessed that he should feel
astonishment and not very much more. I suggest that every
theatre-goer who gets out of that Wimbledon and Haslemere train
will feel about Ibsen's self-tormenting couple very much what
Lemaître felt about the self-tormenting Œdipus of Sophocles.
Such a theatre-goer will probably come to the prosaic conclusion
that infants should not be left lying unattended on tables or moon-
struck little boys be allowed on piers without a nurse. This will
not be a whole criticism of the play because these things are only
the machinery to get the real drama going, the concern of that
drama being the fiendish delight with which two people supposed
to be one flesh tear each other limb from limb.

But how do we fare if we suppose the drama to be particular
and local instead of universal? Is it not the case that Ibsen applies
his excessive cerebration to the formulating of rules for a humanity
which, thank Heaven, has considerably fewer brains? Like all
exorbitant thinkers Ibsen is never so happy as when he is knocking
his head against one of Nature's unshakable walls. The whole
burden of *Little Eyolf* is that marriage should be a disinterested,
rationalistic partnership instead of that sentimental contract
whereby two people claim the power to possess and, it is alleged,
so destroy each other. It is the old conflict between the laws of
Nature and the niceties of Great Thought. Blundering, sentimental, wrong-minded marriages continue to take place; the only
argument against marriage as prescribed by great thinkers is the
practical one that nobody will undertake it. Nor will Ibsen consent that his characters should muddle through or jog along; if
there is an obstacle they must bark their shins. He will not let
them see the road for pitfalls or allow them any use for milestones
except to hang round the neck! We, living in the twentieth century, have heard of compromise; Ibsen's Norwegians cannot abide
it. It comes to this, then, that it is a wise policy to take the art-
value of the plays as cash, and leave the moral credit to the days
when husbands in deer-stalkers and wives in leg-of-mutton sleeves

pedalled round Battersea Park on the newly-invented safety bicycle.

The acting was of three kinds — brilliant, adequate, and praiseworthy. As Rita Miss Jean Forbes-Robertson showed the most remarkable advance in an actress's art that has ever come under my observation. She was formerly a child, playing with all a child's grace and earnestness and, by some accident of divination, rightly. She is now grown to woman's stature and has become an actress, able to play not only Cordelia but Regan, not only Viola but Rita. Her exquisite beauty and fragility remain, and, being the artist that she is, she does not try to force her portrayal of Ibsen's difficult character beyond the limits imposed by her physique. Janet Achurch made Rita a physically superb, ranting, roaring tigress. Miss Forbes-Robertson has neither the voice nor the presence for this, and she wisely softened Rita to something less than her full animalism. For the rest her performance had subtlety, power, beauty of pose and movement and gesture, of tone and phrasing, and, most important in an Ibsen play, gave you the certainty that the actress was never in intention one second behind her author.

As Asta, a noble creature who cannot help being flatter than a pancake, Miss Dorothy Holmes-Gore made the necessary sacrifices. As the Rat Wife Miss Marie Ault was Ibsen's 'thin little shrunken figure, old and grey-haired' to the life. But if Mrs. Campbell was right, the Rat Wife should partly tread the floor of mysticism and not wholly that wretched suburban carpet. Miss Ault played this supernatural part very well except that she omitted the supernatural: her Rat Wife was anybody's charwoman. As Allmers Mr. Ernest Milton whined and moaned, tossed an aloof head, looked unutterable things, and, in general, resembled Bunthorne without any of that poet's innocent fun. But the character is deadly anyhow and should be relegated to the index of the unactable. As the ghastly Eyolf Master Peter Penrose, looking as if he would have been happier picking a peck of pickled peppers, acted nicely; and as Borgheim, the road-mender, Mr. Robert Speaight, wearing one of yesterday's Norfolk suits, gave the impression that he would

have preferred repairing one of to-day's roads to mending this
shocking part.

October 15, 1930

JOHN GABRIEL BORKMAN
('Q')

VICTOR LEWISOHN, MRS. PATRICK CAMPBELL

THE question has been asked, 'What, exactly, are we supposed to
learn from the educational drama? Is it suggested that anyone
goes to the theatre in order to obtain light on philosophy,
economics, sociology, politics, eugenics?' The question could not
have been more happily framed. Yes, it is so suggested. The
essential function of art, including that of the 'educational' drama,
is to give forth illumination. But thereby is not meant the bull's-
eye of the policeman, the beacon of the coastguard, the X-ray of
the consultant. These partake, in Bacon's phrase, of the 'dry
light' of the man of science. When the specialist turns a narrow
beam into the cavern of your throat, he uses the torch in a way
essentially non-artistic. When, sinking the case in the individual,
he turns his apprehension upon you, suffusing it with emotion
of his own, he becomes the artist, and the light he uses is the
sacred lamp. Art has nothing to do with discovery, elucidation,
or moral precept. Its function is simply to invigorate the imagination. The theatre is not a night-school. Its drama illumines
philosophy, sociology, politics, and the rest by reflection, in that
it lights up the philosopher, the sociologist, and the politician.
Shakespeare delights in the essential quality of his characters. He
brings men's talk home to their business and bosoms. Every inch
of Lear is absorbed in kingship. Henry V is greatest, not in his
sentimental rhapsodies, but in his acceptance of responsibility.
Falstaff, taking three pounds to free Mouldy and Bullcalf, throws
a light on Elizabethan tribunals. Angelo is any chairman of

86

Watch Committees. There is hardly a figure in the plays which has not its quota of philosophic, political, and social significance. But to call Shakespeare an 'educational' dramatist is nonsense. There's no such thing. Dramatists are either good or bad. Shakespeare happens to be good.

Mark how another good dramatist, Ibsen, treats the theme of *John Gabriel Borkman*, and think how a less good dramatist would have treated it. Can we not see the excitement which the inferior playwright would have got out of this feuilleton of misappropriation and treachery, Borkman's sacrifice of one earnest sister and espousal of that gallsome other, his detection, imprisonment, and downfall? Ibsen raises the curtain exactly where the other would have dropped it. Five years have passed, the mansion's only traffic is the solitary pacing in the garret. The man is prisoner to his own soul. Not for a moment will Ibsen leave the miner in Borkman out of account. The great passage: 'I love you, prisoned millions, as you lie there spell-bound in the deeps and the darkness! I love you, unborn treasures yearning for the light! I love you with all your shining train of power and glory!' gives significance to Borkman's first words: 'I am a miner's son.' He lends point to Stevenson's 'I have heard the best kind of talk on technicalities from such rare and happy persons as both know and love their business'. From the actual misfortune of his mines and misappropriations, Borkman rises to the spiritual plane. 'He had gone to ruin with a kind of kingly *abandon*, like one who condescended; but once ruined, with the lights all out, he fought as for a kingdom.' Something of this is the clue to the play. Borkman was never nearer to life than in the moment of his death. This masterpiece, for it is a masterpiece, gives 'exact information' about power and the effect of power on the human mind. It gives a clearer apprehension of Ibsen himself, of Napoleon, of Lord Northcliffe, of Jabez Balfour. It teaches more philosophy than all your pragmatists put together. It is the answer to the question with which we began.

The play, in the theatre, is apt to be 'difficult'. There is no positive virtue in dingy parlours hung with penitential gloom.

These things should be minimized by the producer and not accentuated. (Mr. Theodore Komisarjevsky, at the Everyman Theatre, raised his curtain on total night. Slowly we became aware of something that might be firelight, chairs, tables, human lineaments. It was all rather like the grave giving up its dead. The actors spoke from another world; their features were 'composed'. The tones of Borkman came from the cellerage of his past. With his sombrero, frock-coat, and stout boots he was, to outward showing, substantial. But with his grey beard and glittering eye, he was a man 'all light, a seraph-man', standing on his own corse. Mr. Dyall's Borkman was intellectually magnificent, and Mr. Dodd's Foldal brought tears.) The ladies to-night were overweighted. I should like to suggest that Mrs. Wilton's insistence upon Erhart's goloshes be omitted. There is something peculiarly repugnant about 'goloshes'. Then the whole play should be taken much faster, allowing us no time to reflect that people do not enter upon heart-to-heart talks after years of absence and a journey in Norwegian mid-winter without at least a dish of tea, or propose to spend the rest of their lives upon snowbound plateaux unprovided with the smallest suit-case. Ibsen should be played with less obsequiousness, just as though he were an ordinary playwright writing for the ordinary theatre. Which, of course, he was.

October 16, 1928

WHEN WE DEAD AWAKEN
(Torch)

WILFRID GRANTHAM, KATHARINE MORLEY

No author, says Mr. Shaw, in his account of the last creakings and crankings of Ibsen's mighty mind, can give his characters greater souls than his own. Equally no critic can exceed his own statute, however mightily he be pitted. Ibsen's last play is a great bringer-to-trial. It sought out and immediately found the weakness in William Archer, who assumed that because Ibsen was getting at something out of Archer's reach, he must be getting at something beyond his own grasp. *Ergo* Ibsen was off his head, the dour, logical Scot not seeing the possiblity that Ibsen might be no more than off Archer's head!

Walkley was content to be polite to the old giant, merely flicking a few questions from the play's surface, like dust from a top-hat. Grein — good honest fellow! — could be found writing: 'I have intentionally traced the course of the drama with some precision, *in order to make the writer's meaning clear.*' Italics mine. Montague hid behind a display of pyrotechnics, while, also in the North, Professor Herford, who was accustomed to knowing far more about Ibsen's plays than Ibsen himself, retired behind a smoke-screen of Nordic metaphysics, Manchester fog, and his own personal beard. How about Mr. Shaw? Well, our best critical pioneer was always a famous clearer of undergrowth, and in the account of this play in *The Quintessence* we are not surprised that it should be only after eleven pages of closely packed reasoning that we come to the words: 'And now the play begins!' And then, just as we settle down to a good read, Mr. Shaw finishes in just over a page. Which is a polite way of saying that Ibsen finished with his critic in just over a page.

The play, implied Mr. Shaw, had never really been difficult; it was merely thought to be difficult because the Women's Suffrage Movement, which explained it so easily, was not due for another few years. It is, of course, easy to be wise after the event. But it has always seemed to me that, even without that preposterous agitation, anybody who studied this play would perceive that one of the things Ibsen was getting at was this proposition: It is impermissible for one human being to 'use' another under any pretext or plea whatsoever. In other words, a great artist must not, to feed his art, use any other soul, if 'use' means 'use up', whereby that soul, by being absorbed in another, is destroyed. Really it would seem that so simple a truth needed no viragoes chained to railings to bring it home! But bless me! If the play meant no more than that Rubeck, the sculptor, had erred when his statue was finished in discarding Irene with the rest of the other chips, it was all as simple as kiss the back of Nora Helmer's hand. No. Mr. Shaw's brevity about this most difficult of all Ibsen's plays was not only suspect, but a complete give-away. All rumours to the contrary, Mr. Shaw has always been human, and he wanted the last thing in Ibsen's mind to be the first thing in Mr. Shaw's mind. But Ibsen, a difficult man to dictate to even before he had written a play, was the very devil to argue with when he had written it, and the trouble with *When We Dead Awaken* is that the queer, tough drama insists on behaving like a bad witness who goes on talking when his counsel is aching for him to sit down. It goes on to say ever so much more than Mr. Shaw wanted.

And why suppose that the old man at the end of his play-writing life should adopt entirely new tactics? Why expect an arch-qualifier to end on a bald statement? Why imagine that a dogmatist who all his life had no sooner laid down one proposition than he started on another to contradict it, should suddenly change his tactics? Surely it was obvious that the last and final play would present both dogma and contradiction together? As a social economist Ibsen was a suffragist to the whisker-tips. As artist he loathed the umbrella-waving pack. (Max once wrote: 'It was not the strong-minded women he cared for, poor dears; it was only the scrimmage.') As dramatist he saw that the Irenes of this world have no use for art anyhow, care nothing of what happens to the statue so long as they are known to have been its model, and would at any time give the entire contents of the Pitti Palace for a yard of baby-ribbon.

But Ibsen knew a deal more than this. He knew that to the true artist nothing matters except creation, and that the artist shows himself most like God when he creates, and most like Man when he fritters himself away on moral questions which are merely the internal economy of the thing created. Now this creation-fever ends in something very like rivalry with God. It is an old story that, the mountain-top being reached, nothing for Man remains but the avalanche. Which is why Rubeck and Irene, who is his embodied inspiration, perish; there was just nothing else they could do. How little Ibsen cared for his Women's Suffrage motif is proved by his dismissal of the other two characters who claim their equal rights to whatever it is. This is the most contemptuous leave-taking in the whole of drama. And here — with compliments to the strenuous and often helpful acting of Messrs. Wilfrid Grantham and William Hutchison and Mesdames Katharine Morley and Iris Baker — I must leave this play hoping that I have not made it too clear.

November 20, 1938

FOREIGN PLAYS

A MONTH IN THE COUNTRY
BY IVAN TURGENEV
(Royalty)

GILLIAN SCAIFE

GEORGE CALDERON tells us that the Western stage play is *centripetal*, the attention being concentrated upon a group of individuals. The Russian drama he declares to be *centrifugal*, the object being to draw the mind away from the particular events to contemplation of life in general. Such a dramatic philosophy is akin, we are to understand, to that modern theory of physics which does not look to subordinate matter for the last word, but regards it as a break in the continuity of the superior ether. The actors must show by different tone and gesture whether they are speaking to the action or to the atmosphere, the alternation of action-line and atmosphere-line being sometimes so rapid that the surface of a Russian play becomes as rough as that of a French 'vibrationist' picture seen close at hand.

Shall we say more simply that these Russians, instead of depicting extraordinary persons in extraordinary situations, present ordinary people in ordinary conditions? Their plays exhibit no impossibly romantic world in the throes of unheard-of dilemmas, quandaries, concatenations. But there is this further difference. The Russian realist, inviting subjection of the spectator's mood, consents that he shall still remain master of his intelligence; the English romancer insists upon surrender not only of mood, but of mind. A Tchehov, writing about a cheque-destroying lady, would have told us not only the last things about Mrs. Cheyney, but also the first, so that the action, diminishing in importance, would have been sunk in the background of character. To an English playwright, writing for the light-hearted amusement of an English audience, the matter presents itself differently. A cheque for ten thousand pounds is a thesis in itself, and to witness its tearing up is to be in at an emotional and dramatic event, by whomsoever it is torn up, and for whatsoever reason. The action, and not the character, is the material thing; the gap in Nature is the lady herself, who does not really exist. Whereas these Russian characters, who do so little, are as much alive as the people next door.

In his introduction to the printed edition of his plays Turgenev said modestly that he did not perceive in himself dramatic talent. The first act of *A Month in the Country* is sufficient confutation. Let me admit that I am not sufficiently familiar with the Russian theatre to know whether in the 'sixties or 'seventies its more advanced spirits deemed the presentation of uncertain mood and imperfect consciousness to be acceptable as drama. The year of Turgenev's deprecatory preface was the last year of the run in this country of *Our Boys*. Tom Robertson's milk jug had scarcely done waving, and London had still to wait ten years for the comparatively explicit *Doll's House*. Whatever, then, Moscow and St. Petersburg may have thought of Turgenev's tenuous atmospherics, it is certain that contemporary English taste would have made little of them. But we have definitely changed all that, and thanks to the plays of Tchehov we can now understand this comedy of Turgenev. To our awakened sense nothing could be more dramatic than the first act of this play. The drawing-up of the curtain discloses one of those melancholy, sun-lit verandahs with which Mr. Komisarjevsky has made us familiar. In a corner is one of those groups which we have come to know so well. It contains an old lady who is probably the mother of the owner of the house, a female of uncertain age and aspect who may be companion or governess, a nondescript male who could be a steward. These three are quarrelling over a game of cards, which we know is being played without stakes.

Nearer the audience is another little group containing two

persons only. One, who is the lady of the house, is sewing. She is virtuous, discontented, and unhappy, dependent upon, yet not returning the love of the poor fish who sighs aloud, rather than reads, passages from a French novel. Natalia is *distraite*, and does not listen. Then occurs an astonishing piece of stagecraft. Natalia tells Rakitin that, without consulting him — which 'places' their relationship — she has engaged for her son a new tutor who looks like becoming a famous man. Rakitin says his curiosity is aroused, and Natalia has a rather scornful 'Really?' She bids Rakitin read on, and immediately interrupts him to ask where Viera is. And at once we know that the play is to be about the passion inspired by the tutor in an elder and a younger woman. In quick succession we are shown the unconscious stirring of first-love in Viera, Natalia's manœuvring for position after the manner of Fielding's Lady Booby, with all that is grotesque in such a passion softened into pathos, and the complete indifference of the young man. In the meantime an intermediary has arrived with a proposal for Viera's hand. The suitor is wildly impossible, and at first Natalia, who has some kindness for her goddaughter and realizes that she is still only a child, scouts the idea. But presently, having some jealous inkling how the land lies, she goes in to lunch on the intermediary's arm, telling him that she will think the proposition over.

This is perfect writing for the stage. The play is as well made as though it concerned nothing in particular. The subtlety throughout is extraordinary, and Turgenev pays our minds a compliment by leaving the most important things unsaid. Natalia's anguish in declining self-respect, Viera's transition from the child to the woman who knows that her life will never be lived — these things have no words, yet they move us deeply. Ultimately both the languid lover and the tutor go away, leaving Viera to a loveless marriage and Natalia to the house which the presence of her well-meaning husband makes all the emptier. There is no climax, but, then, why should there be? A gentle melancholy suffuses this piece, and like Shelley's wave, gives an 'intenser day' to all that it envelops. Possibly we are inclined to take this sadness a little more seriously than the Russians intend. For at the last, when we expect our feelings to be most lacerated, lo and behold the piece takes a comic twist. Fun is poked not only at the lover and the tutor, but also at two other characters, all óf whom are said to be running away like partridges because they are afflicted with some notion of honesty. That which we should call a tragedy Turgenev calls a comedy, and we reflect that Tchehov intended *The Cherry Orchard* to be played as farce.

Frankly may one suggest that the 'vibrationist' theory of acting is all rather nonsense, and that the best kind in the art with which we are familiar will do for any of the Russians? All that is necessary is the absence of a star-actor and the refusal of the company, whenever the star opens his mouth, to suspend animation like a golf crowd watching Hagen drive off the last tee with a four for the championship. The piece was admirably produced, and acted with great intelligence if with something less than the proper intensity. As Natalia and Viera Miss Gillian Scaife and Miss Natalie Moya gave performances of great competence, though possibly something a little more heartrending and febrile was wanted. Mr. Christopher Oldham's boyish uncouthness was exactly right, and the excrescent humours of Messrs. Michael Sherbrooke and Craighall Sherry could not have been better.

July 11, 1926

THE SEA-GULL

BY ANTON TCHEHOV
(Fortune)

GLEN BYAM SHAW, MIRIAM LEWES, VALERIE TAYLOR

THE spectators who emerged from the first performances of Ibsen's *The Pillars of Society* must have resolved to a man never again to wave the banner of the ideal. Between eleven and twelve on the first night of Mr. Galsworthy's *Justice* more than one prison governor was certainly rung up. Who can doubt that if *Mrs. Warren's Profession* had been performed in the year in which it was written we should all have written urgent letters to the papers demanding a rise in wages for barmaids in railway refreshment-rooms? Tchehov is not of the order of effectual angels. He is not filled with righteous wrath against anything or anybody; as Calderon points out, he would not have condemned the Pharisees but would have written short stories to explain their attitude. 'People are like this!' is all that Tchehov has to say about his characters; they are static in the sense that nothing can be done about them. Almost you might say that they are figures on a Russian urn. Constantine, beside that lake, will never write, and Nina will never act, that play; nor ever will their lives be anything but bare. And so it goes on. Take all the characters in *The Sea-Gull*, and note how they are fixed in time almost as a photograph is fixed. Throughout eternity Madame Arcadina will be an egotistical, chattering first-rate actress, jealous of her son; Nina, the indifferent actress, will know vanity and passion and be betrayed by her lack of art and by Trigorin; Trigorin, the second-rate writer and lover, will fish in his own emotions for the stuff of future novels and write down his catches in a note-book. To the end of time each of the half-dozen lovers in this play will pursue another and see that other in pursuit of someone else. Then there are the quests other than those of love and glory. Trigorin has fame, but does not value it; he would have his youth again. Sorin, dying, clutches at the life which has passed him by; Medvedenko wants affection; Masha seeks an anodyne; the doctor wants to talk and put his little world right about everything. His desires alone are fulfilled: all others in this play are frustrate.

Looking on at the piece one has the sensation of gazing at a photograph of a group of people all of whom are dead. The personages in *The Sea-Gull* are doubly dead. There was never anything to be remedied about Madame Arcadina, Nina, Constantine and the rest, for the simple reason that there is never anything to be done about anybody unless they do it themselves. (There was never anything to be done about Ibsen's flag-waver, though one felt that later Hialmars might be discouraged from making idealistic asses of themselves.) But something has happened in Russia, or we are told that it has. The Russia of Madame Arcadina has passed away. Even she was conscious of that passing: 'Ten or fifteen years ago there were six big country-houses round the shore. It was all laughter, and noise, and the firing of guns, and love-making, love-making without end.' To-day they have something else to do in Russia besides making love. But it is precisely because Tchehov's drifting, hopeless lovers have passed away that they are imperishable. Whether their passing is good for them is not the point. There is too much making free with other people's lives to suit our own comfort, too much easy fortitude akin to that of Scotch elders happy to see their daughters coffined at their feet rather than endure their existence outside the Scotch canon. Schiller patted Gustavus Adolphus on the back for making his exit at thirty-eight before he had time to abuse his new-found power, and only the other day some noodle congratulated Nelson upon dying before Emma had time to weary him with her vulgarities. There is too much of this 'better dead' nonsense. Whether annihilation and being in Hamlet's sense 'reformed altogether' is what Tchehov's world would have best desired for itself is not our concern; the point is that in Tchehov's art that world lives for ever.

There has been some talk of brightening the present production, presumably by taking the action a little faster and by a greater insistence upon the play's comic aspects. This is an old story. Whenever any English producer finds melancholy in *The Cherry Orchard* somebody is sure to point out that Tchehov wrote the thing as a farce; and indeed in this author there is always more of Bunthorne's innocent fun than the casual critic might imagine. But in *The Sea-Gull* there is surely every excuse for a Gummidgean atmosphere. Every creetur' in this play is lone; every one is lorn; and 'everythink goes contrairy' with all of them. The play is one huge haystack of despondency, with not more than three tiny needles of glinting humour. Presumably it is not for nothing that Masha pirouettes to that melancholy waltz, and that Sorin prates about gusto from his bath-chair. And then there is Shamraev, the steward, whose obsession about old actors must be meant for comic relief after the manner of Gayef's billiards in *The Cherry Orchard* and Kosykh's incessant bridge chatter in *Ivanov*. But there the humour in this play ends. Now, if Calderon is right in insisting that Tchehov's characters 'see their misfortunes, without malice, from the remote comedic point of view', it may be that the finest playing of Tchehov would show his characters agonizing, so to speak, at one remove. In the present production Masha and Sorin, when they speak, become centres of tragedy instead of remaining decorations to more important woe. Is it just possible that the more faithful way of dealing with Tchehov would be to play him for a little less than he is worth? Certainly the Russian players we have seen over here make understatement their principal virtue. Personally I shall not fall foul of the present producer or his methods, though it may be that Mr. Filmer feels Tchehov's tragedy 'more than anybody else'. But I am going to confess that I like him to feel it so, for the simple reason that the piece and the playing and the production as I saw them on the second night at the Fortune Theatre filled me with as poignant a pleasure as I am capable of feeling. On the whole I am not for speeding up this production. Tchehov's drama is not a dirt-track. Perhaps the music played 'off' at the end of the first act should have been Chopin instead of Glinka. Perhaps also the setting for the fourth act should have been darker in tone, with the window at the back set further away from the audience. But producers are only human, and the deep from which they must conjure up their treasures may not always be vasty enough. Anyhow, Mr. James Whale's first and second settings are lovely, and the lighting throughout was excellent.

It is certain that there needs no producer come from Moscow to tell Miss Miriam Lewes how to play Madame Arcadina. Her interpretation is extraordinarily subtle and perceptive, her voice and her inflections are admirably just, and her use of arms and hands constitutes one of the most brilliant pieces of fulfilment of, and embroidery to, meaning I have seen for many a long day. In short, until I see a better performance I shall regard this actress's Madame Arcadina as perfect. Miss Valerie Taylor has deepened the beauty of her first three acts, though she now, I think, underplays the last act a little. Or can it be that with increased familiarity the emotional shock is less? Nevertheless I suggest that Miss Taylor might heighten the note here and give, as she did before, the impression of physical distress, want and hunger. But nearly all her acting is lovely, and I offer her congratulations on the complete disappearance of what was once a faulty enunciation. Mr. Glen Byam Shaw as Constantine is a little overweighted by the last act, but excellent elsewhere. That careful actor, Mr. Martin Lewis, makes a fair shot at Trigórin, who wants more presence and authority; Miss Margaret Swallow does, perhaps, too complete justice to Masha; and Mr. Oliver Johnston, though acting well, just fails to give us all he knows about Sorin. But the play is a very difficult one, and to ask for its perfect presentation is to demand at least ten performances of genius.

September 25, 1929

UNCLE VANYA
BY ANTON TCHEHOV
(Everyman)

LEON QUARTERMAINE, JOSEPH DODD, CATHLEEN NESBITT

TCHEHOV's *Uncle Vanya* is an embroidery upon the theme of apprenticeship to sorrow: 'L'homme est un apprenti, la douleur est son maître'. It is a theme which no age or country escapes. Musset may sing it after one fashion, Shakespeare after another. Yet it has been known to cause the practical mind to suffer impatience when it comprehends that Tchehov's sorrowful apprentices are *fainéants*. Vanya, the sentimentalist, unpacks his heart

with words, nags at the fate he will not unbend his idealistic soul
to conquer. Astrov, the man of action, gives his life to drunkenness and the cultivation of trees. Serebryakov, the invalid, is
pure humbug. His wife Elena, loving Astrov, lacks the courage
of adultery; she is in no sense moral. Sonia, his daughter, loving
Astrov, is a sick lily. We watch these people curiously, but without
comprehension and almost without pity. They are, oh, so ex-
asperatingly Russian! 'At last', says Stevenson of the death of
Bragelonne, 'the little Viscount has done something. C'est, ma foi!
bien heureux.' But these Tchehovians do nothing. C'est, ma
foi! bien malheureux. They do not even commit suicide, and
when they shoot to kill, they miss. They make up that most helpless of corporations, the spineless introspective. They do not
indulge in that last Western consolation: 'No dog so wretched but
he wags his tail sometimes.' We English have few wounds which
a ride to hounds will not heal. Your Russian, we are always told,
is a great huntsman. But these characters of Tchehov do not hunt;
they are hunted. The ideal pursues them, flays them with a whip.

I am as certain that this play of castigation is a masterpiece as
I am that I shall never get into touch with the whipped. Who to
me says Russian says Czecho-Slovakian, Magyar, Turk. A witty
French lady once declared that she drew her line at Lucerne.
East of that line, 'ce sont des crocodiles'. (Have not the tears of
that species been observed as far West as Geneva?) The books do
not help one very much. I read that 'To the Russian, European
culture and ethic is a virus, working in him like a disease of which
the inflammation comes forth as literature. Since Peter the Great
Russia has been accepting Europe, and seething Europe down in a
curious process of katabolism'. I look this word up, to find that it
means 'Destructive or downward metabolism; retrogressive metamorphism — opposed to *anabolism*. See DISASSIMILATION'. But I
will not pursue the dictionary further. Scratch your Tchehovian
and you find a crocodile, is enough for me. As a play *Uncle Vanya*
is quite perfect. I shall never know exactly 'what it means', but
then I do not know that I hunger for that knowledge. It is, and
that suffices. It was acted with infinite tenderness and suscepti-

bility by that sensitive player, Mr. Leon Quartermaine, with veracity and humour by that tremendous Iago-in-waiting, Mr. Franklin Dyall. As Serebryakov Mr. Hignett was quite pointedly miscast. There is not, nor ever can be, an ounce of humbug in the composition of this charming actor. Miss Cathleen Nesbitt gave very exactly the impression of demanding more from life than it can reasonably hold. She divided Elena accurately into two compatible halves, self-absorption and self-sacrifice. Miss Irene Rathbone, the helpless lily among weeds, just managed to keep her head above water. But my special admiration was reserved for the Telyegen of Mr. Joseph Dodd. Here was unquestioning acceptance of destiny, the only safe shelter from life. Alone of all the characters he kept humility between him and the myriad universes of the night. 'Bless in me' — it is Loti's little steeple which speaks — 'the shield which guards you from the abyss. Seek, in your infinite littleness, to emulate the dead sleeping at my feet, who departed in simple faith, unmindful of the void and without trouble of the stars.' For Telyegen alone of these unquiet Russians there was blessed unquestioning. He kept his face to earth.

December 10, 1921

THE THREE SISTERS

BY ANTON TCHEHOV

(Old Vic)

MARIE NEY, VIVIENNE BENNETT, NANCY HORNSBY

'Pray, Miss Eliza, are not the ——shire Militia removed from Meryton? They must be a great loss to *your* family.'
— Miss Bingley in *Pride and Prejudice*

IF, like Bunthorne, you are fond of touch-and-go jocularity, Tchehov is the shop for it. Now, is there or is there not an overtone in the phrase 'touch-and-go'? Might it not be the title of a play by C. L. Anthony? The speculation here is admittedly abstruse, but it occurs to me that *The Three Sisters* is a purely arbitrary title and that Tchehov would have been just as pleased to name his piece *Call It a Lifetime*. Between you and me, reader, I have always suspected this dramatist of being the lightest of his kind, the C. L. Antonovich of Russia! Tchebutykin, the doctor in this play, knows from the newspapers that there was such a person as Dobrolyubov: 'But what he wrote I can't say!' My idle fancy is that he wrote *serious* Russian plays, the kind of thing which those who have never seen any Tchehov imagine Tchehov to have written.

A great work is known by its power to provoke parallels, even unhappy ones. A gifted colleague has found a resemblance between these three sisters and their brother and the Brontë girls and Branwell. But surely the likeness is superficial? Tchehov's young women cry for Moscow as other people cry for the moon, whereas to the Brontës there was no horizon beyond Haworth's. In the end Tchehov's Andrey pushes a perambulator; Branwell ended by pushing open once too often the doors of the public-house. No! If a parallel is to be sought in English life or literature it can only be with the family of Mr. Bennet. It astonishes even me who make it, how little far is the cry here! Nobody at this time of day is going to rehearse the plot of *Pride and Prejudice*, though it would be rank intellectual snobbery to pretend that everybody remembers what Tchehov's play is about. Let me say, then, that one at least of the many things lying near its core is the havoc wrought in the sisters' hearts when the brigade leaves that small provincial Russian town. Alas! that Masha cannot follow her Vershinin as Lydia Bennet followed the ——shire Militia to Brighton! The reader will probably recall Mr. Bennet's reflection that at Brighton his daughter would be of less importance 'even as a common flirt than she has been here — the officers will find women better worth their notice'.

Perhaps some day Mr. Maurice Baring will write a fifth act transplanting Tchehov's three sisters to Moscow and showing us

what happened to them in that land for which they had invented
so many promises. But Masha's plight, though pitiful enough, is
common; it is perhaps not too much to say that to the wife of any
dull husband there comes at least once in her life knowledge of
Masha's temptation if not surrender. There is greater pitifulness
in Irina's case, since here the tragedy is wanton. Why, even in the
name of all the old Russian gods, should she not be happy with her
Baron in whom for the first time speaks the voice of the new Russia?
The young man has a quarrel forced upon him by a former comrade, a professional bully with the blood of two previous duels on
his hands, and one of the most skilful things in this play is the way
in which Tchehov brings together the passions of Vershinin and
Solyony. Superficially nothing could be wider apart than the
former's sentimento-philosophic hankerings and the latter's
brutal ardours. But Tchehov knows and gives us to know that
both affairs are merely the distractions of bored soldiers who in
Moscow would not have looked at either girl.

Is it reading too much into the play to suggest that there is an
essential difference between Irina and Masha, that whereas Irina
will not easily love again, Masha with her hummings and cogita-
bundities is only Lydia and Kitty Bennet drawn to tragic scale,
and will love the very next officer who has the wit to dress up his
proposals metaphysically? A very few weeks after the departure
of the ——shire Militia, Elizabeth Bennet could hope that Kitty
would presently be able to mention an officer not more than once
a day 'unless, by some cruel and malicious arrangement at the
War Office, another regiment should be quartered in Meryton'.
I feel that if the Russian War Office had been similarly minded,
Masha would not have been long in finding consolation, if only
for the reason that she is wittier and therefore more volatile than
Irina. Indeed, in Masha I find a suspicion of Hedda Gabler,
though declining to allow that red and whopping whale admission
to the present track. Olga is the steadying point of the trio, never
quite gay, yet never wholly sad. Of common, everyday happiness
Olga is to know nothing; she has overstood her market and is not
to marry, and she takes a brave view of what lies before her. Her

name is serenity. It is in her that the play's dissonances are resolved, since to her is given the beautiful passage:

Time will pass, and we shall go away for ever, and we shall be forgotten, our faces will be forgotten, our voices, and how many there were of us; but our sufferings will pass into joy for those who will live after us, happiness and peace will be established upon earth, and they will remember kindly and bless those who have lived before. . . .

It is while this was being spoken that on Tuesday night the audience put away handkerchiefs used not more for tears than for controlling laughter. The Old Vic audience laughed its fill, and was also deeply moved, showing that it had 'got' this play at first shock and sight. Whether an audience of West End fashionables would 'get' it will never be known. For the first condition of 'getting' a play is getting the audience together, and that one refuses to be got!

Mr. Henry Cass, producing with much skill and care, has scrupulously refrained from stealing any of Mr. Komisarjevsky's thunder. He should have stolen it! We badly wanted those shadows dancing on the bedroom wall, and that dancing bear which, in the production at Barnes, so terrified Irina, and frightened her still more when it turned out to be Solyony in mummer's guise. Solyony ought to be the most menacing personage. I suppose Tchehov knew his business best, but the explanation of why Solyony keeps on scenting his hands seems over-long delayed. Or perhaps the scent-bottle should be more obviously a scent-bottle. Or Mr. George Woodbridge should make more of it. Actually the actor gives the impression of unscrewing a fountain-pen and sprinkling the contents over himself, which may be highly Russian, but is not very understandable. I think, too, that Andrey's fiddle should not be as bridgeless as the noses in a Burne-Jones convas. Media should not be mixed, and if Andrey is to carry an Expressionist fiddle he should, when he sits down, fall through an Expressionist chair. On the other hand, the scene in which the young soldiers say good-bye to the echo is most movingly done.

This is one of the play's three strokes of surpassing genius, the others being the famous red-beard incident, and the blazing notion of that arbitrary fire which springs up from nowhere and is as irrelevant and motiveless as an earthquake would be in the middle of *Hamlet*. It is almost as though Tchehov has said to himself: 'Here are a lot of people intensely alive — let's see if they will go on living through something visitational, like flood or smallpox!' and hits on a fire because it is something visible to an audience. The red glare on Skiddaw roused the burghers of Carlisle, and I think something of the same sort should be vouchsafed the burgesses of Waterloo Road. At Barnes we saw the flicker and the glow.

Mr. Ion Swinley is exactly right as Vershinin; one understands why his wife continually tries to commit suicide, and also why she has two children by him. As the young Baron who breaks with aristocratic tradition, Mr. William Devlin plays with much subtlety, and in the last act with much pathos. That the break is only a little one is shown by the dove-coloured frock-coat with the silk facings, still a mile away from to-day's Soviet tunic. The Baron resents having a footman to pull off his military boots; but I suspect that it is the same menial who brushes those civilian trousers. Nobody could fail in the part of the doctor, Tchebutykin, though it takes a clever actor to succeed as measurelessly as does Mr. Cecil Trouncer. Mr. Keneth Kent wheels Andrey's perambulator as to the manner born. Mr. Andrew Leigh as that cocky little dullard, Masha's husband, is excellent until he puts on the red beard, when he does not give sufficient signs of the struggle before compassion wins; he should be suppressing his own tears while trying to laugh away Masha's. As Andrey's vulgar little wife Miss Myrtle Richardson is nearly as irritating as Natasha herself, which is inescapable in the case of an actress whose work one does not know. The ideal casting would be some exquisitely mannered actress, like Miss Fay Compton, who could not be Natasha except by acting; actually I suspect Miss Richardson of acting quite a lot. There has been a lot of suspecting in this article, which I finally suspect of being too long. This must be my excuse for saying nothing about those weeping willows, Miss Marie Ney, Miss Vivienne Bennett, and Miss Nancy Hornsby, who in the old-fashioned world of unlimited space would have had a column all to themselves.

November 12, 1935

THE CHERRY ORCHARD

BY ANTON TCHEHOV

(Lyric, Hammersmith)

JOHN GIELGUD, O. B. CLARENCE, MARY GREY

'IF people are not English, they ought to be,' puts Mr. Podsnap's view of this play in a nutshell. Tchehov's characters maunder and drivel, barren equally of purpose and that last refuge of the shiftless — optimism. There is no 'drive' about them; they do not 'get a move on'; they potter about, Micawbers for whom there is not even a Port Middlebay. Dickens could not refuse his magnanimous shirker a shadowy success, even if it had to be of the antipodean sort. Tchehov makes no such pretence; his 'job-lots' are doomed from the beginning.

Mr. Shaw's Britannus was a barbarian who thought that the customs of his tribe and island were the laws of nature. In judging this play we must not be Britannus. It is possible that in Russian eyes Micawber, my uncle Toby, even Falstaff himself are no more than mindless buffoons. Let us beware of rating Tchehov's company as passive mug-wumps, and refrain from annoyance that they will not *exuberate*, to use Johnson's word, into doers and contrivers. I make this plea purely on behalf of those who must put a work of art to the test of reason rather than emotion. *The Cherry Orchard* is like one of those pictures in which Utrillo invites you to look at a tenement-dwelling in Montmartre. He does not argue that the house is unsanitary, that it shelters crime and vice, that it should be pulled down. He just paints it. You may not

want to live in such a house, but its presentment gives you pleasure. Tchehov too presents, without judging, his *fainéants*. You
would not live with them in the flesh? Try living with them in
the spirit.

Which of these portraits do we like best? Is it that of Leonid
Gayef, the sieve of sentiment, who will pour out his soul to an old
cupboard and almost frighten you with his obsession of billiards?
Have we not all some *trac* indifferently mastered? Or do we prefer
Trophimof, that pathetic student who dislikes solemnity and takes
himself with immense seriousness? Or Lopakhin, the successful
man, who, we feel, will make too much money out of the villas he
is to build on the site of the cherry orchard? Or Pishtchik, the fat,
jovial sponger, who has had two strokes, takes other people's pills,
is as strong as a horse, and deems himself descended from Caligula's ennobled steed? Or Ephikhodof, that marvellous grotesque?
Or Yasha, that child of the steppes with the mentality of a
Parisian *gigolo*? Or Firs, who is your 'old retainer' with a difference? Madame Ranevsky, that indolent reed, leads the women
easily, though Barbara is a great pool of melancholy, and Anya is
vaguely foredoomed to unhappiness. Even Charlotte the
governess, whiling away her antiquated virginity with card-tricks
and ventriloquism, is a terrifying figure. Yet how real they are!
Mad, indeed, should we be to deny that but for the grace of
God . . .

Here these creatures are fixed in this play more enduringly than
if they had walked the earth in flesh and blood. They wander in
and out, missing trains, hunting for mislaid goloshes, rhapsodizing,
soliloquizing, telling one another that they are grown ugly or have
taken to smelling like chickens, consenting to ruin, yet in all their
ineffectiveness as sensible to sight and hearing, as much *there* as if
they had put in an English morning's work and snatched the
afternoon to return an effective card for the golf club's monthly
medal.

Is not one in this play up against the old difficulty of trying to
put into terms of logic a beauty which pours itself into one's
being through every avenue of sense? I want the reader to be

chilled by that early-morning light stealing into the room still called the nursery, and to sadden with the glow of that melancholy sunset filtering through the shutters at the end. I want the reader to see that arabesque of trees against the moon, to hear Ephikhodof moan of unrequited love to the guitar which he miscalls a mandoline. I want him to rub his cheek against Trophimof's thin beard, to feel with his hands the woolly texture of the smock which Pishtchik wears beneath his frock-coat. Even if all this were achieved I should despair of getting anybody to realize, away from the actual theatre, the delicate beauty of that scene in which these spirits in bondage dance home and orchard away to the tune of an old Viennese waltz. The fiddles die down, the partners separate and stand watching the governess at her imbecile card-tricks like the courtiers of Watteau fading beneath the trees which shall outlive them. But there, it's no use talking. *The Cherry Orchard* is an imperishable masterpiece, which will remain as long as men have eyes to see, ears to hear, and the will to comprehend beauty.

But let it not be supposed that the spectator will pass a doleful evening. He won't. These creatures have their comic side, which Tchehov is as quick to see as anybody. Four months before the first production of the play the author wrote to Madame Stanislavsky whose husband was to play Lopahkin: 'It has turned out, not a drama but a comedy, in parts a farce.' Those, then, who like laughing at a play, as I do, can laugh their heartiest at these often absurd people without fear of doing the low-brow thing. Ephikhodof, that bundle of misery, excellently played by Mr. James Whale, might have walked into this piece straight out of English musical comedy. The fellow cannot enter a room without tripping, hand a bouquet without dropping it, or play billiards without breaking his cue. Poor Alfred Lester played him often. He is only a small character, yet he has his place, and when he speaks the world centres round him for the space of that utterance. Each character shimmers with continuous life, and joins the others to form a kaleidoscope of which each speaker in turn is the centre.

The piece calls for the finest playing, and Mr. Fagan's company were often very fine. Miss Mary Grey, though physically too magnificent, subdued her soul to the required degree of slightness, and her poise in the second act and her dumb grief in the third were lovely. The two daughters of Miss Virginia Isham and Miss Gwendolen Evans could not have been bettered. I am just a little bothered about the Gayef of Mr. Alan Napier and the Lopakhin of Mr. Fred O'Donovan. Was Gayef a trifle too seedy for a remnant of the old nobility? Was Lopakhin a wee bit too brutal? Mr. O'Donovan gave him a red-handed, destructive shade, whereas I suggest that he, too, belongs to the old order and will pass away with it. His cry of 'Strike up, music!' is ironical, not triumphant. He is ashamed of his success and would drown it. Perhaps the actor, trailed, *malgré lui*, and because of old association, too many clouds of Abbey Theatre boorishness. But within their own conceptions, which is what really matters, both Mr. Napier and Mr. O'Donovan acted very well indeed. Mr. John Gielgud's Perpetual Student was perfection itself, Mr. Smith's Pishtchik was immensely jolly, and Mr. Clarence's Firs must have drawn tears from the policeman in the gallery. In a repertory company one part must go astray, and Miss Ellis as the governess was miscast. She should have been elderly and ridiculous. But the performance as a whole gave immense delight, and the staging and lighting were admirable.

I am always being asked which is the best play in London. This is. For the high-brow? Yes, and for butcher, baker, and candlestick-maker as well. I suggest that *The Cherry Orchard* is one of the great plays of the world. Let your British stalwart consider the educated Chinaman who should have left his almond trees to inquire into European culture. Shall we show him these listless Russian folk, or is it that Mr. Coward's exuberated ladies do our civilization greater credit?

May 25, 1925

THE SEVEN WHO WERE HANGED

BY LEONID ANDREYEV

(Scala)

ISIDOR CACHIER

SOMETIMES one feels that praise may be taken a trifle perfunctorily. It is not an uncommon experience for a critic to find himself slapped on the back and challenged: 'Of course I saw what you wrote about such and such a play. Now, tell me, what is it really like?' I want readers of the *Sunday Times* to take me at my word when I say deliberately, and weighing every syllable, that the performance of *The Seven Who Were Hanged* by these Yiddish players contains more great acting than I have ever seen on any stage in any one piece. The drama, in itself, is a great emotional and spiritual experience. One of the tests of a masterpiece is the inability to shake off experience; since Monday evening last I have spent my waking hours in Russia, in prison with these pitiful wretches. But I ask even more than that readers should take me at my word. I ask that they shall go and judge for themselves. The piece will be played again, on Thursday evening in this week, and it is the duty of every person who takes an intelligent interest in the theatre to witness this extraordinarily fine play with its magnificent presentation. A complete ignorance of the language need not be a deterrent; the programme contains an elaborate synopsis, and the scope of the play puts it above words.

I shall beg leave to give the barest account of what it is all about. A Cabinet Minister is told by the Chief of Police that the authorities have discovered a plot to assassinate him next morning, that His Excellency is in no danger as the conspirators are known and will be arrested in front of his house before the bomb is thrown. In spite of this assurance the Minister is so terrified at the idea of death that he dies of apoplexy. The next act shows us the trial and sentencing of the five anarchists, to whom are joined a half-witted, sub-normal vagrant and a brigand. The third act shows them all in prison, the fourth depicts their behaviour on the train that is to take them to the place of execution. The last act gives the procession on the way to the scaffold.

Told thus, the play must read like an old-time broadsheet, or an excerpt from a modern newspaper report. You would hardly believe that it can be compact of love and fellowship, spiritual kinship and ecstasy. Yet so it is, and so, to judge by their literature, it must always be with this race which thinks so differently from our own. Russia is a queer, big place, where queer, big things happen; and Russian facts are stubborn in this, that they persist in being less facts than indices. Take the Cabinet Minister, for example: at the beginning a figure of farce as the elder Guitry might conceive farce, scenting his waistcoat, hands, and the tufts of hair surrounding his little pig-like ears, then changing to a figment of Grand Guignol with his horrible, stertorous death-agonies. Yet behind this comic monstrosity generation after generation of oppressors loom.

In the police court our sympathies are not maudlinly invoked. We deplore the crime, and are not invited to side with Anarchy. We feel pity, not for the individual prisoners, but for that spirit which would not hurt a fly yet knows no ruth in the cause of revolution. When the five learn that their request — to be hanged together — is granted, their tribulation turns to ineffable joy, and with faces transfigured and shining they chant the revolutionary's creed. The leave-taking scene in the prison has a purely human quality of pathos, and as it is played at the Scala is almost beyond bearing. I do not imagine that a single eye can have remained dry throughout this act. The scene in the train is an essay in brotherhood.

But it is in the last act that the theatre is used at its best. It could be sensational, harrowing, 'effective' in the commonplace way. It is, however, none of these, but draws the piece to a grave liturgical close. It remains in the mind like music. It is difficult for me to say anything about the acting, for the simple reason that it did not seem to be acting at all. There was no flamboyance. But not Duse could have launched you upon seas of diviner pity, nor Bernhardt have moved you to a greater quickening of the spirit. There are eighteen actors in this piece, and it is impossible to make distinctions. But if I must call special attention to any individual performances it would be to that of the Cabinet Minister, Mr. Isidor Cachier, who is to be compared with Lucien Guitry and none other, and to the father, mother, and son of Muni Weizenfreund, Anna Appel, and Alex Tenenholtz. The second of the five Anarchists, a young actress whom I cannot identify, is also extraordinarily good. But in fairness I ought to name the whole cast. The scenery varies from the perfectly dreadful — the set for for the first act could not be worse, no horse ever foaled having such forelegs as the charger in the huge picture — through the formal and expressionistic to a realistic snowstorm of great beauty seen through the tracery of bare boughs. The fainting soldier is a remarkable *coup de théâtre* which one will never forget. But, then, I do not propose ever to forget anything which happens in this play.

May 18, 1924

KATERINA

BY LEONID ANDREYEV

(Barnes)

JOHN GIELGUD, FRANCES CARSON

THE point is whether, if Emilia had snatched the pillow away in time, Desdemona would have been driven into the arms of Cassio out of resentment, disillusion, what you will. And, after Cassio, the 'general camp', to use Othello's phrase. We say no, stoutly and for lots of reasons, but principally because we are English, and Shakespeare was an English dramatist who worked in normal passions. White heat of jealous rage, fiery incandescence of poet's mind — these did not affect the matter of normality. Elizabethan gold remained gold whatever the temperature, and, though Shakespeare could destroy Othello, he could never degrade Desdemona. But times have changed, and the day is with the neurologist turned playwright. At least it would appear to be so in Russia.

We must not be too English if we would get the best out of these studies of a way of life so utterly foreign and antipathetic to our own. 'Fool, who believes that he is not I!' cried Hugo. Oh, wad some power the giftie gie us to see these Russians as they see themselves! Everything that happens to Andreyev's characters is repugnant to the English sense of what would, should, or could happen to people laying claim to ordinary, i.e. English sanity. This being so, the temptation is to cast about for excuses, to pity Russia for having been left out of the Roman march, and so passing from barbarism to decadence without knowing civilization, or to talk about 'retrogressive metamorphism' and the way this country has been steadily breaking Europe down ever since, in the time of Peter the Great, she first began to absorb European culture. Or we may just shake our head and talk about calling in the alienist. But surely it is putting the cart before the horse to be quick with the excuse and tardy with the acceptance. Let us grant Andreyev the truth and probability of his characters, the sex obsession, the maundering delight in debauch, the maudlin itch for fine living and thinking — maudlin because it is as drunkard's chatter, unbacked by intention — the morbid delight in revolvers and six-storey windows as means of compassing death. Granted these things, how shall we English best find enjoyment in a play which sets them forth?

Well, the first thing to do is not to arrive late, since within ten seconds of the rise of the curtain the whole matter is set forth in a way which only a master of the theatre could devise. The stage is empty. We hear a fearful din going on in the next room, and not only know what the quarrel is about, but divine that a husband is at that point in rage at which Othello has his fit of epilepsy. A wife rushes across the stage, followed by a husband, who fires his revolver three times and misses. As his fit subsides, hers grows. And at once we know that two Russians being scratched, two Tartars are revealed — the male still a savage beneath his veneer, the female one of those exotic, hyper-aesthetic creatures who are all sensibility and no sense. She is a Russian, and we may look to her for cold and calculated revenge. But there is to be more to it than that. How much more we must wait to see, for Andreyev devotes the rest of the act to ensuring the actuality of his characters and putting them into their furniture and surroundings. So, while Katerina is dressing herself and the children preparatory to leaving the house, we are made to realize that even a husband who has failed to shoot his wife at one o'clock in the morning has still to sleep somewhere. Therefore we see Georg's mother interrupting her floods of tears to fuss about with blankets. Then comes a wonderful touch. The children's governess, bored at having to get up in the middle of the night, enters to obtain some instructions, and, of course, can get nothing out of Georg, who is on his knees, with his mother's arms round him. So she shrugs her shoulders and goes out again. This it is which puts the chairs and tables round these tragic creatures. They may be mad, but we know that they live in a world of method, where, besides loving and hating, people must also eat and drink and sleep. This is great playwriting, since it connotes the world we know, in which though tears are ridiculous and dying is ugly tragedy is believed. Contrast the unrealities of Sheik drama, alleged by us to be about normal people, where lovers swoon from morn to midnight without mention of a chop, or die on sofas uttering sublimities with nobody believing a word.

Having made us accept his world and his people, Andreyev then proceeds to develop his thesis, which is that the fall of Katerina's pride and vanity has brought the whole woman toppling down. The second act shows us Katerina languishing on the verandah in her mother's house. She has given herself to the nonentity, Mentikov, who was the object of her husband's unfounded suspicions. She regards her lover now with the utmost distaste, and as we view this beautiful creature adrift among her dimly-guessed passions we think of a fair ship at the mercy of wind and waves. For Miss Frances Carson does make Katerina a beautiful creature — there can be no doubt about that. Whether we quite believe that the injury sustained would have turned into utter trash a good woman who had no precedent taint is, perhaps, not the point. Our own poet has told us that 'lilies that fester smell far worse than weeds', and perhaps we may think that they also decay faster. But as yet degeneration has hardly begun, and the mood is no more than one of exquisite melancholy. Miss Carson looked very lovely and very Russian here, her dress being so devised as to suggest something bruised and violated; and she played the scene of reconciliation with the husband with great finesse and understanding. The kisses which she gives are almost from another world, since we feel that the soul of her who gives them is dead. The act ends with a fine piece of 'theatre'. Katerina goes within doors, and on the piano plays to Georg, who remains sitting in the sunlight, something remembered from their courtship days. The piece is Debussy's *Plus que lente*. The atmosphere of subtle melancholy is rudely broken by Mentikov, who proffers fearsome banalities, to which Georg hardly replies. Then he offers a cigarette, and by accepting the husband conveys the measure of his contempt. The curtain comes down.

The third act brings on the scene a *raisonneur*, a painter named Koromislov, whom we, not being Russian, should simply call a cad. For though he has been one of Katerina's increasing number of lovers, we find him lecturing both wife and husband. He advises Katerina to throw herself out of his studio window, which she very nearly does, and suggests to Georg that his best atonement for having missed his wife is to take better aim at himself. The fourth act shows a supper party in the studio. Here we see Katerina posing as Salome and drunk with wine, the flattery of the men about her, and her own desires. The picture of degeneracy is complete. Not only Katerina's degeneracy, but also that of Georg, for the husband has now plumbed the depths of complaisance. He takes affectionate leave of Katerina, as she goes off with the soberest of her lovers. The party breaks up, and once more Mentikov offers a cigarette to Georg, who is lost in thought. This time he sketches a refusal, and we know that he is debating whether he shall strangle Katerina or shoot himself, or both. The play might seem sordid here if the scene had not been contrived by Andreyev with so much ingenuity and invention, and produced by Mr. Komisarjevsky with so much virtuosity. To get the supper party and the piano playing, the posing and painting on to the ten-foot stage, and delight the eye with movement and grouping, was a miracle in itself. But Mr. Komisarjevsky achieves more than this; it is a whole web of sight and sound which he presents, so that the play becomes an orchestrated score. This is beauty in which dramatist and producer have an equal hand, and I am not convinced that beauty can demoralize. Or, if we must grant the thematic material to be sordid, we must also admit that sordidness is shown for what it is. The fall of wife and husband does not obscure the heights from which they fell. Thinking on our own smart comedies, in which the deject are not thrown down from anywhere but just grovel about as though mud were the jolliest, and even the only, state of existence imaginable — reflecting on some recent English plays, we are chastened. Consolation comes from thinking that perhaps our comedies are not intended to be more than make-believe, whereas this Russian tragedy is real life. Item, in real life an English husband would probably have neither gone in for nor messed up the shooting, but would certainly have made a success of booting his wife's lover out of door.

Miss Carson was excellent throughout, except, perhaps, at the end of the third act, where Andreyev makes her get down from the window-sill, decline from suicide, put on her gloves, and go home. Katerina has a flood of uneasy flippancies to deliver here, and the scene must be very difficult. But why did Mr. Komisarjevsky consent to that tasteless last-act costume? A Russian woman like Katerina would have devised for Salome something that did not suggest the cabaret. Ineluctable is not a word one uses every day, but it has to be used about Mr. John Gielgud's

Georg. The wretch never could have got away from his tragedy. Mr. Gielgud is becoming one of our most admirable actors; there is mind behind everything he does. Only he must avoid the snag of portentousness, of being intense about nothing in particular. Twice in this play he has to make an entry upstairs from below stage. The first time is an occasion of great solemnity, but on the second he is merely paying a friendly call, to do which it is unnecessary to put on the manner of one rising from the grave. Lots of people were frightfully good, Mr. Ernest Milton playing the painter with so much authority that one lost contempt for the character. Perhaps there is even a certain grandeur in a pot which can call two kettles black.

April 3, 1926

THE SPOOK SONATA
BY AUGUST STRINDBERG
(Globe)

ALLAN JEAYES, GLEN BYAM SHAW, MARY GREY

'THERE is a transcendentality of delirium,' said Gilbert's Lady Jane, 'which the earthy might mistake for indigestion.' If one were forced to find a receipt for the transcendentalities of Strindberg's most difficult play, one might suggest Shakespeare's sixty-sixth sonnet, Hamlet's worm-and-Emperor mood, Lear's 'luxury' speech, something of Poe, Baudelaire, and Wedekind. Set these to simmer and take off the scum, and *The Spook Sonata* is the residuum. To explain away this piece would probably be easier than to explain it; indeed, the upshot of communal elucidations in the foyer after the first and second acts seemed to be that Strindberg at one time inhabited a lunatic asylum, and that the play proved it. But that cock will not fight, since the author's sequestration was in the early 'nineties, and this play was not written until ten years after his return to health. Probably if there had been a third intermission we should all have agreed that enlightenment of one sort or another had come to us, each in his own way. For there is a point in the third act at which the fog lifts. That point occurs when something in the Student's brain pulls a trigger; and it is we as well as he who begin to see more clearly. Each, of course, must still pierce the mist for himself. For myself I can only say that the play took on the aspect of a line of orbit travelling through incidents related only after the manner of points on a circumference, and held together by the attraction of some central truth. If one could find the particular truth, all well and good. None, I think, could doubt the existence in Strindberg's mind of some centre to his circle, for without it the play must have been chaos, and chaos it undoubtedly was not. Behind the most utter-seeming nonsense there was mind, declaring itself in riddles and incomprehensible symbols, but still mind.

Seated in the theatre it is difficult to renounce the old notions of drama as something based upon normal logic and human consistency, and all the more difficult when the renunciation called for is allowed to be intermittent. We grasp that the Old Man in the bath-chair is Malevolence, and that the cold, vice-like grip in which he holds the Student's hand is his eighty evil years. What we don't grasp so easily is that the play which ensues is not Drama but Masque. Incidents crowd upon us, alternating between the comprehensible and the incomprehensible. We register one success in the matter of the Old Man's courtship of the beggars whom he fobs off with the hint of a treat at his funeral — is not this savagery at the dishonest politician's expense? We notch another success in the matter of the Old Man's power over his man-servant — this is understandable blackmail. No difficulty, either, about that figure of the dead man which in its cere-cloths stalks out of the house to glut vanity on the flag at half-mast. But here our lucky hits stop, and we enter precariously upon the no-man's-land of incomprehensibility. Why should the Nobleman who is also a Colonel prove to belong neither to the peerage nor to the army? Why should his wife voluntarily immure herself in a cupboard whence after twenty years she emerges with the voice of a parrot? What is the meaning of the statue; of the Old Man's Fiancée, now eighty years of age, who never speaks; of the screen which the butler places round the living as a sign that they are going to die? What, oh what are those hyacinths? For last poser to end this most weird of questionnaires, what are we to understand by the mad tea-party at which the Old Man and the Parrot-wife, the Daughter, the Fiancée, and one other guest meet once a week for twenty years to nibble biscuits in silence? 'Curiouser and curiouser!' we murmur, when suddenly the play again becomes semi-comprehensible. The Old Man forces his way into the tea-party, ploughs up the visage of each guest, and is himself seized in the beak of the Parrot-wife, who tears the mask from his face and strips his evil soul. This done, she bids him take her place in the cupboard, and calls to the factotum to bring the screen.

The third act contains the love-making of the Student and the Daughter, and throughout this act the Colonel and his Parrot-wife sit silently in an alcove. After a time the play takes a sudden dive into what might be conscious burlesque. There is a long diatribe against table-legs which need propping, ill-fitting windows, dirty lamp-glasses, clogged ink-bottles. This rises to full persecution-mania with the terrifying figure of the Cook, who, instead of nourishing the family, drains its life-blood, and flourishes, as dire presage and embodiment, a bottle of colouring-matter normally associated with soup and gravy. 'Bring the screen!' now cries the Daughter, from whose cheeks all colouring-matter has fled. And in the twinkling of an eye the nonsense fades and the spirit is bathed in pure poetry as, through the chinks of the screen, the Student breathes to the dying girl his message of deliverance.

If there is method in this madness — and one is convinced there is — it can only be in the existence of the central key of which one spoke earlier on. In the 'trigger' speech the Student describes the Old Man's funeral. He has been moved to tears by the noble utterances of the clergyman and the dead man's best friend, only to learn next day that the lives of all covered abysses of infamy. Is not the key we are looking for here, and is not that key the falsity and lying hypocrisy of human relations? Shroud and mummy-wrapping, parrot-cry, and cold marble — are not these so many symbols of untruth? Tired with all these and what they stand for, Strindberg would be gone. But not before he has pursued them with a hate which turned to frenzy, and, at last, in his already shaken mind, to exaggerative paranoia. I do not suggest that this is the whole truth about this play; I hope it may be a bit of it.

June 14, 1927

THE DANCE OF DEATH

BY AUGUST STRINDBERG

(Apollo)

ROBERT LORAINE, MIRIAM LEWES

This play proves once more that art possesses a logic of its own which may with impunity run counter to any other kind of logic. Their creators postulated, but could not explain, Iago and Medea, with the result that those who must account for a thing before accepting it have been forced into daemonism to explain the daemonic hate and daemonic jealousy of two inexplicable beings. And as nobody really believes in daemonism, we are exactly where we started.

The Dance of Death invites to the same kind of metaphysical tail-chasing. In this play Iago is married to Medea, and those who base enjoyment upon probability, or even the old business of purgation by pity and terror, are in for a thin time. Captain Edgar and his wife do not, and could not, exist outside a madhouse. It follows that we do not believe in them, and can have none of the Aristotelian fear that by our own folly we should run upon similar disaster. But that is to judge Strindberg's creations by the logic of the world we know. In terms of their own logic and their own world, which is under Strindberg's hat, and nowhere else, the pair have a terrific and a terrifying reality. Strindberg's power of *creating* character is so great that you accept his monstrous originals more readily than the faithful copies of lesser dramatists. The unnatural and direful elements are so mixed in Edgar and Alice that we proclaim them not the recognizable man and woman of our world, but logical and consistent inhabitants of the world devised in Strindberg's tortured brain.

The curtain has not been up ten minutes before we perceive that we are not dealing with falsification of the familiar, but with a different kind of new truth. If we could be translated to another planet we should not be on that planet ten minutes, I suggest, without perceiving that its inhabitants were consistent with themselves, and that that consistency was not impaired by what we had hitherto known of sentient beings. So it is with Strindberg. It is not the point that his world is a paranoic conception having behind it this or that pathological explanation. It is very elaborately not the point that an inefficient captain and a mediocre actress — the inefficiency is explained in the first part of the play now presented, and the mediocrity in the unperformed sequel — could not and would not in our world remain on an island for twenty-five years chained together by pure hate and forging fresh links of loathing in case the old should wear out. It is very definitely the point that Strindberg has put a world round these two people in which this thing is credible. Being brought into a state of belief, our enjoyment consists in sitting in the theatre and, to use a colloquialism, watching the fur fly. And as it flies we are conscious of an exhilaration in which there is a quality of awe.

In terms of our logic, we might describe Captain Edgar as a megalomaniac suffering from an inferiority complex and persecution mania. His overweening arrogance, his contemptible bullying, his cringing towards superiors, his comfortable familiarity with subordinates — all these are touched off with a technical brilliance which not even Ibsen has exceeded. Nor has any master created any single figure approaching the malignity of Alice. Pile the calculating animalism of Hardy's Arabella upon the repressions of Rosa Dartle, season these with something of

Lady Macbeth and a complete Florentine ruthlessness, and the result still falls short of this tigress with the viper's heart who, when her husband dies at the long last, has these words: 'I'll not act as undertaker to a rotting beast! Drain-men and dissectors may dispose of him! A garden bed would be too good for that barrowful of filth!' Yet both characters are touched to a kind of greatness. For just as Strindberg cannot handle any subject without saying something worth while about it, so when he draws a wicked man and a wicked woman they become cartoons, Michelangelesque and Miltonic. When the Captain, who had been struck with something which we thought was death, returned helmeted and cloaked from his ceremonial visit to the Colonel, we knew that he was no longer man but spectre, and that the cold figure had come hot from Hell. Mr. Loraine's playing here was superb, and the stage shone with evil. His imminent cruelties were so convincingly formulated that we, sitting in the theatre, were as much deceived as Alice, goaded to put the match to the fire which she had been vengefully laying for twenty-five years.

At this point the play fails us, translation into our world takes place, and sentimentalities ensue. There is a very serious breakdown in logic. Within less than a minute of attempting to murder his wife, the Captain makes complete *volte-face*, declares that he has seen the other side of the grave and been granted a vision inculcating redemption by kindness. What in that case becomes of the fearsome threats which immediately succeeded that vision? Frankly, the play goes altogether to pieces in the last five minutes, and both Edgar and Alice, contradicting everything we have been told about them, deny the logic of Strindberg's or any other world. Probably, if the whole piece were given, that which we deem to be a breakdown would prove to be only a breathing-space. Part Two shows the Captain unimpaired in animus yet reduced physically to a shell of evil, and working his mischief through other people, including his own child. And at the end of the complete play, which terminates in fiendish ecstasy, we are back again in Strindberg's world. One did not believe in the ending at the Apollo Theatre, and perhaps the programme should have told us that the piece as performed is only half of Strindberg's work, and that the sentimental close is not an ending, but a halt.

Mr. Loraine's acting was magnificent throughout, and as masterly in its implications as in its detailed craftsmanship. While fully satisfying the eye in the matter of the paralytic stroke and so forth, he kept our minds occupied not with the tricks of the crumbling body but with the cancerous sweep of evil imagination. Whatever else Mr. Loraine may or may not play well his Strindberg is fine. The malignancy in Miss Miriam Lewes's portrayal of Alice was marvellously contrived, though possibly this clever actress was the least little bit inclined to under-act. The exact note must be extremely difficult to hit if a slanging-match is to be avoided, but there were one or two occasions when a greater volume of tone might have been beneficial. Apart from this, which I put forward tentatively, the performance was perfect. As Curt, through whose eyes much of the tragedy is seen, Mr. Edmund Gwenn, though obviously intellectually master of his part, could not be more sensitive than his chubby, sea-going appearance permitted. One wondered what that jolly naval officer was doing in that miserable galley, and one doubted his capitulation to Alice. But within the actor's physical means the performance was excellent. The staging, lighting, and production in general were particularly good, though some holes appeared to have been made in the text. Possibly the caged birds will never again sing as indefatigably as they did on Thursday afternoon.

January 22, 1928

LA RONDE

BY ARTHUR SCHNITZLER

(Arts)

THE PITOËFFS

The French have a taste for lecturing, and the English a dislike of it. Therefore it would have been a kindness to explain this to M. Pitoëff, who preceded this Viennese masterpiece with a twenty-five minutes' oration whereby he eventually raised his curtain on a house seething with exasperation. It should also have been explained to M. Pitoëff that the audience at the Arts Theatre is not a collection of nasty-minded schoolboys and school-girls, but is made up of highly skilled playgoers who can be trusted to know a work of art from a tale of bawdry. Our *conférencier* insisted at enormous length that *La Ronde* is not a scabrous play, whereas a better point would have been that *La Ronde* is scabrous because certain facets of life presented in it are what puritans call scabrous, though to a generation which has ceased to muffle its piano-legs those facets are no more than natural.

Stendhal's well-known handbook lays it down that love is a matter of getting as closely as possible to the object desired and possessing it with every sense, whereas a later Fountain gushes forth the pellucid information that love is or ought to be a 'per-durable hypostasis'. Much virtue in 'ought'! The trouble, of course, is the old matter of words, since it would be absurd to suppose that the word 'love' has meant the same thing to Caligula and Calvin, Nero and Knox. But the misunderstanding has always been collective rather than individual. 'Nature created the female and Man the feminine', said Balzac, implying that the whole business of culture has been to invent a gloss for which Nature has seen no necessity. Yet some individuals still insist upon misunderstanding. Thus I find a distinguished colleague writing *à propos* of this play: 'A serious inquiry into the nature of love cannot go hand in hand with propriety.' Substitute 'frivolous' for 'serious' and I agree.

This play consists of one anecdote told ten times over, and exhibits in each case the intoxicated gallop to passion and the sober retreat therefrom. This is the common experience of all whose youth has not, in Stevenson's phrase, been depressed by exceptional aesthetic surroundings, and it is probably the one universal experience about which most writers have been constrained to a false modesty. Yet there is a well-known Latin proverb built on this particular anti-climax, and it was not a disreputable poet who wrote:

> Mad in pursuit, and in possession so;
>   Had, having, and in quest to have, extreme;
> A bliss in proof — and prov'd, a very woe,
>   Before, a joy propos'd; behind, a dream:
> All this the world well knows; yet none knows well
> To shun the heaven that leads men to this hell.

'All this the world well knows.' Yet forty years after Schnitzler wrote his play it declines to license the exhibition. Perhaps the most cruel thing about the piece is the continued lack of feminine comprehension in this matter, since every one of the ten scenes shows the woman continuing to chatter about heaven to the man entangled in his self-made hell.

There are five women in Schnitzler's play, a cocotte, a servant-girl, a *femme du monde*, a little dressmaker, and an actress, each of whom is seen first with one lover and then with another or her husband. The cocotte meets a sailor, who leaves her for a servant-girl dancing in a café. The servant-girl pretends to be seduced by a young man who has an affair with the *femme du monde*, who allows her husband to lecture her on the beauty of faithfulness, after which he deceives her with the little dressmaker. The little dressmaker makes love to a famous dramatist, who has an episode with an actress, who grants favours to a count, who spends a night with the cocotte with whom the play began. And so the chain is complete.

The five women were played by Mme. Pitoëff, whose delineation of the varying social strata had the same sharpness of definition which a music-hall artist would have given it. If I fault her perfect mastery of this business of instantaneous projection it is because I found her society woman a little too bourgeoise in the scene with her lover, which was perhaps too much like Maupassant in his middle-class vein. To those who have known Mme. Pitoëff only in tragic rôles this series of characterizations must have come as a revelation of comic genius. In the scene in which the actress lured the dramatist into what looked like a houseboat, and, on pretence of the need for *campagne, pureté*, and all the rest of the Dumasian caboodle, never ceased to talk about herself and her triumphs and to bring the scent of the footlights well into the hay — here Mme. Pitoëff maliciously suggested what I shall call the exotricks of Sarah Bernhardt framing her tousled mop in a window in pasteboard imitation of Roxane or Francesca. In the following tableau Mme. Pitoëff showed even greater malice in suggesting the ineffable bunk of a Duse speechlessly unhappy about bygone desertions but not letting present lover escape those tragic hands. Mme. Pitoëff is an actress who acts with her whole body, and whereas lesser talent would have tried to cram a quart of acting into this pint pot of a play, Mme. Pitoëff effortlessly extracted twice as much significance as Schnitzler can have intended. M. Pitoëff acted two parts with fine imagination, and there were two brilliant studies by M. Louis Salou.

Owing to the smallness of the stage, the complicated production was necessarily higgledy and even piggledy, and from time to time one had supererogatory glimpses of one scene-shifter in braces and another adjusting something or other with a boat-hook. However, the theatre admittedly has its pictorial side, and this last desperate effort to retrieve a slipping sea had the charm of a Manet. All playgoers with any taste for something terrifically first-class should find themselves at the Arts Theatre during the next fortnight. But, of course, the play must be banned for all except specialized audiences. Harringay, using Miss Cicely Courtneidge's finest accent, is always entitled to put the question:

'And what is h'all this about, may I h'ask?' A truthful answer would hardly exhale that propriety for which my colleague is so concerned.

February 16, 1933

MAGDA

BY HERMANN SUDERMANN
(New)

GWEN FFRANGCON-DAVIES

As I am in duty bound to scold Miss Gwen Ffrangcon-Davies for possessing the defect of the highest quality proper to any actress, let me begin by defining that quality. Briefly, it is the belief that the player can so discipline technical powers as to be able to use the whole or any part of them to carry out every conception of which his imagination is capable, given the will to put that belief into action. The defect of that highest quality is the reluctance to perceive that expression is necessarily subject to physical limitations. 'We'll e'en to it like French falconers, fly at anything we see,' said Hamlet. To show with what avidity Miss Ffrangcon-Davies has flown at anything and everything she has seen, I will jot down some of the parts which she has played in the last three or four years: Maya, Tess, Cordelia, Titania, Mr. Shaw's Cleopatra, Eleonora in Strindberg's *Easter*, Juliet, Ophelia, Mrs. Herbert in *The Lady with a Lamp*, Lady Macbeth, Nora. It is unnecessary to insist upon the intellectual enterprise which this list shows, and it is not my purpose to appraise the wealth and fluidity of the achievement. My intention is rather to point to certain failures, using the word to connote the discarding of the author's character and the substitution of other exquisiteness. Ransack Marseilles from end to end and you would not find such a Maya; this Lady Macbeth could not have looked upon a dagger; that Tess was as far removed from the elemental creature of the soil as Dresden is from earthenware. Yet in each case disparity was made good with so much imaginative subtlety that though the senses were starved the mind was satisfied. Offer a hungry navvy nectar and ambrosia in place of his expected bottle of beer and steak, and he may well think that he has enjoyed a feast without having had a meal. One repeats that the one admissible charge against Miss Ffrangcon-Davies's artistry is its refusal to recognize that her physical means are finite.

This actress cannot 'look at' Magda, yet by the end of the evening she has contrived to do quite extraordinary justice to Sudermann's heroine. Remember Magda's first appearance, how it is delayed until the second act, and how the first act, though ostensibly devoted to painting the patriarchal household, is really a superb piece of working-up for the actress's entry. In the way of keeping an audience in a fever of expectation Magda has Millamant and Madame Ranevsky and Paula Tanqueray beaten to a frazzle. We hear of the great operatic star's reception at the official soirée, how she came down the room on His Excellency's arm, her corsage blazing with orders. We see Magda's little sister run to the window, and hear her describe the descent from the carriage and orb-like progress up the stairs. Then the door opens and . . . Now, what are we to suppose a great opera-singer of 1893 looked like? The world was just hearing the last of its Lucias, Leonoras, Violettas, and all those somnambulistic, indefatigable aria-mongers whose weakness of mind could have been conceivably housed, though it rarely was, in fragility of body. For better or worse the world had taken the Wagnerian turn, and large against the Bayreuth sky loomed the bulk of Venus and Brynnhilde, while mighty Elizabeths strode down giant Halls whose pillars rocked at their Greetings, and on wide champaigns Isoldas came to anchor like ten-ton lorries. Yes, the opera-singers of 1893 were, to use Lady Jane's adjective, massive. I forget how Duse accomplished Magda's entry, because one never remembers any of her entries; the stage was empty, and then Duse would be sadly, ineffably, remotely present. Bernhardt's entry combined the airs of all the Graces with the business-like efficiency of the old warhorse who has a fair notion as to how much money there is in the house. And one will never forget how in the old days that door would open and the room would suddenly be full of Mrs. Patrick Campbell, a world-ranging eagle swooping down upon little Marie, the home-keeping dove.

Miss Ffrangcon-Davies, who has any amount of brains, is obviously alive to the physical difficulty and flutters up to her comparatively strapping sister with such bravura of fan and brocade that the entry is almost covered, though it still remains that of an opera-singer up to Micaela's weight and no more. But the trouble is not ended. There remain those impudences to her father's visitors which fell from Duse like sour benedictions, from Sarah with the cabotine's natural, slightly vulgar good nature, and from Mrs. Campbell in sheer gusto. When Miss Ffrangcon-Davies says them they are the impertinences of a little girl trying to be naughty. Vocally, too, she does not quite fill this large theatre, and the laugh which should obliterate von Keller at his proposal to keep the child dark hardly incommodes him. This business of criticism is mighty difficult. There is perfect beauty in the English Lakes, as has been sufficiently pointed out, and nobody who has not just had three weeks and twenty-nine guineas' worth of the Engadine is going to bother about the scale of our English fells. But Magda is an Alpine part, and we cannot help remembering the prowess the great climbers achieved in it. Putting recollection on one side and trying not to hear Pastor Heffterdingt's: 'When you stood before me in your primitive strength,' we see Miss Ffrangcon-Davies's performance for what it intrinsically is — a lovely thing. Mr. Shaw claimed for Duse that when her Magda had got over the first reception of von Keller and had time to take stock of her old lover she began to blush so that her face visibly reddened and she had to hide it in her hands. This has always seemed to me to be part of Duse's hocus-pocus of ineradicable nobility and no part of Magda, for the woman who could say to the unoffending Pastor: 'I could never bear the sight of you!' is not the woman to blush before that insignificant insect which is von Keller, though he may be the father of her child. When Miss Ffrangcon-Davies receives the man her face grows white; and that, I think, is better. But these things are as the actress feels, for Sudermann is not Ibsen, and Magda is not a real character but a leading-lady, old school, pitchforked into a problem play, new school. To-day's self-supporting young women would tell their twaddlesome old fathers not to be silly and pat their antiquated cheeks. But in the 'nineties 'What shall we do with our parents?' was a serious problem for young womanhood, and in this play Sudermann tried to make the best of the new drama and the old heroine. That Magda could have again submitted to parental rule and consented to marry von Keller was always incredible if Magda was a real woman, though one accepted it for the sake of all the good theatricalism to follow. As we know, Magda finally refused to marry her seducer, and asked her father why he should insist upon burdening that worthy Councillor with a wife who had had other lovers, whereupon the old man had a stroke and died. The difference between Ibsen the dramatist of reality and Sudermann, the man of the theatre coquetting with the new ideas, is that Ibsen would have begun his play about ten minutes before Sudermann left off. Nearly all that takes place in Sudermann's drama would have happened before Ibsen's curtain went up. When it did, Magda would be married to von Keller, her father would be staying in the house, and not only we, but the old man, would be devastatingly shown what happens to a woman who obeys a code of morality in which she does not believe. 'I did what I thought was right,' says Magda. Ibsen would have shown us what comes of doing what one doesn't think right. Nevertheless, *Magda* as a *pièce de théâtre* wears admirably, and one still gets something of the old thrill which made all the young people of the 'nineties emerge from this play determined to run away from home, become great opera singers, and have generous flings into the bargain.

May 12, 1930

THE MAN AND THE MASSES

BY ERNST TOLLER

(Stage Society)

GEORGE HAYES

FIRST, all honour to the Stage Society that it should have produced this play. Ernst Toller was president of the Council in
Munich during the short Soviet *régime* of March, 1919. The veto
upon the work is still absolute in that town, and its author is still
a prisoner in the fortress of Niederschönenfeld. He will be released
in July after five years' expiation of a political offence. That we,
in free England, should produce the work of a German fighting
for what he deems to be Liberty is a gesture of, at least, intellectual
brotherhood.

A correspondent has suggested that I have 'fallen to the propa-
ganda of Andreyev's *The Seven who were Hanged* . . . Done into
English, it may do no more harm than the ineffable Toller's *Man
and the Masses*'. And I am warned that in praising these plays I
am accelerating the final disintegration of British society and the
ruin of the workers. I am reminded here of a passage in *King
Solomon's Mines*. One of the Englishmen is telling the African
natives that he and his party have made intentional descent from
the moon, in support whereof he cites his preliminary study of the
Zulu language. 'Only, my lord', objects an astute savage, 'thou
hast learnt it very badly.' My correspondent has learned Toller's
lesson worse than badly; he has not learned it at all. And I do
not feel that he has got at the root of Andreyev. In my notice of
that play I said explicitly: 'Our sympathies are not maudlinly
invoked. We deplore the crime, and are not invited to side with
Anarchy.' That statement is not, I submit, open to misconstruc-
tion. Andreyev's piece has nothing to do with political right or
wrong. It is a study of ecstasy in martyrdom; and, incidentally,
the spectator is made to feel extraordinarily sorry for the fat little

Governor who should have been done to death. I admit that the play shows signs of revolutionary stress. But is it not arguable that a country in which nobody wants to rebel against anything is likely to go, in Henley's words, 'fattening, mellowing, dozing, rotting down into a rich deliquium of decay'? And I suggest that if my correspondent will refer to Shakespeare's Sonnet LXVI he will find a protest against Privilege which must have annoyed the Shallows and Silences of his day. Doubtless they, too, had the itch to 'keep such a firebrand in gaol'.

The time has gone past when we can pretend that in considering any burning testament we can entirely divorce manner from matter. It would be absurd to pretend that what advanced minds are thinking in Russia and in Germany is, for us, a question of aesthetics only. *Man and the Masses* is not entertainment alone. If Toller's piece were the most flaming revolutionary manifesto ever devised, it would still be my duty to set it forth with all the accuracy of which I am capable, and to leave political judgment to my readers. The case happens, however, to be exactly and expressly contrary. Toller teaches just what our own Mr. Halcott Glover taught in *Wat Tyler*. His John Ball urged the mob to holy war; Glover showed it returning drunk with pillage and slaughter. Ball propped the mass above earth, and we are told how the very spirituality of that support was the undoing of the individual. Man, Toller points out, is not Mass, and never can be.

The Woman, as she is simply called, seems to me to preach the creed of John Ball. She is strong in dreams and weak in actions. What she would highly, that would she holily; and, like all leaders of new thought, she reckons without the mob which is to translate words into deeds. She forgets that you cannot indict a social order, or, rather, that the only practicable form which indictment can take is violence to the individual, on the heels of which follows the still greater injury to the violent, who rush together in mutual destruction. 'Wat Tyler and John Ball destroy each other to the end of time. Only Hodge remains.' Mass destroys Mass, says Toller; only Man remains. I do not remember that we put or wished to put Mr. Glover in gaol.

It may be said that this is a very poor 'story of the play'. I hardly mean it to be a definite story, for the simple reason that, upon a single hearing, I would not venture to tie this work to a single interpretation. Toller was poet, not propagandist, but he wrote in prison, and in a time of great national strain. He chose a purely 'expressionistic' medium, and his 'characters' are neither individuals nor types. They are the mouthpieces of the Idea. The Husband — or so I take it — is Freedom broadening down from precedent to precedent, and a great deal too slowly for the Nameless One, or impatient torch of revolution. There are choruses of Workmen, Convicts, Courtesans, Bankers, Gaolers, Sentries, etc., etc., and their convolutions might have been arranged by some Expressionist painter. The thing is virtually ballet, and it would not surprise you to read on your programme: 'Choreography by Mr. Mark Gertler.'

The staging was extraordinarily good, and one remembers some striking pictures: the platform resting literally upon masses of men lifting despairing arms, the doll-like, jazzing Bankers, the dance of The Condemned, the Mob beginning to see Red, its Agony and Betrayal. Set over against these was the calm figure of the Woman who has created a child and discovered in it a Cain. The highest praise must be accorded to Miss Thorndike for her presentment of the Woman. She spoke exquisitely throughout, and touched Beauty at the lines:

> O path through the ripe wheat fields
> In August days . . .
> Wandering in the wintry mountains
> Before dawn . . .
> Tiny beetles in the breath of noon . . .
> O world . . .

To imprison a poet who could write this does not seem to me the highest form of sense. Mr. George Hayes played the Nameless One as he played Aaron, with immense gusto and perception. Among the rest of the cast I detected in doing right Messrs. Raymond Massey, Victor Lewisohn, Milton Rosmer, Eugene

Leahy, Bruce Winston, and Mesdames Marie Ault and Drusilla Wills. But the whole of the big cast acted very well, and the production will rank high in the Society's annals. The scenery of Mr. Aubrey Hammond and the music of Mr. J. H. Foulds vied in imagination and significance. To Mr. Casson, for his overseeing, immense praise is due.

May 25, 1924

FROM MORN TILL MIDNIGHT
BY GEORG KAISER
(Regent)

CLAUDE RAINS

You might say simply of this play that it is a yelp from the underdog. But its translator will not let us off so lightly. He tells us that it is an example of an art whose gestures are 'a vigorous clenching of the smooth palm of actuality'. By my troth, Mr. Translator, these are very bitter words, we murmur after Mistress Quickly. The hero 'sets his question mark against the world asking whether this or that is real'. Which sets us asking in our turn whether the play's title should not be *Pirandello's Ghost*. Rest, rest, perturbéd spirit; we thought we had laid you long ago.

But I quite see Mr. Dukes's difficulty. Confronted with, and delighted by, a highly significant form of presentation, he is not content unless he can find high significance in the thing presented. There can be no doubt as to the value in the theatre of the expressionist method. When in the old days you glanced down at your theatre programme and saw the words 'Bathroom in the Palace of the Emperor Hadrian', you fell at once to wondering two things — first, what cranes had been used to haul those giant and marble blocks so noiselessly into place, and second, why the programme should fib, since you were obviously enjoying an expensive set in the beautiful London theatre of the Emperor

Beerbohm. But when they tell you at the Regent that the scene is the 'Interior of a Small Bank' you quite perfectly believe it. The actors, sharply defined against the vague background — in which there are neither walls nor doors — can these be characters in a bank? Yes, because there is a square yard or so of tortured grating to suggest the cramped lives of those who must spend their days raking in and paying out other people's money. Can cavernous gloom with a few dimly flying flags and four excited gentlemen in evening dress waving top-hats suggest a 'Velodrome during Cycle Races'? Again, yes; because the top-hats are sema-phores keeping us in touch with the crowd on the stands and signalling messages of cupidity and greed. All expressionist scenery has this two-fold appeal; it stimulates the eye by the little which it puts in, and the mind through all that it leaves out.

Now what of the drama so vividly presented? Is *From Morn till Midnight* a tone poem of modern unrest? Yes, but we are to remember also that it is a vision of society seen through the eyes of an absconding cashier who, in his 'search for reality' is at the same time 'questioner and interpreter'. Now what are the facts, as prosaic coroner or magistrate might say, since even expressionist drama must use events for its bricks and mortar? The cashier goes off with 60,000 crowns for love of a lady who, being virtuous, declines truck with him. Therefore the fellow has quite a lot of money to burn before midnight, when the police may reasonably be expected to get him. He begins by apostrophizing in a snow-field Life, Death, and a pair of dirty cuffs, using a great many words to say what I submit, in the smallest possible whisper, is just nothing at all. Now he goes home, where he is revolted by the wife who cooks endless chops, one daughter who endlessly darns, and another who ceaselessly strums upon the piano. His old mother dies, and the callous-scrupulous fellow abandons his whole family, leaving behind his honest savings, which, one reflects, will barely pay for the funeral. He next proceeds to the Velodrome, where he offers fantastic prizes, thus proving that he can purchase not the decent wretches who race, but the pig-eye'd, bull-neck'd backers and layers.

After this comes a scene in a cabaret, where money is shown to procure for his delight ladies who are tipsy, hideous, or possessed of wooden legs. And last our cashier hies him to a Salvation Army hall, where, after making some play with the stool of Repentance, he shoots himself, and so baulks the police. Now, frankly, is there more here than a pot-house tale? Is the story, in spite of its pot-house origin, natural? Is what a great poet has called the 'true pathos and sublime' of human life a pure illusion? Are our Cup-tie crowds, which we may suppose to correspond to those of the Velodrome, howling mobs of insensate beasts? Can money be put to no uses save the base and ignoble?

I suggest that more is claimed for these facts than a tale of vulgar debauch, for the reason that the expressionist medium must tell more or be wasted. What this medium does, it does very well. The peculiar virtue of expressionism is that it goes one better in the way of presenting things to the mind than the representational method which presents them to the eye. Compare the Velodrome scene with any of the old racing melodramas of Drury Lane, and you realize at once how much the definition is sharper in the case where nothing is seen. It is impossible to explain why four men waving silk hats with the co-ordinated rhythm of a lunatic ballet should be nearer to the truth of race meetings than a photographic representation of correct, stewardly behaviour. The fact remains that it is so. Possibly a point to be made here is that as soon as expressionism comes in at the door explanation in terms of words flies out of the window. For the thing has become abstract, like painting or music. But the fact that a dramatist should have found a magnificent way of saying something must not bluff one into the belief that the thing said is magnificent. I tried with might and main to see spiritual significance in Mr. Kaiser's turgid bombinations, but all I could see, or rather hear, was a small cashier talking at enormous length through a very large hat. But I take off mine to the setting, which whetted the appetite to an extraordinary degree, though, with all respect to everybody concerned, I could not find that there was much of a meal.

Mr. Claude Rains put his accustomed virtuosity at the cashier's disposal, and thus demonstrated one of the humbugging qualities of the theatre — that an actor may impress you very considerably without conveying any considerable notion as to what his part means. Whether Mr. Rains knew is his secret. There was a very large cast, among whom one would praise highly Messrs. Nat Lewis and Henry Ford, and Mesdames Betty Potter, Caroline Keith, Colette O'Neil, and Irene Barnett.

March 14, 1926

THE RISING SUN

BY HERMAN HEIJERMANS

(Kingsway)

FRANK CELLIER, ANGELA BADDELEY

'I ADMIRE the way you try to get out of difficulties,' said Balzac's Mme. Mercadet to her husband, tottering on the verge of bankruptcy. 'What I cannot stand is your pretending that they don't exist.' To which Mercadet replied: 'My dear, if I had been one to pull a long face I should have thrown myself into the river before now. Don't you realize that a hundredweight of worry doesn't pay a ha'porth of debts?' This succinct exposition of the philosophy of debtors was first uttered by the great French actor Got on the stage of the Gymnase in the year 1851. Balzac, who knew as much about debt as any man who ever lived, remarks elsewhere that a debt is an imaginative masterpiece which the creditor can never understand. And, again: 'Debt is a martyrdom without any heaven for recompense.' Those three things are, as Lady Bracknell might well observe, all there is to be said about debt. Matthew Strong, the bankrupt hero of Heijermans's play, may have thought the last two things, but, being a petty tradesman, he did not utter them. But he did very definitely and almost word for word repeat Mercadet's observations on the expediency of the bold front. The greater the difficulty the greater the necessity for the brave face.

Matthew, you see, was distinctly up against it. His shop was heavily mortgaged, and the big stores next door had begun to swamp his custom very much as their big lights had swamped the meagre gas-jets which he could hardly afford to keep burning. He had borrowed, hazardously invested, and finally lost his daughter's young man's elderly mother's life's savings, and was hardly more worried by the transaction than I am to explain it concisely. The rent was due, the bank was peevish, and even the petty cash had given up the ghost. But Strong remained true to his name. Incidentally, he was president of the local dramatic society, the point being that he was familiar with the great poets, upon whom he drew for comfort in circumstances in which poetry, great or small, is of little avail.

> Love, I am full of lead.
> Some wine, within there, and our viands! Fortune knows
> We scorn her most when most she offers blows —

was among Strong's mental trumpetings when he came back from his long, despairing walk in the snow, and brought home to the querulous partner of his sorrows the bag of sausage-rolls which, together with a bottle of rum-punch, he proposed to wave in the face of Fortune. The gesture, though perhaps new to Holland, could not be new to a French audience, or to us who know all about the 'Beggared Outcast' of the night before radiating jollity on the back seat of next morning's London coach, 'eating walnuts out of a paper-bag with a bottle sticking out of his breast-pocket'.

Perhaps some such comparisons and analogies were necessary to beguile something which tactlessness might call the tedium of the first two acts. For a dramatist of the standing of Heijermans there seemed so very little 'doing'. The minute painting of a Dutch interior, and that interior not more exciting than a shop-parlour; the careful drawing of characters kith and kin with those of a greater writer and including the characteristic half-witted grandfather, the epileptic child, the dull schoolmaster, and the elderly female relative with money to lose; the almost anxious reproduction of Ibsen's 'yesterday's cold mutton' atmosphere — there must, one felt, be something impending, something beating up to make these unexciting things worth while. Perhaps the difference between the greater and the lesser dramatist is shown in this, that in Ibsen you know the moment the curtain goes up that spiritual momentum is, so to speak, afoot, whereas, watching Heijermans's play, one wondered whether anything of the sort is going to happen. Eventually, towards the end of the second act, the change took place. 'Love, I am full of lead —' It was on this quality of lead which was always in the heart of Strong, and not in Micawber's whole composition, that the meaning of the play turned. Up to this point the one hint of tragic import in the play had been the understanding between Strong and his daughter Sonia. It was she who divined that the long walk in the snow, which ended in the purchase of sausage-rolls and the appearance of junketing, had nearly been the prelude to a suicide. It was Sonia who upset the lamp and, purposely failing to retrieve it, committed the sacrifice of deliberate crime in order to obtain the insurance money for her father. At this point what had looked like trivialities receded; and with the third act the play's smallish beer was changed into a wine of the grand order. For Sonia's crime had bigger consequences than she intended; she forgot the epileptic child upstairs, who was burned to death.

This act is one of enormous power. Strong, half-guessing at the truth and putting on another kind of virtue, declines to take the insurance-money, and prefers to face the world with a clear conscience, thus proving that his previous courage was more than the careless pluck of irresponsibility. He arrives at this decision even when he is still uncertain as to the truth about the accident. And Sonia? Sonia cannot stand the drip-drip of the water coming through the ceiling at the very spot where the child's bed had been. She is driven by nervous terror to make confession to the family, and in the enlargement of that confession is supported by her father, because to make confession general is to confess to God. No praise could be too high for the depth and control of passion in Mr. Cellier's playing towards the end of this scene. But I should like to suggest to him that he does not pull out the tragic stop quite soon enough. The turning-point of the play is when Strong comes in from his walk after contemplating suicide. Sonia divines this, but it would make it easier for the audience and give the play better balance if we were allowed to perceive from the actor's face that the promenade has been tragic.

As for Miss Baddeley, I will only say that, confronted with matter in which a little hysteria would have been excusable, she gave to the long and difficult scene its full power while keeping perfect grasp of measure and containment. But I am inclined to think that the production did not give her full support. Sonia's expressed and her father's contained emotion are the dramatic pie here, and the subsidiary characters should be strictly kept from sticking their fingers in it. We know what they are feeling, and do not need to be shown. The thing is difficult, for Sonia must be up-stage at the spot where the water drips, and this gives the front of the stage to the unimportant people. But I suggest that a little experimenting might do no harm. In conclusion, if all London flocks to see this play, all London will be right.

October 9, 1929

LILIOM

BY FERENCZ MOLNAR

(Duke of York's)

IVOR NOVELLO, FAY COMPTON

ACTORS, like everybody else, cannot have matters both ways. They cannot expect to play parts for which their personalities fit them like gloves and then suddenly achieve success in something which is the direct opposite of their personalities. Or if they are going to do that they must begin to act, which is the last thing a celebrity wants to do who has obtained fame on the strength of

seraphic innocence and/or cherubic calves. Some little time ago
Mr. Ivor Novello appeared as the youthful Benvenuto Cellini, and
was fifty-fifty Florentine grace and engaging young Englishman
de nos jours. Later he played the part of a public schoolboy, whose
life proved that if you spent your youth in Quixotism and getting
expelled for your chum's sake, your end could only be drink,
dope, and the Thames Embankment. This part also Mr. Novello
filled out very entertainingly with beautiful profile and baby
grace, being quite perfectly the spoilt darling.

Now comes a Hungarian melodrama which, begging everybody's pardon, is pure highbrow gammon. It is gammon because
it persuades the highbrow, alive to Budapest as the spiritual home
of writers for little theatres, to cast about for symbolical, metaphysical, or poetical interpretations which the play simply will
not bear. It is the reverse of the fairy story; the clothes exist, but
no emperor is inside them. Liliom is a cut-throat with a heart of
gold, an Eulenspiegel turned sentimentalist. In the beginning he
is 'barker', fancy man, and *gigolo* to a lusty circus proprietress,
whom he deserts for a maid-servant. He beats the girl, but upon
hearing that she is to have a baby, cries the news to the housetops.
Next he arranges to murder a cashier, but, awaiting his victim,
babbles of sparrows and telegraph wires. There's not the smallest
telegraph pole but in its sentinelship like an angel sings. So, he
reflects, is it with the music of cut-throats' lives. Awaiting their
victim Liliom and his accomplice fall to gaming, at which Liliom
loses his share of the presently accruing spoil. Query: Would not
Liliom at once withdraw from the business? Why commit a profit-
less murder? However, the attempt is made and fails. Liliom
commits suicide, and is projected into a celestial police court, the
architecture of which is copied from the Early Lavatory style of
the National Liberal Club, where the celestial beak sentences him
to sixteen years' imprisonment with one day on earth in which
to do a kindness to his child. Returned to earth he strikes his
daughter without hurting her, which the mother declares to be a
common phenomenon, since to be struck by the beloved is not
displeasing. And we reflect that we are in Hungary, and that

Leopold von Sacher-Masoch was a Hungarian novelist. Finally, it all turns out to be a nightmare.

Surely it should be obvious to everybody that this hulking brute must be a brute who hulks, and that to present him with the aquiline grace and Latin effrontery of Mr. Novello at his most polished is to court disaster. As a blustering, throat-slitting bully this charming actor failed charmingly; as Mr. Bernard Shaw's Louis Dubedat he was delightful. The only possible view of this character is that hidden somewhere in thew and muscle is a spark of something men call soul. The fellow should be totally unable to explain himself, whereas Mr. Novello, one felt, could have explained anything and everything from Lord Beaverbrook's politics to the esoteric mystery of the Black Bottom. The character should have the maximum of physical ill-grace and clumsiness, with just a spark of something taking fire at the beauty of good sparrows, good women, and good telegraph wires. Mr. Novello gave us the exact opposite. His body was a river of grace, his thighs were cascades of loveliness, and his soul shone with a glow like that of a fountain lit up by coloured electric lights. Liliom was presented as a public-school Adonis with fastidious intonation, careful aspirates, and a sixth-form use of 'whom' in conjunction with prepositions. In a word, Mr. Novello was altogether too 'dossy'. His sweetheart, who should have been a sister to Miss Dorice Fordred's little slavey in *Riverside Nights*, was prettified by Miss Fay Compton into the drawing-room ornament we know so well, a conventional figure of innocence made up of one of Bellini's Madonnas, most of Ophelia, all of Mary Rose, and a dash of Mr. Milne's sophisticated chits. I do not refuse perfection to these impersonations of Miss Compton, but I do deny that a picture-gallery in Venice, the Court of Elsinore, Mr. Milne's drawing-rooms, and the kitchen in a Hungarian lodging-house are one and the same place. I suggest that what was wanted for the woman was not the percipient, lady-like parlourmaid wearing a halo instead of a cap, but an untutored servant wench, clumsy of manner and gait, with thick, strong arms and probably slightly bowed legs.

LILIOM

'Beefy face an' grubby 'and —
Law! wot do they understand?'

wrote Mr. Kipling. Miss Compton, asked by the police-inspector to show her hands for the purpose of proving that she really was a housemaid, produced a pair of ineffabilities, pink-tipped like the lotus buds of Shalimar, and crooned her references with all the saccharine sophistication of the Cromwell Road. All of which was exceedingly nice, and very good Compton, and brought this lady's admirers, among the more ardent of whom I count myself, to the seventy-seventh heaven of bliss. But I also like Molnar, or at least want to like him. And to introduce into his *naïve*, earth-bound fairy story a modish wistfulness is to do this author the greatest possible violence.

It may be that it would not be possible to cast this play with English actors. I could cast the woman's part quite easily in America, and should choose two actresses, both of whom would be entirely different and entirely right. The first would be Miss Jo Wallace, who played the stupid housemaid in *Is Ƶat So?* with so much brilliance and understanding. The second would be Miss Sara Haden, who acted here in *Sun Up*. But in each case I should insist on producing the play myself. That is to say, I should still hand over the main business of production to Mr. Komisarjevsky, and confine myself to warning the actress every evening, and five minutes before she took the stage, that if she went one-thousandth part of an inch towards favour and prettiness I would, speaking Shakespeareanly, 'chop her into messes'. As to Mr. Novello's part, I should probably have greater difficulty. Doubtless the actor for it lives, and lives also in America. I imagine him riding in cow-punching costume on a roaring broncho down some wild and woolly cañon, entering a tea-shop, depositing a revolver on the counter, and demanding a bottle of Johnnie Bootlegger.

December 26, 1926

THOU SHALT NOT
Translated from Zola's *Thérèse Raquin*
BY ALEXANDER TEXEIRA DE MATTOS
(Playhouse)

HENRY OSCAR, CATHLEEN NESBITT

A DISTINGUISHED critic has made three points of the greatest possible interest in connection with this revival. But first, in case people have forgotten Zola's play, let me run through the plot. The setting is a small draper's shop in a squalid corner of Paris, presided over by the strong-willed, doting Madame Raquin, whose weakling son, Camille, has married her niece Thérèse. The marriage is one of name only. Presently Thérèse takes a lover, who, with his mistress's connivance, murders Camille by tipping him out of a boat on one of those Sunday excursions by the Seine dear to the French *petit bourgeois*. A year later the guilty pair marry. But they cannot sleep; Camille's drowned face has murdered sleep. In the course of a quarrel they reveal their guilt to the old woman, who has a stroke. For a time she can neither speak nor write, and they live in daily fear of her recovery and that denunciation which they read in her eyes. One day it becomes obvious that she is getting better. Whereupon the pair take poison.

An eminent colleague tells us first that the play's attack, though magnificent, is not true. Second, that, though a woman is more than her crime, Zola writes as if the crime were all Thérèse. Third, that the story would have been more deeply moving if Zola 'had permitted us to witness the longing and thwarted attempts of Thérèse and Laurent to love each other, if he had allowed them still to hope as men and women do; above all, if he had been able to communicate the truth that no murderer is, to himself, as other murderers are, but exceptional, pitiable, isolated by special circumstances, desiring appeasement as a child desires refuge from a storm!' 'All this' — Mr. Morgan goes on to say — 'Zola misses and — let there be no mistake — deliberately sacrifices.' I propose to show that there *is* mistake, that Zola sacrifices nothing because there is nothing to sacrifice. Indeed at this point I find myself wondering whether Mr. Morgan can have forgotten that preface to the second edition of the novel specially written by Zola to make just this point of non-sacrifice. 'This tragedy is not true', writes my colleague, 'but it is magnificent.' Zola's point is that his tragedy is sordid, but of intense reality.

The argument that Thérèse should be more than her crime brings up a matter that has been insufficiently probed — the aura of past impersonations by familiar players. Over and over again we have admired the subtlety of Miss Cathleen Nesbitt's creations — bloodless women without appetite, dependent on their nerves as a puppet on his wires, so many Hedda Gablers. But is Thérèse such a creature? I think not. Remember Zola's description in the novel: 'One was conscious that beneath that apparent torpor were suppleness wholly feline, strong muscles, and a vast capacity for passion . . . Beneath a purposefully calm exterior Thérèse concealed the fierce ardours of her nature . . . To the outward eye she was calm and indifferent; her inner life was one of burning, uncontrollable desire.' Miss Nesbitt wonderfully suggests this torridity of flesh, these damped-down bodily fires. But why must we draw the inference that Thérèse is a spiritual volcano? Why not be satisfied with Zola's statement that Thérèse's complicity in the murder is brought about by the frustration of her physical senses?

I am going to suggest that it is the miscasting of that admirable actor Mr. Henry Oscar which has led Mr. Morgan to see in Zola's play more than Zola intended anybody to see. Mr. Oscar normally gives me more pleasure than almost any other player. The best actor in the world for suggesting compunction's natural prey, Mr. Oscar is wildly wrong as a *grand gaillard* possessed of broad shoulders, the neck of a bull, hands to fell an ox — the build of your all-in wrestler. It is just that quality of physical clumsiness which, in Charles Bovary, so displeased Emma that

Thérèse finds enchanting. And Laurent's mind goes with his physique. He is a healthy animal who takes Thérèse for mistress because she will cost him less than the women of the streets. He murders Camille out of prudence, and after the murder his trouble is not remorse, but the fear of Camille's ghost. In what way, then, does Mr. Morgan want these two criminals to be more than their crime? Are they to indulge in speculations on the nature of murder? But they are not the speculative sort. Are they to explore that apartness from other murderers for which William Bolitho coined the phrase 'demoniac Narcissism'? But they are not aware of any such apartness.

Now Zola, while steadily refusing to give us more of the criminal than their crime, expands that crime to include what comes after. I have no doubt the ultra-sensitive school would like this to mean that Thérèse and Laurent lie awake o' nights exchanging confidences of the order of 'The time has been, that, when the water was in, the man was out', and 'Who would have thought a drowned man swelled so horribly?' But our couple have long ago put all that behind them; their only fear is that old Madame Raquin may recover. Except that after a time Laurent becomes conscious of another fear. He has begun to notice a change in Thérèse. She goes out more than she used to. Can it be that her nerves are driving her towards confession? Confession to whom? A priest? The police? Laurent watches her and discovers that her rendezvous is of the most ordinary. 'But that's all right' is his relieved comment. 'A lover will keep her mind busy. What a bit of luck! No trouble with the police now.' And he wonders why he has not thought of the same thing. After a bit he does think of it, and it is Thérèse who finds the money for his succession of mistresses. It goes without saying that none of this could have been put on the stage of the 'eighties, which, in Paris, was still glued to the old Dumasian ethics. In France, as everywhere else except Norway, the drama was fifty years behind the novel.

When Zola's book first came out there had been a howl of execration. The French reviewers, with their talk of *ordure et puanteur*, said the same things the English dramatic critics were presently to say about Ibsen. It was the old story of scenting moral implications where an author has merely nosed for facts. An ulcer, said Zola, is an ulcer, and for a demonstrator to point one out to his students is neither moral nor immoral: 'I write as analyst pure and simple. I may be absorbed in putrefaction, but it is the absorption of the surgeon in his operating theatre.' And now for the operative passage which so utterly demolishes any theory of a larger life for Zola's characters: '*Thérèse Raquin* is intended as a study not of character but of temperament. This is the whole book. I have chosen two persons entirely dominated by their nerves and blood-stream, knowing nothing whatever about free will, and whose every act is dictated by impulses of the flesh. Thérèse and Laurent are brutes in the guise of human beings, nothing more. I have tried to show, step by step, the way passion works in these brutes; how they are swayed by their instincts; how they cannot escape the mental deterioration which follows on the heels of nervous excitement. The love-making of my precious couple is the satisfaction of a need; the murder they commit proceeds from their adultery, and is looked upon by them as wolves look upon the murder of a sheep. Finally, what I have called remorse is no more than physical disorder, the protest of two nervous systems which have reached breaking-point. Soul is entirely lacking, I am happy to say, and principally because I have willed it so.' Here, then, is the subnormal humanity of Mr. James Cain. Thérèse and Laurent are the Cora and Frank of *The Postman Always Rings Twice* fifty years before their time.

Zola wrote his preface to remove any possibility of future mis-understanding. Alas for the vanity of human wishes! Either Mr. Morgan or I have misunderstood him. My colleague says: 'The dreadful consistency of Zola's work is at once its power as a theatrical onslaught and its defect as an interpretation of life.' But how can that fail to be an interpretation which is not intended to be one? Zola ruled out interpretation when he wrote: 'They are brutes, nothing more.' 'There is', says Mr. Morgan, 'in life, a certain moderation, an irregularity in the working of Fate; she plays her victims or, in Hardy's language, has "sport" with them.'

But did Hardy use sport in quite this sense? Isn't his sentence —
I quote from memory — 'The President of the Immortals, in
Æschylean phrase, had ended his sport with Tess'? Meaning,
surely, not that the god had finished playing Tess like a fish, but
that the fun of cat-and-mouse with this particular mouse was
exhausted. Perhaps Mr. Morgan and I are not very far apart here.
Where we differ is in thinking that high-souled Æschylus has any
business in a galley of soulless brutes. What would Mr. Morgan
say if one set up Zola's soulless brutes as the standard by which to
measure soulful adumbrations in a play by Mr. Morgan?

I am in abstract discussion stepp'd in too far to get back to the
material performance. I can only offer apologies to Miss Nancy
Price, Mr. Bromley-Davenport, Mr. Morris Harvey, and Mr.
Brian Oulton for saying nothing about their contributions to an
evening of exceptional interest.

August 24, 1938

CYRANO DE BERGERAC
BY EDMOND ROSTAND
(Apollo)

ROBERT LORAINE

THE odds are tremendous against any poem remaining poetry in
a literal translation. Think what nonsense a French translator,
translating literally, must make of: 'And smale fowles maken
melodye' and: 'Sweete Themmes! runne softly till I end my song.'
Consider the dangers of 'Petits oiseaux' and 'Douce Tamise!'
What should we, as Englishmen, think if on the strength of such
journey-work Frenchmen were to proclaim Chaucer and Spenser
to be small beer? With the poet of conceits the injustice is still
greater. Rostand's conceits are immense, and all his plays are
tricked out with staggering felicity. His Muse prates of the stars
and breaks into the spangles of the sky-rocket. *Cyrano* is the

Crystal Palace of poetry. In this play, Rostand says nothing with unexampled virtuosity. So untranslatable is this virtuosity that the best-known of the great speeches has been abandoned by the translators as altogether impracticable.

This is the famous speech of fifty-four lines which rings the changes on the theme of Cyrano's nose.

Agressif: 'Moi, monsieur, si j'avais un tel nez,
Il faudrait sur le champ que je me l'amputasse!'
Amical: 'Mais il doit tremper dans votre tasse:
Pour boire, faites-vous fabriquer un hanap!'
Descriptif: 'C'est un roc! ... c'est un pic! ...
                                        c'est un cap!
Que dis-je, c'est un cap? ... C'est une péninsule!"
Curieux: 'De quoi sert cette oblongue capsule?
D'écritoire, monsieur, ou de boîte à ciseaux?'
Gracieux: 'Aimez-vous à ce point les oiseaux
Que paternellement vous vous préoccupâtes
De tendre ce perchoir à leurs petites pattes?'

And so on through the entire carillon, including the truculent, sympathetic, pedantic, dramatic, lyrical, bucolic. All of this has had to be omitted.

Then take the magnificent cadenza which Rostand and Coquelin wrought upon the vowel 'o':

Voici les cadets de Gascogne
Qui font cocus tous les jaloux!
O femme, adorable carogne,
Voici les cadets de Gascogne!
Que le vieil époux se renfrogne:
Sonnez, clairons! chantez, coucous!
Voici les cadets de Gascogne
Qui font cocus tous les jaloux!

This has been Englished into a characterless hotch-potch of vowels:

> Cadets of Gascony are these.
> A woman smiles — they're on their knees.
> A glance will bring them to their knees
> From brown or black eyes, grey or blue,
> Maid, wife, or widow, prude or shrew,
> They swiftly win who hotly woo.
> Cadets of Gascony are these.

We reflect that the French language as spoken by natives has its points, and that Nicholas Nickleby was right when he said that it 'admits of elegant conversation about everything'. Even about Woman considered as 'adorable carogne'.

In nothing does Rostand show his virtuosity better than in his mastery of rhyme. *Cyrano* in the French tinkles from end to end with pretty jingles, and the verse chosen by our translators hardly amounts to blank. Compare the happy, childish, self-satisfied delight of:

> Ton nom est dans mon cœur comme dans un grelot,
> Et comme tout le temps, Roxane, je frissonne,
> Tout le temps le grelot s'agite, et le nom sonne!

with

> Thy name is in my heart as in a sheep-bell,
> And as I ever tremble, thinking of thee,
> Ever the bell shakes, ever thy name ringeth!

In the one you can almost see the poet patting himself on the back; in the other you can visualize the translators labouring at a stiff job. And so it goes, all the way through. A rose must be *muscade* because in it Love hides *en ambuscade*. If Cyrano's blood runs cold at the thought of an amputated comma, it is because *virgule* is a jolly rhyme to *coagule*. 'Climb, you sluggard, climb!' is not so good as: 'Monte donc, animal!' for the double reason that *animal* drives the rhyme home, and also the point that Christian is no more than handsome clay. I do not suggest:

CHRISTIAN: How may I climb? Perchance this ivied chute?
CYRANO: Climb as thou wilt, but climb, thou handsome brute!

because it is neither poetic nor literal. But I defy anybody to say that it does not give the exact sense and feeling of the passage. 'Sluggard' was never the point. The whole poem being a Gasconnade, it follows that its most melancholy passages are a-shimmer with wit. The French play is an epic declaimed by a tight-rope walker; any Englishing must bring the funambulist to earth, where his performance loses its wonder.

It has always been a commonplace of criticism that Rostand's rhetoric has no *crescendo* and is not cumulative, and that you could miss out three-quarters and only miss Coquelin's delivery of it. The action in performance actually impedes the emotion. In the duel-scene the fighting gets in the way of the words, and even Coquelin was not very effective here. In the balcony scene you must wonder that Roxane can be such a little donkey as not to be able to distinguish between Christian's youthful bleat and passionate middle-age. The fourth act, in which the cadets, warned of an attack, sit down to lunch with Roxane but without any sentry posted, was always nonsense, serving no purpose except to get Christian killed. One may even think that the whole of Cyrano's Gazette is no more than an ingenious display-piece leading up to that last firework:

> Et samedi, vingt-six, une heure avant dîné,
> Monsieur de Bergerac est mort assassiné.

The reading of the letter is better theatre, and it was a fault of production that a spotlight should be turned full on the paper, making it the only visible thing in the darkness. Nevertheless, one would say that the last scene was the most dramatic. Though the performance at the Apollo could not have been more spirited, the play seemed curiously stagnant and to lose all the bustle which it undoubtedly has in reading. But, then, the bustle is in Rostand's words, and not in his characters, which never come to life. Or you might put it another way and say that a poet conceived a fantasy and then got actors to play it, whereas the dramatist visualizes his characters first and sets them down on paper afterwards.

It is an old saying that no rider can come without the horse, and

it is equally true that no actor can soar when his words keep close
to ground. Is it possible that Mr. Loraine is not a romantic actor,
and consequently has little feeling for the rhapsodical? He gave
us a reasoned and reasonable Cyrano, and was tender and witty
by turns, though he could not hang out the verse against the sky as
Coquelin did — there was no verse to hang — or attain to that
peculiar blend of laughter and tears which is the note of this play.
As a sober-minded Cyrano nobody could have been better, and
all his quiet passages were excellent. But he was hardly Cyrano-
esque. Messieurs Francis Lister and John Wyse were sufficiently
agreeable and odious as Christian and the Comte de Guiche.
Miss Winifred Wynne was obviously insufficiently experienced to
give distinction to Roxane, a part essentially demanding practice
of the stage. As usual, all the French words which had been
retained were mispronounced. Thus *rue* became *roo, madame* was
turned into *madarm,* all in the best public-school manner. But the
most annoying thing was the persistent pronunciation of *Cyrano* as
Cyrahno with the accent on the second syllable. Those who wish to
know how this name should be pronounced should study the
little verse:

> Monsieur de Cyrano
> Vraiment nous tyrannise;
> Malgré ce tyranneau
> On jouera *la Clorise.*

But these were minor blemishes. The point is that Mr. Loraine has
revived a play which is a great piece of French literature, and
which many people will enjoy, even in its English, ill-fitting dress.

November 13, 1927

THE YEARS BETWEEN
BY JEAN-JACQUES BERNARD
(Everyman)

LAWRENCE ANDERSON, BEATRICE WILSON

LET me state quite simply that *The Years Between* is one of the best plays performed in London for a very long time. The author has something to say, and says it with extraordinary delicacy, point, and finish. Or you might put it that he is content to supply clues and leave the mind to conduct its own investigation.

M. Jean-Jacques Bernard, the immensely serious son of one of the most frolicsome of French writers, has taken as his motive the love of mother and daughter for the same man. This theme is the basis of that novel which many people consider to be Maupassant's finest. Except that in *Fort comme la Mort* the man fell in love with the daughter after he had been the mother's lover. In *Le Printemps des Autres* there is no guilty relationship. The husband never knows the older woman's secret, and the daughter learns it only a few moments before the curtain falls. We, in the audience, do not know exactly at what point the mother herself becomes conscious of her impolitic, unlawful, but not unnatural passion. One understands that throughout at least two of the three acts the author desires the actress who is playing Clarisse to convey the idea of imperfect realization. She is to be tormented by she knows not what, to respond to incitements without knowing that they exist, to feel pangs without realizing that they are those of jealousy, to endure remorse without committal of sin.

I am not quite sure that in insisting upon this M. Bernard has not made the converse mistake to that of the playwright who put in his stage directions: 'Enter Jane, having drunk three cups of tea.' No actress can convey what in the nature of things the audience cannot possibly guess. But we know that Clarisse is in love with Maurice, and it is Clarisse who tells us. Everything that she says and does is unmistakable, and must point to this. Now, M. Bernard demands that Clarisse should be presented like a signpost which should know nothing of the directions written on it. I suggest that the more frantic Pirandellists should meet together to debate whether such a feat as being explicit, yet unconscious, can be within the competence of any player however skilful. Can the character impersonated remain ignorant of those cups of tea when she has to tell us all about them through the mouth of the impersonating actress? Let the Pirandellists decide. Frankly, my own view is that this is to demand too much from the art of the player, and to mistake the acted scene for the novelist's page. Fortunately, the piece loses nothing even if Clarisse knows all about her passion. That was my view of her whatever the author's intentions, and whichever of us is right I still hold that this is one of the very best plays I have seen for a long time. It is a small masterpiece.

Technically, M. Bernard's piece is superb. There is no plot in the ordinary sense, the spectators being concerned with extraordinarily delicate adjustments of relationships. Half-formed sentences reveal half-formed thoughts, impulses, motives, and you know that this is life as people really live it. No high and tragic horse is ridden, and though momentous issues are being decided, the quarrel is ostensibly about a cook or whether the young couple shall spend their holiday with Clarisse or by themselves. This is not a piece for the vulgar, who will see nothing in it, but for the connoisseur in craftsmanship. Miss Beatrice Wilson's acting in this play is the finest thing to be seen in London at the present time. She cannot give that unconsciousness which her author bids her, because nobody could. But in respect of every other intellectual subtlety her acting is in a class by itself. Miss Beatrix Thomson and Mr. Lawrence Anderson play with a corresponding brilliance of understanding and certainty of execution.

June 20, 1926

THE SULKY FIRE

BY JEAN-JACQUES BERNARD

(R.A.D.A. Players)

AUSTIN TREVOR, UNA VENNING

PROBABLY it was a disservice to M. Jean-Jacques Bernard to produce this early play immediately after his later and very much better work at the Everyman Theatre. *The Sulky Fire* is not, one suggests, a very good translation of the French *Le Feu Qui Reprend Mal*. A sulky fire is surely one which has never exhibited any inclination towards kindling, whereas the fire in this piece is supposed to have burnt brightly at the beginning, to have gone out through no fault of its own, and to have found difficulty in recovering its former heat. Better, one suggests, to have borrowed from *Othello* and called the piece *The Light Relumed*.

This is the story. When André Merin went into the trenches, the mayor billeted on André's wife a single American officer. Blanche fell in love with him, but remained 'correct'. Then the Armistice came, the officer went away, the husband returned, and Blanche, who loved him quite as well as the American, only differently, tidied up the domestic hearth and prepared to relight the fire. All this early part of the piece was extremely well done. The theory that a virtuous woman in addition to resisting temptation must not know temptation when she meets it, thus achieving victory without any cost to herself — this theory of feminine virtue dies hard on the sentimental stage. But M. Bernard had thoroughly aroused interest in, and sympathy for, a good woman who had won through to faithfulness at considerable expense of the sensibilities. Then Blanche did what all wives must do who are married to insanely jealous husbands — she denied both victory and cost, and pretended there had never been any battle. Unfortunately, Blanche had a friend. Jeanne was the most respected married woman in the village, but it was Jeanne's name which

155

had been murmured by one of André's comrades in his last agony. André is immensely disquieted by this. If Jeanne can lie, why should not Blanche lie also? For two hours the remorseless interrogatory went on, and frankly we got a little tired of it.

So tired, in fact, that we relieved the tedium by inventing Blanche's answers for her. Why didn't Blanche blurt out the truthful 'I wanted to be unfaithful, dear, but I *wasn't*'? And in the event of this failing, as of course it would have failed, why didn't she propose the alternative 'I didn't *want* to be unfaithful, old thing, but I *was*'? But neither the absolute yea or nay, nor any half-way state would have satisfied André. All he knew was that he would never know! The piece has a sentimental ending of the last fatuity. Blanche was preparing to go to America when André's father came in and said that he was eighty and lonely. Whereupon Blanche fell into André's arms, and André pretended to believe her for reasons infinitely less valid than any she had hitherto advanced. And we knew that the quarrel would start all over again immediately after supper, or probably half-way through.

The trouble about this piece is the extreme illiberality of its point of view. Let me invite all French playwrights to read again Diderot's *Supplément au Voyage de Bougainville* and consider again that witty philosopher's views 'on the inexpediency of attaching moral ideas to certain physical actions which have nothing to do with them'. The lesson to be learnt from M. Bernard's play is not that chastity is a virtue, but that Blanche's reward for exercising that virtue is so scant as to discourage all wives similarly circumstanced. One would invite serious French dramatists to consider afresh 'a precept which forbids the change which is in all nature; which orders a constancy which cannot be found in it, and which violates the liberty of the male and of the female by tying them to one another for ever; a fidelity confining the most capricious of pleasures to one and the same individual; a view of immutability between two creatures of flesh and blood, under a sky which is never for two minutes the same, in grottos which threaten ruin, at the base of crumbling rocks, beneath falling trees, on the unstable stones'.

The essence of M. Bernard's piece is the distress which goes on in the mind of a mean and pettifogging schoolmaster who cannot decide whether his wife is or is not telling tarradiddles. This makes for a dull play, just as *Othello* would be a dull play if you were to shear the words of their poetry, deprive the Moor of his splendour, and turn him into a jazz-drummer of splenetic temper. We, in this country, have heard all that M. Bernard has to tell us about jealousy since we could first read poetry, and a thousand times better put. And in any case, his schoolmaster is worrying about something which either never happened or is all over and done with. What we really wanted him to tackle was the situation arising if Blanche had had something to confess, and if she had met him with confession. There would have been room for new thought here, the question of believing or disbelieving a wife who may or may not be telling the truth having long been worn to rags.

It is quite possible, of course, that this sort of play appeals more to our neighbours than it does to us. It is possible that in France love and passion occupy a larger share of the attention than they do in this country. I cannot imagine any Englishman who has intellectual hobbies, or even goes in for golf, being solely absorbed by the passion of jealousy to the obliteration of every other interest, nor can I imagine any woman allowing herself to be manhandled and treated as if she were a favourite iron which some other golfer has pinched out of her husband's bag.

Miss Una Venning managed to create a good deal of sympathy for Blanche, though how she made the character keep her temper with her idiotic husband I have no notion. One imagines that Mr. Austin Trevor played the impolite lunatic exactly as his author would have had him played. That is to say, he made us all sympathize enormously with the American. Was it this actor who played the unendurable Frenchman in *Fallen Angels*? One certainly remembers that he was cast for Alec d'Urberville. And now comes the egregious André. It is possible that in disliking these three characters to the maximum point of dislike one is unconsciously paying a tribute to the actor. It is improbable, I suggest, that anybody could be quite so boring as Mr. Andrew Church-

man's Old Mérin, who spoke every word with the deliberation of
one cutting an epitaph in stone.

June 27, 1926

THE UNQUIET SPIRIT

BY JEAN-JACQUES BERNARD

(Westminster)

GILLIAN SCAIFE

ADEQUATELY acted, this play is one of the most beautiful that the
theatre has given us in the last fifty years. It is concerned on the
material plane with a questing woman and a discontented man.
Marceline has had several love-affairs, none of which has satisfied
her, since she pitched illusion too high, and reality can never come
up to the illusory. Out of ennui, for want of something better, or
for safety's sake, she has married Philip, as kind as he is unimaginative, taking to him as a traveller buffeted in Alpine storms will take
to a rest hut. But this satisfaction is also illusory. For Marceline
has cravings like those of the drug-taker deprived of his drug,
except that they are emotional and proceed from some unknown
yet necessary source. If this were a sentimental play our difficulty
as playgoers would be less. One would recognize that Marceline
has leapt too early and is looking too late, and that the rest of the
piece could only be a transposition into the feminine key of Romeo's
difficulty if he had married Rosaline before becoming aware
of Juliet.

But M. Jean-Jacques Bernard has much subtler and more
difficult fish to fry. Already he has given us a hint of his drama's
strange complexity by making Marceline, who is on her way to
Biarritz with her husband, insist on breaking their journey at St.
Jean de Luz for a reason which is as irresistible as it is inexplicable.
There is nothing of the minx about Marceline; she just does not
know the nature or the cause of her compulsion. Her brother

158

Robert detects her unhappiness, and knows, too, that Philip is not, in the phrase of the Victorian writer for schoolgirls, Mr. Right. Every complete soul, he tells her, is half male and half female, and one half must ever wander through the world till it finds its twin, which, living in Patagonia, may be separated in Space, or, not being born, may, as Maeterlinck suggests in *The Blue Bird*, be separated in Time. We feel that the boy has not cited his best authority, which is Schopenhauer in *Metaphysics of Love*:

> As a matter of fact, love determines nothing less than the establishment of the next generation. The existence and nature of the dramatis personae who come on to the scene when we have made our exit have been determined by some frivolous love-affair. The real aim of the whole of love's romance, although the persons concerned are unconscious of the fact, is that a particular being may come into the world; and the way and manner in which it is accomplished is a secondary consideration. However much those of lofty sentiments, and especially those in love, may refute the gross realism of my argument, they are nevertheless in the wrong.

Only, of course, our present love-affair is not frivolous to those taking part in it. It is the reverse of frivolous to Marceline, who in the same breath bids her husband hold her closer and asks if there is not somebody else in the room. There is, but it is only a very ordinary hotel-guest turning over magazines on a table.

Once again, and in the second act, Marceline meets this hotel-guest in a public garden in Paris. She is sitting on one form, and he, who has been a bank-clerk and is dropping in the social scale, is sitting on another and giving her *congé* to the girl who has been his mistress. The third act begins some years later with an explanation by Philip to Robert of his sister's strange malady which keeps them apart though they still live together. Then Marceline enters and repeats the request to be taken in her husband's arms which she made when, in the first act, she sensed some other presence. She is near hysteria, and in a long outburst relates how she has been compelled to sit outside prisons and hospitals without reason, and how equally without reason she has been able to abandon her vigils. And, of course, we realize that these have coincided with the hotel-guest's incarcerations and liberations. During this recital we have seen the figure of the unknown, now reduced to penury, creep past the house, and we know that it is his proximity which has brought on Marceline's hysteria. He leans against the door which Marceline bids her husband open, and falls dead. The curtain descends, and Marceline with the cry of 'Starved!' presents us with the key to the whole drama.

Whether the piece is a part of beauty or belongs to the higher tomfoolery must depend entirely upon the way in which Marceline is acted. Miss Gillian Scaife's difficulties are that physically she does not suggest the woman postulated, and that her technical means are insufficient. The late Clare Eames, in her beautiful and memorable performance for the Stage Society three years ago, was largely helped by a personality which suggested the unrest occasioned by a soul too eager for the body. Here, one felt, was the kind of woman likely to be subject to a stress as unusual as that postulated in this play. In Clare Eames's case the nerves were, so to speak, too near the surface of the body. Miss Scaife gives the contrary impression, that of reposeful domesticity, and one's immediate and continuing impression of her Marceline is that she is not a subject for the influences, quarter spiritual, quarter psychic, quarter physical, and quarter goodness-knows-what that M. Bernard indicates. Now the actress who plays Marceline has to accomplish everything there is in the play before she is given the words with which to tackle it. When Clare Eames played the scene in the Paris garden she expressed in her face, and even in her body, all we were afterwards to know of Marceline, so that we believed the husband's account of his wife's vagaries and her confession of them because the actress had already convinced us that here was the woman capable of them. Miss Scaife does nothing with this scene any more than she makes anything of that first encounter with and instinctive recoil from the stranger, in which her predecessor, by some miracle of suggestion, foretold the play. In addition Miss Scaife's enunciation makes it difficult for us to hear her. Mr. Kynaston Reeves repeats his sensitive performance of the husband, and as the brother Mr. Denys Blakelock is, as usual, enormously intelligent. In the part of the stranger, so well played by Mr. George Zucco, Mr. Richard Southern startles by an accent which if it be art makes him the finest character-actor of the day, but of which, if it be not art, he should get rid at the earliest opportunity.

I regret to have to say ungrateful things about this indifferent presentation of an exquisite piece, infinitely preferring to laud the management's perception that this is an exquisite piece which ought to be put on.

November 23, 1931

MARTINE
BY JEAN-JACQUES BERNARD
(Ambassadors)

ROGER LIVESEY, VICTORIA HOPPER

IF only people would not explain things! Or take care that their explanations are at least intelligent! It was surely a pity to burden this lovely little play with one of the most measurelessly silly prefaces which can ever have been printed in a programme. 'The originality of Jean-Jacques Bernard's works and the aesthetic processes by which he has vitalized them place him far above the few deft psychologists and dexterous dramatists who uphold the prestige and the *éclat* of comedy in France.' But since M. Bernard is easily the deftest of France's psychologists and the most dexterous of her dramatists, it follows that his 'aesthetic processes' have been so vital as to place him above himself. Which is absurd. The only person who is above himself is the writer of this nonsense.

Next we are to note that M. Bernard is 'not distinguished for the originality or strangeness of his subjects'. But doesn't his best-known play, *L'Ame en Peine*, deal with a woman of fashion so much in love with a man she has never seen, but only sensed, that she must sit outside the prison in which she doesn't even know him to be confined? It seems to me that such an interlude would be considered strange and original by most husbands, if not by most playwrights. Then there is something about it being harder to write an unwitty play than a witty one, after which M. Bernard is introduced as the arch-explainer of himself. He says: 'The theatre, above all, is the art of the unexpressed. It is less according to the rejoinders themselves than by the effect of the rejoinders that the most profound sentiments ought to be revealed. In addition to the dialogue which is heard, it is necessary to bring out a subjacent dialogue and to render this intelligible to the audience. . . . The logic of the theatre does not admit sentiments which the situation does not demand, and if the situation demands them it is not necessary to express them. Spoken words in themselves are poor instruments to express all that we wish to say. They have no more value than a violin string in repose, but what marvellous meaning may be drawn therefrom!'

Great artists should always be protected against themselves. What this very fine playwright means is that the theatre is a house of many mansions, one of which may properly be set aside for 'the art of the unexpressed'. As *Martine* proves, this can be a lovely little mansion, and in this line M. Bernard is easily the world's foremost painter and decorator. But just as all rooms in a house should not be alike, so it is nonsense to say that the theatre 'above all' ought to be this, that, or the other thing. Long before M. Bernard 'the logic of the theatre' did not admit sentiments which the situation did not demand. Otherwise we should have heard Goneril interrupting her father's curse and telling the old man to put a sock in it.

I confess to being a little staggered at the statement that the sentiments demanded by a situation should not be expressed. Æschylus and that lot did not impose this restriction on their wordy selves. Racine and Corneille were not exactly mum, and one way and another Shakespeare himself did a lot of talking. If 'Come, seeling night' and all that follows is mere catgut, then 'twere well *Macbeth* were acted in dumb show. The truth, of course, is that it is not M. Bernard's intention to call every dramatist unpacking his heart with words the naughty thing that Hamlet called himself. It is the old story of arguing from the particular to the general, with a spot of bad logic thrown in. That some cats have no tails does not mean that all cats must be tailless. That one kind of drama may be implicit does not rule out all the explicit kinds.

At this point the reader may be asking what all this theoretical and Shakespearean pother has to do with the love affair of a French peasant girl, which is all that *Martine* is about. The answer is that not I but the programme began it. If a thing is printed the presumption is that it is to be read, and it is surely a mistake to mystify willing playgoers at the Ambassadors with the statement that the piece they are about to see 'most aptly illustrates this doctrine of antagonism between literature and the theatre'. It doesn't. There is no antagonism. *Macbeth* is tolerable literature and fairly good theatre. Maeterlinck's *Intérieur*, in which hardly anything is said and nothing happens, is fairly good literature and tolerable theatre. The whole trouble is that the writer of this prefatory note thinks that literature means a lot of fine words. It may mean that or it may mean a few simple ones; and each kind can render its own theatre perfect service.

It only remains to be said that the theme of *Martine* is exquisitely suited not so much to the idiom as to the self-denying ordinance which M. Bernard has invented for and passed upon himself. But I have to say that in my opinion he has cheated. His theatre proclaims itself as relying not on dialogue which is heard, but upon subjacent dialogue which is not; its heard melodies may be sweet or sour, but those unheard are to be the ones that matter. Surely if this theory is to be at all valid it should be applied to people who have a power of expression which, because of the dramatist's self-imposed discipline, they must not use? Silence is only golden because speech is silver, and dumbness is no virtue in a man who cannot speak. If, therefore, there were any serious theory of play-writing involved, the characters in this play must be capable not only of knowing what they are suffering, but of expressing that knowledge. Whereas the tragedy in this piece is the exact opposite, since it is the tragedy of dumb animals who do not need any theory of non-expression to explain their inability to talk. Again, what a fearful pother, and all because a playwright has not been protected from himself!

Martine's tragedy has happened a million times. The young gentleman comes down to the farm, trifles innocently with Martine's affections, marries the daughter of the local landed proprietor, and goes out of the peasant girl's life for ever. She must now marry a brutalizing if not brutal clod and bear him children, with only a grave at the end of forty, fifty, sixty empty years. It is a play of infinite contrivance, because here is the last word in simplification. It is utterly heartrending. It is more poignant than Hardy's *Woodlanders*, because Marty South had not to marry, whereas little Martine must become the instrument of that fecundity which is at once the burden and the meaning of France. 'When you have had your baby', says one of the couple who have unwittingly wrecked Martine's life, 'you must come and see us in Paris!' And the oafish husband argues that this must be impossible, since there will be another baby on the way. In this dread and masterly sentence Martine's tragedy stands revealed.

The piece is beautifully acted. Since Miss Victoria Hopper, who must instantly change her name, is making her first appearance, it is too early to tell how good an actress she may become; the simplicity and unforced pathos of her Martine are this play's justification. Miss Hilda Trevelyan gives the most delicate and tender value to the scene in which, almost without words, she breaks to the child what her tragedy is to be. Mr. Roger Livesey with great skill avoids forcing the note of the uncomprehending clod, Mr. Hubert Gregg gives a sensitive rendering of the unwitting mischief-maker, while as his wife Miss Rosalinde Fuller by doing one-tenth of her normal execution is ten times more successful than I have ever seen her. The piece must be the best that our theatre will know this year, for though a little masterpiece it is an impeccable one. I do not always see eye to eye with Mr. Carroll in his productions. To this one I take off my best hat.

May 23, 1933

N O E

BY ANDRÉ OBEY
(Théâtre du Vieux-Colombier. Arts)

AUGUSTE BOVÉRIO

THERE is an old story of a journalist who called on Lucien Guitry and asked him what his son was writing. 'A play!' mumbled the old actor, who was at breakfast. 'Upon what subject?' asked the journalist, and through a barricade of sustenance the old man was understood to reply: 'The Book of Genesis.' 'Who for?' pursued the interviewer. 'Sarah Bernhardt!' said Guitry with finality. But the other was not to be dismissed so easily. 'What part is Sarah to play?' he persisted. Guitry looked the young man full in the face and said: 'Noah!' That which took place at the Arts Theatre on Friday night was not that play!

Not that one would put this theme beyond, as the nursemaids say, our Sacha; history, scriptural or secular, can have few bogeys for the man who can conceive the third Napoleon as hero. But M. Obey's piece has a background of seriousness not hitherto envisaged by our first boulevardier. At the beginning his piece would appear to be conceived in the vein of Halévy, who, in *Le Rêve*, could write of Le Père Eternel 'wearing his Early Italian manner'. We see Noah tinkering away at, and putting the last touches to, his ark. He has already had what I can only describe as a confab with the Almighty, and now says: 'Excusez-moi! Je regrette infiniment de vous déranger encore, mais faut-il mettre un gouvernail?' The question of the rudder being settled, the animals appear — the bear, the lion, the baboon, the tiger, the heifer, the lamb, the wolf, and last the elephant — all wearing that humanized air of being slightly pleased with themselves so characteristic of the plates in Buffon. They go aboard, and now Noah's sons appear. On being shown the new construction Sem says: 'C'est charmant! Qu'est-ce que c'est?' whereas Japhet is content to pronounce it 'épatant', and Cham mildly wonders what has put the idea of a ship into the old man's head. Presently the mother arrives, and one gathers that married life with Noah has taught her not to be surprised at anything. Then enter the three virgins who are destined to re-people the earth, and finally we come to The Man, symbol of unthinking brute, who takes Noah for a sorcerer. Up to this point the play has worn the air of an operette without the music, as who should say 'Le Beau Noé' instead of 'La Belle Hélène'. But now all Noah's world deems him mad with his talk of rain in a season of drought, of sailing over parched land a hundred miles from the sea. Then falls the first drop. It falls upon the forehead of the brute, and with it a primitive earnestness comes into the play.

The second act shows us the deck of the ark forty days later. It is the first day of sun, and whoso wants to realize the atmosphere here has only to bethink him of the opening bars of Grieg's *Morning*. Noah devises a romp for his family, in which all join. But the waste of waters continues, and the third act sees general discouragement. In his trouble Noah confides in the animals, telling them that they are not abandoned, but only a little neglected of God. With them he addresses a last confident prayer, and as he lies down to sleep the wind arises. This is a scene of simple and utter loveliness, for which, so far as I know, the author is indebted to nobody, though this in truth should be said of the whole play. In the fourth act Noah sends out his emissaries, and here again the quality of the emotion, compounded of simple writing and exquisite acting, amazes. The last act shows the grounding of the ark, the quarrel of the sons, their departure with their wives to the ends of the earth, and Noah, sufficient to himself provided God is with him, tackling a new habitation. 'Seigneur, êtes-vous content de moi?' he asks. The rainbow is his answer.

LE VIOL DE LUCRÈCE

This artless little play, put together with an infinity of contrivance, moves with perfect poise on twin planes of amusement and emotion. In the beginning we are reminded of some round-game for children, primitive 'Happy Families', let us say. But long before the end we know that we have been in touch with a mind which, having acquired all sophistication, has yet lost nothing of simplicity. As a work of art the thing is flawless and unique, or perhaps it would be more proper to say that I know nothing from which it can be derived. As a last impression let me suggest a poem by Blake acted by figures in a Gauguin canvas come to life and talking the everyday jargon of Paris. The playing throughout was superb, and in M. Auguste Bovério one respectfully salutes a very fine actor.

June 12, 1931

LE VIOL DE LUCRÈCE

BY ANDRÉ OBEY

(Théâtre du Vieux-Colombier. Arts)

AUGUSTE BOVÉRIO, MLLE. DASTÉ

'CE bon Brutus! Ça, tu sais, c'est un numéro!' says the first soldier, talking to-day's *argot*. Brutus is the quipster whose lips turn to bronze when at the end he promises the populace that the wild boar, Tarquin, is 'for it', as we, in our lingo, would say. 'Pourquoi Tarquin fait-il cette gueule-là?' asks the second soldier. His comrade explains that Tarquin is 'fed up', since a nobody like Collatin can be so richly married while he, a King's son, still lacks a wife. Note that in making his Roman soldiers talk like this, M. Obey merely repeats Shakespeare's trick of making his Athenian workmen talk like the Warwickshire rustics of his own time. This is the only way in which to bring the past to life again; anything else is mummification.

Now the roysterers have left the tent of Collatin, the secure and happy husband, and sought their own. But Tarquin bids his groom saddle his horse, whose head he is to turn towards Rome. Now we see Lucrèce at her needle among her maidens babbling like novices in a convent, but so grouped and each assuming disposition of such loveliness that about and over them is the clarity of a thirteenth-century painting. But Lucrèce is more mysteriously attended. For here come the Reciter and Recitress, two half-masked figures who fulfil the triple rôle of Chorus, Messenger and Mouthpiece. Chorus interpreting the emotion of the scene is familiar, and Messenger is a little less than Greek in the sense that the messages brought concern not things too horrific for visual presentation, but merely matters not convenient to be seen. Yet even here the device is intensely dramatic, as when the Recitress verbalizes the brooding scene:

> Elle file. Comme tous les soirs, comme chaque soir, comme hier soir, Lucrèce file la laine au milieu de ses femmes —

and is capped by the Reciter's clamant picture not only of Tarquin's ravishing stride but of his horse's gallop:

> Il est parti! Tarquin est parti! Le Seigneur Tarquin est parti! ... Il galope! Comme il galope! Vous entendez? Entendez-vous les quatre fers de son cheval carillonner sur les pavés de la route romaine?

We see Lucrèce's chamber, empty save the bed round which the curtains are drawn. The Reciter and Recitress have mounted pulpits on each side of the stage, as who should say Joel and the Erythraean Sybil on Michael Angelo's ceiling. Now o'er this half of the world Nature seeming dead, the Woman who is Mouthpiece for Lucrèce makes for us an image of her quiet slumber. She hears no more than the crooning of the doves, whereas the Man, alarum'd by Tarquin's sentinel, bids us hear the wolf. At last comes Tarquin, in the full light of the stage stealing along black corridors and fumbling at dark doors while the Reciter explains what he does and the emotions tearing his breast. He enters the chamber and draws aside the curtains of the bed. Here follows a scene of unmitigated grandeur, in which Tarquin confesses full knowledge of the colour of his deed and its consequences to their utmost ramification of remorse and shame. The last thing which should restrain him is his kingship, voiced by the Reciter crying four times in tones to wake the conscience of the dead: 'Tarquin-roi! Roi des Romains! Roi! Roi!' But in vain.

The next act begins with the gentle chatter of the maidens going to attend their mistress's rising. This is followed by a long, but not too long, tableau of the distress of Lucrèce, beautifully commented by the Recitress while the Reciter shocks us to further realization with a vignette of Tarquin returning to camp, throwing himself off his horse, and boisterous with his 'Bonjour, Collatin, tu as une mine superbe, haha! une mine de pape!' It is the Reciter who, as the crowd gathers to listen to Lucrèce's avowal, puts the whole thing back in time:

> La grande Rome est en histoire. Athènes, jadis, à ses grandes heures, fut en beauté; Babylone, en amour; Troie, en alarmes. Un jour, Berlin sera en guerre et Paris, en révolution. Rome, aujourd'hui, est en histoire.

Collatin comes, and has his terrible: 'Tarquin est resté ici?' there being that in his tones which reveals the eternal Latin across whose mind the notion of his wife as drab is beginning to flit. Falteringly Lucrèce tells her story of the threat under which Tarquin forced her submission. But Collatin hardly listens, Lucrèce despatches herself in the high Roman fashion, and the tragedy is complete. The last word is with Brutus, who declares that she whom Tarquin has violated is not only Lucrèce but their common mother, Rome.

This magnificent and austere tragedy is perfectly staged and acted. Throughout the play the tones of M. Bovério's voice, ranging from organ bass to shrill trumpet, are something which the English stage has not heard in my day. Adding this player's Reciter to his Noé, we are entitled, I think, to acclaim not only the fine but the great actor. Mlle. Suzanne Bing brings immense perception to the long and difficult rôle of the Recitress, while for the spiritual tenderness and beauty of Mlle. Marie-Hélène Dasté's

Lucrèce no praise can be too high. M. Jean Dasté gives to Collatin some of the glamour of old legend, the representatives of the flower-like maidens fulfil their tasks perfectly, and one should not overlook M. Jean Villard's sketch of a major-domo. Remains only the Tarquin of M. Aman Maistre, and of this good actor it shall be said that his portrait shows the firm drawing of an old master. These distinguished visitors are to move to-morrow to the Ambassadors Theatre for a short season, where it is to be hoped that not only the general public but our English actors will contrive to see them. Everything that the leaders do is a part of great acting, whilst the enunciation of the company's humblest member puts our mumblers to shame.

June 17, 1931

BATAILLE DE LA MARNE
BY ANDRÉ OBEY
(Compagnie des Quinze. New)

AUGUSTE BOVÉRIO, MLLE. DASTÉ

On the stage nothing save a few dun hangings veiling the bare theatre walls, and the floor artificially raked to enable the actors to move in different planes. Off the stage an immense distance away a military band is playing, and in the wings the armies of France go by. We see them through the eyes of five or six peasant women clothed in black and grouped as you may see them in the fields of France or the canvases of Millet.

Enter the Messenger wearing his *carrick* or coat with three capes. Strange combination, the wear of French coachmen and the symbol of French military genius. And now the events of August 1914 come to us through the Messenger, good and bad news being conveyed through the ringing and awed tones of his voice, through the blaze and darkening of his eye. The gay troops in their pre-war blue and red have reached Mulhouse. The houses of Altkirch are bright with flags that have not waved since 1870. An old peasant promises himself to renew old friendships at Strasbourg and make the journey on foot.

The calm is excessive. 'Hist!' says the Messenger, lending an ear to that which is happening far away. 'A check!' Brusquely he leaves the scene. The figure of France enters, and we see in Mlle. Dasté's aspect that France is anxious. The Messenger re-enters with tidings that the mind rejects — the news that a million German soldiers are on French soil — and his words are already a carillon of defeat: 'Echec de la première et de la deuxième armées en Alsace! Echec des troisième et quatrième armées dans le Luxembourg belge. Echec de la cinquième armée sur la Sambre! Echec du corps expéditionnaire britannique à Mons! Echec sur toute la ligne!'

Women arrive from the invaded districts. In one village a game-keeper has fired on the Germans, who, in reprisal, have shot the mayor. Here we find a pointer to this play's compression and momentum, since in a dozen words we receive the full impact of that, in other hands, full-length tragedy, *The Burgomaster of Stilemonde*. Then a handful of soldiers drag themselves over the ground, destroyed by that fatigue in comparison with which defeat and victory are meaningless. Now the Messenger has that to impart which strikes France to the ground so that he must speak to her with bent head and as to the dying.

The Cathedral of Rheims has been bombarded. The images of the saints have been destroyed. Alone the statue of Joan of Arc . . . But enough of portents. The enemy continues to advance and has passed St. Quentin. Why does the General hold his hand? He is well, has never been better. Rises at six, bed at ten. The mid-day meal at noon, dinner at eight, a little walk after dinner for the digestion, the sleep of a child. Round their chief the officers of the General Staff rage in nightmare impotence. He sleeps. Why? The tension increases. The soldiers who should defend Paris retreat and again retreat. The women taunt them and ask whether Marseilles will be far enough. France joins in the jeers and hurls at her children the unforgivable among insults:

Lâches! lâches! Eh! lâches! . . . Vous savez ce qu'ils disent de vous? Hein? Ce qu'ils écrivent de vous à leur famille? Oui, on a trouvé une lettre sur un prisonnier allemand — car mes troupes ont fait un prisonnier, ha! ha! — la lettre commence comme ça: 'Cette fameuse armée francaise qui f . . . le camp . . .' Vous avez entendu! . . . Quoi? . . . Oh! je vous en prie! Ne vous gênez pas pour moi! . . . Rien, je vous dis . . . Je ne vous demande rien . . . Allez, hop! . . . F . . . le camp!

As the curtain falls on the first part a German soldier takes the stage. Alone the Messenger has not lost hope, since high up in the sky he has heard the song of a lark.

In the second part the Messenger describes the General's stupor of contemplation before his maps, and how it has not been stupor. Then comes the finest thing in the play, a *récit* which will become famous in French literature. This is the story of the taxi-driver describing how he took to the front a corporal and four soldiers, a Limousin, a Morvandiau, a Tourangeau, and a Breton, who as they neared the lines began to sing each the song of his people. This is followed by something belonging to another loveliness.

France, sensing the new hope, bids her soldiers take new courage. Still in that summer the old men and women shall gather the grapes in vineyards which the soldiers of France will have protected. France smiles at an old woman filling that basket for which she, the embodiment of a country, forgets the local name. A soldier from the vine districts prompts her. France continues. The corn shall still be harvested and threshed, and from the farms will rise again that golden dust which is properly called . . . A soldier who has laboured at the harvesting prompts her.

And now the piece draws to an end. During their retreat the soldiers have continually advanced towards the footlights, and now, physically in the theatre, can go no further. 'En avant!' cries France, and the superb right-about turn is the image which tells us that the Battle of the Marne has begun. The victorious Generals are saluted by name. Manoury! French! Foch! Sarrail! Castelnau! Joffre! One name is singled out for its mere beauty of sound. 'Général Franchet d'Espérey! Vous dont le nom est beau comme une devise!' We recognize, in this apostrophe, unthinkable in any other language, the *panache* which is France, and see again the blue and gold of her statues to the Maid.

I seem to have read that this piece is not successful. I can only say that I saw nearly all of it through a mist, and that I will never pronounce a piece unsuccessful which, as this play did on Thursday afternoon, reduces a whole audience to tears. Is it objected that the Gallic cock crows a little too loudly over a battle which was rather lost by the Germans than won by the French? Such considerations are the dull stuff of staff lectures at the Ecole Militaire; they do not concern the work of art which is this piece. Further, we who are English must remember that M. Obey is a Frenchman writing for a people whose spirit cannot be o'ercrowed. It is unnecessary to say how Mlle. Dasté limns France and how M. Bovério delivers her message. Hardly anything happens on the stage, yet owing to the astonishing talent of this dramatist aided by these two great artists the play begins its significance where realism ends.

Mlle. Bing, in the tiny part of the mother of one of the soldiers, again reveals herself as one of the notable actresses of our time, and the whole cast plays with a perfection of understanding and a mastery of ensemble beyond praise. This is great, perhaps the greatest acting, since on a bare stage the actors recreate not the passion of one or two, but the agony of a nation.

February 4, 1932

L'ÉCOLE DES MARIS
BY MOLIÈRE

LE CHANDELIER
BY ALFRED DE MUSSET

Á QUOI RÊVENT LES JEUNES FILLES
BY ALFRED DE MUSSET

LE LÉGATAIRE UNIVERSEL
BY JEAN-FRANÇOIS REGNARD
(Savoy)

LA COMÉDIE FRANÇAISE

That the House of Molière must start with a play by Molière is a self-evident proposition. But a proposition attended with some danger, since it too often means *Le Misanthrope*, which inaugurated the famous visit of 1879 and of which Sarcey wrote: 'Il était à craindre que *Le Misanthrope* n'ennuyât quelque peu son monde. Dame! entre nous, *Le Misanthrope*, même à Paris, n'est pas toujours régalant; on l'écoute avec respect, mais sans transport.' Joseph Knight, dealing with the same visit and the same play, has the following:

> *Le Misanthrope* is a difficult play wherewith to please an English audience. Without either action or situation, it seeks to interest by purely psychological processes, and exposes to vulgar gaze a nature which vulgar perceptions can never penetrate. It is painful, if edifying, to watch the efforts to force into drollery the biting phrases of Alceste, out of regard for a public which, hearing of Molière as a comic writer, waits for comic scenes.

But the scenes in *L'École des Maris*, now preferred by our visitors,

174

are comic. They expose to English gaze that which English perception has no difficulty in penetrating. Sganarelle, the eternal *niais*, is universal in the sense that Sancho Panza and Aguecheek, to whom he is first and second cousin, are universal; it is only their manners which they wear with a difference. Every drama in the world has had its gallant, Valère; our own Shakespeare found it convenient to unite wideawake heroine and knowing serving-maid in the person of Maria; and the valet, Ergaste, is our old friend Figaro all over again. Only the presentation is French, and here Hazlitt . . .

'Pest upon the fellow!' I can hear the reader saying. 'Why can't he tell us what he thinks and not what other people have thought?' The point is that I cannot, and perhaps will not, divorce myself from what better men have thought and better expressed on this great subject. Hazlitt said of *L'École des Maris*:

> The plot is charming, and the style is profuse of sense and wit; but there is this remark to be made here, as of other of Molière's plays, that however elegant, ingenious, or natural, the scene must be laid in France, that the whole passes under that empire of words, which is confined to her airy limits, and that there is a credulous and unqualified assent to verbal professions necessary to carry on the plot, which can be found nowhere but in France.

The piece was deliciously presented and, as far as one knows, traditionally, except that in Ergaste Molière appeared to have foreseen the Russian Ballet, the actor in this case, M. Robert Manuel, contributing a literally skipping wit·which added greatly to the visual excitement of the piece. Gorgeously caparisoned, M. Jean Weber raised the clowning of Valère, if that be not too gross a word, to heights independent of language. In the short part of Léonor Mlle. Irène Brillant showed how galleons move; and as Isabelle Mlle. Lise Delamare was a little rogue in samite. But the keystone of the play must always be the Sganarelle, and here M. Max Lafon's performance struck us as the perfect piece of engineering, holding the plot together and meeting its strains and stresses with perfect understanding and imperturbable good humour.

Musset's *Le Chandelier* was for an English audience much more difficult. For here the passion of love is exposed to our gaze in an aspect of which until recently English sense has by no means approved. Truth insists that for 'love' in the foregoing sentence one should read 'adultery'. Now this was the period in which Musset was most in thrall to Byron — indeed his detractors dubbed him 'Byronet' and even 'Mademoiselle Byron' — that enslaver of reason whose system of ethics, compounded, according to Macaulay, of misanthropy and voluptuousness, knew only two commandments, to hate your neighbour and to love your neighbour's wife. But it is not Musset's immorality, if you pass the word, in this play which affrights the modern English sense: our own Mr. Coward has given us a wholly French courage. The point is Musset's brand of melancholy, which is still alien to the English temperament. To quote Macaulay again:

> We know very few persons engaged in active life, who, even if they were to procure stools to be melancholy upon, would be able to enjoy much of what somebody calls the 'ecstasy of woe'.

But Musset's Fortunio is just such an ecstatic; he does nothing but weep, and the English sense cannot wholly sympathize with this overflowing urn. We feel that Fortunio belongs to that part of Dickens's world which contains Job Trotter and the Rev. Stiggins, and that his name is Dick Sniveller.

Our visitors did their gracious best to put this play across not only the footlights but the Channel. M. Gaston Baty's production and the décor of M. Marty were both sentimental and effective, to the point when looking at this play was like listening to a Chopin ballade by candlelight. Jacqueline was given a quite unimaginable finesse by Mlle. Madeleine Renaud, who made her a 'keepsake' of the period and look all the virtues she does not possess. So much for the first evening.

The second was more understandable and altogether jollier, though not so Britannically jolly that the programme was entitled

to declare Musset's *À Quoi Rêvent les Jeunes Filles* to be in prose!
It isn't. It is in verse, and verse in which the wit and sensibility,
equally matched, are so much part of each other that you think
of the result as a compound rather than a mixture. If it were
possible to cavil at the acting of this company during the week
it would be at M. Denis d'Ines's 'throwing away' of the exquisite
soliloquy beginning:

> Mon Dieu! tu m'as béni. — Tu m'as donné deux filles;
> Autour de mon trésor je n'ai jamais veillé . . .

and ending:

> Je te livre, ô mon Dieu! ces deux herbes tremblantes.
> Donne-leur le bonheur, si je l'ai mérité.

But this is dangerous ground; it is possible that what is sentimentality to us may be sentiment to a nation whose peculiar genius it
is to know in any art exactly how much to put into any scale at
any moment. It is all very well for the programme to prattle of
music by Debussy and Delibes. The décor of Marie Laurencin, the
faintly balletic charm of Mlles. Mony Dalmès and Françoise Delille,
M. Pierre Bertin's stressing but not over-stressing of the extrava-
gances of *le fat*, Irus, and the grave charm of M. Julien Bertheau's
Silvio — all of these combined to keep the comedy in its Chopin-
esque dimension, the music in our ears being, I do not hesitate to
affirm, the Valse in C sharp minor.

Regnard's great farce of *Le Légataire Universel* brings us back
to the battleground of argument where we make the surprising
discovery that our neighbours are capable of flirting with that to
which the Englishman is wedded — the moral justification of his
pleasures. We all remember how Charles Lamb provided
Restoration comedy with a moral coating when, of course, he
should have said: 'Vice is its own reward — see Restoration
comedy!' The editor of my Regnard actually seeks to justify the
insensibilities of a piece which makes a mock at a dying man!

Et voici le prestigieux tour d'adresse: c'est d'un sujet funèbre
que jaillit ce rire intarissable, d'un spectacle en soi propre à

faire naître la pitié et l'horreur. Géronte, cet affligeant exem-
plaire de l'humaine misère, est gourmandé, rudoyé à plaisir par
trois gredins qui exploitent sa crédulité et son agonie. Le
spectateur devrait, semble-t-il, compatir et s'indigner. Comment l'artiste s'y est-il pris pour éviter le drame qui est au fond
des choses, et même le moindre commencement d'émotion
douloureuse? Il a éloigné de la victime la sympathie et l'estime.
Au physique et au moral, Géronte est répugnant, à la fois tout
à fait ridicule et tout à fait odieux. . . .

And so on and so forth. But why not be content with the ridiculous
part of the business and never mind about the odious? The piece
is hateful only if Punch-and-Judy is hateful. It is a quasi-
mediæval snook cocked at the major catastrophes. Here are the
body and mind of an old man falling apart like a worn-out type-
writer, and the spectacle is very, very funny. At least it is when
there is a great French comedian to make it so. M. Fernand
Ledoux is such a comedian. What cackling proceeded from his
bosom when bronchial derangement permitted anything to proceed at all! Did ever human legs so vacillate? Except perhaps
Grandfather Smallweed, was ever anybody so laid out in his chair
by those hoping to lay him out in his coffin?

The spring of mischief was the Crispin of M. Pierre Dux, who
in this part contrived to run the entire gamut of the *cocasse* without
respect to clime or time. Some such span as in our own country
might begin with Ben Jonson's Mosca and end at a pantomime
dame by Mr. Douglas Byng. This was the perfection of acting,
and one might remark about both players not only their intellectual and artistic but their physical fitness. The very pores of
their skin seemed to act, and in this piece they had to. I have no
space left to pay more than formal but sincere compliments to
Mlle. Béatrice Bretty and the other players. It would be improper
to let our visitors depart without an expression of admiration for
the enormous technical skill which has brought these four elaborate
productions on an unfamiliar stage to a complete and hitchless
success. Every seat throughout the week was taken, and the

audiences were as discriminating as they were enthusiastic. The second because of the first.

February 28, March 3, 1939

SIX CHARACTERS IN SEARCH OF AN AUTHOR

BY LUIGI PIRANDELLO
(New Oxford)

HENRY IV (in Italian)

BY LUIGI PIRANDELLO
(New Oxford)

RUGGERO RUGGERI, MARTA ABBA

HENRY IV (in English)

BY LUIGI PIRANDELLO
(Everyman)

ERNEST MILTON

AND THAT'S THE TRUTH

BY LUIGI PIRANDELLO
(Lyric, Hammersmith)

NIGEL PLAYFAIR, CLAUDE RAINS, NANCY PRICE, DOROTHY GREEN

THIS week has been for me a defeat, if not a complete rout. I do not know, alas, a single word of Italian, and to sit stone-deaf before two plays, every word of which is an intellectual challenge, induces in me maximum exasperation. It is like taking a picture-lover into a gallery, blindfolding him, and bidding him judge a Cézanne by his finger-tips. All that follows here, then, is a hodge-

179

podge of the printed page and the visible, entirely unintelligible superficies of the plays in performance. Add the lesson taught by the early critics of Ibsen and Shaw, unlearned as yet by the detractors of Tchehov and Glaspell, and the reader must see how pathetically anxious I am not to be mistaken in Pirandello. At the same time I will never be bluffed into deeming any play 'marvellous', in Mr. Coward's lingo, simply because I cannot understand it.

These things being said, let me suggest that I find Pirandello to be a great dramatist for those very reasons which the Pirandellists deny. They insist that the master has broken the bounds set to the old-fashioned 'sentimental' Latin play, and abandoned those largely ethical motivations of the 'old' theatre which developed spiritual crises from the conflict of impulses with a rigid framework of law and convention. What, then, has Pirandello substituted? Simply the theory of Relativity as applied to persons instead of to formulae. I confess that this seems to me to be not very new. The idea that two people, having a different sense and value of things, can never really communicate is sufficiently familiar. To me a person whose soul is centred in the acquisition of used, or even unused, postage-stamps is demented; to your fresh-air fiend a man who for pleasure spends a fine summer evening mewed up in a stuffy theatre is obviously a lunatic. How can the words 'good' and 'bad' have any meaning between people who have such different standards of what is desirable and undesirable? It is only a step from this to the imperfect differentiation between sane and insane, real and unreal.

Are characters in a book real? An English poet has written of those legendary heroes 'who soon as we are born are straight our friends'. Is not Mr. Micawber the friend of every Englishman from the day of his birth? Is he less *real* than the thousands of actual people who, once seen, are never remembered? Would Mr. Micawber have existed if Dickens, dissatisfied with his novel, had never given it to the press? That's the whole burden of *Six Characters in Search of an Author*. The Pirandellists are particularly anxious that we should look upon these works as stage-dramas and not as philosophical dissertations. I humbly suggest that in the theatre the comedy, if not the tragedy, comes off excellently. First you have the stage filled with a company of actors complete with manager, prompter, and stage hands. Could any collection of people be more real? We think no, and are immediately confuted. For the Six Characters, never quite brought to birth by their author and 'side-tracked' by him, now appear, looking not so much like the unborn as the recently-interred. And at once they put up a show of living, the fierce intensity of which makes ghosts of the real people on the stage. Perhaps the most stupid objection to Matisse, Picasso and their kind is that they can't draw, the only possible semblance of a real point being that they won't, preferring to do something else. It jumps to the eyes in this comedy that if Pirandello cared to write a straightforward play he would have no superior living. The reaction of these Six Characters among themselves is magnificent drama, though no more tortured way of presenting it could be imagined. It is their story — belonging incidentally to the old 'sentimental' theatre as defined above — which interests us, though the main theme of the play is their superiority to the flesh-and-blood, 'real' people. Yet one would not dogmatize. No moment in the terrible story of the Father and the Stepdaughter has quite so much 'theatre' in it as the evocation of Madame Pace — who is Mr. Shaw's Mrs. Warren — by the reconstitution of the material surroundings in which she carried on her nefarious trade.

June 15, 1925

Frankly, of *Henry IV* in cold print I could make nothing at all. Let not the Pirandellists rage too furiously together; I speak for myself, not for them. Of the play in the theatre I made something, but only for such periods as the King was on the stage. When he was absent — for immense periods, alas! — the play seemed to me to be one long wilderness of dementia. Large tracts of it were concerned with the re-incarnation of a mother in her daughter — a theme which both Maupassant and our own Hardy have handled with tragic pity. But I do not believe anybody in the theatre could have told me whether, at any particular moment, the mother was speaking in her own person, or in that of her former self, or as the embodiment of the eleventh-century Marchioness she had impersonated. The Marchioness, in other words, obscured the drama — 'an obstacle that came between', as Lewis Carroll might have put it, 'her and ourselves and it'. But the madness was the thing. Henry's diseased brain was like those calceolarias invented by Des Esseintes to resemble tumours, and glowed with a colour and energy denied to healthy blooms. And just as the Six Characters were more alive than the real people, so Henry's mind, working in terms of an unknown reason, was obviously made of more perceptive stuff than that in which our more familiar logic works. Henry's lucidity, like Lear's, shone most when his mind was what we should call darkest, for we must remember that mad people ratiocinate intensively within the circle of their own reason, though that reason is not ours. Henry's intellectuality was such that when sanity overcame him he still towered above his court like genius among valetry. If only Pirandello would abandon those wretched metaphysics! But I suppose you might as well ask Cubist painters to draw cows which look like cows. That's not what they're after: and Pirandello was certainly not after writing a simple tragedy like *Hamlet*, which any fellow can understand.

Are we, I wonder, in for a wave of portentous abstraction? As I write, an American magazine comes tumbling from the skies containing a story by Maxim Gorky. It is about a woman who meets a novelist and 'adopts a cautious attitude towards him'. He is a man *who does not exist*, and though his physical self is present his soul, however attractive it seems to be, is absent! The woman goes for a walk and meets a character out of her friend's novel. The character has been deserted by his wife, and does not know whether he is supposed to meet her again, the rest of his story not being written. This shadowy personage, the unnatural movements of whose body remind the woman of a sheet shaken in a breeze, then soliloquizes: 'One sits and thinks: how boring, how foolish and prolix real people can be, and how much more interesting we imaginary creations are! We are 'always more spiritually concentrated, we have more poetry and romance about us. And to think that we exist solely for the amusement of these dull real people!' Will the Pirandellists forgive me if I 'adopt a cautious attitude' towards their idol's plays, and if I draw a parallel between the master's concern for his precious metaphysics and Wagner's craze for philosophic theory?

Ruggero Ruggeri is a really fine tragic actor, possessing all that Barrymore owns together with all which that actor lacks, and Marta Abba shows herself to be of the stuff of which Duses are made.

June 18, 1925

Of all people in the world your high-brow is the easiest to take in. A foreign author, baggy-trousered disciples, half-a-dozen undergraduates disposed about the stage like the lovesick maidens in *Patience*, an entirely unintelligible plot — and he falls for the thing at once. 'The dust of an earthy to-day is the earth of a dusty to-morrow', says Signor Pirandello, or words to that effect; and the high-brow concatenation shrieks out the 'Too perfectly marvellous!' which is to-day's equivalent of the eighties' 'Too utterly utter!' Let me, emerging from Hampstead's tulgy heath, draw an honest, vorpal blade, and declare that *Henry IV* is pretentious nonsense, and that the high-brow frenzy for it is largely composed of the feeling that not to enthuse is to be out of the fashionable swim.

Only the other day my wise and witty colleague, Mr. Ernest Newman, was telling us that if one man says that Yankee Doodle is a good tune, and another man says that it isn't, there is really no use in going on with the discussion. All you can do with a tune is to sing it over again. But you can go some way towards deciding whether a play is a good one or not by paraphrasing it. A is persuaded by Mrs. A to murder their host B. If B is a king, then Mr. and Mrs. A bag his kingdom; if a private individual, they collar the insurance money. The happiness of the As is complete except for B's ghost, and their own consciences. The tragedy lies largely in the fact that A is a poet and Mrs. A a loving wife and capable 'manager'. Yes, *Macbeth* in the baldest paraphrase is obviously a good play. Now let us do the same thing for *Henry IV.* X twenty years ago was kicked on the head by his horse, and has been potty ever since. Potty, that is, according to the standards of people who have not been kicked on the head by a horse. X's madness induces him to believe that he is still the eleventh-century monarch impersonated by him in a pageant at the time of the accident. He recovers his wits for a space, and proceeds to round upon his keepers, who have decently humoured him when they might have clapped him into a strait-jacket. In a pet he commits murder, and then to save his neck has to pretend that he is still mad. But he has already decided that a life of pretended insanity is better than other people's sanity.

It is not the question of madness or non-madness that I find worrying. It is possible that the moon may be made of green cheese, that the earth is flat, that men and trees and houses are holes in the solid ether, that the whole universe is but a corpuscle in the blood of a gnat, that a smile may exist without a Cheshire cat to support it. I am perfectly willing that a play should take all these suppositions for a working hypothesis. What is worrying me is that I find it impossible to care whether this pretended Henry IV is mad or not. 'Oh, what a noble mind is here o'er-thrown' was said of Hamlet, whom to know is to love. Is there anything lovable about the Italian hero? Is there anything human, as there is about the Macbeths? Do we care whether he lives or dies? Take that speech to his valets:

> Do you think it's a joke that the dead continue to live . . .
> But get out into the live world! Ah, you say; what a beautiful
> sunrise — for us! All time is before us! — Dawn! We will do
> what we like with this day — . Ah, yes! To Hell with tradition,
> the old conventions! Well, go on! You will do nothing but
> repeat the old, old words, while you imagine you are living!

Then consider his proposals as to how these young men might more usefully employ their lives:

I say that — you are fools! You ought to have known how to create a fantasy for yourselves, naturally, simply, day by day, before nobody, feeling yourselves alive in the history of the eleventh century . . . You would have drunk it in with the air you breathed, yet knowing all the time that it was a dream, so you could better enjoy the privilege afforded you of having to do nothing else but live this dream, this far-off and yet actual dream. And to think that at a distance of eight centuries from this remote age of ours, so coloured and so sepulchral, the men of the twentieth century are torturing themselves in ceaseless anxiety to know how their fates and fortunes will work out. Whereas you are already in history with me. . . .

To reject life for the sake of a mouldy dream seems to me to be the very poison of decadence. To plead that the man is mad is no excuse. Hamlet did not urge us to drink up Eisel or eat crocodiles. Every word uttered by Henry is pessimistic to the point of corruption. And therefore I deem the play evil. There is not in it, I maintain, one single shred of ordinary, decent, human feeling. 'What is there then to arouse so much enthusiasm?' I asked one frantic Pirandellist. He replied: 'Well, I like the different angles from which the problem of reality is surveyed. I like the grouping, I like the stage-patterns, the gestures, and attitudes of the actors. I like Mr. Milton's bedroom slippers. Of course, there is no human interest, but I like the visible surface of the thing: I like it as ballet. I should like it just as well if it were in Chinese.' 'But it is in Chinese,' I murmured.

Let me suggest that Signor Pirandello has hoodwinked my friend by his amazing faculty for presentation. This dramatist possesses a technical equipment as elaborate as that of Ibsen, Labiche, or our own Pinero; and he uses his wonderful crafts-manship to conceal the fact that he has nothing whatever to say. Nothing, that is, outside the realm of metaphysical speculation. The madman will hold out his arm, feel his wrist, and exclaim 'Sometimes I am even afraid of my own blood pulsing loudly in my arteries in the silence of night, like the sound of a distant step in a lonely corridor'. Here the world seems to stand still for the utterance. But there's nothing in it beyond the glib, deft gesture. Next moment he is off on some nonsense about living his madness with the most lucid consciousness; he would revenge himself on the brutality of the stone which has dinted his head. And so on and so forth. There is no thought in this play, only the elaborately-fashioned Pirandellish shell of thinking.

No good actor can fail to be impressive who is allowed to take the limelight in a white wig, sackcloth, and felt slippers, and who has the Larger Lunacy to draw upon for words. The Pirandellists signified by their applause that, in their view, Mr. Ernest Milton had given a fine performance. I shall not be so impertinent as to offer an opinion upon this clever actor's interpretation of that which I deem to be plain gibberish. There was one piece of acting which excited my complete admiration, and that was Mr. Geoffrey Wincott's Berthold. This young man was ordained to shrink against the wainscotting throughout the whole piece in complete and total bewilderment at every word uttered. This the actor realized quite perfectly.

July 16, 1925

I remember once being driven in a hansom cab down a street that turned out to be a *cul de sac*, and brought us bang up against a wall. The driver and I simultaneously said something. But I said: "That'll never do!" and the cabman said, "This is all right!"

— G. K. CHESTERTON

Was there ever bonnet-bee of such buzz and persistency as that which afflicts poor Signor Pirandello? The hum of this insect was the ground bass to Thursday night's proceedings at Hammersmith, and the high-brow audience reciprocated with the whirr of brains in maximum cerebration. The house applauded systematically as each favourite in Mr. Playfair's team made extrance or exit, and altogether it was a noisy evening. But I venture to say, with enormous diffidence, that I have not the least intention of being bounced into liking a play which I regard as inherently wrong from beginning to end. *And That's the Truth* is such a play.

There's nothing either good or bad but thinking makes it so, is a self-evident proposition. There has never been pretence that 'good' and 'bad' are anything but expressions of opinion. And human opinion, too. That it is good for men to eat beef is accepted by most of us, but not, one imagines, by the oxen. That it is lawful to snap up human beings is a view held by sharks and contradicted by Polynesian natives. Man finds tobacco-smoke delightful, whereas the greenfly holds it to be obnoxious, and holds this opinion so strongly that it makes no bones about dying for it. It all depends upon the point of view. And now comes Signor Pirandello, who would have it that there's nothing true or untrue, but thinking makes it so. Here is the snag which our intellectuals will not perceive.

Take three persons, A, B, and C. A is kind to B and unkind to C. A, then, in B's opinion, must be a kind man, in C's an unkind one. But cannot our relativists see that A's make-up contains both kindness and cruelty, and that the measure of these two ingredients is in no way determined by the incomplete knowledge of them held by B and C? Kindness and cruelty, charity and meanness, and a thousand other qualities — what we call A's character — cannot be perfectly known to anybody except himself, and may even not be known by him. But it exists, absolute at any moment yet with all its potentialities of change, and at all times in the old devout phrase 'known unto God'. 'They say the owl was a baker's daughter', moaned wandering Ophelia. But is not it obvious that the owl's paternity was definite, and independent of whatever the baker may have thought about it? What Signor Pirandello will not see is that Relativity is concerned only with the happiness or unhappiness of the baker according to the view he holds of the matter. The present play is made to hang upon the recognition or denial of the fact that one person cannot be himself and somebody else at the same time. Signor Pirandello neither confirms nor denies this; he says you can think what you like about it. Which is nonsense.

Signor Ponza has immured his wife, and allows her mother, Signora Frola, to converse with her from a distance only. Provincial Italian society is anxious to know why this should be. Signora Frola's version is as follows: The immured Signora Ponza is really her daughter who, some years earlier, fell ill. This illness so distressed Ponza that he was sent to an asylum. The wife recovered, but Ponza remained mad in so far as he maintained that his wife was dead, and remarried her in the belief that she was another woman. To humour him, Signora Frola pretends that she is a lunatic who mistakes the second wife for her own dead daughter. Ponza's story, on the other hand, is that his first wife did actually die, and that it is his mother-in-law who is out of her mind. He, in his turn, confesses to pretended madness out of regard for the other. These are the statements of the first act.

The second act poses the question: which of the two is a lunatic? They are confronted, and their real and simulated derangements at once set up multiple reflections like opposing mirrors. In the third act the bright idea occurs to somebody: Why not send for the wife and let her declare who she is? The suggestion is thrown out that Signora Ponza may be a Mrs. Harris, that Ponza is living with the ghost of a memory and Signora Frola cherishing a phantom regret. For we are to mark that nobody has seen the woman, and that the whole argument up to now has been based on the lines of Mr. Justice Stareleigh's famous summing-up. If Signora Bardell-Frola is right, it is perfectly clear that Signor Pickwick-Ponza is wrong, and if the audience-jury think the evidence of Signora Cluppins worthy of credence they will believe it, and, if they don't, why they won't. So the vital witness comes in to settle the matter, and when she appears veiled we know that our worst suspicions are confirmed. At once she declares herself to be either the first wife or the second, or both together, or anything anybody likes. The audience has paid its half-guinea and is at liberty to make its own choice.

Signor Pirandello has tacked Relativity on to a matter which cannot possibly be subject to Relativity. The dramatic significance in this play should lie not at all in the question of identity — which

is what we are made to pursue throughout the whole evening —
but in the influence upon the husband and mother-in-law of
their views as to that identity. Is it better to be sane and lose a
cherished object, or mad and keep it? This is the true drama,
whereas the poser which Signor Pirandello prefers is whether we
take the object to be teacup or teacaddy. Relativity is Signor
Pirandello's bane; a few precious people may hold it to be his
virtue, but precious few will agree with them. Relativity has, in
my judgment, entirely ruined every play of his that I have seen,
for the simple reason that it has led him to use a magnificent
technical equipment to dethrone that human interest which in the
theatre should be paramount. What is moving in *Six Characters*
is not whether these unborn creatures may be said to exist, but the
tragedy which they want to tell us. What interests me in the
present play is the 'story' behind grief of such momentum that its
impact destroys reason. But that is the tale Signor Pirandello will
not tell, preferring that we should spend the evening guessing
which of two lunatics is the likelier.

The piece was admirably acted. Mr. Playfair contributed a
masterpiece of aplomb, Mr. Claude Rains one of virtuosity, and
Mr. Guy Lefeuvre one of finicking meddlesomeness. Miss Nancy
Price gave a good study of a withered beldam, half harpy and
half crone, with some moments of pathos. Miss Dorothy Green's
five minutes at the end snatched up the piece into those regions
wherein it was highly, if wrongly, conceived.

September 17, 1925

THE KINGDOM OF GOD

BY G. MARTINEZ SIERRA

(Strand)

S. J. WARMINGTON, GILLIAN SCAIFE

MARTINEZ SIERRA has written forty plays. Of these I am un-
fortunate enough only to know four that have been produced in

this country — *The Romantic Young Lady*, *Wife to a Famous Man*, *The Cradle Song*, and now *The Kingdom of God*. Two of these struck me as being light, insubstantial pieces for which the theatre was almost too gross a medium, and two to be concerned with themes for which the theatre is no place at all. Probably I am wrong in all four cases, and in view of the slightness of my knowledge of this dramatist I am not going to pretend to be right. Horribly conscious of insufficiency, I have been at pains to look up what the better-informed have to tell us about this writer.

Mr. Ashley Dukes, in *The Youngest Drama*, is not helpful. He does not mention Sierra. Mr. John Garrett Underhill, who has translated many of the plays, says that the first decade of Sierra's productivity suggests little of the theatre, and is 'quietistic in feeling, essentially contemplative, a communion with idyllic and elegiac poets'. A clumsier way of putting this might be to say that the early plays are dull. Of his later theatre he says: 'No other plays convey so convincingly, or with equal grace, the implications of environment as it interprets itself in terms of character, not symbolically or in any didactic way, but directly and visually so that the ambient becomes the protagonist rather than the individual, and the spirit of the *milieu* is felt to express more clearly than words the fundamentals which condition its life.' Which passage, presumably, must be taken to mean what it says. Mr. Granville-Barker, Sierra's official champion in this country, tells us that *The Kingdom of God* is 'a very stirring play'. Reading this writer's analysis I am abashed and discomfited to discover that the one thing which stirred me in this piece was very elaborately not Sierra's point, and that his case, as Mr. Barker explains it, moved me very little as an argument, and as theatrical entertainment not at all. Perpend.

In the first act we see eighteen-year-old Sister Gracia, who belongs to the Order of St. Vincent de Paul, ministering in an asylum for old men who, Mr. Granville-Barker admits, are foolish and tiresome. She is visited by her father, mother, and sister. The father is null, the mother is impossibly-mannered, and neither is amusing. A half-witted negro, homesick for Cuba and its cigars, is comforted by Sister Gracia. (This little part was endowed by Mr. James Whale with very real pathos.) Sister Gracia defines her position: 'One must give one's life, one's whole life . . . to the last breath and the last drop of blood, if one wants to atone for the wickedness of the world. For misery is wickedness and want is a crime . . . because God gave His world to us all alike . . . and our daily bread. And if His children starve and are homeless . . . that's a crime, yes, a crime. And the man who keeps more than he needs robs the man who's in need.' The parents leave, and the old pensioners come back drunk as Trinculo and Stephano and less amusing. Darkness descends on the asylum.

The second act takes place in a maternity home. Ten years have passed, and the point of the act is the same which Sierra made over and over again in *The Cradle Song.* Rudyard Kipling says somewhere that 'single men in barracks don't grow into plaster saints'. Sierra shows in both plays that healthy young women immured in convents grow up into saints only with the greatest difficulty. The doctor is called in to Sister Gracia, whose mentality does not enable her to distinguish between the Life-Force which is not yet stifled within her and the misdirection of that Force of which the poor mothers around her are the victims. 'You dare to speak to me of love . . . here . . . where we see how it all ends.' To this the doctor has the perfectly adequate reply: 'It isn't love that comes to such an end . . . that has eaten like a cancer into these lives. True love between men and women is health and strength to both.' He proposes that she shall marry him and as his wife carry on her good works. Sister Gracia, who is not a nun but belongs to an order which she may leave at any time, refuses this reasonable proposal — reasonable since she is obviously in love with the man — for motives which are not a part of this world's logic. One respects these motives, and the whole act is one of undeniable beauty. The third act takes place forty years later. Now Sister Gracia is head of an orphanage, and, despite the advent of a bull-fighter who comes to pay tribute to his former mother, I must confess to finding the proceedings insufferably tedious.

The reader will have observed the chain of significance in the settings. Mr. Granville-Barker puts it that Sierra 'relies upon making as clear in his picture to us, as in the reality it was clear to Sister Gracia, the human needs and their claim upon us of disreputable age, sordid sins of the flesh, and of childhood that will bate no claim, and should not, since upon it all the claims of the world must fall'. We are not to be concerned, he tells us, with the growth or wane of the woman's religious belief, nor yet with her mental reaction to her environment. But how if the belief and the reaction are the things which most excite the spectator's interest? There needs no playwright come from Spain to tell us that we must be kind to old men, orphans, and unmarried mothers. On the other hand, how can a play which shows us a woman divided between natural instincts and the dictates of the spirit not provoke us to take up arms on one side or the other? How can one stand aside dispassionately and regard such a play as a pattern in aesthetics?

It seems to me that interest in Sister Gracia cannot be divorced from the general question of self-mortification. A subject may be bigger and more stirring than the play that is written round it. Sierra's piece certainly stirred one playgoer to passionate protest. Is it moral that to do good to other people the individual must do harm to himself? Is it not obvious that only those fitted for seclusion should seek seclusion, and that if good works demand more assistants than there are natural celibates, unnatural celibacy should not be insisted upon? Considered dispassionately as a work of art one would say that this play has quality, is well-written, contains some vivid snatches of character, but that, with the exception of the one vital thing which is not supposed to be its point, it is not always enthralling. This is not to affirm that many people were not enthralled. I must write as I feel, and the play's reception proved overwhelmingly that a very large audience felt quite otherwise.

The piece, which has been very well translated, was beautifully produced by Mr. A. E. Filmer, and given some really beautiful stage-settings, which, it was interesting to note, were by Mr. James Whale, the actor responsible for the lovely performance of the Cuban pensioner. But the acting throughout was wholly admirable. Miss Gillian Scaife, whose talent for getting her to a nunnery is almost the equal to Duse's, composed for the occasion an admirable mask — a mask all breathing human passion far above, and from which the trivial records of normal sensibility had been wiped away. She exhaled the celestial ravishment and terrestrial stupidity of the *dévotee enragée*, and, whenever her author would allow her, was very moving. I take it that the part could not have been better played. Capital performances were given by Mesdames Ivy Des Voeux, Dorothy Darke, Barbara Everest, Efga Myers, and particularly by a very young actress, Miss Barbara Listova. Miss Kathleen O'Regan as one of the lapsed and lost gave a broth of a performance. Mr. S. J. Warmington's playing of the doctor puts me in some difficulty. A well-known writer who knows his theatre expressed to me the view that this actor's performance was inadequate, whereas it seemed to me that any greater stressing would have been perilous. In fact, I thought that Mr. Warmington got round, through, and under the part's appalling difficulties with extraordinary discretion. He held attention and succeeded in not being diverting; and, after all, it should be remembered that he was asked to make love to one who was to all intents and purposes a nun. The play was presented by Mr. Anmer Hall in conjunction, laudably, with Mr. George Grossmith.

October 30, 1927

FORTUNATO AND THE LADY FROM ALFAQUEQUE

BY SERAFIN AND JOAQUIN ALVAREZ QUINTERO

(Court)

O. B. CLARENCE, GILLIAN SCAIFE

To attempt to describe the peculiar delight in the theatre of *Fortunato* is to make one more shot at that baffling, and altogether useless, job of describing one art in terms of another. It isn't difficult to say what this little play is about. It is about a beggar who is indifferently thief and martyr, and preserves his soul equally in both situations. He steals for his children's sake, and in the end for his children's sake props himself up in the attitude of a Saint Sebastian against a target while a lion-tamer's daughter makes a pattern round him with a pop-gun. 'My children will have bread,' he cries in an ecstasy of fear and gratitude. The play is called a tragic farce and would, I think, have been the entire and perfect chrysolite if the authors had taken their courage in both hands and sent a bullet through Fortunato, as the talk of Amaranta's failing skill did at one time hint. However, the poor fellow is permitted to live and carry bread home to his children, which is rather like allowing Lear to take up his bed and toddle back to a restored palace. A preposterous simile? No, because the tragic spirit remains the same whatever the size of the tragedy. Our translators allude in their preface to their authors' 'benevolently humorous eyes', which perhaps explains why they, the brothers, ran away from their own tragedy and fobbed us off with a 'tragic farce'.

Anyhow, it is a lovely, lovely farce to be relished only in the theatre. Ensconced there the spectator may, if he be so inclined, attempt to resolve his entertainment into its component parts. Can one of them be Mr. James Whale's corner of a village-street, and the flood of sunshine which proclaim that we are in Spain? Is another the jovial, successful beggar of Mr. Fewlass Llewellyn, who could obviously give a capital account of our own Falstaff? Does he find a third in the metallic stridency in the voice of Miss Miriam Lewes, who as the menagerie's bright particular star takes the stage with inconceivable gusto? I remember pronouncing in these columns upon the absence of a sense of humour in this distinguished player. Her present performance cries aloud for a withdrawal, and publicly I abase myself. Is the final factor the very sensitive and moving performance of Mr. O. B. Clarence? What matter what it is! This little piece is exquisite, and the first-night audience rose to and at it in quite extraordinary fashion.

The rest of the evening was not so good. Our authors set out to tell a little tale with as much circumstance as if it had been a world-history with all time to tell it in. Actually the piece was a storyette about a foolish lady's inability to resist anybody who 'lisped the magic name of Alfaqueque'. The simplicity of the lady who is alleged to perform this feat having been sufficiently established at half-past ten, there were reasonable hopes of getting out of the theatre by eleven. But, no! At ten minutes past this exhausting lady got her third or fourth wind with the phrase: 'I have so much to say that I hardly know how to begin!' But she began all right, and concluded at twenty-five minutes past eleven exactly. There were amusing performances by Messieurs Eric Stanley, Geoffrey Wincott, and Anthony Ireland, and for once Mr. John Gielgud was right in his Byronic suggestions. The homeliness of the homesick lady was admirably rendered by Miss Gillian Scaife. I suggest that half an hour or forty minutes should be cut out of this piece, and the order of the plays reversed. The translations seemed to me to be quite perfect, with one tiny exception. The beggar-boy's 'You're a corker!' brought us out of Spain and back to England with a bump.

October 28, 1928

A HUNDRED YEARS OLD

BY SERAFIN AND JOAQUIN ALVAREZ QUINTERO
(Lyric, Hammersmith)

HORACE HODGES

A LITTLE eventless, shall we be ungracious enough to say? Our translators in their admirable introduction to the printed version of this play have already discounted this ungenerous, unseeing criticism. The particular gift of the Quinteros, they tell us, is to adjust the dramatic balance between the individual and society. More simply, they put a lot of people on the stage and 'seem quite unable to take one side against another'. They are the playwrights of placidity, and their plays have a pervading temper 'so gentle, so full of compassion, that hate and anger and violence will seem to have no place there'. Do our translators, then, suggest a definition of drama as that which is too full for sound or foam, put together on the scientific principle that deep waters run still? In this introduction they foresee and burke the question by riding off on other issues. They tell us that the Quinteros, unlike Ibsen, Shaw, and Tchehov, are not seething with a message; but then, better no philosophy than a sham one. This play is as unashamedly senti-mental as Tom Robertson; but then, why not? We are not to look down our noses at the simple thing. If anybody thinks there is nothing in writing plays of this order, let him try! And so on and so forth. For final recommendation the eyes of these Spanish brothers are 'benevolently humorous'. In other words, the eventlessness is admitted, but it is held for a gracious eventlessness.

Papa Juan will in a few days attain his 100th birthday. He proposes on the great day to gather round him all his family, down to his remotest great-grandchild. Tact will be called for in the handling of, for example, Doña Filomena, his son's needy relict and epitome of all that Lamb had to say about the female Poor Relation, in the handling again of that other impoverished descendant whose pride is proper and not touchy, of the Com-munist tippler, of the grand-daughter fled to the big city. The achievement of these things, the attainment of the birthday and the party make up the whole play. But not quite. Papa Juan, even at 100, has still something to live for—a great-great-grandchild. To this end he asks his niece Currita and his nephew Trino whether they do not hear an infant crying for the light. Where-upon we ask ourselves whether, if the old gentleman had known whose philosophy he was voicing, he would not have been as much astonished as M. Jourdain in that little matter about the prose. But we cannot imagine the Quinteros allowing even a cen-tenarian to say anything in the key of Schopenhauer. So Papa Juan must say what he has to say in the manner of—Sir James Barrie. As night falls on the birthday the lovers clasp hands. And that, really, is all.

The play centres, then, in Papa Juan and the Quinteros' view of extreme old age. Think for a moment of other projections of senility. Think of that empty repository who is Justice Shallow, of that bundle of impotent venom who is Grandfather Smallweed. These are exactly the types to which the Quinteros shut their 'benevolently humorous eyes'. They will not have us believe in the drawing nigh of the years when man shall say he has no pleasure in them. Theirs is not the pessimism which made Flaubert end his account of the funeral of M. Dambreuse with the words 'dont il ne sera plus question sur cette terre', and the implication that there wouldn't be any question of him any other where.

Rejecting the long grey beard, glittering eye, and skinny hand of ancient mariners approaching the end of their voyage, they have presented a cherubic residue, pink and rosy as his outlook, an Abbé Liszt grown passionless, a Walt Whitman in subsidence, a deliciously venerable Bede. In short, certainly not the old man whose demise is hailed as a blessed relief, meaning a relief to his caretakers, but most definitely the old gentleman who not only 'sits and thinks', but thinks shrewdly and pithily to the general edification and entertainment. Mr. Horace Hodges, resisting all temptation to stray from his authors into realism, gave a most admirable performance. In appearance he contrived to look something between a pianoless Pachmann and the prints of Mr. Gladstone which still hang over Welsh mantelpieces. Considerations of space make it impossible for me to say all that I would of this piece of delicate, unforced playing, and of the really excellent acting of Mr. Herbert Ross as a poor but honest gardener, of Miss Winifred Evans who had to do nothing over too long a period, and of Miss Angela Baddeley, who contrived to be an *ingénue* without being a ninny. And last of Miss Mabel Terry-Lewis, in seeing whom in a state of simulated intoxication one feels one has bagged a collector's piece of virtuosity. I feel that too little has been said of the charm of this piece, of its atmosphere, its complete absence of vulgarity, stridency, over-accentuation, and all the other faults of playwriting *à la mode*, of its truth — so far as I can judge — to

197

Spanish character, its easy humour and kindly glow, its integrity as a work of art. And, after all, why boggle about realism when that which is offered is a benediction?

November 25, 1928

THE INTRUDER

BY FRANÇOIS MAURIAC

(Wyndham's)

ERIC PORTMAN, MARY HINTON

THERE are certainly four and possibly six plays in this remarkable piece, according as we take for pivot any one of the four or six principal characters. Does the play belong to the widowed Mme. de Barthas, so like and yet so unlike our own Mrs. Bardell, seeing that jealousy of a daughter of marriageable age is a situation to which this mother must compose herself since to this situation she must inevitably come? Or does the play belong to Emmanuele, exquisitely placed in the centre of it, a young girl hovering on the threshold of ecstasies mystical and the reverse, and generously confounding them? A French audience would understand better than an English one how a young girl can be induced to believe the death of the senses to be the life of the soul. If it were possible for dramatists of different nationalities to collaborate I should hanker after that scene of conversational twistings and turnings in which M. Mauriac's Emmanuele and Mr. Shaw's Ann Whitefield should have a straight talk together.

Or does the play belong to Blaise Lebel, that very odd creature who, nominally the tutor of the son of the house, is consumed with a passion for its mistress, makes a meal of the governess, and what Miss Dorothy Parker would call a pass at the daughter? I was reading the other day that if ever the energy in a pound of uranium is liberated by the simple process of splitting the atom, that energy will split still more atoms with the result that London,

England, Europe, the earth, the solar system, the universe, and ultimately the cosmos — you recall how schoolboys write their addresses in the fly-leaves of text-books! — will be annihilated. For the more we examine into the character of Lebel, the more engines of destruction does he turn out to be. Mark that one writes 'examine' and not 'explain', since the fellow is at least as inexplicable as Iago. Add quite a lot of Heathcliff, more than a dash of Quilp, a hint of Mr. Littimer, plus a hanging-about-ness which would have given yet another turn to Henry James's screw.

Then what of Mademoiselle, the governess who wants her attachment to this monster to be regular if not regularized, and is fobbed off with regular and irregular verbs? One feels that an entire circulating library of novels by the Brontës is tucked away in that brain. Well, that is four of this play's possible dramas. The fifth would centre in the good-looking English boy who has come to live for two months with this French family *au pair*, and does not realize that whereas English boys never think about the tender passion, in France they are regarded as young men and as such are not expected to think about anything else. There is a hint of wicked malice *à la* Maurois here which pleases me greatly. Within a day or two of his arrival Harry is actually walking with the widowed châtelaine in her moonlit park, putting his scarf about her shoulders, and instinctively performing those little offices which a French young man would intuitively avoid. This is what on the Continent is meant by English hypocrisy, whereas it is merely our good-mannered stupidity in full and innocent flower.

Lastly the play might be the private property of the Curé who has an entire and perfect sympathy for Emmanuele and looks over everybody's shoulder as though he were watching a game of chess. To him alone are the board's shifting situations plain. The piece has been written about as though it were a mirage, a nebulosity, a web of tone, a tissue of sensitivity. I, on the contrary, find nine-tenths of it hard, precise, and net. I find those nine-tenths no more difficult than, say, *Sweet Lavender*, the only difference between the two plays being that M. Mauriac is an adult playwright writing for an adult audience, whereas Pinero, whose mind must

always remain a puzzle to the sophisticated foreigner, was writing for
the unsophisticated English of the 'eighties. Perhaps instead of *Sweet
Lavender* I should have instanced *The Elder Miss Blossom*, that
nicest of drawing-room comedies in which Mrs. Kendal would
nightly go through the tortures of Mme. de Barthas, conceived
in terms of aunt and niece, engagements and wedding breakfasts,
relieved by jokes about toast-racks and fish-slices.

As for the incomprehensible residue, I say boldly that this is the
fault of M. Mauriac. I do not think I am worried by the fact that
Lebel, while consumed by a major passion for Mme. de Barthas,
permits himself lesser excitations and appeasements. That sort of
thing understands itself. What I cannot follow is the attraction he
possesses for Madame, to whom it is categorically stated that he is
necessary. Not for a long time have we heard in the theatre anything more full of doom than Madame's concluding words to her
daughter: 'But, darling, I am not alone; I have M. Lebel to keep
me company!' And we reflect that the poor lady does not speak
the whole truth here, that besides Lebel she has for eternal company a long-distance jealousy of her daughter and a near-hand
jealousy of her governess. So merry is this little hell that one feels
the Devil will be a long time before gathering its occupants to
himself.

Talking of the Devil, I suggest that another difficulty is provided
by the play's title, *Asmodée*, that its Diable Boiteux is not Harry,
the straight-limbed English Galahad, but the wry-backed tutor
lifting the lid to inspect troubles of his own brewing. Apart from
these minor difficulties, I repeat that I find the play crystal clear.
If I were asked which were the best intimate plays I have seen on
the English stage in the last twenty years, I should mention
M. Jean-Jacques Bernard's *The Unquiet Spirit*, *The Years Between*,
and *Martine*, Turgenev's *A Month in the Country*, and this piece,
which might be called *Two Months in Another Country*.

Miss Mary Hinton's acting in the part of Mme. de Barthas is
exquisite in tone and recalls cherished performances by Miss
Beatrice Wilson and the late Clare Eames. Overdoing neither
the graciousness of the first half of the play nor the selfishness of the

second, she demands and receives sympathy for a character real and unsentimentalized. Nor would it, I think, be possible to better Miss Jill Furse's Emmanuele, who is given all the pathos of the opening bud. Miss Marian Spencer with a rare tact knows the governess's dramatic place and keeps it, resisting every temptation to mistake her for the heroine. Mr. Peter Coke's Intruder is played with the proper kind of forthright charm and boyish sincerity, and Mr. Leslie Frith gives the Curé his precise value. The real burden of the play must, of course, be borne by whoever plays Lebel. It gives one great pleasure to see Mr. Eric Portman square up to this very difficult part. The best actor in the world cannot make clear that which his author has left in obscurity; short of this Mr. Portman, in my view, completely succeeds. This is a performance of both power and subtlety over which evil broods, though the actor throughout rightly resists the melo-dramatic temptation to make our flesh creep.

And now is it presuming too much to invite the playgoer who is always complaining about the mediocrity of the modern theatre to hurry up and see a piece which is head and shoulders above everything else in the London theatre of to-day? It would be unfair to make no mention of the translation, which reproduces with perfect fidelity the spare and taut quality of the original.

May 7, 1939

LES PARENTS TERRIBLES

BY JEAN COCTEAU

(Gate)

HENRY OSCAR, CYRIL CUSACK, MARY HINTON, VIVIENNE BENNETT, MARTITA HUNT

'I DON'T know', says the husband in M. Jean Cocteau's *Les Parents Terribles*, 'whether what is happening to us all is a tragedy or a farce. It is certainly a masterpiece!' The 'all' to which the husband refers is a group of five persons only. The first of these is himself, a man who is on the outside any husband and any father. But any husband postulates any wife, and it is difficult to believe that the wife and mother in this play has any relation to normal wifehood and motherdom. She is dying of diabetes, she is a slattern, and her emotional reactions to everybody around her exceed the limits which the old Greek dramatists set themselves in the matter of decorum. When her son confesses to a love affair, her perturbation goes far beyond that of the normal mother fearful that her offspring has fallen into the toils of some harpy. Jealousy is only too obviously the ruling passion here, but the boy is less than wideawake, and as unsuspecting as Hippolyte before, in Racine's version, Phèdre has her: 'Ah, cruel! Tu m'as trop entendue!' Sitting at the Gate Theatre we expect the young man to break at any moment into Hippolyte's famous couplet:

> Dieux! qu'est-ce que j'entends? Madame, oubliez-vous
> Que Thésée est mon père, et qu'il est votre époux?

But the young man's thoughts are not on his mother but on his mistress, whom he wants to marry. Whereby, to use an English vulgarism, the fat is in the fire, and the fire becomes a raging furnace when it turns out that the young lady whom the boy insists on marrying has already, unknown to him, been his father's mistress.

In the second act we are introduced to the young person, and a full examination of the case from her angle. She is a decent young woman and has little difficulty in persuading even an English audience that a genuine affection for the older man can be coexistent with an equally genuine love for the younger. You are to suppose that if another French parallel be permitted — and after all this is a French play — Balzac's Esther Gobseck entertains gratitude towards the Baron Nucingen as well as a passion for Lucien de Rubempré. Does the reader object that Lucien is not the Baron's son? Quite so, but then neither does the young woman know until the second act that her lover is the son of her protector. It is essential in the interests of the play that M. Cocteau's 'too, too

French French beans' should not all be spilled; in other words, that the secret of the young woman's liaison with the elder man should be kept from the son altogether and from the mother until the last act.

Now, how is the secret to be kept? What new dust had the innovating M. Cocteau to throw into the eyes of the persons to be blinded? To my astonishment the dust turned out to be the oldest in the world, that thrown by Dumas's Lady of the Camellias into the eyes of Armand in the Vaudeville Theatre, Paris, on the night of February 2, 1852. The boy knows that his mistress has an older lover but is unaware of his identity, and the young woman must now invent a third lover, whose existence will, of course, disgust the young man utterly. The reason why the young woman must accept this shameful proposition is that if she does not the father will reveal his monstrous secret. And again one rubs one's eyes, for M. Cocteau is a modern of the moderns, and his personages are certainly not recognizably old-fashioned in their outlook! Sitting in the theatre the other evening I tried to put myself into the position of the young man in this play and to ask myself which, as a young Frenchman, I should find the more shocking — the revelation that my fiancée's former protector was my own father, or the fact that by pretending to be in love with me she was carrying on an affair with yet another man. I found I had no difficulty whatever in deciding that the second alternative was the more terrible. What, then, would have happened if the young lady, putting herself in the boy's place, had realized this, and then declined to be blackmailed?

Actually in the play the blackmail is allowed to succeed, which paves the way for a third act in which everybody is so prostrate with emotion that there is hardly a sufficient number of persons left upstanding to carry on the drama. However, it contrives to get carried on somehow, and at last I have space to mention the wife's sister, the unrequited lover of the husband, the boy's aunt, and the fiancée's understanding friend — who are, of course, like Pooh-Bah, all one and the same person. Her rôle in the piece is to say 'Pooh!' to all the characters in turn, and 'Bah!' to each and every complication as it turns up. The ending of the piece is a happy one, if you can associate happiness with a diabetic woman in the throes of suicide! The formidable aunt sums the matter up in the sentence that the mother was better dead. This at least enables the rest of the characters to resolve themselves into two more or less happy families — the young man with his mistress, and the father with his sister-in-law. And afterwards? This, the point at which Ibsen would have begun, is the play which M. Cocteau must now write.

One understands that the author regards this play as a tragedy in the key of farce. It may or may not be a masterpiece; it is certainly a brilliant piece of theatre. It occasionally falls down into what our English sense terms absurdity, but its recoveries are remarkable. The difference between the average well-groomed English drama and M. Cocteau's careless extravagance is rather like that between a flawless round of golf and a round played by the great American golfer, Walter Hagen. Between some British champion's perfectly played 4, and Hagen's drive into a bunker followed by that pitch which, laying the ball dead, wins the hole in 3. The acting is brilliant, the quintet being made up of Mesdames Mary Hinton, Vivienne Bennett, Martita Hunt, and Messrs. Henry Oscar and Cyril Cusack.

May 31, 1940

NEW PLAYS

ROBERT E. LEE

BY JOHN DRINKWATER

(Regent)

FELIX AYLMER

WHETHER we are admirers of the chronicle-form or not, a new work by Mr. Drinkwater is a great event, the show of a fine mind in noble poise. I take *Robert E. Lee* to be this writer's best play, judged by the standard of performance in the theatre. And this for three reasons.

First, because its 'message' is both good and clear. Now I am not one of those who look upon a dramatist as a kind of moral postman with a bagful of letters addressed to our best selves. But if a dramatist must knock at our moral consciousness, then at least he should do so both intelligibly and intelligently. The message of *Robert E. Lee* is that nations must use defeat as a stepping-stone to something higher than that for which they fought. 'Virginia!' cries that local patriot, Lee, at the end of the first act: 'America!' he breathes at the end. And David, the poet-volunteer who acts throughout as chorus, expands this. To a comrade desiring to know what, after defeat, remains, he replies, 'There will be graves — and a story — and America!'

My second reason for preferring this play is that it does no violence to known fact. Perhaps Lee is a trifle sententious. Perhaps he and Lincoln wear too much the air of an American Romulus and Remus suckled by the same motherly sheep. Be that as it may, one felt that one was in the presence of Lee himself, and not of some mislabelled, poetic figment. Third reason. Except for the long pow-wow between Lee and Jefferson Davis the play is theatrically effective, holding not only the mind but also the eye and ear, arousing expectation and satisfying it in such way that from satisfaction springs fresh demand.

Nevertheless, I have little doubt that the play will be pronounced 'undramatic' and lacking in 'development of character'. Surely this is to use words as masters instead of slaves? If 'drama' cannot be stretched to cover Mr. Drinkwater's spiritual progressions then we must discard it for a word that will. For that 'development' which consists in exposing character bit by bit — first a hand and then a foot, next an elbow and now the tip of an ear — I have the same admiration that I have for the cheapjack displaying his table in a doorway and withdrawing it inch by inch until he has filled his shop with a literally nose-led crowd. I do not bewail Mr. Drinkwater's short measure in minor virtuosity. As for 'evolution of character', there was nothing in Lee to evolve. You remember what a relief it was when the *longueurs* of *Abraham Lincoln* were broken up by that incident of the sleeping sentry? This play has plenty of this kind of material shock. Soldiers fall thick, and in the hail of bullets Lee will not budge. There are heroisms after the manner of 'Sapper', and dyings *à la* Hay. Yet in spite of these the play moves symphonically, full of contrasted yet inwardly related movements. It maintains throughout a spiritual whole, co-ordinating the *allegro* of Lee's independence, the *adagio* of his farewell, the *scherzo* in the woods which is the young men's joy of war, and the grave, liturgical close.

The scenery was as simple as the *toilette* of a perfectly dressed woman, and as ruinously expensive in time. Darkened waits of ten minutes between scenes simply won't do, and Mr. Playfair might be well advised to retain his expressive outdoor scenes and formalize his interiors. Declamation was something in the air; and even Lee so far played the conscious hero as to act his letter of surrender to his secretary instead of dictating it. And that, as all authors know, is a pure waste of emotion. Individually, the actors were very, very good. Mr. Felix Aylmer's Lee, though noble and austere, was a little soft, just a little reminiscent of the Vicar of Wakefield, though, probably, given the text, he could not have been otherwise. Mr. Gordon Harker extricated himself with dignity from the appalling futilities of Jefferson Davis. Mr. Edmund Willard, as 'Stonewall' Jackson, made fine use of his glorious voice and aptness for berserk fury; Mr. Harvey Adams, as Colonel Hewitt, died as became a soldier. And there were two pieces of acting which filled me with the greatest admiration — the David Peel of Mr. Claude Rains and the Ray Warrenton of Mr. Harold Anstruther. Mr. Rains showed authentic passion, pathos, and feeling for beauty. Mr. Anstruther was exquisite by implication, his broken soldier speaking, through his very silences, for our dumb fields in France.

June 24, 1923

HEARTBREAK HOUSE

BY BERNARD SHAW

(Court)

BREMBER WILLS, MARY GREY, EDITH EVANS

FOUR hours of persistent button-holing at the Court Theatre convinced the dramatic critics that as a simple entertainment *Heartbreak House* was a failure. But what else it might be they did not try to find out. They hurled at the author the quite meaningless epithet of 'Shavian' — as though it were his business to be Tchehovian or Dickensian or anybody-elsian except himself — and then ran away like children playing a game of 'tick'. What is there about Mr. Shaw that he should break so many heads as well as hearts? In and out of season, from his preface-tops, he has proclaimed that he is no leisurely horticulturist, pottering about Nature's garden and pruning it into trim shapes. The tragedy and comedy of life, he has shouted, come from founding our institutions — and in these he certainly includes our plays — on half-satisfied passions instead of on a genuinely scientific natural history. Well, here is natural history preached with all the fury of the Salvationist. With Shaw fanaticism means the blind espousal of reason, a marriage which, in the theatre, turns out to be something joyless. But what, this disciple would ask, in comparison with truth and reason are such petty virtues as good play-writing, good manners and good taste? Truth, like everything else, is relative; and what is truth to the sentimental, loose-reasoning playgoer is not necessarily truth to the unsentimental, logical playwright. 'A fool sees not the same tree that a wise man sees.' 'If a man can be partaker of God's theatre, he shall likewise be partaker of God's rest', says Bacon. But if truth be the thing which Shaw will have most, rest is that which he will have not at all. If we will be partakers of Shaw's theatre we must be prepared to be partakers of his fierce unrest.

But then no thinker would ever desire to lay up any other reward. When Whitman writes: 'I have said that the soul is not more than the body, And I have said that the body is not more than the soul, And nothing, not God, is greater to one than one-self is', we must either assent or dissent. Simply to cry out 'Whit-manesque!' is no way out. When Ibsen writes a play to prove that building happy homes for happy human beings is not the highest peak of human endeavour, leaving us to find out what higher summit there may be, he intends us to use our brains. It is beside the point to cry out 'How like Ibsen!' *Heartbreak House* is a re-statement of these two themes. You have to get Ibsen thoroughly in mind if you are not to find the Zeppelin at the end of Shaw's play merely monstrous. It has already destroyed the people who achieve; it is to come again to lighten the talkers' darkness, and at the peril of all the happy homes in the neighbour-hood. You will do well to keep Whitman in mind when you hear the old sea-captain bellowing with a thousand different intona-tions and qualities of emphasis: 'Be yourself, do not sleep.' I do not mean, of course, that Shaw had these two themes actually in mind when he set about this maundering, Tchehovian rhapsody. But they have long been part of his mental make-up, and he cannot escape them or their implications. The difficulty seems to be in the implications. Is a man to persist in being himself if

HEARTBREAK HOUSE

that self run counter to God, or the interests of parish, nation, the community at large? The characters in this play are nearer to apes and goats than to men and women. Shall they nevertheless persist in being themselves, or shall they pray to be Zeppelin-destroyed and born again? The tragedy of the women is the very ordinary one of having married the wrong man. But all these men — liars and humbugs, ineffectual, hysterical, neurasthenic — are wrong men. The play, in so far as it has a material plot, is an affair of grotesque and horrid accouplements. It is monstrous for the young girl to mate in any natural sense with a, superficially considered, rather disgusting old man. Shall she take him in the spirit as a spiritual mate? Shaw holds that she shall, and that in the theatre even spiritual truth shall prevail over formal prettiness.

It were easy to find a surface resemblance between *Heartbreak House* and *Crotchet Castle*, to transfer to our author the coat-of-arms Peacock found for his hero: 'Crest, a crochet rampant; Arms, three empty bladders, turgescent.' The fact that opinions are held with the whole force of belief prevents them from being crotchets. Nor would I agree to 'bladders'. You have seen those little carts piled with iridescent and splendiferous balloons, some delicately moored, afloat in thin air. So this play of wooden plot and inflated symbol. The cart may plough through ruts or sink axle-deep in mud, the balloons are buoyant still. Rude urchins may fling dirt — the owner of the cart is not averse, when the mood takes him, from bespattering himself — the balloons still soar or are made free of the ether. Their vendor is the old sea-captain, a hawker of ideals. As this world goes he is mad. With him we are to climb Solness's steeple all over again, to catch at 'harps in the air'. To ears not ghostly attuned he talks a jargon nigh to nonsense; yet through him booms the voice of that restless Force which is Shaw's conception of God. Happiness is the sleepy pear ripening to decay. This is pure Ibsen. So, too, is the hymn to appetite and rum, two things from which our author has held himself rigidly aloof. 'It is not drunkenness so long as you do not drift; they are drunkards who sleep in their cabins, though they

209

have but drunk of the waters of Jordan.' I quote from memory. The old man with his soul divinely loose about him, has something of the moral grandeur of Job, the intellectual stature of Isaiah. There is pathos in him. 'I can't bear to be answered; it discourages me', is the plea of waning power. And still he talks, shunning, postponing severance from life, 'seeking to ward off the last word ever so little ... garrulous to the very last'. I imagine this is the one portrait in all the long gallery which the author will 'ever with pleas'd smile keep on, ever and ever owning' — the one to which he, here and now, signing for soul and body, sets his name.

The play stands or falls exactly as we get or miss this spiritual hang. As an entertainment pure and simple it is dull and incoherent — even for Shaw. It has all the author's prolixities and perversities. It has the old fault of combining thinking on a high level with joking on a low one. There is the old confusion of planes. There is the plane upon which the old man and the young girl, spiritual adventurers both, after the manner of Solness and Hilda Wangel, are fitting spiritual mates; but there is also the plane upon which the girl says: 'I am his white wife; he has a black one already.' The play is full of the 'tormented unreticence of the very pure'. Spirituality chambers with lewdness revealed: beauty beds with nastiness which any but the nicest mind had instinctively avoided. On all planes but the highest these people induce nausea. Throughout the evening Stevenson's 'I say, Archer — my God, what women!' came to mind over and over again. 'What a captain!' one said in ecstasy, but in the next breath, 'What a crew!' This, however, was merely the expression of a predilection. Shaw is concerned with the salvation of all his characters. Nowhere in this play do I find him with his tongue in his cheek. I refuse to believe that his Zeppelin is an irrelevant joke, a device for waking the audience up. If I did not take the author to be perfectly serious I should dismiss the play as a senile impertinence. I found it quite definitely exhilarating and deeply moving, and it therefore ranks for me among the great testaments. When I saw it at the Court Theatre it was admirably acted. The old captain

of Mr. Brember Wills was magnificently distraught — Ibsen and
Shaw, Whitman and General Booth rolled into one.

October 21, 1921

SAINT JOAN

BY BERNARD SHAW

(New)

SYBIL THORNDIKE

MR. SHAW's preface to the newly printed version of *Saint Joan* is
compact, as all this writer's prefaces are, of awful sanity, incredible
erudition, and unbelievable flippancy. There is enough horse-
sense in these sixty odd pages to keep the solar system going for a
twelve-month. There is enough imaginative and reconstructive
stuff about the Middle Ages to suggest that the author's power of
divining the past is at least as great as Mr. Wells's capacity to
guess the future. The joking is first-rate.

Mr. Shaw is at enormous pains to prove that Joan was really
one of Mr. Arnold Bennett's heroines born some five hundred
years before her time. 'She was very capable; a born boss.' He
makes us believe in the actuality of this Joan, mainly by adducing
the wrong reasons. Joan is sane because the modern woman who
allows her child to be vaccinated is insane. She is nineteen and
healthy-minded because the people who in their old age take to
monkey glands are diseased. We are to believe that she heard
voices because people of a later date have been what is known as
'Galtonic visualisers'—like, one supposes, the folk who play blind-
fold chess. And so on, and so forth, at a fascinating length. Watch
the brilliant fellow lay about him. The 'legal compulsion to take
the doctor's prescription, however poisonous, is carried on to an
extent that would have horrified the Inquisition and staggered
Archbishop Laud'. Burning at the stake, breaking on the wheel,
drawing and quartering did not inflict on the victims 'the misery,

degradation and conscious waste and loss of life suffered in our modern prisons, especially the model ones'. The reason people formerly believed that the earth was flat 'is because their senses told them so'. Their senses told them nothing of the sort. What about boats hull-down on the horizon? But perhaps Mr. Shaw is alluding to the days before boats. The preface is called 'a sober essay on the facts', though you might not call it that off-handedly.

The Maid in Literature gives Mr. Shaw his head. Shakespeare's Joan is 'as little authentic as the popular English view of the German Crown Prince in 1915 or Lenin in 1917'. Voltaire and Schiller are laughed off the page. Mark Twain's heroine 'skirted to the ground, and with as many petticoats as Noah's wife in a toy ark, is an attempt to combine Bayard with Esther Summerson from *Bleak House* into an unimpeachable American school-teacher in armour'. If Twain was a street arab, Andrew Lang was a simpleton who, like Walter Scott, 'enjoyed mediaeval history as a string of Border romances rather than as the record of a high European civilization based on a catholic faith'. Anatole France is 'anti-clerical, anti-mystic, and fundamentally unable to believe that there ever was any such person as the real Joan'. In other words, Mr. Shaw's Joan must be right because everybody else's has been wrong. One would rather say that the latest Joan is right by virtue of her own truth. The others have nothing to do with the case.

But one would not, in short space, undertake to discuss either comprehensively or in detail this closely packed piece of argument. As a piece of reasoning it is both wayward and flawless; as a piece of writing it is first-rate. It is all so extraordinarily 'cute. The difficulty now is not the mud which Shakespeare, or some other, threw at Joan, but the dirt which, later and for some hundreds of years, has been allowed to bespatter her judges, and the whitewash with which it became fashionable to coat their victim. This is so obvious that only a big man would have thought of saying it. Shakespeare's kings, Mr. Shaw points out a little later, are not statesmen, and his cardinals have no religion. His world is not governed by forces in the shape of religions and laws, but by vulgarly ambitious individuals who make rows. This is perfectly true; but who else would have thought it noteworthy?

There follows a good passage showing that essential truth may demand an inexact picture of accidental facts:

> It is the business of the stage to make its figures more intelligible to themselves than they would be in real life; for by no other means can they be made intelligible to the audience. Cauchon and Lemaître have to make intelligible not only themselves but the Church and the Inquisition, just as Warwick has to make the feudal system intelligible, the three between them having thus to make a twentieth century audience conscious of an epoch fundamentally different from its own. Obviously, the real Cauchon, Lemaître, and Warwick could not have done this: they were part of the Middle Ages themselves, and therefore as unconscious of its peculiarities as of the atomic formula of the air they breathed. But the play would be unintelligible if I had not endowed them with enough of this consciousness to enable them to explain their attitude to the twentieth century.

Well, they *do* explain it, and the author regrets that he cannot have twelve hours to do it in instead of three and a half. Will Mr. Shaw never realize that the better the stuff the less you can stand of it? The scene in the Cathedral failed with me for the simple reason that my mind had been exhausted in the precedent struggle to cope with the aforesaid Church, Inquisition and Feudal System. Mr. Shaw defends his epilogue on the ground that it is essential. One would attack it on the ground that it is redundant; to the perceptive it is implicit in all that has gone before. But perhaps all playgoers are not perceptive. Perhaps some of them are like the average jury, to whom counsel must say everything three times over. Once, because the box hears that counsel is speaking but does not distinguish the words. Twice, because it distinguishes the words but does not grasp their meaning. Three times, because, with luck, the jury may at last understand who is speaking to whom and what is being said. Mr. Shaw's epilogue is for those who are hard both of hearing and understanding.

'It is always hard for superior wits to understand the fury roused by their exposures of the stupidities of comparative dullards.' To which the correct retort is: 'Art thou there, truepenny?' Cannot Mr. Shaw understand the fury roused in the devout breast on reading that Joan is the most notable Warrior Saint in the Christian Calendar, and the 'queerest fish' among the eccentric worthies of the Middle Ages?

June 29

The thing to do with a new work by Mr. Shaw — and, indeed, with any new work — is to find out its particular quality of interest, enlightenment, ecstasy, and provocation, to discover the exact kind and degree of emotion which that particular work, and not some other, contains. The point is to get at an author's meaning, and not to attempt to discover corroboration of your own conceptions. What like is Mr. Shaw's *Joan*? For the moment nobody else's matters. You are not to find yourself aggrieved because her memorialist has not seen fit to bathe his subject in the sentimental mysticism of M. Anatole France, or to make her the central figure of some romantic melodrama, all gilt armour and mellifluence, unfurling her replies to her judges in words silken as the banner of France. Incidentally, if ever you saw Sarah's Maid, half angel and half bird — who, to the charge of being a witch, retorted, 'Si je l'étais, je ser-r-r-ais déjà loin!' with a gentleness and ineffability unknown to celestial choir or cooing dove — incidentally, if you remembered this most pathetic impersonation, the thing to do was to forget it and put it out of your consciousness altogether.

You are not, I suggest, to 'worrit' because Joan is not really the principal personage in the play, nor yet because the drama does not pan out quite as you would have it. Let me admit that it is a trifle disconcerting to see Joan plunged at the rising of the curtain into so very much the middle of things, ordering a noble lord about as though she were one of Mr. Arnold Bennett's 'managing' young women. It would have been pleasant and romantic to find Joan tending sheep in her native fields of Domremy, hearing her 'voices', and rejecting some loutish suit. It is, to the conservative playgoer, distressing to have no glimpse of the coronation in Rheims Cathedral — what a 'set' they would have made of it in the old Lyceum days! — and to be fobbed off with the less important cloisters, and what for a time looks like mere desultory chatter. But I must not waste space in describing what the play is not, but rather try to make plain what it is.

Saint Joan seems to me — and I stand open to any amount of correction — to be a history of privilege. It is in seven scenes. The first sets the play going in so far as it establishes the immaculacy and immunity of the Maid, and provides her with armour, horses, men, and means of access to the Dauphin. The second scene shows her conquest of the Court. Let me say here, since I may not have space later on, that the Dauphin was beautifully played by Mr. Thesiger, who showed beneath his astonishing grotesquerie the pity and pathos of all weakness. It is during this scene that Mr. Shaw strikes one of his very few false notes. Joan is challenged: 'You tell us that Saint Catherine and Saint Margaret talk to you every day?' 'They do!' comes the retort. 'Through your imagination?' they suggest to her, and she replies, 'That is the way God talks to us'. Now Joan never said that and never believed it. If I am wrong, then we must deem her to have been five hundred years in advance of her time. Similarly, an Archbishop who defines a miracle as 'an event which creates faith', in contradistinction to a supernatural happening which has to be believed whether you like it or not — such a cleric has read rather more Herbert Spencer than is good for, or probable in, a fifteenth-century divine. The third scene shows a miracle — the change of wind — happening before Joan prays for it, which seems to indicate that Mr. Shaw would have belief follow in the wake of reason. But I would not be dogmatic here. Throughout the play the author is at his old trick of what in music I think they call 'overtones'. Simpler, perhaps, to say that he runs two hares at once, and that the value which accrues when old speeches are informed with present-day meaning must obviously be at some cost of authenticity.

The real play begins with the fourth scene, in which the Bishop of Beauvais, the Earl of Warwick, and Chaplain de Stogumber assemble round a table and 'get down to it'. The English peer wants Joan burned, not so much because her continued prestige is a danger to English arms, but because, by going direct to the Dauphin and not through the intermediacy of the Court, she has struck at the very existence, and reason for being, of the peerage. The Bishop wants Joan burned because she pretends to the ear of God by ways other than through his Ministers. This scene is enormously long; we lose sight of Joan; and there is danger, as the trio review the whole field of religion and politics from 1429 to the present day, and we sit and hope in vain that each fresh turn in the argument will be the last—there is danger, I repeat, of both physical and intellectual cramp. Will Mr. Shaw never learn to distinguish between length and significance? Cut this scene in two and you double its meaning; quarter it and you quadruple its effect. One was so weary of the flood of talk that the ensuing colloquy in the Cathedral hardly got the attention it deserved. There was great pathos in the repeated warnings of Archbishop, General, and King that not one prayer, man or louis would be expended on Joan's salvation, should she fall into enemy hands. Joan had her second opportunity here, and her passage comparing the loneliness of the human soul with the loneliness of God was immensely fine.

After the much-needed interval came the Trial scene in the Hall at Rouen. In an Author's Note on the programme, Mr. Shaw states that Joan's confessions, recantation, relapse, and execution, which actually occupied several days, on the stage occupy forty minutes. This is inaccurate. The scene lasts forty minutes, but for the first half of it Joan is still in her cell, and the time is taken up with an exhaustive and exhausting disquisition on heresy. It may be true that all evil begins in good, but the lecture, or so much of it, held up the action and ultimately became a weariness. However good the cackle—and it *was* good — one was conscious of a growing impatience for the 'osses. The trial and all that followed was masterly. When Warwick entered, called for attendants, and received no answer, the silence betokening that all that little world had gone to the burning, you realized that the theatre was being put to its proper purpose. And this was reinforced when Stogumber rushed in with the horror of the accomplished martyrdom written on his face, its terror quaking in his voice, his whole soul shaking with the sudden realization of cruelty. There was another sermon here — one-tenth the length of the others and ten times more effective.

The play then draws rapidly to what ought to be its close. Warwick ascertains from the executioner that not a nail, not a hair, not a vestige which might become a relic remains. The legend of Joan is destroyed. But the priest who held the Cross before her dying eyes avows that it has just begun. 'I wonder!' says the English murderer as the curtain falls. This should have been the end. There is a faintly jovial, quasi-satirical, and wholly unnecessary epilogue, conceived in a vein of lesser exaltation. Mr. Shaw excuses this on the ground that without it the play would be 'only a sensational tale of a girl who was burnt'. Do not believe it; Mr. Shaw does himself injustice here. There is not an ounce of sensation anywhere in his piece, and the epilogue is implicit in all that has gone before. It is the greatest compliment to this play to say that at its tragic climax every eye was dry, so overwhelmingly had its philosophic import mastered sentiment. None in the audience would have saved Joan, even if he could.

The production was beyond any praise of mine. The scenery, designed by Mr. Charles Ricketts, was neither frankly representational nor uncompromisingly expressionistic, but a happy blend of the two. The dresses made a kind of music in the air, and at the end Joan was allowed to stand for a moment in all that ecstasy of tinsel and blue in which French image-makers enshrine her memory. As Joan Miss Thorndike had three admirable moments: when she said 'They do!', when she listened in the Ambulatory to the pronouncement of desertion to come, and when she listened to the reading of her recantation. May I beseech Mr. Shaw to allow her to drop her dialect? Whatever the quality of Lorraine peasant-speech, it cannot have been Lancashire, and there was too much the smack of Oldham about such sentences as 'Ah call that muck!' and 'Th'art not King yet, lad; th'art nobbut t'Dauphin!' Apart from these eccentricities, which were not of the actress's seeking, Joan was excellent — boyish, brusque, inspired, exalted, mannerless, tactless, and obviously, once she had served her turn, a nuisance to everybody. The part is one which no actress who is leading lady only and not artist would look at. But Miss Thorndike is a noble artist, and did nobly.

It is in keeping with the spirit of the play that the character which remains most with me is not Joan. Since Thursday I find myself thinking continually of Mr. Lyall Swete's Warwick, who was the materialistic fox of the Middle Ages come to life, and of Mr. O. B. Clarence's Inquisitor, about whose silver serenity there was real awe, and whose long speech was a very notable performance. Mr. Casson, in his outburst on cruelty, gave one more proof of those talents as to which he is altogether too modest; and there should be good words for Messrs. Robert Horton, Eugene Leahy, Lawrence Anderson (very sincere and moving as Joan's comforter), Victor Lewisohn, Milton Rosmer, Bruce Winston, Raymond Massey, and Shayle Gardner.

March 30, 1924

OUR BETTERS

BY SOMERSET MAUGHAM
(Globe)

ALFRED DRAYTON, MARGARET BANNERMAN, CONSTANCE COLLIER

MR. MAUGHAM, in this brilliant, heartless comedy, has rewritten one of Henry James's short stories in the manner of Congreve. His Elizabeth Saunders, Bessie for short, is Bessie Alden all over again, the young American heiress immensely taken with the idea of living in a castle. Young Lord Lambeth, in the book, 'went with' Branches, and we remember that James's Bessie rather liked him. In the play Bleanes Castle presumably goes with young Lord Bleane, and we gather that Mr. Maugham's Bessie would have made a good show of liking his Lordship. Both young men are exceedingly well-mannered. The parallel here is really very close. It is true that the play has no Duchess of Bayswater, 'large, and with a fine fresh colour', nor any Countess of Pimlico, pretty and elegant, to overawe Bessie Saunders with their fine ways and their grandeur, and make her '*lâcher prise*'. It is Bessie's own fineness of character which at the last makes her let go. But isn't Bessie Alden's sensitiveness the *clou* of the story also?

Perhaps the play would have been more interesting to an English audience if the author had included in his satire some less negligible English characters. To have one's withers delicately wrung is one of the choicest treats the theatre can offer; to watch one's cousins wince is less intimately amusing. Mr. Maugham states in a note on the programme that the characters in the play are entirely imaginary — an advice to which the great satirist of two hundred years ago devoted the epilogue of his greatest play. *Our Betters* does not

'stoop so meanly low,
As any one abstracted fop to show'.

Mr. Maugham, in this *Way of America's World*, does

'in one piece expose
Whole *belles assemblées* of coquettes and beaux'.

And he is really much nearer to Congreve than he is to James. The parallel we noted above is merely a trick of the plot; were it not for the trifle of heart, the ultimate concession to a belief in human nature, we should be acclaiming in Mr. Maugham the very spirit of Congreve.

Here again is that comedy of manners which depicts what the author himself would probably admit to be only a very small section of society. Here again is the old picture of well-bred immorality lit up by flashes of hard, conscienceless, compunctionless wit. Mr. Maugham's characters, like those of Congreve, confess their narrow interest in life, and flit before us, as we have heard so often, without impinging upon our moral sense. Their meanness and vulgarity amuse us a little, perhaps; these qualities have certainly no power to offend. You do not ask whether a butterfly conforms to a moral standard; you pin it down and try not to destroy the bloom upon its wings. Mr. Maugham has secured a very brilliant specimen in Lady George Grayston, and with her capture has enriched that national collection which has come down to us from the Restoration.

This play is really extraordinarily deft, and its matter is handled with any amount of 'style'. Think, for a moment, of the way in which heavier-handed, more 'sincere' playwrights would have treated that cold, calculating blonde, Lady George Grayston, that lightning calculator with the air of an inconscient feather-brain. Is it to be imagined that Mr. Sutro, for example, would have been content to leave her at the end in perfect poise upon her brazen pinnacle? Would not that husband of hers, whom Mr. Maugham keeps so adroitly in London out of discovery's way, have come trumpeting to Grayston, razed those improper towers and hauled the châtelaine off to Alaska, or some abode of Arctic chastity? Would not Sir Arthur Pinero have plunged her into suicide on the discovery that some day she must grow old? Would not Mr. Jones have probed beneath that brassy bosom to a heart of gold? Would not Wilde have let off innumerable squibs round a bonfire of sodden sentiment till the playhouse resembled a smoky backyard on a wet Fifth?

How would any one of these playwrights have treated that dark and common beauty, the Duchesse de Surennes, divided between passion and parsimony, torn between her sentiment — forgive the word — for Gilbert Paxton and that blackguard's drain upon her purse? Would not Sir James Barrie have discovered the 'mother-instinct' in disguise? Would not that eager gardener, Mr. Shaw, have exterminated her and her kind with three acts of weed-killer, maximum strength? And would not Mr. Galsworthy have found fresh cause for pity? Mr. Arnold Bennett . . . ?

All these are fine playwrights; yet I cannot conceive that they would have held themselves so icily aloof from their miserable creatures as does Mr. Maugham. Any one of them — and I will add for this purpose the late Haddon Chambers — might have put together that excellent second act, the 'great' scene in which the imprudent lady is surprised with the Duchess's lover. But would they — I do not say could they — have kept the 'situation' so rigorously on the plane of heartlessness? Would there not have been question of sentiment? It seems a paradoxical thing to say, but I think this play would have been even finer if it had been shorn of its two honest characters, the little American back-woodsman or great-heart from the candy-store — a creation, this, after Mr. Sutro's own fancy — and the sentimentalizing Princi-pessa, a romantic creature whose marriage to a foreign prince had apparently been brought about by a too-persistent perusal of the *Songs before Sunrise* and the Italian Debrett. These two bring a blurring to the hard lines of the picture, translate us to a world where decency is, and so suggest questions of moral censure.

It is a long time since I saw a play quite so perfectly acted. It stands or falls by the two women. As Lady George, Miss Margaret Bannerman is quite ravishingly good, continually calling to mind Woodley's remark in the James story: 'Here comes a great cele-brity — Lady Beatrice Bellevue. She's awfully fast; see what little steps she takes.' Miss Bannerman has acquired a wonderful carriage of the head — half the drawings by Charles Dana Gibson, so popular a few years ago, and half Herkomer's idea of the *maintien* of great ladies. She exhibits a very perfect sense of well-bred comedy, and makes not the smallest concession to any kind of bourgeois decency. There is so much sparkle about her per-formance that whenever she appears it is as though the lights in the theatre have suddenly gone up. I am forced to make two criti-cisms. One is that this actress is just the least little bit inclined to talk 'upstairs', as the vulgar say. The other is that she cannot be trusted with pronouns, every one of which she endows with an entirely unnatural emphasis. '*You* must write to *your* mother', she will say, when there is no question of anybody else writing to anybody else's mother. 'Of course, if *you've* made up *your* mind', she will declare in exactly the same way. This trick — for it is no more than a thoughtless habit — struck my ear early on in the evening, and became a positive affliction and martyrdom. I went in dread of the entrance of each character lest he should be received with a 'And how do *you* do?' This apart, Miss Bannerman gives an extraordinarily fine performance, which places her amongst our most accomplished actresses. Miss Constance Collier, as her *vis-à-vis*, was richly comic. She trailed behind her clouds of the pork-packing business, yet wore her clothes and her manners with an air. She was, you felt, vulgar only of soul. Her archness, her fatuousness, the ridiculousness of the Duchess's passionate forties was a pure joy. I should deem it almost an impertinence to praise the acting of Miss Marion Terry, whose art has been a standing wonder for two generations. Sometimes I think that merely to watch this actress move to an exit is to attend whole sessions of our academies of dramatic art. There is that in the mere organ-swell of her voice which moves me unreasonably. Bessie was difficult to do and Miss Alice Moseley put up a game fight.

Mr. Reginald Owen played the extremely difficult part of the Duchess's gallant with the very nicest tact. It could have been extraordinarily unpleasant, and the actor's avoidance of quite shocking pitfalls was a veritable *tour de force*. Mr. Alfred Drayton's strong man, an inversion of Mr. Sutro's sublimest projection, was indeed capital. It is a curious thing that all young American 'leads' should be so uniformly pleasant, and pleasing in the same way. Mr. Stuart Sage's Fleming Harvey, the young, unsophisticated backwoodsman, was entirely disarming. To listen to him you seemed to be hearing Merton of the Movies all over again. Bathos lurked in the part; Mr. Sage succeeded in being both adroit and moving. Mr. Yorke Stephens was by no means hateful in an odious part, and five minutes of Mr. Henry Ford's dancing-partner were full of entertainment.

September 16, 1923

FOR SERVICES RENDERED
BY SOMERSET MAUGHAM
(Globe)

CEDRIC HARDWICKE, FLORA ROBSON

'WHEN I love, I *do* love', is Drury Lane's chief contribution to the season's gaiety, and the converse hits off this play exactly. When Mr. Maugham hates he *does* hate, and the new piece shows him basking in his famous bitterness, apparently unaware that jaundice, like beauty, is in the eye of the beholder. Now what exactly are we to deduce from the title chosen by this splenetic master? I suggest that *For Services Rendered* implies the indictment, the whole of the indictment, and nothing but the indictment, of this country's failure to recompense the renderers of service. Failure either through black ingratitude, or the equally damaging grey of bungled intention and the backsliding inherent in the scheme of things. Of all passions gratitude is the hardest to keep fresh. The fondest and nearest relative knows how nursing drags; that is why professional nurses are better. But in healing a nation's wounds we are distant relatives at best, and all of us are amateurs. Mr. Maugham forgets this, and is too busy being bitter about our lack of pity to find time for pity of his own. He is a modern Thersites who has come into the theatre wholly to rail. Well, there is room for a dramatist of too much brain and too little heart, and the opposite of that drawing-room sort which, in the language of the scurrilous Grecian, 'wears his wit in his belly and his guts in his head'.

But a playwright with the bitter pretence must be logic-perfect, and I suggest that this play as a war indictment fails on too many counts, since the things which it· alleges against war are chiefly the things for which war is not responsible. The great evil of the war years was that they demoralized character; Mr. Maugham in his bitterness has chosen a set of people who would be worthless with Peace piping her hardest. It is true that when the flower of a country's manhood is destroyed sex-starvation must be experienced by the country's womanhood, and Mr. Maugham shows the most delicate sympathy with Eva, the elder unmarried daughter of the country solicitor upon whose household the play turns. The girl lost her lover in the war, and her desperate wooing of the next best is done with extraordinary insight. But how about her sister, Lois, who at twenty-six sees herself threatened with Eva's fate? Does Lois go off with a man whom she likes, which would be understandable and not wholly discreditable? No, she rejects one sensualist who makes some kind of appeal to her and chooses another because she does not love him, because he is rich, and because 'to care nothing for a man who is passionately in love with a girl gives her immense power over him'. Can it reasonably be argued that the war determined the nature of this baggage? Or that a nation of exemplary gratitude could save Lois from herself? Then what could any nation do for Sydney, the blind son, who after fifteen years still moons about the house meditating murderous epigrams? Might not this young man have better spent those fifteen years making inquiry as to what it is that gilds the faces of so many of his fellows in like situation? We hear nothing of any such effort, and in my view to blame the war for Sydney shows as much bias as to praise it for St. Dunstan's.

Then how about the ex-naval officer who, retiring after twenty years with the rank of Commander and the D.S.O., is now the unprosperous owner of a garage? Overdrawn at the bank and informed that no further cheques will be honoured, he nevertheless insists upon giving a number of stumers, and, to avoid arrest, commits suicide. Honestly, I cannot see how the war is to be blamed for this. 'He was a good sailor, but he knew nothing of business', says the old solicitor, and the blind son makes a sensational hit when he replies: 'Why not put that on his tombstone?' But is the hit so good after all? Twenty years in the Navy should not, and do not, stupefy a gallant officer to the point of not knowing that whereas a bank's Yea is sometimes Yea, its Nay is invariably Nay. Actually the one thing which every ex-officer in either service knows all about is the nice conduct of an unclouded cheque-book, which has nothing whatever to do with business.

I must be brief in this tale of blame, for there is much to praise. But I cannot pass over the fact that the two sensualists and the hyena-like wife of one of them are not war-products, but a part of Nature's wilful and persistent ugliness. Or that Mrs. Ardsley's cancer is a tragic patch torn out of some other fabric and imposed upon this drama. That the solicitor who, without perception of a wife dying and a daughter gibbering and with a suicide fresh on his hands, can indulge in afternoon rhetoric about the political situation does not exist except as the head of Mr. Maugham's nightmare household and owner of his Villa Coloquintida.

But an argument, though manifestly unsound, may be magnificently marshalled. Indeed, to achieve this is the hall-mark of your first-class politician and advocate, and I do not see why it should not be that of your dramatist. As sheer playwriting our stage has seen nothing so good for a very long time. The piece is put together like an Ibsen puzzle in which every bit fits. The business of blowing up the Ardsley household is conducted slowly, a little wedge of potential dynamite being inserted here and another little wedge driven in there, the explosion being reserved for the last act and the last minute of the last act, where the craftsmanship is electrifying. The old solicitor has just finished maundering his tea-table version of the toast in *Cavalcade*, whereupon his daughter, Eva, in the cracked voice of Ophelia's madness, falls to singing the National Anthem.

The dialogue is spare and taut with never a word too much or too little, and each character, complete in itself, provides a first-class chance for each and every actor. There comes a moment when the son, hearing his mother's death-sentence, crosses over to the sofa and, without a word, lightly kisses her. The mother makes no fuss and says simply: 'As you are up, Sydney, you might ring the bell.' It is not often that our players are given such a chance as this, and that Miss Louise Hampton and Mr. Cedric

Hardwicke should take it so grandly proves that up to this point they have utterly fulfilled everything given them by the author to speak, to think and to look. In the part of the sex-starved daughter Miss Flora Robson contrives to give both the undercurrent of deep emotion and its ultimate flood, though I think her hysterics would gain in force if she would put a little less power into them. This is no time to argue the paradox of acting, but Miss Robson is a good enough artist to realize that because a character is at the end of its tether is no reason why the actress should be at the end of hers. In fact, she must not be. As Lois, Miss Marjorie Mars presents an accurate and clever study of calculation veneered by niceness, while the two sensualists and the Commander are perfectly realized and turned into highly individual portraits by Messrs. Cronin Wilson, S. J. Warmington and Ralph Richardson. There is a very difficult part for Miss Marda Vanne, who, herself a young actress, must simulate the middle forties made up to look like the twenties, and be outwardly gracious while inwardly ridiculous. Miss Vanne's work here is well worth attention, and deserves respect, though it cannot quite succeed, and, in addition, she is the victim of Mr. Maugham's one technical mistake in this play — that of giving this character a hysterical outburst less important than the one immediately preceding it. Mr. C. V. France does the ratiocinative dodderer perfectly, even to the extent of putting a palisade of plausibility round him, and Mr. David Hawthorne and Miss Phyllis Shand fill in agreeably as the family's doctor and parlourmaid. One character remains unaccounted for, and it is evidence of the wealth of interest that I have been unable to find room for it in my précis. This is the third daughter who in the war days fell in love with a uniform and married its wearer. The character is performed by Miss Diana Hamilton, who by her blazing mastery of the unspectacular contributes a piece of acting which I have half a mind to single out as the best thing of the evening. But perhaps it is safer to say that where all is good there can be no best. Mr. Shelving's scenery is exceptionally satisfying, and I take Mr. Ayliff's production to be faultless, since it fulfils the author's intention with obvious exactness.

To conclude, the truth about this play can be put in three short sentences. It is faulty in argument. It is a piece of dramatic carpentry of which the English theatre may justly be proud. It is the work of a man possessed of something like genius. Let us hope that we shall not be able to put the truth about the English playgoer into one still shorter sentence: This play did not run.

November 1, 1932

HASSAN

BY JAMES ELROY FLECKER
(His Majesty's)

HENRY AINLEY

Hassan, in the theatre, is a fine play. We knew that it was poetry; now we know that it is at least handsome melodrama. None can have watched the ghosts of Rafi and Pervaneh wanly climb the Staircase of Torture without some ache of pity. The play has philosophy too, and this, though pessimistic, is not utterly despairing. Since death is but a sleep and a forgetting, and 'the memories of the dead are thinner than their dreams', golden, while we may yet travel, is the journey to Samarkand.

Let me leave it alike to the 'bookful blockhead ignorantly read' and the student of exquisite taste to decide whether or no *Hassan* is a literary masterpiece to be mentioned in the same breath with those of Shakespeare. (My own view is that whoever first coupled these authors together is a prize idiot.) Let us agree that in the theatre the play is episodic and something broken-backed. Hassan, *philosophe*, is no Hamlet. He squats at the divan of the Caliph with never a word to say, and is mum before the pronouncement of the lovers' doom. Shakespeare would not have forgotten him so. But the next scene brings a quality of mingled ecstasy and agony which is neither greater nor less than Shakespeare, but is simply not to be found in that poet. Rafi, the king of the beggars who have

227

conspired against the Caliph, and his lover, Pervaneh, are to be granted their lives on condition that he shall go into exile and that she shall become the Caliph's lawful wife. The alternative is one day of love, and death together in utmost torment. It is the man who holds life dear, who knows that love fades, and muses on his own country, his people, his white-walled house, his books and old friends, his garden of flowers and trees. The voice is the voice of Rafi, but the heart is old Montaigne. He wavers:

> What have I decided? . . . You locked the silver fetters round my neck, and I forgot these manacles of iron: your perfumed me with your hair till this cell became a meadow: you turned towards me eyes in whose night the seven deep oceans flashed their drowned stars, and all your body asked without speech, 'Wilt thou die for love?'

And again:

> Shall we choose laughter and tears, sorrow and desire, speech and silence, and the shout of the man behind the hill?

We catch echoes of Synge and Stevenson, but perhaps we are listening to all the poets singing together who have loved life and hated easeful death. Pervaneh pleads for love and doom lest the Trumpeter of Immortality be shamed, and in the sure and certain hope that in some garden she and her lover will walk side by side.

If I am to make any criticism of Mr. Basil Dean's extraordinarily faithful arrangement for the stage it is that he has not found some means of giving the ensuing *colloque sentimental* between these ghostly lovers who find themselves betrayed.

> 'Te souvient-il de notre extase ancienne?'
> 'Pourquoi voulez-vous donc qu'il m'en souvienne?'
>
> 'Qu'il était bleu, le ciel, et grand, l'espoir!'
> 'L'espoir a fui, vaincu, vers le ciel noir.'

These ghosts talk their Verlaine unwittingly. 'Speak to me, speak to me, Rafi', Pervaneh cries: 'Speak to thy love!' But all that the ghost of Rafi, now scarcely visible and very faint, may make for answer is 'Cold . . . cold . . . cold'. And the wind sweeps these spectres out of the garden *solitaire et glacé*. So torture and death have been in vain, and even hope has died under the dark sky. I am inclined to think that the ghosts' silent tableau is more likely to suggest reunion to those who have not read the play. The implication in the constant interval between them is too subtle to reach all minds. Will not Mr. Dean reconsider this, since great, if unintentional, violence is done to Flecker here?

What, all this time, has become of Hassan? You may well ask. Flecker in this play is like a composer whose second theme has taken on such an intensity of dramatic significance that he forgets to go back to his first, and only at the last, and out of compunction, bethinks him of it as coda. The epilogue, although it brings us back to human aspiration and romance, and also to this Persian Mr. Polly, the confectioner with a soul for poetry, flowers, friendship, and good design in carpets, remains something tacked on. But since good playgoers will watch a play of wit 'with the same spirit that its author writ', let us admit boldly that Flecker was torn by two exquisite themes, and did them justice in turn. Exploitation of all kinds of beauty, and not their reconciliation, was his game. And against Hassan's spiritual burgeonings we are to set the Caliph's passion for a world made after the heart of Théophile Gautier — a world of bronze and marble, and passions like purple velvet.

Mr. Malcolm Keen's Caliph was a shining and sinister performance. Few actors could have stepped so authentically out of the *Arabian Nights*. Mr. Basil Gill gave us the figure of Rafi, but hardly the underlying poet. Mr. Ainley did, perhaps, less than was possible with Hassan, and he was bound by his part to remain, let us say, in the middle distance. And I think his ghazel, beginning 'How splendid in the morning glows the lily', was too full-throated. The lines did not hang in the air as they should. The thing is a cadenza to be caressed, and Mr. Ainley proclaimed it something after the manner of battalion orders. As the explicit and confessed poet, Mr. Leon Quartermaine was exquisite. This was verse as it ought to be said, though the actual metre was that of prose. Mr. Willard's Executioner was capital. Miss Cathleen Nesbitt made a pretty show of abandonment in which I did not quite believe, and Miss Laura Cowie loved with a wild and passionate devotion of which Bunthorne would have entirely approved. She yearned and yearned and yearned . . .

The music of Delius has the quality of being too subtle and too modern to be easily caught by me at a first hearing. I seem to hear the horns of *Scriabinsky* too pronouncedly blowing. And shouldn't the Bacchanal sow riot in the blood? *Schéhérazade* lifts even the unmusical out of his seat; yet I, who have been listening to music all my life, get no tingling in the ears out of the dance themes, which might have accompanied elders in synod losing their tempers. But some of the music is recognizably exquisite, and the processional march is grand. The setting is wholly superb; never has the texture of stone and marble been so delightedly conveyed. Scene follows scene with a most admirable propriety in loveliness. M. Fokine's ballets are such as we should expect, and the Procession of Protracted Death is a fine thing. The chorus and ballet are good, and the production as a whole is one of considerable beauty.

September 23, 1923

JUNO AND THE PAYCOCK
BY SEAN O'CASEY
(Royalty)

ARTHUR SINCLAIR, SARA ALLGOOD

THREE-QUARTERS of a century ago Henry Morley made the discovery that the English temper jibs at undiluted tragedy. Whether for good or ill, the English audience, says Morley, has a habit of looking out for something upon which to feed its appetite for the absurd. The orthodox writer of melodrama satisfies that hunger with a comic underplot, and by so doing 'saves his terrors whole'. It is impossible, I suggest, to imagine an Englishman taking his wife and family to a State theatre on a Sunday afternoon to follow the humourless progress of *Polyeucte, Bajazet* and *Mithridate*. We are not built that way, and Shakespeare knew it when he gave Lear his Fool and wrote in the porter's scene in *Macbeth*. Morley ends an admirable argument with a sentence which is highly significant to-day: 'There must be a deeper earnestness than plays can demand, in whatever serious thing Englishmen are to look at without exercise of that sense of the humorous which is part of their life; so natural a part that every man in every grade of society is regarded as a bore who lacks it; and the very phrase with thousands even among our educated men for not finding a thing acceptable is "seing no fun" in it.'

The Irish, who are popularly supposed not to know what they want on their side of the Channel, would appear to have a very accurate idea of what we English want on ours. Or, at least one of them, Mr. Sean O'Casey, has an adequate notion. *Juno and the Paycock* is as much a tragedy as *Macbeth*, but it is a tragedy taking place in the porter's family. Mr. O'Casey's extraordinary knowledge of English taste — that he wrote his play for the Abbey Theatre, Dublin, is not going to be allowed to disturb my argument — is shown by the fact that the tragic element in it occupies at the most some twenty minutes, and that for the remaining two hours and a half the piece is given up to gorgeous and incredible fooling. 'Juno', it should perhaps be explained here, is a woman of the Dublin slums, born, courted and married in the month of June; her husband is called 'the Paycock' because he prefers taking the floor of a public-house in strutting magnificence to doing a day's work. The tragedy that befalls their son and daughter is felt in repercussion by the mother, and not at all by the father. The daughter's affair is comparatively commonplace. She is courted by the lawyer's clerk who brings the news of the family's sudden prosperity, and is at once abandoned by him when that prosperity proves chimerical. The son's tragedy is

conditioned by the drama's place and time. The scene is a tene-
ment house in Dublin, and the time is 1922, during the fighting
between the Free Staters and the Republican Die-hards. One is
a little uncertain about the value and amount of the tragic surprise
in this play. I happened to have read the piece, and therefore
knew the fate in store for Johnny Boyle — which is to be dragged
out and shot for treachery — and the full value to be assigned to
his terrors. It would be interesting to know at what point exactly
a spectator coming fresh to the play would connect Johnny's state
of panic with the shooting of the boy lying dead in the same tene-
ment. Would such a spectator get an inkling of the connection
before the entrance of the Irregular Mobilizer at the end of the
second act? To anyone who is aware of what is to come the com-
forting of the terrified boy by his mother in the middle of this act
has an extraordinary poignancy, lacking, I suggest, if the cause
of the boy's terror is not revealed. But perhaps the shadow is
sufficiently forecast; I simply cannot tell. Probably Mr. O'Casey
knows from performances in Dublin how far his intentions here are
fulfilled. My own feeling is that as the value of surprise is very small
in comparison with the value of apprehension, the tragic matter
should be exposed to the audience from the beginning. There are
some tremendous moments in this piece, and the ironic close — in
which the drunken porter returns to his lodging unconscious of
his son's death, daughter's flight to river or streets, and wife's
desertion — is the work of a master.

Mr. Arthur Sinclair has never before been seen in such a fine
part. He stands four-square to all the winds of the grotesque,
ruminating in a bemused rapture of self-delight. He has the
hooded eye of some intoxicated owl wise in its own conceit. This,
we feel, is a full man, though that wherewith he is filled be folly.
Miss Sara Allgood lags but little behind in the way of humour;
her geniality has its bite of shrewdness while her causticities hardly
sear. I do not find myself quite in agreement with Miss Allgood's
rendering of the distressful side of her part. Here Juno seemed to
me to abandon the character and accent of a Dublin charwoman
and to make ascent to Duse-like ineffabilities of grief. It is in my

mind that at the news of her son's murder such a woman would be inclined to 'carry on' in the pre-war sense, and give sorrow noisy and vulgar words. The fault is probably Mr. O'Casey's, since he has given Miss Allgood nothing to be noisy and vulgar with. Instead, he makes Mrs. Boyle repeat what that other bereaved mother had said in an earlier act. Sentiment and words are in themselves sublime, and may easily be supposed to rise in the mind of one whose grief, like Mrs. Tancred's, is some hours old. But it is difficult to believe that any newly-stricken mother would at once fall to praying for murdering hate to be taken away, though the echo has a certain dramatic value. Miss Allgood's performance, granted feasibility, was very fine.

There were many admirable pieces of acting in the play, but I must be content to single out two — an amusing character creation by Mr. Sydney Morgan and a piece of careful truth by Mr. Harry Hutchinson. *Bis dat qui cito dat,* says the Latin proverb, which being translated, means that from the managerial point of view that playgoer visits the theatre twice who visits it quickly. Messrs. J. B. Fagan and Dennis Eadie, who present this piece, are entitled to the fullest measure of support. For this is a great play, in which both educated and uneducated will see any amount of that fun which Morley declared to be our heritage.

November 16, 1925

THE PLOUGH AND THE STARS
BY SEAN O'CASEY
(Fortune)

ARTHUR SINCLAIR, SARA ALLGOOD, MAIRE O'NEILL

THIS piece contains that greatness which is something different from the sum of small perfections. The strength of a beam is measured by its weakest part, of a man by his strongest. Greatness in a man and in a work of art is a matter not of faults but of excellences, and of a pervading spirit. The world, people say, has been too full of tragic scenes in these recent years for us to welcome them on the stage. But tragedy is unescapable both in this work and in the mind which conceived it. *The Plough and the Stars* is the outcome of a spirit strongly moved by the events which happened in Dublin between November, 1915, and the following Easter. Its personages are the rag, tag and bobtail of the Dublin slums, shiftless of character and romantic of temperament, great phrase-makers and soil for the most grandiose flowers of speech. Yet what a lot they are if we stop to consider them dispassionately! Consider Fluther Good, the drunken carpenter, whose abhorrence of the 'derogatory' is only equalled by his knack of falling into it; Young Covey, the fitter, who has a passion for Communism in the abstract and a practical taste in plunder and loot; Clitheroe, the bricklayer, whose patriotism and personal ambition are like a pair of horses pulling away from one another; Peter Flynn, the mindless labourer, eternally maundering about the grave of some patriot of long ago; Mrs. Gogan, the charwoman, with a ghoulish delight in all the appurtenances of death and burial; Bessie Burgess, the fruit-vendor, with vileness on her tongue and something that is not vileness in her heart; Rosie Redmond, street walker and pure pragmatist.

But it is the business of the dramatist to consider passionately, to abound so much in sympathy for his creatures that they take on life. Mr. O'Casey has done what Balzac and Dickens did — he has created an entirely new gallery of living men and women. These projections of his imagination live, and live with such an urgency and veracity that you feel moral censure to be impertinent. You may be appalled, but you do not blame; these people are alive, and you refrain from judging them. But it would be a mistake to think that this piece is gloomy throughout. It isn't. It moves to its tragic close through scenes of high humour and rich, racy fooling, about which there is something of Elizabethan gusto. Young Covey roars his gospel of economic regeneration with the emphasis of Pistol; there is a Falstaffian ring about Fluther, mercurial excitability taking the place of the lethargic sweep; old Flynn is Shallow all over again; and Rosie is pure Doll. It may be that the first two acts are something meandering, and that at the end of them we feel that though we have been tremendously amused the piece has not got sufficiently under way. This is largely owing to the fact that Mr. O'Casey's people talk too much but not dramatically enough. In the printed version of the piece the speeches read magnificently, because the eye, having the power to dwell, may linger long enough for the mind to take them in. But with the ear the case is different. Many of Mr. O'Casey's sentences are too long, too much involved and too parenthetical to be easy of apprehension. For example:

> Take your rovin' lumps o' hands from pattin' th' bassinette, if you please, ma'am; an' steppin' from th' threshold of good manners, let me tell you, Mrs. Burgess, that it's a fat wondher to Jennie Gogan that a lady-like singer o' hymns like yourself would lower her thoughts from sky-thinkin' to sthretch out her arm in a sly-seekin' way to pinch anything dhriven asthray in th' confusion of th' battle our boys is makin' for th' freedom of their country!

I submit that it is impossible for any actress to deliver this effectively. The play is full of chunks of mere verbiage which remind one of the journalist who applied for a post as leader-writer. 'What's your line?' asked the editor. 'Invective', replied the applicant. 'Invective about what?' pursued the editor. 'Nothing in particular', was the reply, 'just invective.' Yet Mr. O'Casey can make his people come to the point as when the charwoman says to her lady-friend: 'You mind your own business, ma'am, and stupify your foolishness by gettin' dhrunk.' It may even be that these first two acts put you in mind of the justification of the Scotchman for eating a dish of singed sheep's head. '*Dish*, Sir, do you call that a dish?' asked the Englishman. 'Dish or no dish', rejoined the Scotchman, 'there's a deal o' fine confused feedin' aboot it, let me tell you.' Despite the confusion there is a fine dramatic meal in this play. There is a magnificent passage

235

in the public-house, in which the officers of the Citizen Army pledge themselves to imprisonment, wounds and death. They go out, and then Rosie and Fluther enact a scene of dalliance which might be a pendant to the amours of the fat knight and his mistress.

The terror and suspense of the third act are masterly. Death is in the house, in the street outside, and in the mind. In the room is the coffin containing the child whom we have seen wasted by consumption; at its foot the familiar riff-raff are playing cards. In the next room is Nora Clitheroe, who has lost her new-born baby and her reason, and does not yet know of her husband's death. In one corner is Bessie asleep and worn out with sacrifice and vigil, in another is Clitheroe's second-in-command relating the commandant's miserable end and how the General has described it as a 'beam of glory'. The English soldiery are about, and next door there is a sniper. Nora goes to the window and Bessie, dragging her away, is shot. The curtain descends upon the soldiery drinking tea.

Miss Sara Allgood, Miss Maire O'Neill, Mr. Arthur Sinclair and Mr. Sydney Morgan have never acted better. Miss Eileen Carey, who played the immensely difficult part of Nora, is perhaps not a highly accomplished actress at present, though she may become one.

May 16, 1926

THE VORTEX

BY NOEL COWARD

(Everyman)

NOEL COWARD, LILIAN BRAITHWAITE

LIKE the lady of fashion, your theatre manager is always declaring that he has nothing to put on. Well, here is a piece which is the *dernier cri* in the theatrical mode, 'un peu schoking', perhaps, but no less popular on that account. It has a cast of moderate size, and as for setting, its demands are exorbitant only in the way of good taste. The reception of the piece was as extravagant and sincere as any author would desire, and I should not be surprised to learn that on the following morning Mr. Coward had to engage a secretary to help him to turn down the offers. But could no West End manager foresee that the piece could not fail? And will none of those now so sorely disappointed ones commission this very clever young playwright to prepare a new piece specially for him? Must the risks accepted by these gentry always be the absurd ones? Brains must ultimately come by their own, even in the theatre; and Mr. Coward has brains to spare.

The first act is a-shimmer with wit of the best theatrical kind — the non-literary sort that has to be spoken in the situation. The *milieu* is that of *Our Betters*, without the Americans. Into this viciously-silly and crazily-perverted minority, which makes a noise entirely disproportionate to its numbers, importance or influence, comes one Nicky Lancaster, who has been finishing his schooling in Paris. He finds his mother languishing on the breast of Tom Veryan, a sturdy young Guards officer — a 'tame cat', in Pinero's old phrase. Nicky is himself tarred with the degenerate brush. He dopes, his tongue takes the convenient path of the 'too adorable', 'too divine', and 'too perfectly marvellous'. But Nicky is not 'too foul'. He has some notion of decency, and is in love with a comparatively 'nice' girl, one Bunty Mainwaring. There is this to be said for Bunty — that she is a frank little savage, who likes to be a-moral, but does not believe in giving vice a halo. And now it appears that Bunty and Veryan are, again to use Pinero's phraseology, not strangers to one another. 'Tis a pretty kettle of fish, even for a young man of 1924, to come home and find that his sweetheart's former lover is the *amant en titre* of his mother. The scene of the discovery is as good a bit of theatre as I have seen for a long time. It might be just disagreeable, but Mr. Coward, by a stroke of pure genius, lifts it into the region of philosophic comment. Nicky is by way of being a pianist, and he covers up his mother's outburst of jealousy with a crescendo of discordant jazz. You feel that he will go to his mother by and by.

And so he does. The third act is a very fine piece of work. Florence has offended not only the boy's father, but the boy himself. Yet Nicky is not all denunciation; the century has altered. He tells his mother how he has watched her jig, amble, and lisp, and forces her to a confession. But he is no severe judge, and would understand wantonness. Has his mother a case? She has, but it is a wretched one, and the boy tears it to pieces. It will be all different in the morning, he knows, but let them look truth in the face for one night. He loves her, and if she be but the least bit desirous to be blessed he'll blessing beg of her. And as he lays his sobbing head upon his mother's knees the curtain comes down. There is the imprint of truth upon this play. These creatures are nauseating as animalculae in a pond, but they interest.

The piece was magnificently acted. First by Mr. Coward, who lived the part with his nerves, and was so life-like that you seemed to be in the same room with him. Next by Miss Lilian Braithwaite, who gave a display of comic artifice and emotional power far in excess of anything she has been allowed to do for a very long time. Why should this clever actress be so often condemned merely to simper and pour out tea? Miss Molly Kerr, with her vanity, and her sleek aristocratic head prepared for the mob's guillotine, was admirable; while Mr. Kinsey Peile and Mr. Bromley Davenport, each in his so different way, was perfect. Only Miss Millie Sim was not quite right in her suggestion of the chorus.

I have four criticisms to offer. The caricature of the well-known novelist is offensive, and should be deleted. The third act is too long, there is too much piano playing in the second, and ladies do not exhale cigarette smoke through the nose.

December 7, 1924

HAY FEVER

BY NOEL COWARD

(Ambassadors)

MARIE TEMPEST

MR. NOEL COWARD has four plays running in the town, and all of them as barren of emotion as a moneylender is of generosity. *The Vortex* has a certain quality of hectic excitement which may make the galled Society jade wince, but will not wring the withers of the man in the street. Comparatively few of us, after all, possess mothers who go off with their son's sweetheart's discarded lover. It is not to be imagined that if Mr. Coward's Queen Gertrude and her precious son, Hamlet, were drowned in a bucket of disinfectant — a consummation devoutly to be wished — it is not thinkable that in the course of three hundred performances one single tear would be dropped. Charles Lamb declared that if one of Congreve's or Wycherley's personages were placed in a modern play his virtuous indignation 'shall rise against the profligate wretch as warmly as the Catos of the pit could desire'. Why does not our virtuous indignation rise against those two profligate madams in *Fallen Angels*, seeing that they are placed in a modern play where we are supposed to judge of the right and the wrong? The reason is because neither creature has ever had, or ever could have, an emotion, their sentimental peripatetics being dictated solely by appetite. We are certain that our wives, mothers, sisters, and daughters are not made in this mould, and we are as much amused and as little touched as if the spectacle were that of a Hottentot *ménage*.

It is not denied that in the concoction of trivialities Mr. Coward cannot be excelled. But the point I want to make is that the English theatre, or rather that part of it which has its home in Shaftesbury Avenue, is in process of starvation. The average playgoer cries out for the bread of emotion, and Mr. Coward offers him a Noelism. His new piece of unpretentious fooling is a *moue* made at those of his mentors who insist that he shall grow up into a writer of 'serious' plays. Not that *The Vortex* hadn't a moral. It had. It had lots of morals, sufficient in any case to make you feel that the writer had dabbled in low things out of the highest motives. Was there an uneasy suspicion that after all her son's haranguing the mother would backslide? *Tant pis*; and in any case we reflected that there was precedent, since in the moral play of *Hamlet* the Queen seems to have gone back on her midnight resolution long before the day of the duelling. Then came *Fallen Angels*, and the case for the author as scourger of modern manners seemed pretty thin. Wasn't the naughty part of it done with too much relish?

After the curtain had fallen upon *Hay Fever*, Mr. Coward came forward and said that though we might have found the piece excessively dreary we must admit that it was as clean as a whistle. I beg to take exceptions to both halves of this statement. The piece is by no means dreary, and I am not to be cajoled into mistaking anaemia for morality. There is neither health nor cleanness about any of Mr. Coward's characters, who are still the same vicious babies sprawling upon the floor of their unwholesome crèche. Take any one of the characters you like. Take the boy Simon. His mother regrets that he cannot be taught to box — 'he's so dreadfully un — that sort of thing'. He is helpless on the river, thanks God that his sister is not 'a fresh, open-air girl with a passion for games', abuses the word 'marvellous', and when they want an adverb for a guessing-competition suggests 'winsomely'. The mother, Judith, spends the afternoon, in the words of a visitor, 'bouncing about on the sofa with a hearty young thing in flannels', and is capable of warning her daughter that because she is a vigorous *ingénue* of nineteen she is not to expect a monopoly of amorous adventure. Are there such mothers? Does any one of the characters exist?

But it would be foolish to insist upon attacking this play on the score of truth or morality. Mr. Coward began it, as they say, with his talk of whistles. But even a whistle has to exist before it can be either 'convincing', or clean. There is no theme here to be either moral or immoral. As a piece of brilliant, impudent, and sustained fooling the play is very pleasant entertainment, and well enough 'made' to delight a Frenchman. The ex-actress who cannot have an emotion without merging it in one of her old parts or the more dithyrambic passages of her husband's vile novels, the quartet of week-end visitors who flirt with anybody except the person they were invited down to the country cottage to flirt with — all this is excellent.

And then there is the dialogue, for which Mr. Coward's simile would be much more apt. This is clean indeed, in the sense that it is whittled and pared to an admirable fineness. Take that passage in which two visitors, having arrived together, find themselves alone and neglected. It should be said that Jackie is a girl:

JACKIE Have you travelled a lot?

RICHARD (*modestly*) A good deal.

JACKIE How lovely.

[*There is a pause.*]

RICHARD Spain is very beautiful.

JACKIE Yes, I've always heard Spain was awfully nice.

RICHARD Except for the bull-fights. No one who ever really loved horses would enjoy a bull-fight.

JACKIE Nor anyone who loved bulls either.

RICHARD Exactly.

JACKIE Italy's awfully nice, isn't it?

RICHARD Oh, yes, charming.

JACKIE I've always wanted to go to Italy.

RICHARD Rome is a beautiful city.

JACKIE Yes, I've always heard Rome was lovely.

RICHARD Have you ever been abroad at all?

JACKIE Oh, yes; I went to Dieppe once — we had a house there for the summer.

RICHARD (*kindly*) Dear little place — Dieppe.

JACKIE Yes, it was lovely.

RICHARD Russia used to be a wonderful place before the war —

etc., etc.

I venture to suggest that many moral plays are not enlivened with such delicate imbecility. On this score at least, my heartiest congratulations. Mr. Coward is credited with the capacity to turn out these very highly polished pieces of writing in an incredibly short time. And if rumour and the illustrated weeklies are to be believed, he writes his plays in a flowered dressing-gown and before breakfast. But what I want to know is what kind of work he intends to do after breakfast, when he is clothed and in his right mind.

I want to make two points here. The first is that the nursery vein is a thin one, and there are signs in the present play that for this writer it is almost worked out. It has been said that the characters in *Hay Fever* are Tchehovian. They are, but with a difference. Those Russian maunderers and drivellers lie back in their cherry orchard mouthing grandiose futilities at the stars; these English ones sprawl on their stomachs wittily picking the nursery hearthrug to pieces. Let their author stick to his rod, but let him spare us more of these silly children. My second point is that such plays are bad for the theatre. They appeal to an infinitesimally small and, I believe, purely Metropolitan audience. Their success is one almost entirely of curiosity, even of a more or less prurient itch from which the country as a whole is free. Your good dramatist is welcome on Humber as on Thames. Will Mr. Coward risk a fall with Hull? All the provincial managers are crying out against the 'sex-play'. Will not Mr. Coward see to it in the future that he has something to say to the country as well as the town? My advice to him is to forget all about that which he vaguely deems to be 'Society', and to go down to Southend and spend a week amongst dead winkles and people who are really alive, and to bask on the beach with any novel by Charles Dickens. Let this playwright forget that genius has been attributed to him in the portrayal of those classes about whom nobody cares anything at all, and let him show us whether he has the talent to depict people who really exist. It was a capital mistake to come forward and say, as he virtually did say, 'You tell me I can't write a clean comedy. Well, here is a clean comedy, as clean as a whistle, and see how little inspiration I find in cleanliness!'

The piece was played a great deal better than it deserved by Miss Marie Tempest and her company. Miss Tempest has, I understand, been out of England for a considerable period, and she would do well to get some woman to tell her what kind of frocks are worn during week-ends in this country.

June 8, 1925

PRIVATE LIVES
BY NOEL COWARD
(Phœnix)

NOEL COWARD, GERTRUDE LAWRENCE

'YES', people said, 'but suppose it were not so well acted?' Which is rather like saying that our intrepid aviatrix might not have got to wherever it is she did get to if another had made the journey in her place. For Mr. Coward wrote the leading man's part in this play knowing he would play it, taking a leaf out of Sacha Guitry's book at the same time that he borrowed a familiar page from French comedy. When, round about the sixties, France was promised her new divorce laws Sardou at once saw that old chains are not so easily broken. It is a feather in Mr. Coward's cap that the old bird from whom he plucked it would have approved the wit which has gone to adorn the new version of his old play. At first one thought that in the matter of model Mr. Coward was going to prefer Capus. The point of *Les Deux Écoles*, that other comedy of ill-assorted couples, was that the husband about to desert a staid spouse for an excitable chit realized in time that he was only exchanging one boring bargain for another still more tedious. Mr. Coward envisages the same situation, but fails to exploit it. Elyot has separated from Amanda, who has her elegances, to fall into the arms of Sybil, who is not elegant at all. But the parallel is not pursued, Mr. Coward obviously preferring to invent new adornments for his tale rather than point its own moral.

Elyot, newly married to Sybil, proposes to start his honeymoon at the same hotel at which Amanda, newly married to the cloddish Victor, also proposes to stay. They meet on the hotel balcony, their respective bride and groom having made themselves scarce in fits of dudgeon which look as though the new marriages will turn out no better-tempered than the old. Elyot and Amanda now perceive that they bitterly regret their parting of five years earlier, that the happiness of each consists in being bound to the other, that theirs is an essential marriage admitting no impediment in the fact that neither is fit to live with. This scene is beautifully done and stamps Mr. Coward as a man of the theatre for the reason that only a born playwright could have written it. It contains a great deal of skilfully modulated and finely shaded emotion, and it is nothing to the point that we do not approve of the people who are moved, that they do not belong to the world's workers, and that this place of travail will be no better for their having passed through it. 'In respect that it is private, it is a very vile life.' Whether the people leading their private lives in this play are vile or virtuous is not the touchstone here; they have a butterfly melancholy, and the only question is whether the playwright has given that melancholy its butterfly texture. Mr. Coward has done this perfectly. But I suggest that he should end his first act with the lepidoptera taking wing to Paris, since the rest is anti-climax. The second act shows the pretty creatures tearing each other to pieces. The third shows Victor and Sybil quarrelling not wittily, but as people without breeding quarrel. And under cover of this brawl the prettier pair steal hand in hand away.

Perhaps the middle act should be a trifle shortened, and the hurly-burlys on the sofa mitigated. But this is a small point, and I would rather enlarge upon a talent which can devise so many ingenious variations on the outworn theme of lovers' quarrels. No man can be wise at all times, or witty either; and occasionally Mr. Coward's wit declines from champagne to the minuscule sparkle of a Vouvray. 'Lady Bundle was in great form blowing shrimps through her ear-trumpet', and 'Is not that the Grand Duchess Olga lying under the piano?' are not brighter things than less gifted young people have achieved. But there are compensations, and that Mr. Coward writes for the theatre is proved by the fact that to tear them from their context is to do them unfairness. Mr. Coward's genius consists in this, that he catches admirably the conversational tone of the day, the fool-born jests of the wise, the world-weary banter of the modish restaurant's most privileged table. To talk even of Wilde or Hankin would be uncritical; for the wit of these wears down the ages, and Mr. Coward's hardly reaches the theatre door. 'Women should be beaten regularly, like gongs!' will not be marvelled at by our children's children, but it amuses till it is relieved a fraction of time later by a fresh impertinence.

The piece, as has been suggested, is brilliantly acted. Mr. Laurence Olivier and Miss Adrianne Allen handsomely pretend to absence of brains and breeding. Mr. Coward runs the full and familiar gamut of grimace, giggle, and gaminerie; in the sumptuous décor he is the exotic baby sprawling upon Aubusson. As for Miss Gertrude Lawrence I will only say that to assess her talent I should assemble as jury Mesdames Tempest and Printemps, Fontanne and Arnaud. For these artists know what is what, and Miss Lawrence answers expectation's every beck and call. She has extraordinary variety of expression, and the supreme gift of the artist in comedy, that of thinking with her features so that you know exactly the significance of every sentence. The words may be uttered in the same tone; but there is that in the face which tells you whether we are listening to trumpet truth, the full-blown lie, or the artfulness of feminine compromise. But this artist is superb throughout, physically as well as mentally; there is humour in the ripple of her shoulders, fun in her head's poise, and even her elbows are witty. The new theatre deserves a column to itself; it is unnecessary to hope that all London will flock to see the Phœnix and the turtle-doves.

September 24, 1930

DESIGN FOR LIVING

BY NOEL COWARD

(Haymarket)

ANTON WALBROOK, REX HARRISON, DIANA WYNYARD

> Trois pigeons s'entr'aimaient d'amour tendre!
> — *The New La Fontaine*

THIS play, which might have been an airy, debateless excursion into Cloud-Cuckoo-Land, is an elaborate and painstaking examination of the case for cloud-cuckoos. This being so, one cannot make for it the excuse that Lamb made for Restoration comedy — that it all happens in an amoral world in which the moral sense cannot be offended because it does not exist. 'Of what consequence is it to Virtue', asks Elia, 'who is the father of Lord Froth's or Sir Paul Pliant's children?' Hear now Mr. Coward's chamberer:

> We're not doing any harm to anyone else. We're not peppering the world with illegitimate children. The only people we could possibly mess up are ourselves, and that's our look-out.

And what is that look-out? To answer we need only put to Otto one of Elia's questions. Would Otto's principles universally acted upon reduce the frame of things to chaos? It is the second of this play's chamberers who supplies the answer: 'We all love each other a lot, far too much, *and we've made a bloody mess of it!*'

For Mr. Coward sees as clearly as the sternest moralist could wish that flouting convention is a form of parasitism. 'The passion to *épater le bourgeois*', wrote Montague in his essay on ᾽Wilde, 'to knock the stupid party all of a heap each time you open your mouth, is itself a form of parasitism: for where would you be without the *bourgeois* to keep you going with his horror?' Whence do parasitic Otto and Leo and Gilda imagine they are going to draw their sustenance when, having cut themselves off from normal society, they have exhausted themselves as sources of entertainment? Here Mr. Coward uses his moral as dagger and turns it in the wound. Otto goes on:

> Our lives are diametrically opposed to ordinary social conventions; and it's no use grabbing at those conventions to hold us up when we find we're in deep water. We've jilted them and eliminated them, and we've got to find our own solutions for our own peculiar moral problems ... There's no sense in stamping about and saying how degrading it all is. Of course it's degrading ... Therefore the only thing left is to enjoy it thoroughly, every rich moment of it, every thrilling second.

Until, of course, the seconds cease to be thrilling and the moments rich. And now comes the dramatic point: can those solutions be found, and is it good fun sitting in the theatre while the characters find them?

The play might make easier watching if Mr. Coward, normally so nattily minded, were less vague in his use of the word 'love', to which he gives a plurality of meanings. It is as though Dickens had employed the same word to cover Mrs. Nickleby's affection for her spouse, Sir Mulberry Hawk's eye for her daughter, Mr. Crummles's emotion on first beholding Mrs. Crummles inverted on her spear, Mr. Mantalini's adoration of Madame, the altruistic fervour of the Brothers Cheeryble, and the friendship of Nicholas for Smike. Is this far-fetched? I think not. Hear Leo: 'I love you. You love me. You love Otto. I love Otto. Otto loves you. Otto loves me.' This is where Leo and Otto and Gilda make their mistake. Nobody in this play loves anybody. For to love in any grown-up sense you must be grown up, which Leo and Otto and Gilda are not. They are naughty children occupying the same perambulator and sharing a bag of sweets which they snatch from one another. Does this make an entertaining evening, or does it not? For me, not. If I am interested in that triangle which was Von Bülow, Cosima, and Richard Wagner it is because one of them was a Wagner. Put that on the stage, and even then what I want to see is the curtain falling on the first night of *Tannhäuser* in

Paris. Contrariwise, if that on which the dramatist raises his curtain is nothing more than the trio's sleeping arrangements, why, then I go to sleep myself! In Mr. Coward's play there is perfunctory talk of Otto being a painter, Leo a playwright, and Gilda an interior-decorator. But I do not believe this. The play has but one interest, the plot but one aim, and the wit but one point, and to these three things, which are but one thing, Mr. Coward sticks with the single-mindedness of a sleeping-car attendant. *Et c'est moi qui dors!*

How is the play acted? I am reminded of a story about Oscar Wilde who, during a heat-wave in New York, was seen on Fifth Avenue in heavy boots, a mackintosh, and carrying an open umbrella. Being asked for an explanation, he replied: 'They tell me it is raining in London!' Similarly I shall say here that the present play was magnificently acted — in New York! But there Miss Fontanne and Messrs. Lunt and Coward had the easy task of exploiting their own genius for the tart, cynical, and impish, for presenting human beings as gargoyles. The task before Miss Diana Wynyard and Messrs. Anton Walbrook and Rex Harrison was quite other, and one reflected that honey can never suggest vinegar. The note of Gilda, however you try to disguise it, is, in the last resort, an elegant sluttishness. Valiantly though Miss Wynyard attempted this, she achieved only elegance, and the result was like St. Cecilia in full blast on her organ failing to swing it on the voix-céleste. Mr. Anton Walbrook and Mr. Rex Harrison tried very hard. But trying was not enough. We felt that at heart both Otto and Leo were decent fellows. Vice should have proceeded out of these adolescents, and possessed us. It did not. Mr. Coward's message to his characters was obviously: 'Destroy yourselves and like it!' Which, of course, made it a moral play. His English cast lets him down by its very niceness. Otto and Leo and Gilda have no notion of destruction. They flit before us neither in Lamb's 'palpable darkness', nor even in his 'privation of moral light'. They pretend that the day is sunny, and ask us to join in their basking. Which makes it not at all the moral play that Mr. Coward intended. January 25, 1939

CAVALCADE

CAVALCADE

BY NOEL COWARD

(Drury Lane)

MARY CLARE

CHELSEA and Bloomsbury, foregathering in the foyer, made no secret of the fact that this production had not their approval. Stage-pictures, they said, did not make a play; there was no wit, and such stirring of the emotions as they detected was obviously vulgar. A rude answer would be to laugh, but I shall choose the patient method and ask the highbrows to consider how far Mr. Coward achieved that which he intended and not something else that they would have preferred and he did not attempt. What did Mr. Coward set out to do? Make a present of a Commedia dell' Arte theme to some four hundred extemporizing mummers? No! Sponsor a mime-ballet with spoken interludes, an entertainment *à la* Diaghilev cum Berners cum a few chosen Noelisms? No! Turn *Post Mortem* into a musical comedy? Again, no! Mr. Coward's job was to bethink him of Drury Lane Theatre, the old autumn melodrama, *Rose Marie*, *The Land of Smiles*, and find a successor *in that line*, for if it was not in that line there could be no hope of filling Drury Lane, which holds 2600 people, nine times a week, for fifty-two weeks. This amounts to close on a million and a quarter of people, and if Chelsea and Bloomsbury have a better play which they think can draw this audience, will they please stop grumbling and trot it out?

Mr. Coward had the happy idea of presenting as drama to the eye the principal events of the last thirty years. But since Drury Lane stage does not revolve, he was compelled, while the big scenes were being set, to have little front scenes of a narrative value. Now what sort of narrative could possibly connect national events throughout thirty years? Obviously a family which, *ex hypothesi*, shall take a part in each event as it comes along. This being so, it is absurd to complain of the coincidence which presents the Marryots as being at the hub of every happening. Mr. Coward's thread is thin, but so is the string which holds a number of beads together, and this play consists, and is intended to consist, of a number of highly-coloured beads strung together. Mr. Coward is not a conspicuously bungling technician, and it may be supposed that if he had intended to present a Marryot Saga he could and would have made his string stronger. Only then, of course, there wouldn't be room for the beads, the play wouldn't be happening at Drury Lane, and he would not be doing the job with which he was entrusted.

The worst of the hyper-aesthetes is that give them an inch and they want to know why they have not been given the whole ell. Mr. Coward has given Chelsea and Bloomsbury one or two scenes for their peculiar satisfaction. There is Church Parade on the Sunday after Queen Victoria's funeral, a scene in dumb show admirably low in tone. There is the funeral which passes out of sight while we see its effect on the Marryot family. There is another scene in which enlistment is decked out with a rewarding and faintly erotic romanticism — *On Monday I Walk out with a Soldier, Military Mary*, and so forth. This is followed by a vision of the departing armies, by bad news, and the recital of the same songs in the accents of horrified realization. All these things are first-class because they are not underlined and because Mr. Coward is writing here for a section of his audience which can take a thing in. But the gallery at Drury Lane is a long way off, and subtlety runs the risk of becoming mere ineffectiveness. A precious Strachey-esque account of the last thirty years would be one good thing; bound volumes of the illustrated papers of the period are another. And it is the second sort of good thing which Mr. Coward has achieved with something like genius. If the charge that the emotions are vulgarly stirred means that the appeal is couched in a way which simple folk will understand, I agree.

The scenes which aroused the greatest excitement, and over which one's recollection lingers longest are Mafeking Night at the theatre, Petticoat Lane, the front at Brighton with the band playing *The Gondoliers* and the crowd startled by what must surely be Blériot's monoplane, a picture of Waterloo Station during the tragic years, and last, Armistice Night in Trafalgar Square. 'I hope', said Mr. Coward at the end, 'that this play has made us feel that despite our national troubles it is still a pretty exciting thing to be English.' That, in a nutshell, is his play. Miss Mary Clare, sustaining the chief part of Mrs. Marryot, fills it with deep womanliness and gives it the value of her own personal dignity. At the beginning she looks like a Renoir, and as the play proceeds she ages in the fearless old fashion while Miss Irene Browne, also acting brilliantly, rejuvenates in the fearless new.

Miss Una O'Connor, as the maidservant to whom Time and the war bring sables, provides another dazzling commentary, and one should on no account overlook the fun provided by Miss Strella Wilson as a musical-comedy heroine. The men have not much opportunity, and Mr. Fred Groves is easily the best. Here and there are one or two tiny faults, for instance an anachronistic use of the word 'gesture' and a honeymooning young lady who looks as bridal as Matthew Arnold. But I shall not dwell upon occasional and minute blemishes, preferring to insist upon the beauty of Mrs. Calthrop's scenery and dresses and the unparalleled virtuosity of those stage pictures which are this play's merit. I enjoyed every moment of it, and propose with Mr. Cochran's leave to be present at the hundredth night, the two-hundredth, and so ad infinitum.

October 13, 1931

THE LAST OF MRS. CHEYNEY

BY FREDERICK LONSDALE

(St. James's)

RONALD SQUIRE, GLADYS COOPER

. . . popular preference for fun, fashionable dresses, a little music, and even an exhibition of eating and drinking by people with an expensive air.—BERNARD SHAW.

The world is still deceived with ornament.—SHAKESPEARE.

FINE feathers make fine birds, and fine birds make fine plays, or at least paying propositions. Countless plays have proved beyond shadow of doubt the managerial contention that the number of playgoers in London alive to and immediately curious about the intellectual theatre is at the most forty thousand, and may be very much less. But take forty thousand from seven millions and a considerable balance remains, to entertain which is a complicated business. The complications are lessened as soon as the playwright realizes that the West End audience takes no interest in low life except on condition that it is above stairs. Nearly all successful playwrights owe their success to the perfect realization of this fact. There is no secret about successful playwriting. Avoidance of any kind of truth, wit which does not rise out of character but is an impartial distribution from the author's private pepper-pot, and, as to players, stars of whoppingest magnitude with no nonsense about team work — this cannot be wrong. The success of *The Last of Mrs. Cheyney* will, I imagine, be found to correspond exactly with the faithful carrying out of this formula. It is not a good sort of play, but it is a very good play of its sort.

Mr. Lonsdale's curtain rises on a gilded saloon, giving on to the garden in which vicious owners of the land are entertaining the virtuous tillers thereof. Presently Mr. Ronald Squire enters

disguised as a butler, yet cinct and girt with an Oxford manner.
To him comes an indefatigably inquisitive young footman, to
whom Charles explains that their mistress's guests must be the
best people since they have the worst manners. And now the
garden party draws to a close — there are to be no fireworks, since
Charles has let them all off within doors. The characters enter
in inverse order of significance, like an England eleven
which should go in tail first. They, too, coruscate. There are two
lords, one of whom is an old fool, the other a debonair drunkard.
Which will Mrs. Cheyney prefer — the rent-roll or the *mauvais
garçon*? And then the scene changes. The shades of eve have fallen
fast, the eldest villager has humbly bent his last sad spectral hairs,
the nobility has gone to dress for dinner, leaving the world to
darkness and Mrs. Cheyney, her piano and Scriabin. The first
footman enters, and, having drawn the curtains with ceremony,
produces from his pocket a packet of 'fags', one of which he 'puts
on'. The lady continues to address herself to Scriabin. The
second footman and the chauffeur enter and sit about at their
ease. Still no rebuke from the piano. Finally, Charles enters,
smoking an admirable cigar. The first footman, weary of Scriabin,
comes straight to the point: 'What about them pearls?' (It used
to be 'sparklers', but other times other jewels.) Mrs. Cheyney is
a crook counting major-domo and vassalage her accomplices. She
says she is 'getting warm'. The under-footman calls for a livelier
tune, and foots it as the curtain descends to the thumping of *I want
to be Happy*.

All this has been very good, but from this point the play, as a
piece of nature or observation, goes steadily to pieces. And this
because the author must needs forsake the primrose path of pearl-
snatching for the steep and thorny road of popular psychology.
Or let us say heart-interest, the gateway of popular taste. Who,
after a good dinner, could doubt that a thief clever enough to
know real pearls from imitation will know quite perfectly the
value of the jewel locked in her own breast? Who, when the
mauvais garçon offered the lady choice between five years in gaol
and a night of gallantry, could doubt again that she would throw

the rest of the champagne in Quex's face and ring Sophy Ful-
garney's bell? Or that upon the entry of the awakened
household the pair would exchange prodigies of gumptionless self-
sacrifice? It would seem now that there is nothing to save the
poor girl from gaol. But stay! We learn at next morning's breakfast table—the board at which high society adjudicates upon the
events of the night before — that the stupid lord has written a
letter to Mrs. Cheyney in which he not only proposes marriage,
but gives away the character of every member of the house-party.
If they prosecute, the woman will, or so we are told, produce the
letter in court and make everybody ridiculous. Whereupon
everybody invites blackmail, and finally thrusts freedom, a ticket
for Australia, and ten thousand pounds upon the blackmailer.
But Mrs. Cheyney has yet another jewel up her sleeve — her love
for the rascal who bade her ring upon the bell. She tears up the
cheque as, she now confesses, she has torn up the letter of which
no honourable thief could possibly make use. The cricket team
slinks back into the pavilion, and the thief falls into the noble
toper's arms. We leave the theatre reflecting that though Hamlet
could not bear to look upon Ophelia as a breeder of sinners, our
hero must be a manlier fellow in that he looks forward without
dismay to becoming the founder of a race of pickpockets and
dipsomaniacs.

The cast was made up of fashionable players, each of whom,
finding nothing human to act, proceeded to give an impersonation
of a familiar self at its greatest point of superbity, nonchalance,
and what not. Thus Sir Gerald du Maurier flaunted his old
impenitent grace, Miss Gladys Cooper aired her practised
elegance, Mr. Ronald Squire fired off the Roman candles of his
punctilious wit, Mr. Basil Loder edited whole volumes of bucolics,
Dame May Whitty gave her exposition of mothering, and Miss
Ellis Jeffreys soared into the empyrean of her own technique. The
whole thing was a marvel of timing, and as much a miracle of
getting out of each other's way as taxi-driving in the Strand on a
Saturday night. One piece of indifferent acting came from that
very distinguished artist, Mr. Dawson Milward. Indifferent,

because Mr. Milward never persuaded me for a moment that he was really stupid. He simulated the outward semblance, but not the core, of all that is crass; if, however, to have suggested the possibility of gentleness in such surroundings was to be successful, then Mr. Milward scored a great triumph. But the best performance of all seemed to me to be the junior footman of Mr. Frank Lawton. The London streets are full of *gamins* who have put on astonishment with their first livery, whereas I have never to my knowledge set eyes on any of Mr. Lonsdale's pearl-wearers and pearl-snatchers. I suggest *Thomas in Wonderland* as an alternative title. The house, as soon as it had taken the measure of the bulge in Mr. Lonsdale's cheek, enjoyed itself famously.

September 22, 1925

DANGEROUS CORNER

BY J. B. PRIESTLEY

(Lyric)

RICHARD BIRD, WILLIAM FOX, FRANK ALLENBY, MARIE NEY, FLORA ROBSON

MR. PRIESTLEY has rung the bell, scored a bull's-eye, or whatever sporting simile you prefer to denote the complete artistic success. It is the merest accident of time that a pronouncement which has achieved a certain notoriety — 'the best first play written by any English playwright during the last forty years' — was not affixed to his play instead of to Mr. Mackenzie's. That there is no point of similarity between these two pieces should not dissuade the enterprising critic from declaring ways in which they surpass and yield to one another. I take *Musical Chairs* to be the more enjoyable because every one of its characters has some aspect of lovableness and because zest and fun abound, whereas all the characters in *Dangerous Corner* are hateful, zest has become an eager, prying morbidity, and the fun is a kind of ghoulish licking of the chops.

255

But among the more childish blunders of criticism is to confound the enjoyment derived from a play on account of its subject with the delight in the craft that has gone to its making. In the case of these two plays I shall say that Mr. Priestley has put up a more easily recognizable display of playwriting skill, considered absolutely, and granted that playwriting is a matter of putting on to paper words that later are to be spoken from a stage.

There is no suggestion of any debt to any other playwright, and perhaps Mr. Mackenzie owed more to Mr. Komisarjevsky than Mr. Priestley owes to clever Mr. Tyrone Guthrie. That atmospheric play was not so perfect that bad production could not easily have ruined it; whereas the present affair is of that cut-and-dried order which would require producing of malicious and wilful ingenuity to hurt it. There is the plot and there are the words; the actors have only to get on with both. Here, again, the discriminating reader will demand that I should differentiate between two kinds of playwriting, which I do with pleasure. There is that kind of playwriting which, like Mr. Mackenzie's, takes into account the visual aspect of a play when it is acted. And there is that kind of playwriting which, like Mr. Priestley's, would be very nearly as exciting if the actors stood with their backs to the audience and read their parts from a book. But every playwright must be given credit for the effect his play has when it is produced to its own infinity along its own lines, wherefore Mr. Mackenzie was entitled, so to speak, to Mr. Komisarjevsky's magnoperative skill, and Mr. Priestley, being obliging enough to do nine-tenths of Mr. Guthrie's work for him, is equally entitled to Mr. Guthrie's modicum remainder.

One said that Mr. Priestley's characters were hateful, by which one meant no more than that the book of everybody's inner life as taken down by the Recording Angel probably bears much closer resemblance to Mr. Joyce's *Ulysses* than to the arithmetic prize at a Girls' High School. The passion of loving is the one most convenient for stage illustration, and it so happens that human nature which ought to love by the Rule of Two — incidentally sufficient for the propagation of the species — insists upon loving by the Rule of Three. Mr. Priestley's characters are six in number, not counting a lady-novelist. Some of these six characters are intermarried and some are not, but each loves and is loved by the wrong person, and each has been guilty in thought or deed, while all of them have been victimized, irrespective of the normal divisions of sex and in the way of love, friendship and money, by a character who, we learn, shot himself six months before the piece opens.

The whole of the play hangs upon a chance remark of one of the women, 'chance' in the sense that she incautiously lets out of the bag of polite concealment a bit of the truth, not foreseeing how terribly sharp Pussy's claws can prove. So sharp that before the end there is not a shred of decency left on anybody, whereupon Mr. Priestley starts his play all over again, till we come to the fatal remark which on this occasion the lady refrains from making. If this is not a brilliant device I do not grasp the meaning of either word, and if the plot is not a piece of sustained ingenuity of the highest technical accomplishment, I am, not an impercipient donkey, but an ass who has perceived too much. In fact, I regard the whole play as original in design, first-class in execution, and marked throughout by the one thing that really matters — quality. It is about something. The characters are alive, by which one means that their speech is their mind's betrayal rather than a dramatist's lines, which again means that having been set in motion they appear to go on by their own volition; they do not say a word too much or too little; they keep the spectator in a state of tension, and finally, though this is on a lower plane, they present him not only with a credible study in real life, but also with an excellent puzzle of such extreme complication that a précis here is impossible.

Let me meet two objections, that in real life the husband who insists on uncovering the cesspool would have desisted at the first hint of a bad smell, and second, that plays ought not to be about bad smells. The answer is that every playwright must be allowed the peg on which to hang his play. Otherwise Macbeth's answer to Lady Macbeth's 'Was the hope drunk?' was simply 'Yes!'

followed by a mixed foursome with the Banquos. May we not have morbid plays? Come, come! Subdivision: must not the treatment of morbid subjects be in itself superficially morbid? I do not see how to avoid it; you cannot investigate drains with the expression of one inspecting an eau-de-Cologne factory. Incidentally Mr. Priestley has treated with skill and understanding a matter which on the stage is usually a subject for facetiousness, and I congratulate the Censor on having passed what must have been a difficult play. It is extraordinarily well acted by Mesdames Marie Ney, Flora Robson, Isla Bevan and Esmé Church, and by Messrs. Richard Bird, William Fox and Frank Allenby, among whom I shall make no distinctions. I hope it will be sufficient to say that each and every one of these players attacks and successfully overthrows a part whose difficulties begin where the triumphs of the average commercial piece end. If this play does not take the town it will be the town's fault. In Mr. Priestley we have an obviously first-class play-wright in the making. If adequate encouragement is not forthcoming and Mr. Priestley should decide not to go on with the job, the public will have only itself to blame.

May 17, 1932

EDEN END

BY J. B. PRIESTLEY
(Duchess)

EDWARD IRWIN, BEATRIX LEHMANN

A HALF-WIT said to me the other day: 'Did you enjoy *Treacle Tart*?' I said: 'No!' The half-wit went on: 'But you gave it a good notice.' I said: 'I thought it an excellent musical comedy!' and left him. After the first night of Mr. Priestley's play another conversation of like refreshing clarity took place, this time between a distinguished intellectual and a dramatic critic:

D.I. I read your notice of *The Busy Bee*. I must say that play entertained me immensely, though you say there wasn't a word of truth in it. Now, to-night's play may be true. But I just didn't want to see it.

D.C. Oh!

D.I. You see, I go to the theatre purely to be entertained.

D.C. Ah!

D.I. And therefore I don't care whether a play is true or not. The kind of falsehood which you say upsets you in a theatre upsets me if I find it in a book. But then I take my reading seriously.

D.C. Yes?

D.I. You see, I don't think the theatre's the place for serious plays!

D.C. No?

D.I. Of course there's Tchehov. But that's different.

D.C. Is it? ´

D.I. What I mean is ... Sorry, here's my car. Good night! Intellectual disappears, and Critic turns into the Strand wondering how an art can survive when the half-wits only like it when it is bad and the intellectuals won't have it when it is good.

I have decided that what follows shall be addressed neither to the one class nor the other, but to that utterly reasonable person, the middle-brow, who will not scoff if I mention the name of William Archer. Archer laid it down that there were three things to be asked of any play. (1) Is it true to the visible and audible surfaces of life? (2) Does it use the mechanism of the theatre in such a way as to beget 'interest, suspense, anticipation, sudden and vivid realization'? (3) Does the end of the play find the audience morally the better and intellectually the richer for it, and does the play say and mean something? I shall return to these three questions presently. The point is now to report Mr. Priestley's play as accurately as memory and the necessary condensation permit.

It is October, 1912, when the curtain rises on the sitting-room of Dr. Kirby's house at Eden End in the North of England. Sarah (Miss Nellie Bowman), the old Yorkshire nurse in the Doctor's family, is alternately petting and scolding Wilfred Kirby (Mr. John Teed), a callow youth on leave from Africa where he has a job with a trading-company. He is at the stage when barmaids attract, and we feel that she will be a lucky Hebe who does not get him for a husband. Wilfred has a sister called Lilian (Miss Alison Leggatt), a hard, unlovable creature who if she ever gets a husband will make him feel meaner than he really is. She hankers after Geoffrey Farrant (Mr. Franklyn Bellamy), a neighbouring gentleman-farmer, whose poetic needs are satisfied by Kipling and who could not spell 'Rachmaninoff', let alone play his concertos! We feel that Geoffrey will be a lucky fellow if he does not fall a victim to Lilian's spidery lure. Then there is old Kirby himself (Mr. Edward Irwin), a country doctor who, after taking his degree, deemed provincial discretion a safer card to play than London valour. Life's more glittering prizes have passed him by, and it is his half-regrets which hold the play together.

They would be whole regrets if it were not for his elder daughter Stella (Miss Beatrix Lehmann), who eight years before the play opens ran away to become a great actress, and has achieved her object. Or so her fond parent believes. This affectionate gullibility is the play's single weakness; the old man is too shrewd in other matters not to know the truth in this one, and, in any case, the jealous Lilian's viperish tongue must have undeceived him. The difference between this anomaly and concerto-playing farmers is the difference between a good suit of armour with a flaw in it, and one which isn't sword-proof anywhere. It is a structural weakness rather than an imperfect realization of character.

Now Stella enters, and we realize from the actress's mien and aura that she is not really a famous player even in the repertory sense. Ostensibly home for a holiday, she is obviously tired out and sick to death of playing second leads in Number Three towns. You might put it that she would shake the yoke of being an inauspicious star from her world-wearied flesh. By the end of the first act Lilian has wormed out of her sister that she is married, though separated from her husband; she will leave it to Stella to tell her father in her own time and way. In the interval Lilian has been busy, for when the curtain rises three days later, we find that she has telegraphed for Charles Appleby (Mr. Ralph Richardson), Stella's husband and a fifth-rate actor and 'good sort' whose spiritual home is the saloon bar. Why has Lilian telegraphed? Because Stella has been setting her cap at Geoffrey, that innocent fly half caught, or so Lilian thinks, in Lilian's web. Here we come upon the play's strength, which is its steady truth to life as it is really lived, and not as it is imagined by greensickly playwrights with Oxford insufficiently out of their systems. Does Lilian, improving the shining hour, swallow half the contents of her father's medicine-shelves so that the way is clear for Stella to marry Geoffrey after divorcing Charles? No. Instead she has a heart-to-heart talk with Stella, and Mr. Priestley is a sufficiently good dramatist to arrange that you cannot easily tell it from a slanging match. Lilian points out to her sister that she has made a mess of everything she has attempted. She ran away to become a famous actress and failed. She has tried marriage with Charles and failed. Now she comes quoting Wordsworth and a lot of guff about starry skies and lonely hills to poor Geoffrey who is perfectly happy with a gun and a few rabbits. In a few months' time she will drop him like a hot potato, and where will they all be then? Lilian is just not going to stand for it, and Stella has the sense to see that right is entirely on her sister's side. There is nothing left to do except pack up, which she literally does. Pretending to her father that she and Charles have two important offers, Stella makes it up with that bemused numskull, who asks for nothing better than to take the road again in double harness. The end of the play finds the Doctor with his dream of vicarious content unbroken, and the curtain descends on a delightful touch. This is that Geoffrey, who cannot have Stella and will not have Lilian, also packs a bag and goes off to a cousin in New Zealand.

Now, is this a good play, or isn't it? Let us go back to Archer's criteria. (1) I suggest that, apart from the unique discrepancy to which allusion has been made, the play is entirely true to the visible and audible surfaces of the life it sets out to present. Wilfred, Lilian and Stella are brother and two sisters, the daughters of this father and not three gowned-and-tailored, unrelated mannequins only to be brought to life when fashionable players consent to put on their clothes. Mr. Priestley's characters move by their own volition before he has started to do and after he has done with them. Charles is the kind of man Stella would marry, and Geoffrey is the kind of gentleman-farmer who would be potting rabbits in that vicinity. In other words, the characters exist and cohere. (2) Is the play all that is conveniently summed up in the word 'interesting'? That depends upon the playgoer. If the playgoer must have Lido-haunting duchesses upbraided by their dukes for choosing their gondolas according to their gondoliers, and cannot bemean himself to a *milieu* where nobody has more than a few paltry hundreds a year, why then this play is not for him. I am afraid my word will have to be taken for Mr. Priestley's craftsmanship and manipulation of incident, which are admirable. This is not one of those plays written round a dozen heads stuck out of a dozen railway-carriage windows to see why a train has stopped and pressing their owners into some fortuitous imbroglio.

(3) Permit me to leave moral improvement out of the question. Archer had to put that in because he was a Scot. Is the playgoer intellectually the richer for this play? That again depends upon the playgoer. If he be a low-brow he has no intellect to be enriched; if he is a distinguished intellectual like my friend of the other evening he wants his theatre to make him not richer but poorer. I am convinced that this play will give the middle-brow something to think about and talk over. What does it say, and what does it mean? I doubt whether Archer himself could have given a satisfactory answer to this question about any play. In connection with the first production of *Little Eyolf* we find him writing: 'I should be puzzled to say off-hand what is 'the good of'' the *Oedipus* or of *Othello*.' And again: 'I must premise with emphasis that it is no set "doctrine", or "moral", or "message", that I profess to expound. I do not even assert that Ibsen deliberately put in the play all that I make out of it. He simply took a cutting from the tree of life, and, planting it in the rich soil of his imagination, let it ramify and burgeon as it would.'

Similarly I shall be content to say that Mr. Priestley has taken a cutting from the tree of Yorkshire life and that its ramifications and burgeonings, with their gentle melancholy and rich humour, moved and amused me as I like to be moved and amused in a theatre. Why 1912? Not for the easy irony of the 'good time coming', but because of the greater poignancy of that passing moment which has all the illusion of urgent life and that we know to be in yesterday's grave. If *Eden End* is not a good play, then all that I know and have learned about plays is wrong, and I must go to school again. My half-wit who enjoyed *Treacle Tart* will probably say to me, provided he retains even that half of wit which he hath: 'I thought *Eden End* was an excellent play. I did not enjoy it.'

On the first night I thought that Miss Lehmann was a little shy of the immensely difficult part of Stella. It is a comparatively easy thing for a great actress to come flaunting on to the stage as a genuine world-famous actress like Sudermann's Magda; all that is necessary is for the player to abound in her own glamour. Miss Lehmann had to tackle the far more difficult job of suggesting an actress trailing clouds of failure. But even unsuccessful actresses visiting the home that lay about them in their infancy bring with them the smell of grease-paint, and the fact that they have not made good only increases their pretentiousness. In other words, Miss Lehmann was not quite actressy enough for Stella. This lovely player is first and foremost an intellectual actress, and I half-suspected her underplaying to be due to the old intellectual snare of team-work. Away with all such repertory nonsense! Stella is a leading part, and whoever plays it must lead. May I then suggest to an actress of extraordinary perception and quality that she should first of all speak up a little more, and then consult some Mrs. Vincent Crummles or other old trouper as to how she may make her gestures and the outline of her acting a little less woolly? If Miss Lehmann can be persuaded to throw her weight about a little more, this beautiful play will draw the town; her colleagues, one and all, are sheer perfection. The production of Miss Irene Hentschel is exceedingly sensitive and skilful, though as a sop to those who go to the theatre 'for entertainment' she would do well to speed it up here and there.

September 13, 1934

TIME AND THE CONWAYS

BY J. B. PRIESTLEY

(Duchess)

JEAN FORBES-ROBERTSON

All the beautiful time is yours for always, for it is life that takes away, changes, and spoils so often—not death, which is really the warden and not the thief of our treasures.

—LADY JEKYLL, in a letter to the Earl of Lytton.

SOMEWHERE in Walkley's essays there is a passage which runs more or less like this:

'Ideas are a godsend to the critic. Give him a thesis, and you have given him his article. He can not only examine the playwright's solution, but suggest another one of his own, and in fact pass in review all the possible permutations and combinations of the problem presented. The result is apt to be a little deceptive about the play itself, because it suits the critic to travel farther afield in the region of ideas than the playwright. Nor is it merely a question of intellectual area covered; the need for logical symmetry, for strict form, in analysis will often have tempted the critic to assume these qualities in the play when they are not, in fact, there. His picture of what the playwright has constructed will be, in Joe Gargery's phrase, a little too "architectooralooral". Hence the playgoer is often disappointed when he goes to see the play for himself. Half the ideas he has read about are not there, and those that are there are not so shipshape.'

Only half of this applies to Mr. Priestley's new play, which is perfectly shipshape, but the other half hits the mark exactly. Half the ideas you are now to read about, dear playgoer, are not

264

in this piece, which I most urgently and insistently beg you to see. I will go further and say that not one-tenth of what this play is really about is contained in it, and that it would be wrong if it were. Mr. Priestley works the reverse way from Mr. Shaw. That metaphysical old cook will take a kettleful of ideas, and so heat them on the fire of his wit that they boil over, leaving hardly any play behind. Our younger *cordon bleu* proceeds the other way about; the idea behind Mr. Priestley's play is no more than the pinch of salt essential to every good dish.

The idea in the present case is the new conception of Time. The old conception of Time was that of a piece of string in which the knots were years, and Infinite Time merely meant more and more string. About twenty years ago it occurred to Somebody that Time might be something in the fourth dimension. Knowing what a mess a three-dimensional world makes of two-dimensional ideas, it dawned upon this Somebody that a fourth dimension must make a similar mess of three-dimensional ideas about everything, including Time and Space. The notion was even conceived that Time, being something four-dimensional, might be a part of four-dimensional Space. Ten knots ago it occurred to Somebody Else to make a mental picture of this new Time similar to that which we can make of the old Space.

Conceive a tourist leaving London and proceeding to Manchester via Birmingham, and imagine him at Birmingham. Now the traveller does not suppose that because he has left London behind, London does not exist, or that because he has not yet arrived at Manchester, Manchester is not in being. In fact he knows that if he could mount sufficiently high in an aeroplane and were provided with a sufficiently powerful telescope he would be able to see London, Birmingham, and Manchester all existing at the same time. This being true of the things we know as places, why, argued Somebody Else, might not the same thing hold good of the things we call dates? If Time is a part of Space and Space a part of Time then even Mr. Curdle would see that dovetailedness cannot end here. If one can get above, and so obtain a bird's-eye view of places, why should not this be feasible with regard to dates?

It needs no more than the simplest metaphysical aeroplane to enable one to get a bird's-eye view of, say, 1066, 1588, and 1815, showing the Norman Conquest, the Defeat of the Armada, and the Battle of Waterloo all happening together and to be still going on.

Recently has come Yet Another — calling himself Mr. Dunne — who conceived the notion of moving about in Time. But just as in a railway train 'cows flash past the window' because it is the traveller who is flashing past the cows, so perhaps, argues this metaphysician, it is not we who move about in Time, but Time which moves about in us. Now when would Time choose to do this? Obviously when we are asleep, with the result that Time's escapades appear to us in the form of dreams. From which it follows that if you, being a lady, dream of meeting a tall, dark handsome stranger you are probably going to meet him, because in this new dimension you have always met him, are always going to meet him, are always meeting him. Well, there is nothing new under the sun. Coming events cast their shadows before, and every servant lass with a dream-book knows all about the tall, dark, handsome stranger. It is easy to make jokes on this subject. Some little time ago I heard a man at a supper party say: 'Why be afraid of Death? Since Time is not absolute, but merely something invented by Man for his convenience, we are already dead. Equally, when we are dead we shall be alive. We are both now. Past, Present, and Future are one.' He then turned to the man sitting next to him and said: 'Will you lunch with me to-morrow?' The man replied: 'Sorry, I'm going to the execution of Charles the First.'

It is, as I say, easy to make a good joke about Mr. Dunne's Experiment. But it is not so easy to make a good play out of it. This is the place and time, and both together and one as much as the other, to say that Mr. Priestley has made a play which is magnificent drama, if you grasp what it is essentially about, and first-class entertainment if you don't. The Conways are a middle-class family living in a suburb of a prosperous manufacturing town. The family consists of the mother, two sons, and four daughters. The War is just over, and it is Kay Conway's twenty-first birthday, which is being marked by a party. The first act is pure exposition, showing what each character is like now and hopes to become. Of the children the elder son is the least adventurous-minded; he is a clerk with a dull job, and doesn't resent his job being dull. Dull jobs must have their dull doers, and why not he? The younger and flashier son is going to make a fortune, probably out of selling motor-cars. One girl is like that daughter of Mr. Bennet's who could be happy in any town provided a regiment of good-looking officers was quartered in it. (Has any critic of Jane Austen observed that her regiments consist entirely of officers?) Another, more serious-minded, is going to reform the world, and incidentally become head of Girton: another is a little bundle of sixteen-year-old life, quivering for the fulfilment of the promises life holds out at sixteen. If these three sisters were Tchehov's how we should praise the skill with which they are drawn! Some shred of justification for the comparison is the figure of the mother, a comfortable English Madame Ranevsky, who cannot conceive that the value of her house will decrease or her shares go down.

Remains the fourth daughter, Kay, who acts as liaison officer between Mr. Priestley and Mr. Dunne. Kay doesn't experiment with Time; it is Time which tries its experiments on Kay. She is visited by waking dreams in which she has foreknowledge of the wreckage made of human hopes by Time — and, of course, by those human foibles which are Time's allies. The second act happens nineteen years later, and has a clear-cut quality worthy of Mr. Granville-Barker at his best. We see what all but one of the members of this family have become, the little bundle of urgent life having died. We see what has happened to the flighty daughter's marriage, and what the younger boy's love affair has turned into. We see that happiness, though of a subdued kind, comes to that member of the family who made least claim to happiness. We see a great deal which cannot be explained here, though I cannot forbear mention of that changelessness which Mr. Priestley has so adroitly allotted to Mrs. Conway. A little older, a little fatter, a little sillier, a little sharper-tempered, and no more.

In the third act we go back to the party, where we see the burgeoning of those hopes which the second act has so cruelly shattered. This last act is emotionally satisfying and, indeed, compulsional, since the poignancy springs directly out of Mr. Priestley's thesis. I have heard a complaint that this act lacks surprise, since it shows us nothing that we have not anticipated. I regard this as the most foolish objection I have heard in the whole of my playgoing life, since novelty in this third act would be the one thing to destroy the thesis which is this play's backbone. One supercilious eyebrow raised itself to say that it couldn't for the life of it see why the play's events were not performed in their proper order. Whereby I suggest to Mr. Priestley that he should adopt this suggestion on alternate nights—the present order of the acts being maintained on Mondays, Wednesdays and Fridays for ordinarily intelligent people, but reversed as to second and third acts on Tuesdays, Thursdays and Saturdays for the benefit of highbrows and cretins. Before the matinées the stage-manager would, of course, toss up!

Now Mr. Priestley, as an experienced man of the theatre, knows that whereas a Russian piece may close in complete gloom to the plaudits of crowded houses, an English piece which did the same thing would play to empty benches. Where was the mitigating ray of sunshine to come from? (Mr. Priestley is too much of an artist to look for the ray which cannot logically exist, and if his piece had been dark with the darkness of the tomb I think he would not have written it.) His characters, he tells us, are to find their consolation in the very nature of this new Time. If the disappointment endures, so, too, does the hope; woe does not extinguish joy. All the beautiful time in life as well as its ugly quarters of an hour is ours for always. This remains true though the quarters lengthen into hours. Not even sunset can do away with sunrise. Night cannot abolish day.

The acting of this piece is so good that it takes away the breath with surprise and gives it back with pleasure. The artists concerned are Mesdames Jean Forbes-Robertson, Barbara Everest, Rosemary Scott, Eileen Erskine, Molly Rankin, and Helen Horsey, and Messrs. Raymond Huntley, Wilfred Babbage, Mervyn Johns, and Alexander Archdale. Space permits me merely to say of their performances that individually and collectively they make up a concatenation of intention and display of achievement which have no parallel on the London stage at the moment. Miss Irene Hentschel has produced very brilliantly. Indeed, I see no reason why, London taste being what it is, this lovely piece should not play to scantier and scantier houses. It is only because Mr. Priestley's pockets are not empty that his play sees the stage at all. For the piece is what your commercial manager insists upon calling uncommercial. By which, of course, he means that it is ten times more enthralling than the rubbish upon which he relies to fill his coffers.

August 26, 1937

I HAVE BEEN HERE BEFORE

BY J. B. PRIESTLEY
(Royalty)

WILFRID LAWSON, LEWIS CASSON, EILEEN BELDON

In his other play, at the Duchess Theatre, Mr. Priestley propounds a theory of Time in which past, present, and future events are like a high tea, in which everything is put on the table together. Aeons later, says Mr. Priestley, tea-time comes round again, and you sit again at the table, find all the dishes there exactly as before, and have the same meal. The idea is that this process goes on for ever and ever, at, of course, aeonic intervals. Even that stern moralist Matthew Arnold would have approved this notion, since if in this life you speak out of turn or steal your neighbour's helping you go on interrupting and stealing throughout eternity, thus making conduct more important than ever.

Now comes this second play, which completely upsets everything laid down in the first. The implication at the Duchess is that we are seeing the Conways sitting down to high tea *for the first time*. The play at the Royalty tells us that the Conways, we, and everybody else have sat down to high tea any number of times before, that the meal has always proceeded in the same fashion, and will do so on the present occasion unless we make that effort which, normally, it does not occur to us to make. But to-day we have a Strange Guest who begins by telling Tommy that he is going to steal Dicky's cake, Mabel that she is about to spill the milk, and Mum and Dad that they will have a row. There is a general chorus of 'How do you know?' The Strange Guest replies: 'Like all prophets, I have the gift of looking into the past. I know what is coming to you because it has all happened before. But there is no need for it to happen again. You, Tommy, can refrain from stealing Dicky's cake. You, Mabel, have only to be more careful with the milk-jug. And you, Mum and Dad, can pull yourselves together!' In the new play the Strange Guest is a German professor, and, being a German professor, he lightly alludes to the foregoing as the Game of Recurrence and Intervention.

Half-way through this piece I was suddenly stung by an idea. This was the the notion of Mr. Priestley as a sentimental molly-coddle and dyed-in-the-wool good-behaviourist, one of those people who insist on moral wish being father to scientific thought! This kind always thinks loosely, as when the Strange Guest asks: 'Why should this great theatre of suns and moons and starlight have been created for the first pitiful charade we can contrive?' Why not? Would Mr. Priestley suggest that the vaults and caverns of Gruyère cheese have been created in order to give cheese-mites a second chance? Our author likes to play at the Game of Recurrence and Intervention because it gives people a second chance, and in the theatre the people who are given second chances invariably lead better lives.

But hold on a bit. The Game is only half of Mr. Priestley's theme. The other half is Pattern. All the people in the new play are as closely inter-related as the threads in a piece of cloth; you cannot alter the life of one without a corresponding change in the lives of all the others. Now let us see where this leads. I am a naughty little boy. My schoolmaster is a brutal fellow who likes using the rod. Its use makes me grow up into a good man, and I die a millionaire at the age of ninety. This happens thousands of times. Then one fine day my schoolmaster stops being a sadist, conceives a positive distaste for the rod, spares it, and so spoils me that I take to drink and die in the workhouse. And that, dear Mr. Priestley, or dear Mr. Ouspensky, just won't do.

Think of the unwarrantable changes that are going to be wrought in our lives if on some future occasion Julius Caesar and William the Norman decide to forgo their invasions of this country. Think of the difference it is going to make if the women who have rejected us suddenly make up their minds to accept. And since, according to Pattern, everybody reacts on everybody else, the number of lives I may have to lead amounts to $1 \times 2 \times 3 \times 4$, and so on, in a progression, the last figure of which is the entire population of these islands! We all remember Carlyle's answer to the lady who told him she accepted the Universe: 'Damn it, ma'am, you'd better!' I accept the effect of other people's Pattern on my life because I have to. But once is enough, and if there is a new Dimension subjecting me to countless millions of contradictory existences because of the whims of other people, I shall do my best to remain outside that Dimension. No, I am afraid Mr. Priestley's new piece, considered metaphysically, is bosh!

This does not prevent *I Have Been Here Before* from being a magnificent play, for it is no argument against a sieve that it fails to hold water. Not one but fifty ideas filter through this piece, which, under its startlingly new guise, one yet perceives to be the very oldest play that was ever written. Janet has fallen out of love with her husband Walter, who suffers from all the neuroses consequent upon too much drink; she is now in love with Oliver, the good-looking young schoolmaster. A German professor who knows his Ouspensky arrives at the Yorkshire inn where the three are staying, and tells them that they are going to make a mess of

things because they have made a mess of them before. Walter
will shoot himself, his business will collapse, and ruin hundreds of
people, including the innkeeper and his daughter and the little
grandson who is at the school to which the wife's lover has been
appointed by the husband who happens to be the governor of that
school. (You note the Pattern?) The young man will lose his job.
The lovers will cease to be lovers and take to quarrelling in
filthy lodgings in Bloomsbury. 'Now children', says Dr. Görtler,
'why not make it a pleasant tea table instead of an unpleasant
one?' In other words, Walter is to behave like a civilized man and
hand Janet over to Oliver, after which Walter will not shoot himself, but devote his attention to turning teetotaller and repairing
the business, thus keeping everybody prosperous. Oliver will
continue in his job at the school, and in the holidays he and Janet
will be on the friendliest terms with the nicest intellectuals in the
tidiest parts of Bloomsbury.

Now what, may one ask, is this except the very oldest theatre?
At the Royalty on Wednesday evening I seemed to be present
once again at the first night of *The Liars* at the old Criterion and
to hear the voice of Wyndham's Sir Christopher Deering booming
away at Faulkner and Lady Jessica. Booming with a difference
it is true, but still booming. The reader will detect the variations
without my help:

'I've nothing to say in the abstract against refusing to run away
with another man's wife. There may be planets in which the
refusal is not only the highest ideal morality, but where it has the
further advantage of being a practical way of carrying on society.
But it has this one fatal defect in our country — it won't work!
You know what we English are, Ned. Take my word for it, my
dear Lady Jessica, my dear Ned, it won't work. You know it's
not an original experiment you're making. This trick of refusing
has been tried before. Have you ever known it to be successful?
Lady Jessica, think of the brave pioneers who have gone before
you in this act of renunciation. They've all perished, and their
bones whiten the matrimonial shore!'

I am not the first to say that there is nothing new under the sun. But perhaps Ecclesiastes was wrong, and Mr. Priestley is right, in which case the whirligig of Time brings not revenges but satisfaction. In this new Dimension races are to the swift, battles to the strong, riches to men of understanding, and full houses to playwrights of skill. For Chance droppeth out, and Time and a Firm Intention to Do Better happeneth to everybody. But what about the firm intention to do worse? Mr. Priestley's reply to this is that if the bad man persists in his badness he sinks to the lowest circle in the spiral and dies. Which seems to me like arguing that cannons go off only when they are fired in a just cause. Will Mr. Priestley never realize that metaphysical thought should be free from moral bias?

The point about this play as a play is that it holds you with or without the metaphysics. Superficially it is the fashionable drama of the 'nineties all over again; actually it explores hell and glimpses heaven. It is a play of wuthering heights and depths, whose acting alone might serve for a whole column. Limitations of space permit me to say only that Mr. Lewis Casson as the German professor gives the best performance, excepting Mr. Bax's Socrates, of his career; that Miss Eileen Beldon as the inn's housekeeper exhibits an understanding and a restraint beyond all praise — she deliberately refuses laughs throughout — and that Miss Patricia Hilliard and Mr. William Fox acquit themselves admirably. Mr. Wilfrid Lawson makes of the husband a middle-aged Hamlet who has married Ophelia and bitterly regrets it. Is this a great actor? Let me shelve the difficulty by boldly stating that he is a grand one, whose present performance is something to dream about.

I advise every reader to see this play, provided that it is still running when this inadequate account of it appears. It is so interesting in thematic material, whether the argument is sound or false, so novel in treatment, so loyally produced, and so flamboyantly and dimly acted according to the integrity of part and moment, so gloriously independent of playgoing fashion — it is, in short, such big stuff that I cannot understand, playgoing taste being what it is, how the bats in this metaphysical belfry have survived to flit across the London sky for a second, third, and even fourth evening!

September 22, 1937

THE FARMER'S WIFE

BY EDEN PHILLPOTTS

(Court)

CEDRIC HARDWICKE

MR. PHILLPOTTS has never had the best of luck with his beloved Dartmoor, very much the younger son in comparison with the Exmoor of an older writer. But for *Lorna Doone* his *Children of the Mist* would have been more generally recognized as the magnificent novel it undoubtedly is. When this author began writing there was, you see, hardly any West of England moorland not pegged out. A giant genius had claims extending from Exonbury, on Dartmoor's right hand, all the way to Quartershot, which is as nearly Surrey as makes no matter. To the left prospecting did not seem more hopeful, at least two stalwarts claiming rights in the rich ore of Cornwall. A lesser lover would have forsaken Devon for some unwritten county, say Huntingdon or Rutland. But faithlessness was not for Mr. Phillpotts, who, at the long last, came into his own, west of Thomas Hardy and south of Blackmore. Who to me says Devon to-day conjures up visions of red earth and a mothy coombe, white bread laden with strawberry jam, clotted cream and wasps, and a belated beam lingering upon this writer's page. This little comedy is very much like that.

At the beginning there was a question of a love affair between young George Smerdon, a Corydon whose charms consisted solely in a legacy of five thousand pounds, and Petronell Sweetland, a sullen, moody Phyllis who liked nothing in her lover save his fortune. This part of the play brought to mind a story by Villiers de l'Isle-Adam, called *Virginie et Paul*. Two cousins have each attained the age of fifteen, and the boy pays court to the girl in the park, under the moon. He is late, having delayed to wheedle a silver piece out of his father. She urges him not to forget his aunt's birthday, since she is to leave them her silver savings. He bids her mark the silvery note of the nightingale. She calls attention to the silvery moon. They avow a common passion for the country, where life is cheaper. He adores 'la chasse', which again may be an economy. It is late. He must fly, lest his father give him no more silver. And the writer concludes: 'As the lovers parted, the walls of the château gave back, not the heavenly murmur of a kiss, but the jingle "De l'argent! un peu d'argent!" '

But to have stressed the five thousand pounds would have meant satire, and Mr. Phillpotts' piece was clearly an idyll. And therefore George and Petronell were not explored, though we felt that the boy would have stood the test better than the girl, who was a mercenary little madam. The play's real motive was the irksomeness of the widower's state to Petronell's father, Samuel Sweetland, who, like a wiser before him, decided to go once more a-wooing. He woo'd in turn a plump rider to hounds who must have kept more than one horse; a faded lady lavishing upon her villa-residence the affection which poor Miss Flite kept for her canaries; a post-mistress, and an hotel-keeper. But there was nobody on hand to bid poor Samuel to beware of widows, or of spinsters either, and to notify him that their Nay is as like as not to turn into Yea. How the good man got out of his quartet of encumbrances I deem it unnecessary to explain. The end had been foreseen before anybody in the piece had spoken a word. Buxom farmers' wives *in posse* don't darn socks with a seraphic air for nothing.

By far the best character in the piece was a battered and crusty henchman, beautifully played by Mr. Cedric Hardwicke. Old Churdles Ash might have come straight out of Borrow, or again you could imagine cantankerous Samuel Butler taking him to his heart. There was a good deal of observation and humour both in the old man and in the actor's playing of him. So lifelike was he that at times he seemed to turn the stage into your own private well of recollection and imagination, being dipped wherein, the other characters put on a new and shining feasibility. There was one moment when, some twenty people being assembled on the stage, one forgot, or almost forgot, about the theatre, and fell to thinking in terms of some native, endeared village. There is tribute here, not only to the player who fused the acting round about him to a sensible whole, but to the producer, whose stage picture at this point was a masterly piece of composition.

Mr. Colin Keith-Johnston put some loutish clothes on that perfect Gauguin which was his Adam, and as the clumsy lover acted with perfect felicity. As the farmer Mr. Melville Cooper was unflagging, and Mesdames Chatwin, Gill, and Thornton lent themselves to the guying of their sex with all conceivable good will. It says a great deal for this comedy that it survives, and survives triumphantly, a theme foreign to perfect chivalry. That little matter apart, this farmer's search for a wife is one of the most joyous excursions the theatre of to-day affords.

March 16, 1924

THE PLEASURE GARDEN

BY BEATRICE MAYOR

(Stage Society)

HAY PETRIE, RICHARD BIRD, MARY BARTON, ATHENE SEYLER

THIS is one of those pieces whose every moment is delightful but whose total gesture is misconceived. Its author is obviously a pessimist like the butler in Wilde's play, who took the wretchedest view of life, yet did his best to give satisfaction. Mrs. Mayor gives, in a series of scenes of great charm and delicacy, an interpretation of life almost Gummidgean in its darkness; her pleasure garden is a 'wale', a pit, a slough of despond, or whatever simile our brightest may have discovered for their extremes of dejection. No community was ever quite so miserable as this, not even in Russia. What is at the bottom of so much despair? Well, principally dying and being born, love and hate, desire, fulfilment, intoxication — all the things which are meat and drink to the artist, and make life worth while for the ordinary man.

When the curtain rises we see a number of people sitting under trees. It is a bright, sunny afternoon. A student is reading a work upon stalk-eyed crustacea. On the form next to him an elderly gentleman is smoking a pipe. In the background an actor is 'resting' and snoring. A young wife sews in the foreground. Then odds and ends of humanity drift on to the stage, and the play begins. A chit of a girl seeks the boy-lover whom she has driven to distraction; a husband and wife engage in as embittered and futile a quarrel as ever graced the pages of Mr. Wells; a poet despairs of his Muse and of his mistress without a mind; a rich woman bullies her maid; a distraught lady makes meaningless moan. This traffic rouses the student, who compares philosophies with the smoker and is persuaded to exchange for the rest of the afternoon the study of shell-fish for that of mankind.

The *va-et-vient* is resumed. A clergyman's wife meets a former schoolmate, now a courtesan. Both are miserable — one because passion has not entered her life, the other because her life has been wrecked by it. The actor wakes up and reveals a past as pretendedly inscrutable as he would have it romantic in a seedy, second-rate way. He is amorist and drunkard, and blabs his affairs to all and sundry. It now appears that the boy-lover and the courtesan are not, in Sir Arthur Pinero's phrase, strangers to one another. The young *ménage* totters, and the chit reveals unexpected depths of silliness and cruelty. The distraught lady — who has been a companion eleven times in fourteen years — opens an abyss of loneliness before our feet. The actor makes up to the courtesan. Two factory girls make a mock of the wander-wit. We see a mourner on his way to a funeral. A child laughs. The student believes that all the world is mad and that only crabs are sane. But that, of course, is only because he knows so little about them. At the end there are only two happy people left — the man with the pipe, who is going to die, and the girl, because she is sewing the proverbial 'little, little things'.

The charm of the play comes from the author's very subtle sense of character, and her abounding fantasy and wit. Everything that she says about her people is true of them at some moment of their lives; it is the implication of continuity that is wrong. Produce these people, as the mathematicians say, even the shortest distance in their present moods, and you would land them in the asylum. But as the companions of an hour they are delightful. The piece went throughout to an audible purr of content, and you could hardly believe that there was 'not a penny in it'. The acting was excellent, every member of the very long cast being quite perfect. There was not enough of Mr. Felix Aylmer, the man with the pipe. He alone kept one's nerves under control, and when he was not on the stage one felt like the sick man among Flaubert's pigmies, 'downcast to see his little physician depart'. Mr. Hay Petrie played the student in an ordinary brown suit and an extraordinary vein of charity. Mr. Richard Bird imparted beauty to the boy-lover; he is really young and not, like so many *jeunes premiers*, merely rejuvenated. As the romantic actor, half gallant and half cad, Mr. Stephen Ewart was wholly admirable. He exuded self-pity, and tawdry, second-hand pathos — a grotesque full of humour. It is difficult to decide between Miss Mary Barton and Miss Athene Seyler, but if I must do so I give the palm to the latter for a straightforward, understandable success. Her part, you see, was as plain as a pikestaff or plainer; and when it comes to seeing the nose on her character's face nobody can beat Miss Seyler. Her courtesan had a careless gaiety that sent a shudder down one's back, and a moment or two of lacerating pathos. Miss Barton dree'd her weird with faint, sad grace and an exquisite poignancy. It was not her fault that the character could not explain itself; and her withdrawals into the half-night of madness, her feeble efforts to express unusual thought in shreds of common-place phrases worn like counters, her hopelessness and resignation — all this was very fine. Miss Jean Cadell was good. Miss Marjorie Gabain and Miss Elsa Lanchester were amusing, and Miss Drusilla Wills, as a waitress, contributed a sketch which was perfectly true and, at the same time, amazingly funny.

June 6, 1924

THE CONSTANT NYMPH

BY MARGARET KENNEDY AND BASIL DEAN
(New)

NOEL COWARD, EDNA BEST, CATHLEEN NESBITT

THIS piece begins with the Artistic Temperament and ends with Heart Disease. I have, unfortunately, not read Miss Kennedy's novel, but I glean from the play that Sanger was a colossal artist who spent the greater part of his existence in dram-drinking, begetting children and other heroic dissipation of energy. There is a lot of nonsense written in connection with this business of being a great artist. It may be that inspiration comes to a man in a mood of exaltation, and is brought about by such different things as a pinch of dope or a climb among mountain tops. But that mood accounts for no more than the original conception. Behind every work of art, behind every poem, painting or piece of acting, there is, there must be, an immense amount of sheer, solid hard work, which can only be executed in soberness. The artist cannot be a creature of dissipation by the very meaning of the word. In fact, one of the disabilities attaching to the artistic profession is that it gives you no time for going to the devil. Let me inconceivably suppose that Mr. Selfridge or Lord Rothermere or Mr. Cochran should drink a thimbleful too much champagne or smoke one cigar too many. Is it thinkable that next morning the Stores would close, the *Daily Mail* default or the Albert Hall fall down? No. Yet in like circumstances the creative artist would have to shut up shop for the day. A man who is always drunk cannot always be composing fine symphonies. And, therefore, I presume that Sanger must have had his lucid intervals, and that in those intervals his lucidity must have been, as Dick Phenyl says, 'devilish'.

I am far more inclined to believe in Sanger's disregard of appearances. After all, no artist who is really an artist cares anything at all for the world outside his art or for anybody outside himself. Always provided, of course, that his disregard of the conventions does not deprive him of his livelihood. The artist who is really an artist and has an independent income of five pounds a week, or even two, cares nothing whatever what the world about him may say. He belongs to a superior race and he knows it. Anybody can build a Forth Bridge, or at least span the river with something or other which will bring Scotchmen and their luggage over the border. Anybody can run a huge store. Or if they can't it doesn't matter, for there will always be somebody to sell one hats and umbrellas. Anybody, in short, can do any job in the world outside the realm of art, *or something that will do as well*. But nobody except Milton could have written *Lycidas*, and nobody except Wagner could have composed *Tristan*. To do them justice, both artists knew it, and to do us justice we know that no other compositions could have taken the places of these two. None would have 'done as well'. Therefore, I would advance my argument a step further and declare the artist to be free of all those shackles and restraints which bind the ordinary man, were it not for the fact that the unbinding would immediately prove fatal, both to the artist and to his art. What it comes to is this: the artist is a superior being who has got to behave himself rather better than the average man under penalty not only of losing his superiority, but of being of less use and service to the world than a pew-opener or·a stockbroker or anybody who has never bothered his head about art.

And now to my notice proper.

There are best sellers and best sellers. There is the confection concerning the loves of Sir Gervase Devereux, Baronet, and Elaine Pigot, the shorthand typist — a cloying sub-Garvicious sweetmeat feverishly absorbed in 'bus or tube and between the hours of ten and six folded in two to fit the hand-bag. The name of the confectioner is unknown even to the millions whom his wares delight. Then there is the high-grade bosh confessing a name sufficiently notorious to act as a deterrent to any connoisseur of dust covers. Next we have the best-seller *pur sang*, which everybody pretends to despise and nobody can help reading if and when the long winter evening comes. But there is yet another class — the best seller by inadvertence. There are two explanations for this type. One is that just as the sun will sometimes shine even in an English summer, so the public will sometimes buy the highest when it is for sale. The other is that the writer, having given his story the sentimental core beloved of the multitude, has had the supreme luck not to offend with the artistry with which he has surrounded that core. This is the class to which, although unfortunately I have only my knowledge of the play to go upon, I instinctively assign Miss Kennedy's novel.

The Constant Nymph must always be happy in three themes which no amount of good writing could ever defeat. First there is the 'heart-of-a-child' theme, perennially refreshing in a world grown sick of war, war debts, labour leading and misleading, and all the other knavish trickeries of the grown spirit. Tessa is flower-like, and it will be a sorry age when we are not moved by the spectacle of virginal purity and fineness of mind going hand in hand with a sense of fun and a healthy knowledge of life. Tessa is a twentieth-century heroine with nothing of that 'softness of mind amounting almost to feebleness' which rendered Lucy dear to Edgar Ravenswood. It is Tessa's firmness of mind which endears her to Lewis Dodd. I am less sure about the validity of the second theme — the early dying. There never was any reason why the naughty heroines of Prévost, Murger, and Dumas should find Heaven by the consumptive route except that death pays all and secures the moral ending. There is no reason that I can see why Miss Kennedy's good little woman should not have borne her husband a brood of sturdy, constant little children. Tessa towards the end becomes uncommonly like Miss Alcott's Beth March with the addition of a grand passion. And since Chance has a place in this world as well as Design, we must perhaps consent that those whom both gods and stalls love shall die young. Certainly Tessa's death scene is very affecting, and it is perhaps foolish to demand that it should have further significance. A good cry is its own justification.

The third theme is the age-long one of the conflict between respectability and the artistic temperament. I am not quite clear whether we are to assume that because Sanger was a great composer he was bound to take to brandy, or that it was brandy which gave him his inspiration and so led to his being a great composer. But whether it is the artistic dog which cannot help wagging a vicious tail or whether it is the vicious tail which gives the dog its temperament, is not really to the point. It is tacitly assumed in the play that Sanger, being the artist he was, could not help doing the things he did, and that he and Lewis Dodd belong to a race which is entitled to make its own laws. 'You expect art to be turned on like the electric light', says Lewis scornfully, and we feel we are expected to forgive in the artist conduct which we should not tolerate in the electrician. I am conscious that this is not the place fully to combat or defend such a thesis. But it is necessary to state it, since it largely explains the play's success. The point is that the public which is most obedient to Mrs. Grundy at home and most likes to flout her in the theatre is the Great English Public which provides ninety-nine per cent of playgoers. In view of these three themes — child-heroine, early demise and the artistic clash — how could *The Constant Nymph* be a failure?

But a piece built on these lines might yet reek horribly of mawkishness. This play is good because, though it contains plenty of sentiment, it is entirely free from sentimentality. It is good because though it is of the theatre it is never theatrical. We can see through it into the lives of people who have had an existence before we came into the play-house, and will go on having one after we have left it. It is good because of the obvious beauty of the principal character. Tessa, besides knowing a child's depth of suffering, has all a child's intuition, and it is a very poignant moment when, taking her imagination by the hand, she declares knowledge of the whole of love, and is misunderstood by Florence. The part was almost unimaginably well played by Miss Edna Best, who looked and breathed the single mind and loyal purpose. This performance had many beautiful moments. There was one when Tessa awoke from her trance at the end of the musical charade, another when Sanger's death made her call out to that other heart of hers beating in the body of Lewis, a third when she broke from Lewis's love-making, and a fourth when she asked him to kiss her as for the last time. But then, Miss Best's playing throughout the whole of that last scene was extraordinarily firm and sensitive. It was as though the childish spirit which hitherto had known nothing perfectly except anguish had been suddenly touched to the full comprehension of womanhood.

The play is good because of the absence of exaggeration in the drawing of Florence, who seems to me to be entirely lifelike. The eager, predatory, absorbing female who, besides marrying the man, wants to mate with the artist so that she can brood over genius and hatch out its works to her own snobbish advancement — the character is admirably caught. 'It must be splendid', Florence says, 'to live with a genius and help him in his work.' And, groaning, we at once foresee for Lewis the dreary vista of musical At Homes at which all the musical nobs will be nobbled and prospective patrons petted. Somebody, I forget who, has talked of *la peinture à quatre mains*; the fate of one who must compose in double harness is equally horrible. The only thing that anybody can do for any genius is to feed him, inspire him at a discreet distance, and keep the bailiffs away. But Florence did not know this. Neither did she know that when her husband realized his love for Tessa the quickest and surest way to bring about catastrophe was to behave badly to the child and talk of doubling her love for Lewis. Had Florence behaved decently to Tessa and doubled her affection without talking about it she would at least have had Lewis's compassion and sense of decency left as spars to cling to. Instead of which she upset the boat and was drowned. All this is very well observed, and Miss Cathleen Nesbitt did perfect justice to the thinly concealed egotism, the quick resentments and returns to surface-calm and affability. The part is not only very difficult; it is against the sympathies of the audience throughout. Miss Nesbitt gave every shade its full and exact value, and her performance was very justly acclaimed. For the first time in my experience a musician of genius was credibly put on the stage, and I even believed in the symphony! Mr. Noel Coward played Lewis very well, with a complete waywardness which lost no hold on virility and an excellent sense of the shifting emotional values.

Probably the play, if it had been conceived as a play, would have been a trifle less stragglesome. Linda, admirably acted by Miss Mary Clare; Kate Sanger, excellently played by Miss Marie Ney; Trigorin, de-Russianized by Mr. Aubrey Mather to the likeness of a typical British taxpayer; Jacob Birnbaum, whose accent and spirit were capitally caught by Mr. Keneth Kent — all these necessarily fade away. Antonia, interpreted by Miss Elissa Landi with great spirit, seems to demand a play to herself, and we want to know more of Miss Helen Spencer's Paulina. But over-crowding is inherent in any adaptation of any novel, and our complaint is really that of a man set down to a banquet with too little time in which to do it justice. Still, I suggest that the first act, which runs to an hour and a quarter, is too long, and that the musical charade might be shortened, preserving however the moment at the end when Lewis and Tessa stare into each other's face and prepare us for all that is to come.

The second and third acts are as taut as the greatest stickler for well-made play-making could desire. The production was admirable throughout, and Mr. Dean has probably never done anything better than that amusing musical party. The last scene was as good as good can be, from the time when Lewis put his feet on the counterpane — a piece of admirable naturalism masking a moment of some difficulty — to the manœuvre at the end which made the lovers sit on the bed side by side and give you their profiles as on a medallion. The exquisiteness of this last scene lingered in the mind long after the curtain had fallen. Good performances were also given by Mesdames Marjorie Gabain and Margot Sieveking, and Messrs. David Hawthorne, Tony de Lungo, and Craighall Sherry. Is it possible that Mr. Harold Scott, though entertaining, was a little too much afraid of speaking up? Miss Margaret Yarde at last gave one an opportunity for something less than fulsomeness: she had obviously steeped herself too much and too recently in Mr. Maugham's Papuan duennas to be quite credible as a Belgian landlady.

But the whole thing — play, production, casting, acting — was really very good. It would be ungracious to insist upon the absence of certain qualities which go to make up a great as distinct from a good play — poetry, atmosphere, strangeness in beauty, and so forth. One would not claim too much for *The Constant Nymph*. But for people who can recognize a plain, unvarnished transcript from life and like a good play 'with no nonsense about it', I can imagine nothing better. Every moment of the piece, except perhaps the over-long charade in the first act, held the house in thrall.

September 19, 1926

BERKELEY SQUARE

BY JOHN L. BALDERSTON AND J. C. SQUIRE
(St. Martin's)

LAWRENCE ANDERSON, JEAN FORBES-ROBERTSON

JACKASSES who would not have tweaked the tail of the living lion have been heard to bray that James the novelist is dead. This may or may not be true, the point being that James has not been dead long enough to get his second wind. All great writers when they die suffer a temporary diminution in popularity, falling often into something very like oblivion to be followed by a come-back, the nature and period of which are variable. An author who was precious to the few may never be read again except by the precious few, or he may in his second innings strike the imagination of the whole reading public. Pondering any page of James and noting the glossy surface, the lustre and the sheen of words, it is surely presumptuous to prophesy annihilation. Yet perhaps the seeds of nothingness are sown in the very elaboration of it all; is it possible that the imperceptible does not admit a hundred viewpoints? And can we stomach four hundred pages of this rich bamboozlement? It is just conceivable that James the novelist may be dead, though one ventures to think not so hopelessly as our door-nailers suppose.

James the dramatist is a different pair of shoes. He cannot be dead who was never alive. One of the most pathetic things in the history of the theatre is the life-long conviction of this narrow refiner in ideas that he could broaden them for the theatre. This is an old fallacy; probably the jeweller never breathed who did not believe that he could make the descent to pots and pans as successfully as any tinker. Yet the gifts are not the same, or anything like the same. A play is not a novel coarsened to delight a serried mob breathing down the back of each other's necks. The remark of the American to the immemorial English butler — 'To whom do you, beautifully, belong?' — sets the novelist's page a-tinkle with mischief and irony; spoken on the stage it is a knell. No word or collection of words can be shy enough to describe the pith of a James story, whispered by the writer and overheard by the reader. Whereas the method of the theatre is the method of the town-crier.

Mr. Balderston, in collaboration with Mr. Squire, has taken his plot from that posthumous fragment *The Sense of the Past*. One knows instinctively what James could, would, and must have made of an American swapping identities with an Englishman living one hundred and forty years earlier. One senses the hesitant delicacy with which James's centuries would kiss and commingle, and the sly chicanery of writing bent on keeping the reader's attention to this or that 'value' and no other. But in the theatre the bonds cannot be drawn so tight. Show the spectator an action and you will have his whole mind; speculate and theorize for him, and he will begin speculating and theorizing for himself.

286

Our authors in their first two acts give the spectator too much time in which to ask himself what he would do if the clock were suddenly to be put back a hundred and forty years. Personally, I should have recited *Dolores* to Doctor Johnson and asked him what he made of *that*. (Always presuming, as this play does, that the Great Man was still alive.) Or I should have tried some of Wilde's best epigrams on Sheridan, or watched Jane's face while I told her about Dorothy and Sir Francis Beekman and Mr. Eisman's theory of education. I should certainly have mentioned the railway and the telephone, and probably journeyed up to Fifeshire to tell the golfers about the rubber-cored ball. But the effect that Peter Standish's later knowledge might have upon a previous generation is quite elaborately not our authors' point, though in the theatre the spectator will insist upon making it. Nor are we to concern ourselves with the inevitable and tragic concomitant to knowledge of the future — the absence of surprise. No material slavery can be comparable to the servitude of predestination, and we wonder how Standish can keep quiet about it.

But the particular 'value', in the Jamesian sense, to which our attention is drawn is Standish's disillusion at meeting his adored eighteenth century face to face. This disillusion really amounts to very little more than that the women have a poor notion of the beauty of old furniture and that the men do not wash sufficiently. It is to establish this that an unconscionable amount of machinery has been requisitioned, including elaborate explanations as to the curvature in Time. Now it would be foolish to argue that not Einstein with all his mathematics can bring back yesterday, nor Pirandello at his most ingenious arrange for a cake to be eaten the day before it is baked. For the theatre has to make a beginning somewhere, and every sensible playgoer will concede that for the purposes of dramatic discussion centuries may be laid on top of one another like a sandwich. Only there must be something of a meal to follow, and for the first two acts this play gave us little except pleasant dresses, vigorous 'period' acting, adumbrations of half-hearted spookery, and some not very pointed irony.

The third act seemed to me to be on an altogether higher plane. This was concerned with the spirit of the modern Peter Standish and its reaching out after the spirit of Helen Pettigrew, who died a hundred years earlier. Here the dry bones of Relativity were stirred by a breath of something human. A timeless epoch was postulated, and it seemed easier to accept this peaceful dimension, in which Time was not, than the wrangling one in which the centuries set one another by the ears. Perhaps I am an inveterate sentimentalist. Certainly I could take little interest in Peter's lessening enchantment in the presence of contemporary *bric-a-brac*, and it is equally certain that I found the love affair to be very moving. There is a fragrance in the young spirit knowing that it cannot encounter love this side of the grave and fading like a flower which has lost hope; and there is pathos in the lover who lives too late. Perhaps the acting was better here than in the earlier parts of the piece. Mr. Lawrence Anderson said his last few words admirably. For they dealt in human emotion, and those who remember this actor in *St. Joan* will realize that he can be as moving in a simple fashion as any actor we have. He said one other line beautifully — 'The veil is thin for you.' But I suggest that the introspective does not lie in this actor's personality. Something daemonic, perturbed, brain-sickly was wanted for this part, and I am prepared to believe that if Signor Ruggeri or Mr. Barrymore or our own Claude Rains had played it the whole effect of the play might have been different. After all, the willingness to abandon your own century and step into another is not a part of normality, and this particular Peter Standish was as normal as a Yorkshire pudding. And Yorkshire pudding, though possibly the most adorable thing on earth, is comparatively useless as an aid to metaphysical questioning.

Miss Jean Forbes-Robertson was quite perfectly in the temper and spirit of her authors throughout. Her approach to her art seems incalculable either by herself or anybody else, and I shall certainly not attempt to calculate it here. Her performance in this piece is eerie and 'fey', and contains something of the quality which makes *La Belle Dame sans Merci* a great poem. What that quality is in either actress or poet I have not the faintest idea. It is there, and that is all there is to be said about it. It may be of some use to a young artist perhaps standing on the threshold of greatness to be told that both the management and the make-up of her hands require more study. Miss Valerie Taylor did very much more with a poor part than almost any actress I can think of could have accomplished, and Miss Beatrice Wilson, having no truck with transcendentalism, gave a very good performance in high comedy. There was some incidental music of a vaguely mystical character. Taking a hint from the play, I should imagine that the score had been bound up in the same volume with one of Mr. Norman O'Neill's.

October 10, 1926

SOCRATES

BY CLIFFORD BAX

(Stage Society)

LEWIS CASSON

IF fair comparisons be odious, what shall be said of the unfair? What shall be said of the kind of criticism which as a condition of praising Dickens must dispraise Thackeray? Writing of Mr. Bax's *Socrates* an eminent colleague, blasted with ecstasy as the young lady in *Hamlet* said, compares this drama of inaction with the drama of action, of whose benighted votaries he goes on to tell us that 'their highest pleasure, we may suppose, is a prize fight or, in the theatre, a horse-race on a revolving stage'. The answer to this is that we may not suppose anything of the sort, and, given a rudimentary sense of logic, will not. It is further suggested that those who stand up for action in the theatre 'have scoffed at the idea that certain Platonic dialogues would be more acceptable, and more entertaining, than the sight of Miss X frantically deciding whether her worthless self shall be bestowed upon the rich gentleman in Monte Carlo or reserved for the romantic artist in St.

John's Wood'. But why compare the best of one kind with the worst of another? I suggest that the fair comparison is between Plato and the Greek dramatist proper, between a talker like Mr. Shaw and a doer like Shakespeare, and not between a lovely mind expressing itself in tranquillity and no-mind making a fuss.

But comparison, even when properly used, may be unenlightening. It is a fine thing to climb a peak in Darien, and a fine thing to sit at the bottom and write a sonnet about peak and climber. The one thing is as good as the other. Yet we have to recognize that to do argumentative wrong that the right conclusion may prevail is one of mankind's oldest weaknesses. There is evidence even in the present play that Socrates himself could turn this weakness to account. Putting the case for meeting death with fortitude he makes the remarkable statement that 'it cannot be a difficult thing to do that which every man has done since the human race began'. Cebes and Simmias murmur assent, and we reflect that either they must have been slow in the uptake or afraid to 'take up' Socrates, who has the hemlock at his lips. For, of course, even a Rugger Blue must know that the correct statement is: 'It cannot be an easy thing to do that which the entire human race has always done with difficulty.' Part of the fun of Monday's performance lay in detecting the exact point at which these fledgeling pupils allowed themselves to be caught in the snares laid by this wiliest of antique birds. Take that bit of dialogue which went more or less as follows:

soc. You admit that to discover truth is the thing most desired by the philosopher?
pup. I do.
soc. You admit that death will bring discovery of the truth?
pup. I do.
soc. Why, then, should a philosopher fear death?
pup. (*cornered*) O Socrates, ask me another.

Of the pupil's three replies, the last, which I will not foist upon Mr. Bax, is the only one worthy of respect, since even the most amateur metaphysician should know that death may bring no discovery at all. But the pitfall was earlier still. What philosophers desire most is not to discover truth but to go on living, a desire they have in common with all other men, with every beast, insect, plant, and all created things. This desire satisfied, philosophers start on their philosophy, the search after truth being to them what art is to artists and good bricklaying to the good bricklayer, as much and no more. 'Crushed again!' replied Lady Jane, after each emotional thwarting. The reason the members of Mr. Bax's debating class in this play are so easily crushed is because he has allowed their reactions, like those of Lady Jane, to be emotional rather than cerebral. The contention that the logic-chopping is Plato and not Mr. Bax will not distress me. A poor argument remains poor, whosoever advances it.

Be all this as it may, the fact remains that for a full hour on Monday we sat rapt as children at the feet of Socrates and, so to speak, read our Plato without tears. These were reserved for the latter half of the play, in which Mr. Bax bethought him of those weaker spirits who deem the current of pure and absolute drama to be none the worse for a snag of action. And so we had Crito warning Socrates of pending arrest and offering escape to Thessaly, Socrates' refusal, the trial, and the death-scene with Crito lamenting that Socrates had not availed himself of his offer. 'Oh, Sammy, Sammy, vy worn't there a alleybi?' as another friend in need put it. Mr. Lewis Casson, by a performance which was both shrewd and affecting, helped us to a fine personal, as well as impersonal, interest; and nobody need be ashamed of having wept at the demise of one who, as well as looking absurdly like Socrates, reminded us in his snub-nosed, venerable ugliness of both Tolstoy and Verlaine, and contrived, such is the whimsey of this actor, to encompass the fun of all three. In conclusion, the Stage Society gave us a lovely afternoon in which the mind, having had its bath of pure sublimity, was permitted those commoner emotions for which actors and the theatre exist. For if those emotions are away there remains no reason why we should make the journey to the theatre, Plato and the fireside sufficing.

March 24, 1930

THE WORLD OF LIGHT

BY ALDOUS HUXLEY

(Royalty)

DENYS BLAKELOCK, MARGARET HALSTAN,
FABIA DRAKE

To say that this play is about spiritualism is like saying that *Much Ado* is about mistaken identity or that *Romeo and Juliet* is based on the defective postal service between Verona and Mantua. Spiritualism is merely its peg, and thereby, as this play's inveterate cliché-monger would put it, hangs a tale. Perhaps not so much a tale as a tally, since there are few things under the sun which are not taken into account, though one frankly admits 'under the sun' to be a niggling interpretation of the scope of Mr. Huxley's mind, which here goes sizzling about all the space there is, consuming itself and us.

The way of it is this, if it be permitted to pin down inter-stellar cerebration to a local habitation and a lot of names. The scene is the drawing-room of some people called Wenham. Mr. Wenham (Mr. Aubrey Mather) is a chartered accountant who sets out on the uncharted sea of spiritualism. He is meek, intellectually honest, though without enough intellect to make that difficult, and wrapped in so much humility that he always speaks of himself in the third person. 'One is a teetotaller. One took a drink once but it disagreed with one.' Mrs. Wenham (Miss Margaret Halstan) is the sheet-anchor of the drifting Wenham *ménage*: 'I do not believe that communication with the dead is possible, and if it were I should not care for it.' And again: 'Heaven and earth may pass away, but there's got to be dinner!' To this pair has been born a son, Hugo (Mr. Denys Blakelock), a young man at Cambridge and presumably a *fainéant*, since he is world-weary without having done a thing in the world to tire him. It is into this character that Mr. Huxley spills some of his familiar brain-sickness just as he uses Hugo's friend, Bill Hamblin (Mr. Sebastian Shaw), as outlet for the famous exuberance. Bill is a talker among talkers, and perhaps this is the place to say that the dialogue throughout is a close web of sheen and shimmer, the warp of everybody else's outlandish speculations being knit together by Mrs. Wenham's home-keeping woof.

The ball is set in motion — that is presuming anything in Mr. Huxley's mind can ever have started from rest — in this way. They are discussing clothes. The volatile Hamblin, for whom the meanest topic is springboard to infinity, jumps from animadversion upon short skirts to a declaration in favour of a well-draped universe with plenty of mystery. 'I hear the Absolute is being worn longer this year!' This is the modulation which gets us from the key of small-talk to that of metaphysics, whence it is only a step to Hamblin's recollection that prior to a visit to Borneo he was an agnostic and would have remained one had not certain dark practices under that high sun turned him into a devil-worshipper. Talking of Borneo, he is off to Guiana, British or otherwise, by aeroplane first thing to-morrow morning. Will Hugo accompany him? Now Hugo happens to be in the devil of a mess. He is loved by Enid Deckle (Miss Fabia Drake), whom he dislikes, but to whom, through some odd blackmailing on the part of his better self, he has become engaged. Hamblin makes Hugo drunk and persuades him to cut the cable of his melancholy love-affair and that still duller professorship at Cambridge which is all that young man's future. Before he knows where he is, Hugo is whisked off to Guiana.

But not before he has let us know where we, the audience, are in the matter of the spiritualism of Wenham *père*. Here Mr. Huxley is at his old trick of beginning with some frivolous remark, idle as a stone thrown into a pond, but having repercussions on the shores of heaven and hell. 'If', says Hugo, parodying his father, 'one doesn't smoke or drink, hang it all, one must have some excitement! If not spirits, why not spiritualism?' Hugo goes on to explain that spiritualism is the result of wrong thinking on the part of the right-minded, and hence the sentimental association of unrelated ideas. Telepathy is one fact, and the dead are another; in spiritualist logic wish and thought are identical, therefore messages received must emanate from the quarter whence they are desired. Let the dead bury their dead! Hugo has impatiently exclaimed, to which — and this is the gist of the play — Mr. Wenham in all devoutness remarks that the author of this saying was a young man. We come here to the play's closest thinking, Wenham's amplification that for the young life is all that is to come, whereas for their elders life is what is past. How can the very old consent to bury that which is become their all? It should be said here that the play is neither for nor against spiritualism, though one detects the bias in the suggestion that it is better to concern ourselves with the living who are at their fullest point of our understanding rather than with the second or millionth best which is all we can hope to know of the dead in their new state.

This play, like some of Ibsen's, is in two storeys, an upper one of thought and a lower one of action. On the ground floor, so to speak, Hugo and Hamblin have crashed, and now Enid must explore an old torment. Can the spirit divorced from its envelope constitute any true survival of personality? What comfort to a lover can there be in abstraction? All this part of the play is immensely serious, and Mr. Huxley does not fear to cite such a phrase as 'in a glass darkly' with all its immensities of reverberation. Miss Drake sustains Enid's agony very finely, and it is not her fault that she cannot make what follows credible. Séances have been established at the Wenhams', and messages are now received from Hugo through the mediumship of one Hubert (Mr. Philip Brandon). This is a preposterous slug who, believing in the fiction of Enid's dead lover, invents the kind of messages Enid would like to receive, and thus works upon her gratitude to the point at which she becomes his mistress, an incredible consummation in which the author permits himself another excursion away from real life. Now old Wenham is in his seventh heaven; his spiritualist theories have been proved, and incidentally he has sold sixteen thousand copies of a work of love and proselytism.

He invites his publisher (witty Mr. Marcus Barron) to a sitting at which Hugo is to prove the truth of spiritualism. In the middle of the séance Hugo walks in! The aeroplane had come down, but neither has been killed, and Hugo pleads that to lie doggo for a period seemed to him and his friend to be no end of a lark.

Wenham is appalled by the prospect of having to make public renunciation of his theories, and there is something in Hugo's gibe that his father would prefer a live faith and a dead son to a whole Hugo and a theory blown to smithereens. Enid's case is even worse; she has become the spiritual wife — since the Hubert affair is on the material and negligible plane — of her idealized Hugo, and now finds that he dislikes her as much as ever. The solution comes from Hugo, who declares that Hubert is not wholly crooked, that there *were* messages not from himself being dead, but from some living and subconscious better self. He decides to go away for good, and so once more give place to that idealized self who will still be stage-managed by Hubert. His father need not write that letter to the Press, since who knows that they are not in the presence of a higher truth? As for Enid, she will console herself by consoling Hamblin, who, in the course of their peregrinations and a very long play, has become blind.

It cannot be said that this ending is satisfactory, since it shelves one difficulty only to create others. Mr. Huxley does not confound the spiritualists, but neither does he support them; the sum of the play's argument is that Hugo not being dead, what is normally meant by spiritualism is not under examination. What is in question is telepathic communication through questionable mediumship between the subconscious mind and the conscious, which strikes one as the roundabout delivery of an impracticable message of doubtful provenance. On the human plane this dragging in of the subconscious is not very satisfying, since human affections have always found body and conscious mind to be sufficient complication. Surely Mr. Huxley must see that to fall in love with the subconscious is rather like stroking the grin in the absence of the Cheshire Cat? But perhaps Enid does see this; it is certainly her tragedy. On the everyday plane, then, the nature of the theme precludes possibility of normal tidying up. But it is a great intellectual adventure to listen to and be present at this play. Throughout, the visible and audible surfaces of life are admirably presented. Space does not permit me to describe the superb acting and how all of it is a glove-fit for the play's intricate convolutions. I must be content to say that in the matter of sustained interpretation the entire cast is beyond praise.

April 1, 1931

AUTUMN CROCUS

BY C. L. ANTHONY

(Lyric)

FRANCIS LEDERER, FAY COMPTON

'Tears, idle tears, I know not what they mean', wrote the poet, and perhaps the audience at the Lyric Theatre had no very clear notion of what it was crying about. For myself I was much too busy examining into the nature of Miss Fay Compton's plight. Miss Compton is supposed to be a fading, bespectacled schoolmistress emanating from Eccles, a suburb of Manchester and the home of the sad cake of that name. Now, I am perfectly well aware that criticism should be impersonal; if, therefore, I mention the fact that it was at Eccles that I first went to school it is not out of egotism but to lend what follows more than a show of authority. Very well, then. Let the readers be assured that bespectacled dames of thirty-five helping to keep a school in Eccles did not when I lisped the alphabet — if that feat be possible — in the least resemble Miss Compton. Taking a wider view, I would say that an exquisite creature, looking at most twenty, and possessed of the heavenliest nose in Christendom, could never, despite the spectacles perched thereon, remain a schoolmistress in Eccles or anywhere except sentimental comedy.

The point is not frivolous, since this is exactly what *Autumn*

Crocus is about. The difficulty is that which always crops up when an author postulates one kind of matter for tears and an audience wants to cry at another kind. Let me explain. Miss Anthony, when she sat down to write, obviously had in mind a depressed, inhibited school-marm who, holidaying in the Tyrol, should fall in love with a young and handsome innkeeper, and on discovering that he is married, go back to her school with her romance shattered, the shattering to be all the more pitiful since, in view of the plain looks and the spectacles and the thirty-five years, romance is supposed to be saying good-bye for ever. Capital matter for the novel, where what is not seen by the physical eye can be glossed over. But in the theatre the eye is first logician, and it will never allow us to believe that an innkeeper, however Tyrolean, is going to fall in love with Plain Jane. Even if he does, no audiences are going to assemble to see him do it. Conversely, if Jane, instead of being unsightly, looks like Miss Compton at her loveliest, one cannot see what all the pother is about.

> Hearts just as pure and fair
> May beat in Belgrave Square
> As in the *upper* air

of the Austrian Tyrol. And, we may be sure, will! This should be as plain as the nose on every face except our heroine's. In fact, I could see no reason for crying except on Wilde's theory that it is a terrible thing to part from people one has only known a very short time.

But the setting is better than the story and one hastens to say that Mr. Basil Dean, aided by some stage-settings admirably designed by Mrs. Calthrop and scenery beautifully painted by Mr. Alick Johnstone, has achieved a strikingly successful production. There is a moment when the company in the inn settles down to listen to a German (Mr. Frederick Ranalow) singing Schumann. His German wife (Miss May Agate) listens with musical understanding and a sympathy all the more rapt because this was probably one of the songs with which her husband wooed her. To this singing the English people present listen uncompromisingly and sitting bolt upright. Then it is Miss Compton's turn to sing. To this the Germans listen indulgently and with the obvious desire to be polite to English music, while upon the English faces dawns something that one might call ballad-receptivity. This is producing of a very fine order, only I suggest that Mr. Dean over-reached himself in the matter of Mr. Goossens's atonal embroideries which must have rendered Eccles dumb.

Good production will not by itself make out of a rather thin little play the great success that *Autumn Crocus* is obviously going to be. This brings us to the acting, which is a hodge-podge of pure delight. Hodge-podge, because a lot of brilliant and clever people accomplish three separate feats. Miss Compton, after some two minutes of dutiful pretence at the unattractive, abandons that fiction and gives herself up to Gilbert's picture of another victim of first love:

> A simple frightened loveliness,
> Whose sacred spirit-part
> Shrank timidly from worldly stress
> And nestled in your heart.

That Miss Compton's acting has very little to do with Miss Anthony's character does not prevent it from being an exposition of dewy fragrance put together with wholly conscious art. Acting of a totally different order, if it is acting at all, delights us when Miss Muriel Aked takes the stage. Or should one say that the stage takes her? — for this tremendous favourite seems hardly to do anything by volition or contrivance. She has no sense either of timing or attack, is apt to be inaudible, and appears to have in her gallery one portrait only — that of some sage and elderly lamb. The character lives, though how much of that conscious creation which is acting has gone to its presentment cannot be known until Miss Aked ceases to be the Universal Aunt and bethinks her of some other incarnation. Meanwhile, one feels grateful to Nature rather than to Art. In the third category, that of impersonating somebody not themselves, were nine or ten other players, among whom one would mention Miss Martita Hunt, brilliant as ever, Miss Jessica Tandy, and Messrs. George Zucco and Jack Hawkins. Last remains Mr. Francis Lederer, the young Czechoslovakian actor who made a great personal success in a recent ill-fated musical play. The whole piece hangs or falls by the innkeeper's charm, and the amount of this commodity produced by Mr. Lederer is so colossal that unless he is very careful he will have a play written for him by Sir James Barrie. In addition, he is an extremely fine actor.

April 6, 1931

THE ANATOMIST

BY JAMES BRIDIE

(Westminster)

HENRY AINLEY, FLORA ROBSON

'One of the anatomies this rogue has set i' the cold yonder in Barber-Chirurgeons' Hall.' — THE DUCHESS OF MALFI

YES. But is not this another case of material which, while good enough to be fact, is not sufficiently well arranged to be fiction, and in particular that branch of fiction which is the theatre? To the argument that Mr. Bridie has stuck to the facts one would simply reply that, if those facts do not make a good play he would have done better to choose others. Not that *The Anatomist* fails. It does not. Indeed, it begins pleasantly, has an enchantingly gruesome middle, and then, when we return for the third act in expectation of the evening's grisly but nevertheless *bonne bouche*, we find, alas, that all is over except that those things which we know already have to be explained to ladies returning from Dieppe! It is the old case of the better being the enemy of the good. Let us see, therefore, how much good there is in this play and what better might have been devised.

The first act takes place in the drawing-room of two Scotch

ladies. These are Miss Mary Dishart, who is being courted by
Walter Anderson, a demonstrator in anatomy, and Miss Amelia
Dishart, at whom Dr. Knox, the famous surgeon of that name,
blows his flute. This act, which is a delightful conversation picture
in the manner of *Quality Street*, establishes two things. First, the
natural leaning of young ladies towards medical students, together
with an equally natural dislike for that which they study. Can we
imagine Arabella Allen · enjoying that 'agreeable anecdote' in
which Mr. Bob Sawyer illustrated the removal of a tumour from
a gentleman's head by means of an oyster-knife and a half-
quartern loaf? Second, the manner of that autocrat of the dissect-
ing table, Dr. Knox, together with his habit which was a compound of Dr. Johnson and Long John Silver, with an eye missing
instead of a leg. Here Mr. Ainley does well enough to send the
mind harking back to the most terrifying thing about Irving — to
wit, his joviality. Yes, you say at the end of the first act, that's a
first-class bit of painting. Now, let us see the monster in action!

But we were not so to see him, and it is no dramatic excuse that
the real Dr. Knox kept himself in the background. The second
act took us to the 'Three Tuns' tavern, where we saw ogreishness at
work, but caught no sight of the ogre. Here, however, were the
young medico, Anderson, driven to drink by the doctor's brutal
scorn, and Raby, the young student sent after him by the doctor
in some stray access of compunction, and Davie Paterson, sent to
bargain with the resurrectionists, and, of course, Burke and Hare.
Here, too, was Mary Paterson, the drab whom these last were to
murder. This scene was made extraordinarily moving by the
astonishing quality of actuality bestowed upon it by Miss Flora
Robson.

But a scene of such importance must either be the big scene in
the play or one leading to something bigger. In the first case the
piece would have been altogether too like *Hamlet* without the
Prince of Denmark, wherefore we settled down to await something
more satisfying still. There was another scene in this act in which
Knox, on Mary Paterson's identity being revealed to him, said
that a good subject on the dissecting-table was better than a bad

subject on the streets. But still one felt that the real play had to come, so much so that when the curtain went up again and showed objects flat-topped and shrouded, one was a little nervous as to the rites presently to be performed. Could this be the dissecting-room in Surgeons' Square? But it couldn't, for the objects were only the Misses Dishart's spinet and console table covered by dust-sheets pending their owners' return from Dieppe, after which the play petered out into some question of Dr. Knox's marriage, and, Burke being hanged, his acclamation by the students siding with their preceptor against the mob.

All this entertained, but it can hardly be denied that the entertainment fell short of that implicit in the subject. Must not the ideal drama have concerned itself with the conflict between the man of science determined to admit no bar to the prosecution of research even if it means conniving at murder, and the man of normal conscience and responsibility? Mr. Bridie might retort that Knox was a being without normal conscience, a super-man by anticipation, in fact the monster we have called him, and as such an unfit subject for ideal treatment. Mr. Bridie may claim to have attempted no more than to tell the story as he found it. Then why not tell the whole story? For there *was* a third act to this play, which Mr. Bridie could have found if he had bethought him of that old question of dramatic conflict. This conflict did not lie essentially in Knox's inability to win his Amelia, which might happen to any old bachelor, but in his futile strugglings against Nemesis. Knox did not end his career, as this play would have one suppose, continuing to lecture to enthusiastic students and living down opprobrium. Actually the doctor fought the rising storm of obloquy for ten years, after which he removed to Glasgow, and, losing all consideration, finally to London where for fifteen years he practised in Hackney obstetrically and obscurely. Here in Lambe Terrace, Hackney, I submit that the last act of this piece should have taken place, and I feel that if Mr. Bridie would re-read Sacha Guitry's *Pasteur* he must agree with me, for it is among the shadows that we should take leave of Knox.

I wish to make it plain that the foregoing presents a purely personal opinion. All that happened in the old-world Edinburgh drawing-room composed a picture of great fragrance, and I cannot help it if I am alone in thinking that the purport of a play about Burke, Hare, and Dr. Knox cannot be to get that kind of fragrance across the footlights. There can be no two opinions about the acting. Mr. Ainley prepared the way magnificently for a truly terrible picture of the a-moral scientist in action, only to find that there was no battle to be fought. Messrs. J. A. O'Rourke and Harry Hutchinson looked the parts of Burke and Hare, and performed them sufficiently. Mr. Craighall Sherry was like a drawing of Rowlandson, and in the part of a likeable innocent Mr. Robert Eddison put up a performance of great charm. As the Misses Dishart, Mesdames Gillian Scaife and Betty Hardy provided pleasant decorations. Of Miss Flora Robson I can only add that she made the evening memorable by an exquisite piece of acting, though doubtless she was helped to this by the fact that here the playwright was expressing something complete and self-contained, and not, as is the piece itself, a fragment of an unrealized whole.

October 7, 1931

JONAH AND THE WHALE

BY JAMES BRIDIE

(Westminster)

EDWARD CHAPMAN

MR. BRIDIE continues in his endeavours to make of every week-day evening a pleasant Sunday afternoon. We now know that in this mood he will take some miracle of compression and expand it, which can only be done by industriously filling in all the bits that the original artist left out. This should make remunerative theatre, since most playgoers are simple people, and the one thing simple people cannot bear is simplicity. Perhaps it requires a certain amount of education to be satisfied with writing as spare as: 'But Jonah . . . went down to Joppa; and he found a ship going to Tarshish; so he paid the fare thereof, and went down unto it.' And anyhow, if you are going to make a two-hours' entertainment out of something that can be read in ten minutes, not only prolixity, but invention, must be the order of the day.

Was it in accordance with this principle, or because Mr. Bridie was struck with the Arnold Bennett touch in 'and paid his fare', that he proceeded to give what the irreverent might call this auld wife's tale furniture solid enough to win the approval even of Mrs. Baines? In the original, Jonah goes on board in the third verse; in the play he takes a whole act which, still like the Baines furniture, is 'good', but dull. Zebulun has to be reconstructed, and most of the fun here comes from making these B.C. Gittah-Hepherites crack to-day's jokes and recall conceits that a Herrick or a Suckling have believed to be original. Thus Bilshan, a commercial traveller, compliments Euodias, who is Jonah's donah, on not dyeing her toes as the wicked Phoenicians do, on not, so to speak, being a Lido lady. Then he hums a music-hall song of the period:

> Rapidly crept, on the one hand,
> Her feet, like small mice in a panic,
> Under her petticoat's fringe.

A little laboured, perhaps, but so are most pleasant Sunday afternoons.

At the other end of the play comes the reconstruction of Nineveh, and here Mr. Bridie has happened upon abysmal and cataclysmic failure, since he shows that naughty city behaving with a blamelessness beyond the dreams of Bournemouth. Now, if Nineveh was worth destroying, the least of its cocktail parties must have been on the scale of Helen's orgy, whereas all that Mr. Bridie offers is an afternoon at the Semiramis Club with Jonah as the guest of honour. Here there is some minor fun at the expense of a chairwoman who takes up the time intended for the speaker. But the fact remains that, as a rival to some cities which shall be nameless if not unmentionable, Nineveh appears to have been a wash-out.

Perhaps the fault lies in the acting. There are some actresses who can run the gamut of all the vices, or convince us that they are doing so, by merely reciting the alphabet, while there are others who would make an unbowdlerised day in the life of Messalina read like a page out of *Little Women and Good Wives*. It is to this second class that Miss Gillian Scaife belongs; she could play 'Marmee' to the life. As the head and front of Nineveh's offending she is frankly incredible, though I have long given up wondering why actresses whose talents lie in the direction of uplifting mothers should invariably be cast for fallen daughters.

The most amusing part of the play is where Jonah is most bored, that is in the belly of the whale. This is amusing, first, because the interior of that leviathan looks exactly like the inside of Rosamund's Purple Jar, and second, because of the whale's address to his guest. In this the monster undertakes inquiry into the nature of matter, but abandons this after deciding that Jonah, the sun, the steerage bugs, and the captain's whiskers are all composed of millions of dancing atoms each behaving in its own orbit like a lunatic star. But that this should be the end of inquiry proves that it is a pre-Einstein whale, since the only meaning of the word 'inexplicable' is the lack of something wherewith to explain, which again means indefinite pursuit. Indeed, the fact that no explanation exists ensures the search for it in perpetuity; the search can only stop on condition that the explanation exists. So it is an idle whale, content with a mere ten or twenty lines of exploration, whereas a Shavian one would have required the rest of the evening and the whole of the next day.

The most dramatic part of the piece is the final scene in which the poor little prophet looks forward to a lifetime's discredit and is comforted only by Euodias who, as though she were Janet in *The Great Adventure*, says: 'You'll forget all about this. You will make hundreds of beautiful prophecies yet.' It is hard to see any moral in the old story except that it goes hard with little people when their betters change their minds — a text which may have some meaning for those of us who are still asking why the ex-Kaiser was not hanged.

Mr. Edward Chapman gives a beautiful performance as the
wee prophet. Here is the man, not without consideration in his
own village, who becomes henchman to authority, swells to a
magnificent importance, and then is horridly let down when
authority forgets about him and pursues some other plan. But
in the original, Authority is more considerate, since Jonah has
not to argue the matter in his own soul but is dealt a blow of logic
whereby he is perforce content. Mr. Chapman's acting is excellent
here since he gives that particular piece of logic growth in his own
soul. But throughout he plays very cleverly, since a minor prophet
is much more difficult to portray than a major one, and because
he doubles Jonah's lack of importance with his lovableness as a
man.

Miss Joan White is very pretty, and the rest of the company
comport themselves as people should do on pleasant Sunday afternoons. Perhaps the best actor in the piece is the electrician who,
doubtless after consultation with that highly imaginative producer,
Mr. Henry Oscar, has devised a glow of lighting which turns the
stage-pictures into coloured plates. Miss Molly McArthur has
found her tasteful scenery and dresses partly in her own clever
imagination and partly in the canvases of Holman Hunt.

December 18, 1932

MR. BOLFRY

BY JAMES BRIDIE
(Westminster)

ALASTAIR SIM, RAYMOND LOVELL, HARRY ROSS

Two young soldiers, a Bloomsbury intellectual and a Cockney,
are billeted on a Calvinistic parson in the West Highlands. Staying
with the parson is his niece, a worker at what I understood to be
the Ministry of Inefficiency. Perhaps the actress was inclined
to swallow her words? Or was I ear-dazzled by a strawberry-

coloured morning wrapper in what I understand the dressmakers call ciré-satin? Anyhow, life at the manse has got on the trio's nerves, and breaking point is reached when they are told that to indulge in tea on Sunday afternoon is to break the Fourth Commandment. Since in the matter of ratiocination they are no match for the Rev. McCrimmon, and since the West Highlands is a spookish kind of place, they decide that night to invoke the Devil by anagrammatizing on the parlour table and drawing a circle on the floor. '*Sint mihi Dei Acherontis propitii!*' mumbles the fellow from Bloomsbury, or words to that effect. And then the Devil appears, not as Faustus in the garb of a Franciscan friar but in the formal, top-hatted umbrella'd get-up of a Scottish clergyman. The accompanying thunderclap wakes the household, and down comes the Rev. McCrimmon *en déshabille* but in the matter of argument armed cap-à-pie. The rest is talk.

Is the talk good? We have all thought so in our time. In any case it is good enough to make the amateur philosopher inside each of us want to answer back. As thus. PROPOSITION A. The man who says, 'I believe the moon is made of green cheese, because something inside me that I cannot explain tells me so' has taken up an unassailable position. But if he follows 'because' with any other words he is lost. If he adduces, say, spectroscopic proof, or any other kind of proof, he is at once vulnerable. In plain English, whoever tries to explain faith in terms of reason is undone before he begins. PROPOSITION B. Since Man cannot think of a number before one he invents a Cause which he can only call First. Vanity and intellectual presumption being very much the same thing, Man must needs start predicating about his First Cause. Deciding upon Omnipotence and Benevolence as essential attributes, the poor fellow, meaning Man, has succeeded in tying himself into knots about predestination and free will, the existence of pain, cruelty, disease, war, and so forth.

This is where Mr. Bridie's Devil comes in, and the play suddenly becomes adult. Just as a scientist once explained to me that if the atoms composing the table on which I am writing were to stop trying to get away from one another the table would collapse, so the Devil in this play explains that if ever we attain to Bickersteth's ideal of 'Peace, perfect peace, in this dark world of sin', this world will collapse in the sense that it will be reduced to a condition of one hundred per cent stagnation-cum-inertia. It is just because of this 'unbearable idea of nothingness', argues the Devil, that peace must continue to be intermittent and war must continue. He points out that Good cannot exist without Evil, and that the primary duty of the First Cause is to keep Evil functioning and give Malevolence its proper place in the scheme of things. Is Man condemned, then, to strive after something which, if realized, would annihilate him? Perhaps striving is Man's business, and the result is the affair of the Unknowable. Or so we read this play's message. There are no flies on this Devil, and no bats in Mr. Bridie's Bolfry.

The author has been generous of his wit. And of his shrewdness, too. 'I never 'as a bob I ain't worked for', says the Cockney. 'That's what I mean by poor', replies the Devil. And beauty, as when somebody calls the boys 'young enemies of death'. The piece is extremely well acted. By Mr. Alastair Sim, who presents McCrimmon as a combination of Mr. Littimer and a celestial shop-walker (Presbyterian Dept.). By Mr. Raymond Lovell with wit, charm, invention, and passion. By Mr. Harry Ross, whose genial Cockney is the one *point de repère* in all this argumentative Cloud-Cuckoo-Land. The audience? It sat rapt and spell-bound as though the theatre were the Royalty, the date 1892, and the occasion Mr. Shaw's first play.

August 8, 1943

MUSICAL CHAIRS

BY RONALD MACKENZIE

(Criterion)

JOHN GIELGUD, FRANK VOSPER, CAROL GOODNER

I HAVE seen this play twice, and am now ready to burn my boats about it. *Musical Chairs* is, in my view, the best first play written by any *English* playwright during the last forty years. It is a better work of art than *Widowers' Houses*, for here the dramatist, as we realized later, bagged a good deal of the credit that was due to the reformer in political economy. It is a better play than *Journey's End*, which owed at least as much to its subject as to its author. It is better than McEvoy's *David Ballard* and Houghton's *Hindle Wakes*, since it reveals a finer mind and a wider sensibility. It is not better than *Berkeley Square*, but that was the work of two authors, one of whom I believe to be an American. And it may not be better than *Nan*, though it is thirty years or so since I saw that tragedy, and I cannot remember whether Mr. Masefield wrote other pieces before it. Leaving first works out of it I say that Mr. Mackenzie's tragic farce is as good as the best work of Mr. Ervine or Mr. Van Druten. I call it a little play because, though it deals with the major themes of life and death, love and sorrow and laughter, it has not to the superficial view that specific gravity which, by their subject matter, the plays of Mr. Shaw, Mr. Galsworthy, and Mr. Drinkwater have the knack of taking to themselves.

My reasons for regarding this play as a small masterpiece are as follows. One, it tells a credible and tragic story about something that matters. Two, that story is enlivened by a magnificent humour. Three, throughout it is as taut and spare as a barrel, which means that it is perfectly made, and put together with maximum economy. Four, the characters are real, vivid, and do not overlap each other. Five, as parts they are magnificently laid out for actors. Six, the interest of the action is so constantly renewed that we do not notice that the scene remains the same. Seven, the play is consistent with itself from first to last. Eight, it has been conceived as a play, which means that the stage is the unique vehicle for the expression of this thing and is perfectly used. Nine, the visible and audible surfaces of life are accurately reproduced. Ten, we come away from the theatre feeling that we have undergone an emotional experience. Eleven, the play could be translated into any language without loss of appeal, which gives the hint of universality. Twelve, this work of art has its own atmosphere, compounded of strangeness, melancholy, and the wildest fun.

Now, is the play original and does it hold out further promise? Is it a tank or a spring? Here I shall temporize. The indebtedness to Tchehov and even Turgeniev is obvious, since the last scene is *The Cherry Orchard* all over again and the whole plot owes something to *A Month in the Country* which, nevertheless, the author may not have seen! And here is the same theme of the ring of serpents each swallowing the tail in front of it. The neurotic, war-destroyed hero who loves, or has a bitter passion for, his step-brother's wholly self-centred fiancée, but is loved by the family drudge, his step-sister. The hero's father, who loves his wife, is bored by her and indulges in a flirtation or worse with a mercenary little girl from the village. Everybody loves where he does not like and likes where he cannot love. The foreign setting — since the framework of the story concerns an oil-field in Galicia — accentuates the derivatory notion. This may be fallacious, and to disprove it the author should, in his next play, exchange Poland for Paddington. Are we to see in Mr. Mackenzie a coming major dramatist? I cannot answer that, and am content to believe that he has done enough to be going on with.

The piece was marvellously well acted, and if I single out only Mr. Gielgud, who played with every nerve in his body and brain, and Mr. Vosper, whose Micawberish old fribble was a riot of pure joy, it is only because I lack space to appraise at their proper worth the lovely performances of Messrs. Finlay Currie and Jack

Livesey, and Mesdames Carol Goodner, Margaret Webster, Amy Veness, and Dorice Fordred. A perfect octet and, in Mr. Komisarjevsky, an inspired arranger of this music. Apropos, there is a remark about Beethoven having been the world's man of greatest courage, to assent to which the old roysterer interrupts his hurlyburly. This may give some hint of this play's extraordinary quality, extraordinary not because somebody is right or wrong about Beethoven, but because all the characters who are competent to do so hold that it is the things of the spirit which are of the greatest interest. 'Insensitiveness, stupidity, vulgarity of soul are God's best gifts, since by them alone can Man be happy.' This may be nonsense, but it is unusual, plucky nonsense. If any reader sees nothing remarkable here let him attend, say, a month of London first nights! Play and players were grandly received, and it looks as though that most miserable of all kinds of success, that of esteem and nothing else, has been avoided.

April 1, 1932

RICHARD OF BORDEAUX

BY GORDON DAVIOT

(New)

JOHN GIELGUD, GWEN FFRANGCON-DAVIES

THE second Richard was, says the Ninth Edition of the *Encyclopaedia Britannica*, 'slight, fair-haired, beardless, with rounded face and elegant but rather feminine features'. Having looked the effeminate King full in his beardless face, this respectable authority then declares that his character must remain an enigma to the historian. J'ever hear such hypocrisy? — as my Lord Castlewood might have said. The 'strange mixture of strength and weakness, courage and irresolution, indolence and energy' constitute an enigma only in the sense that none are so blind as those who will not see, and that the leavened loaf is inexplicable to the baker who denies the existence of leaven.

Richard's character is proclaimed in letters a mile high by that Smithfield exploit in which as a lad of fifteen he rides alone into the mob whose leader has been killed, and induces it to follow him. This feat in itself connotes feminine intuition as well as male courage, and is exactly what Joan of Arc would have done in the circumstances. But the exploit is in two parts, since after Richard has tamed the mob there comes the effort made by his troops to come to his aid, refused by the young man as much out of coquetry as strategy. He has charmed the crowd, and as its charmer he intends to return to London. Now Shakespeare, who *pace* Mr. Shaw was neither a fool nor a humbug, probably knew as much as the *Encyclopaedia Britannica* about Richard. He certainly knew about his friend's play of *Edward II*, a King whose character has never presented any riddle even to an historian. From which we may take it that Shakespeare was perfectly well aware how many abnormal beans make five. But knowing his audience to be still drunk with the virility of that Armada-thwacking age, he may have anticipated Mr. Ivor Brown's view that to some spectators even a hint of the epicene theme can be 'irreparably distasteful'. Yet unless his Richard was to be a complete fake the effeminacy had still to be suggested, and Shakespeare achieved this by diverting the stream of Richard's character into the channel of preciosity and aestheticism which are effeminacy's co-ordinates. Something of the foregoing must be in the mind of any spectator who is not going to find Miss Daviot's Richard wholly enigmatic, and all of it was obviously in the author's mind since she has created a Richard who, in this light, at once becomes wholly understandable.

The play opens with Richard in his 'teens already exhibiting intelligence beyond his years, and opposing his uncles who would still be war-mongering because that is the beefy English tradition. Mr. Gielgud confronts his Council with a high impertinence, the character having previously established likeableness in a delightful five minutes of friendliness towards his Queen and bonhomie towards two pages caught at the medieval equivalent of pitch-and-toss. The same night sees the young King plunged into high passion at the attempt of the nobles to overrule the little authority he actually possesses. The whole of this act is a brilliant essay in the reconstruction of a period and should be a lesson to those who object that they are not interested in fourteenth-century politics. Nobody asks them to be. The point is that the spectacle of living men in desperate conflict enthrals whether the matter of that conflict be rival kingdoms or papal authority or silk duties. The second act shows Richard in intellectual sympathy and partnership with the Queen, who must now die of the plague. Here is the place to say succinctly that if Miss Gwen Ffrangcon-Davies is not the best actress in England there is certainly none better. Her performance is a little miracle of sensitive perception; she creates the woman and sets her in her period as definitely as she created Mrs. Herbert and set her in the age of Victoria and, since critical memory is long, created and rightly dated that Egyptian kitten, Caesar's Cleopatra. A year or two now pass, which brings us to the famous quarrel between Henry of Lancaster and Thomas Mowbray with which every schoolboy is familiar. The third act deals with Richard's downfall, which his power of self-dramatization enables him to enjoy. It is not, however, Miss Daviot's purpose to harp on another playwright's note, and the relish she gives Richard is not that of defeat-savouring but of preserving irony and wit in the face of disaster. Richard, with the horrors of Pontefract Castle looming in front of him, can still make Bolingbroke feel a fool, and his rebuke of Canterbury is masterly and royal. The play ends quietly with the King taking leave of his faithful secretary, beautifully played by Mr. Richard Ainley.

There is a really magnificent cast, and Messrs. Eric Stanley, Frederick Lloyd, Francis Lister, H. R. Hignett, Ben Webster, Henry Mollison, Donald Wolfit, Reyner Barton, George Howe, Kinsey Peile and Walter Hudd will not take offence at this barest mention in a very full week. Sufficient to say that as a team they exhibit the greatest loyalty to their author and to each other, together with that skill which makes the loyalty worth while. I should hate to single out any one performance, and must therefore say nothing about Mr. Stanley's harsh and commanding Gloucester. But the piece is and must be Richard's, and by his really superb performance Mr. Gielgud now makes it impossible for us to deny him some at least of the attributes of greatness; one is chary of the full title only because that must mean not the best of a poor lot but greatness as previous ages have understood it. Thew and sinew are obviously denied this actor, and perhaps he will never play roaring Basanic bulls or any of the breed of those whom Stevenson liked to call ventripotents. But no actor that has ever lived has been omni-sided, and that kind of playing in which Mr. Gielgud is a master permits an actor to be great ten times over since it comprises nine-tenths of the human faculties. Mr. Gielgud has long been known to possess the finer physical graces including that beauty of mask and voice and pose and gesture which are his by inheritance; known to possess, too, store of intellectual subtlety and temperamental fire. The point one has hitherto debated has been his capacity for the pathetic, and his characters' staying power. These things are now cleared up. His last scene showed that he has command of simple pathos, and the whole matter was finally settled when we saw that though the part attained its climax, explosively considered, early in the first act the character could and did in Mr. Gielgud's hands increase in emotional momentum to the end, and this despite diminishing opportunities for virtuosity.

All the players came in for a tremendous ovation in which the play seemed strangely included. But it was foolish of me to use the word 'strangely' since the only thing the West End objects to in a Shakespeare play is Shakespeare's part in it, a poetic handicap absent in the case of Miss Daviot's really fine achievement. The piece was beautifully mounted, and its appeal to the eye continuous. In fact, I am not sure that the exquisiteness of a production flowing like music did not give this work greater quality than it actually possesses.

February 2, 1933

SPRING 1600

BY EMLYN WILLIAMS

(Shaftesbury)

IAN HUNTER, FRANK PETTINGELL, ISABEL JEANS

It is Spring, 1600, and 'sumer is icumen in'. But it is also Spring, 1934, and the point is whether West End audiences will be coming in to see this unusual and charming play. My first job, however, must be to welcome into management Mr. John Gielgud and his partner, who, as Irene Iddesleigh would have phrased it, have flung Mr. Williams's work 'on the oases of futurity', hoping doubtless that the public will not consign it to 'the false bosom of buried scorn'. The first-night reception was wholly favourable, and once more one hopes that the tale told by a first-night audience will not prove to have been too flattering. This would be a pity; obviously the entrancing title is the danger. To the man in the street this can only indicate a kind of play he doesn't think he would like, but which, if he can only be got to see it, enchants him, and which if he never sees it he never stops regretting.

The first act is exceedingly slight, for in it Mr. Williams has no more matter than to explain why Ann Byrd, daughter of William Byrd, the musician, runs away from her home in Essex to become, since female players are not permitted, a boy-player in the company of Richard Burbage. This act is really unnecessary, since this author is craftsman enough to have raised his curtain on Burbage's bedroom and put all that goes before it into a couple of explanatory sentences. But the drama's laws the drama's patrons continue to give, and one of them is that the acts of your West End play must be, as Mr. Belloc used to say about Army Corps, more than two and less than four. As it cannot take a whole act to show Ann declining to wed an unwelcome suitor, there is nothing for Mr. Williams to do except paint the times, which appear to consist in open-air performances of Byrd's madrigals. Whereby one realizes how much in three hundred years has happened to the Gulf Stream; anybody who looks forward to open-air carolling in Spring, 1934, is probably courting a wholly un-Shakespearean rheum. Is it not, by the way, rather a mistake for Ann to call her dad 'the Father of English music', with Tallis, his acknowledged master, still being sung everywhere? 'Smale fowles maken melodye', and perhaps Mr. Williams thought that some of us might need a hint that Byrd was at least high up in the period's musical tree.

While we listen our eyes take in Motley's very pleasant decorations, which do not, however, suggest the worse than Hogarthian frowsts and stenches of the Elizabethan age. Every brick in Byrd's country-house looks as if it were as newly laid as an egg, while even the farm servants have the air of new-emergence from bandboxes. Which appetizingness is, one submits, not a property of hinds. This impression is further accentuated when we come to the opening of Burbage's playhouse, where each and every spectator is less somebody in his Sunday best than the faithful copy of one of Motley's admirable drawings. It is arguable that the Sunday best of Spring, 1600, was still the Sunday best of Autumn, 1580, or earlier; three suits a lifetime was a fair allowance. But perhaps I am carping, though I should some day like to see a stage-setting which should show the soil at the roots of Shakespeare's poetry to be good honest earth, and not a special kind of drawing-room loam.

The second act starts the real fun, which is in places fast enough to make the prudish furious. It has occurred to Mr. Williams that not only Juliet, but each and every one of Richard Crookback's trio of hags must be played by a boy. To what sort of creature will these Queens fall? Obviously a boy-player upon whom long assumption of the feminine has grafted a mature and ridiculous effeminacy. There have been actors who could play such a part without miraculous distortion of their proper selves. But Mr. Frank Pettingell is not such an actor, and those who saw him in *The Good Companions* will not believe until they behold it the incredible expense of observation and mimicry to which he must have been put. He rides the limpid waters of this comedy like a dolphin, and submerges himself like a whale, coming up to blow in the most unexpected places. Here is a riot of tumultuous glee and zest which would shake a laugh out of Freud, always provided that stern psychologist has a laugh in him. More simply, this is a golden-wigged, full-stomached performance which Pélissier himself could not have bettered.

The third act is largely taken up with the story of one of Burbage's light o' loves, and although Miss Isabel Jeans makes a dazzling display I am not at all sure that the character should not have been labelled 'Summer 1660'. One feels that the proper person to emerge from this beauty's closet is the Merry Monarch. What in the meantime has become of Ann, and what of Burbage who should be the play's principal character? Well, the two have never quite loved, and she, after achieving success with her tiger's heart wrapped in a woman's hide, has realized the folly of wanting Burbage all to herself. So she goes home to marry the tender of apricocks and Saturday-night glee-singer, who in the first act has been dangling after her. But none of this is really important, and Mr. Williams has used it because playgoers insist upon a plot. Where the playwright's mind is, there will his treasure be also; whence it follows that the best of this play is its wit and not its seriousness. As dramatic carpentry *Spring 1600* is perhaps not a great achievement; as a *divertissement* it is superb, at least for those realizing that tongue-in-cheek is as much part of the theatre as hand-on-heart. And certainly requires more skill. Only the nicest dramatic sense could have given us a Shakespeare of no account, who merely puts his head in at the door to ask for Mr. Burbage, and as quickly withdraws it.

Miss Joyce Bland gets the right number of ounces out of a part from which a world-actress could be safely trusted to wring overweight; she is gracious and charming and does not pretend that Ann Byrd has more than Rosalind's humour and more than Viola's pathos. As Burbage Mr. Ian Hunter, looking magnificent, carries to a completely successful issue the play's one challenge to eloquence, and it is in this swelling moment that the play declares itself as a labour of love. For the rest, Miss Margaret Webster richly endows Mrs. Burbage with some of Janet Cannot's sterling quality, excellent sketches are contributed by Messrs. H. O. Nicholson, Lawrence Baskcomb, Scott Russell, Valentine Rooke, and Ellis Irving, and Messrs. James Rich and Anthony Bruce make a pleasing pattern in black and white. In conclusion, one might say of this piece that its parts are more entertaining than the whole. There is good Elizabethan humour in Burbage's bedroom, and there are good Restoration frolics in Lady Coperario's. The play may or may not be a popular success, though on the first night gallery and stalls were of one delighted mind about it. It is certainly choice entertainment for the fastidious.

January 31, 1934

LOVE ON THE DOLE
BY RONALD GOW AND WALTER GREENWOOD
(Garrick)

WENDY HILLER

On the principle of horses for courses I amused myself after the first act of this play — which is all about unemployment in that part of Salford where I happen to have been born — in wondering which among the great dramatic critics of my time would best have dealt with it. A. B. Walkley? But then I remembered a sentence of his which ran something like this: 'M. Morand has wandered over London from Ebury Street to the confines of Epping Forest, from Upper Tooting to the route of Motor-bus No. 19, which (he asserts) takes you to Islington.' No, it would not, I think, have been safe to trust this play about short time and short commons to one so delicately nescient. Mr. Max Beerbohm? I have a feeling that our ever regretted dilettante, instinctively shrinking from this tragedy of unfilled working-class

317

bellies, might have given his essay the form of a parody of contemporary Mr. Kipling:

> And the Devil whispered behind the leaves,
> 'It's squalid, but is it art?'

Mr. Shaw? I recalled an article on Shakespeare's *Henry IV*, in which our All Wisest treated himself and us, but more particularly himself, to a dissertation on quite a number of things. On the incompetence of shoemakers. On the new medical practice of painting the tonsils with caustic to cure kidney disease. On the technique of Paderewski. On the reason why the bass part in Mendelssohn's *Son and Stranger* consists of only one note. On Christy Minstrelsy. No! Despite the fact that this article contained a sentence beginning: 'When the operative at his mule in the cotton mill pieces the broken yarn . . . ' I did not feel that our Puckish Solon was the man for Mr. Greenwood's play; I felt that we should have got not so much a criticism of a particular set of hard cases as an indictment of that short-sighted, somnolent, supine, spineless, shirking, shameful, sottish stupidity on the part of our economic rulers which has led to China's dwindling consumption of shirtings and India's decreasing demand for dhootis. Montague? Here there was the risk that the clothes-pegs on Mr. Hardcastle's clothes-line would have become jewels on the thread of that exquisite prose. Archer? But surely the very name of Hardcastle must have lured that learned Scot into long-winded comparison between the state of the drama to-day and its condition in 1773, the year of *She Stoops to Conquer*? One giant remains — Clement Scott. That over-despised critic may not have been overburdened with taste, discrimination, style, though I suspect that these charges are generally preferred by those who have never read a word of him. But he had three essential qualities — a great heart, enthusiasm for a play as something to be acted before a full and excited house, and a capacity for seeing what the point was and making that point in straightforward, understandable English. Clement Scott was the Dickens of dramatic criticism, and he would have been this play's ideal critic just as Dickens would have been the ideal spectator of this tragi-comedy. But you say quickly, *Love on the Dole* is not a tragi-comedy, since in it the comic quality does not enter into and transfuse the tragic as it does in, say, *Juno and the Paycock.* You say that Mr. Greenwood's play is the sum of alternating chunks of both commodities. I agree, and that is the reason why Dickens would have been our ideal spectator, because that is the way in which he wrote his novels.

Following in Scott's footsteps I must perceive what is *not* the point about this piece acted in a London theatre before a London audience. I am to realize that the house cared no jot about the author's narrative skill, type of humour (whether Hogarthian or Dickensian), characterization, and other matters normally the province of the literary critic. No jot about the degree of faithfulness with which these things have been transplanted to the stage, the first business on these occasions of the dramatic critic. No jot about the ironic, even Greek quality of the happy ending which, if the thing is a work of art, must be established beyond question. I am to see that what moved the house was not the art with which the father's, mother's, daughter's, son's predicament was presented—though the attained effect obviously connotes recognition. even if subconscious, of the skill used to produce it — but the predicament itself. Since Scott would not have been ashamed of adjectives like 'naked', 'raw', and 'bleeding' to describe such a situation as that with which this play ends, I must not be ashamed either. The play moved me terribly, and must move anybody who still has about him that old-fashioned thing — a heart.

In case there are readers who do not know what Mr. Greenwood's situation is, I shall briefly recapitulate it. Sally Hardcastle, a mill hand, has lost her lover, killed in a skirmish with the police during an unemployment demonstration. He was consumptive and would have died anyhow. All the family except Sally is out of work, so that she has to keep father, mother, herself, her brother, and the girl whom her brother has got into trouble. There is the dole, but that does not last for ever. And now a wealthy bookmaker makes Sally a proposition. He is married, but if the girl will consent to be his nominal housekeeper he will provide not only for her but for her family also. It was at this point that I feared Walkley's filigree-work on the theme of: 'They drink the champagne wot she sends them, but they never can forgive!' It occurs to me here that some of our moralists might give us the benefit of their cogitations on this theme and tell us what Sally should do. I would ask some bishop, except that bishops do not provide solutions: they deplore. The way for Sally's ultimate decision has been paved in an earlier conversation between her mother and a neighbour who has her head screwed on — in the wrong or right way, but anyhow on! Mrs. Bull's argument is as follows:

> 'Y'want to forget y'self for a bit an' try to understand how t'young 'uns must feel about all these here goings-on in t'world to-day. Every cent they earn being tuk in keeping their owld folks an' any o't' family what comes out o' work. If your Sal had gone on brooding as she was, she'd ha' done what poor sowl did in t'next street yesterday. Guardians towld him he'd t'give five bob to his people what had come under t'Means Test, an' him married wi' a wife and family o' his own. An' what did *he* do? Cut his froat an' jumped through bedroom winder, poor sowl.'

There are some terrible passages before Sally finally decides. Her father calls her unspeakable names. But Sally goes on making her point. She faces up to her father: 'Y'kicked our Harry out because he got married, an' y're kicking me out 'cause Ah ain't.' He knocks her down. Sally goes on: 'Ay, an' Ah'll tell y'summat else. It's sick Ah am o' codging owd clothes t'mek 'em luk summat like. An' sick Ah am o' working week after week an' seeing nowt for it. Ah'm sick o' never havin' nowt but what's bin in pawnshops an' crawling wi' vermin.' In the end Sally goes off with her bookmaker, and we know that some force in her other than her own luxury and riot is driving her to a career which may not wholly displease her though the man does. As she goes she pours

money into her mother's lap and leaves on the table those letters
from her protector which are to obtain jobs for her father and
brother. In a scene for which the only parallel is Balzac's César
Birotteau falling to his knees on the news of his bankruptcy, we
have already heard Sally's father pray for work and take the
name of God not in vain. The end finds him an angry, beaten
man, and his last words are: 'Oh, God, Ah've done me best! Ah've
done me best, haven't Ah?' Well, hasn't he? — I imagine Scott
would have asked. And I ask readers of the *Sunday Times* the same
question. In the days before booms and slumps, when virtue was
as stabilized as the currency, such a father would have plunged
the bread-knife into his daughter's bosom, saying with Macaulay's
Virginius:

> And now, mine own dear little girl,
> There is no way but this.

Are we to-day to condemn Sally? Or her father? How far is a
man justified in using his daughter's immoral earnings to keep
a roof over her mother's head? It may be that in the light of
later reason such earnings may not be immoral. Are they, then,
moral? Since we have mentioned old Hardcastle, perhaps we
might echo Lady Teazle and agree to leave honour, which to-day
we should call morality, out of the argument. Out of the argument, that is, when there is question of empty bellies, and babies
coming into a starving world.

Whether the play is or is not a work of art in the sense that it
will endure when the Lancashire looms are going full time again,
and Chinese and Indians have unlearned the trick we taught them
of weaving their own calicoes and preferring them to the imported
ones — is a matter of purely academic interest. The matter of this
play is here and now. Here is something which brings home to
us the fact that whereas London is one luxurious traffic jam, many
a street in Lancashire has no traffic, and in many a Lancashire
home is neither jam nor the bread to put it on. But it is still my
business to declare that Mr. Gow has made a shapely play out of
Mr. Greenwood's novel, though what one might call the ideal-

istic parts of the book are beyond any manipulation. Nobody is
going to believe the scene on the moors, which is only another
little bit of *Autumn Crocus*. I personally don't believe in the young
workman who, looking at the smoke-cloud hanging like a pall
over the distant city, says: 'It's a queer thing that all that foul
smoke should make beauty for us.' This agitator is played by Mr.
Ballard Berkeley. Now Mr. Berkeley, if I mistake not, is a London
actor, and when it comes to playing Lancashire plays London
players, however good they are, just won't do. They won't do
because they bring with them overtones and echoes from scores
of familiar performances. That Miss Marie Ault was born in
Wigan is no matter; however skilfully she acts, at some time or
other we are going to be reminded that the Amah in *East of Suez*
spoke with that voice. Miss Drusilla Wills is a lovely person, but
here *Yellow Sands* crops up. The same thing applies to Miss
Cathleen Nesbitt and Mr. Arthur Chesney, giving performances
whose brilliance sticks out a mile. This is their undoing, since all
this gloss and polish and careful obliteration of gentility in
favour of Lancashire roughcast is shown up for the artistic, and
therefore make-believe, thing it is the moment it is seen in juxta-
position with the absolute authenticity of Mr. Alex Grandison's
Harry Hardcastle, Mr. Julien Mitchell's Mr. Hardcastle, Miss
Beatrice Varley's Mrs. Bull.

Cézanne's drawing of a brick may be more real than any brick
that was ever made, *but not when somebody hits you with it.* Mr.
Grandison's loutish hobbledehoy, growing out of his clothes and
into man's estate, and his two equal and urgent demands for the
right to wear long trousers and the right to look after his girl —
these are tremendous things to watch; they hit you in the face,
and perhaps the play would have been still nearer to life if this
character had been unbearably killed, instead of the agitator,
which was bearable. Is Mr. Grandison an actor? I don't know
and shall not ask until I have seen him in something else. Is Mr.
Mitchell an actor, and could he play any other part except
Hardcastle? Here again this is not the time to enquire. If Mr.
Mitchell should be a London player his virtue is in being a

London player unknown to me. And Miss Varley? Again the same thing. There is more truth and reality and vigour in one corner of Mrs. Bull's shawl than in the entire casts of the six most popular drawing-room plays now drawing the West End. Miss Wendy Hiller impresses me as having a foot in each camp. As Sally she is very, very good indeed, though there are moments when she is inclined to become actressy; in these she is indistinguishable from a London actress trying to be non-actressy. I wish to state that I am not under the impression that the actors I like in this play are actually out-of-work cotton-operatives. They may be, or they may not, and anyhow it is difficult to believe that they are superlative artists concealing their artistry, because that doctrine is all moonshine. I would prefer to say that they are Lancashire players who know everything about Lancashire life and not enough about London acting to spoil that knowledge. Now let Miss Hiller beware! I can see that six months ago she was a magnificent Sally. On Wednesday night I had the glimmer of a ghost of a notion that here was a very promising young actress giving a magnificent *performance* of Sally.

January 30, 1935

FROLIC WIND

BY RICHARD PRYCE

(Royalty)

BASIL BARTLETT, S. J. WARMINGTON, MABEL TERRY-LEWIS, DOROTHY HOLMES-GORE, HENRIETTA WATSON

If Tchehov had written this play it would have been called *The Four Sisters*. Lady Bernice Jeune (Miss Nina Boucicault) has got to the time of life when, were her blood less blue, she would be a 'body' in the Scotch sense. Lady Athaliah (Miss Henrietta Watson), the descendant of dragonsome dowagers, has rheumatism and lives at the bottom of the garden in a tower upon whose mysterious contents she turns the key. Lady Damaris (Miss Mabel Terry-Lewis) is all that we conjure up in connection with châtelaines of country houses. These three ladies, with their youngest sister Cleone (Miss Dorothy Holmes-Gore), preside over Pagnell Bois in amity like that of china tea-cups which have lived long together, a little chipped, a little stained, and one permits oneself to say that one of them is a little cracked. This is Lady Cleone, who when she was in the forties fell in love with one of the grooms, a handsome rascal instantly dismissed by Lady Athaliah to seek his fortune and favours elsewhere. Lady Cleone has never quite recovered from the shock, and though sometimes not noticeably odd, at others resembles an antiquated Ophelia, daisy-chain and singing mad. These ladies spend their time in the only way that is open to them, that of entertaining. Entertaining whom? Now the houses of the great, unlike flats, insist on being lived in, and for their owners to entertain each other would be too cumbersome a game of general post. Their guests, then, must be chosen from among those who have no castles, and this includes prime ministers, painters, poets ('When Lord Tennyson was here, the rose-garden was reserved for his use alone!') and other prey of these lion-huntresses whom, were there space, one thinks one could acquit of vulgarity. One is made to feel that if any of the Guermantes had visited England, Pagnell Bois is where Proust would have had them stay.

I suppose a good hour is spent in establishing the characters of the four sisters and of Miss Jewell (Miss Veronica Turleigh), the poor relation who arranges Lady Cleone's patience cards backwards so that her games come out; Mr. Charlecote (Sir Basil Bartlett), the young man whose painting is causing a stir; Mr. Roxborough (Mr. Stanley Lathbury), the talkative bore straight out of the pages of Peacock; General Tresmand (Mr. Graveley Edwards), a mindless martinet; Mrs. Murat-Blood (Miss Mignon O'Doherty), who is on the committee of five mental institutes, and the very important Miss Vulliamy (Miss Fabia Drake), an avid spinster whose novel has been all about the right of country girls to have their babies and go on living at home. (I seem to spend my entire life reading novels by Miss Vulliamy and wondering what their authors would do if they met a cow in a lane.) But the hour during which the ground is prepared is not too long, and though the action is cut up into little scenes our interest is not frittered away. Nothing has happened, and there is no sign that anything will happen, and it doesn't matter, and the only question we ask is whether the author can possibly keep his play going on his chosen level, that of a comedy say by Mr. Aldous Huxley, for an audience of the same calibre. But at the very end of the first act there is promise of action. The party is taking tea under the shade and patronage of the oldest cedar in the garden, and the mutter of thunder is echoing the well-bred chatter when the butler announces Sir Lothar Smith (Mr. S. J. Warmington), the self-made millionaire. We know from the glint in Lady Athaliah's eye what is going to happen. Sir Lothar Smith is going to turn out to be Lot Smith, the dismissed groom; the dangerous cat will be out of the bag — for this has always been the closest of secrets — but for Lady Athaliah's watchfulness. Even so one delicate claw protudes, instantly recognized for what it is by Miss Vulliamy, indulging a week-end tenderness for the young painter whose attentions are given to the underling Miss Jewell, and if Miss Vulliamy is not going to enjoy him herself, then, by all that's feminine, misery and shame shall come upon Pagnell Bois!

The second act is a ladies' battle conducted with the utmost elegance. The third act has an immense surprise. Or perhaps one should say that the surprise will be immense for playgoers un-skilled in the mysteries of the human brain and body, which in the theatre are usually made so strangely subservient to those of the heart. We learn now why repression has not wreaked upon Lady Athaliah the same mischief that it did upon Lady Cleone, and as this play's surprise is part of its value I shall not be more particular. The tidying-up at the end — whereby the little under-ling, who turns out to be the daughter of Lady Cleone and the ex-groom, is united to her lover, Miss Vulliamy repents, and the family is brilliantly exhorted by the Princess Rosencrantz-Guildenstern (Miss Martita Hunt) to believe that if they were commoners they would have nothing to be ashamed of — all this tidying is infinitely better than your normal windings-up concerning a cub and a chit and a tennis-racket.

Purists may hold that this is not a good play, and I say, weighing my words, that it is the cause of the best evening I have spent in the theatre at something not strictly a play since Mrs. Mayor's *The Pleasure Garden* and Mr. Huxley's *The World of Light*. (True lovers of Berlioz have been known to say that with such sounds in their ears, pedagogues who call his harmony 'spotty and helpless' can take any one of his chords and with it go hang themselves!) What is there in this play to fill the mind of the true playgoer? The answer is: character-drawing of subtlety and persuasion — the sense that these people, unchallengeably real as in Proust, move and exist on the plane to which they are accredited — dialogue of such point, variety, new invention, and authenticity that you begrudge the rustle of a programme making you miss a word of it — delicate adjustments and revisions of the main situation which engross and satisfy the mind — and the main situation itself, of moment in an age which recognized the social enormity. The modern attitude which would describe the seduction of a lady by her groom as 'rather fun, my sweet' destroys any play on the subject; here is one of the many things Shepherd Market does not know. This is the place to record that one or two of my colleagues have dismissed this piece as 'Meredithian', as though that were a term of disparagement. May I ask whether they prefer the exchanges in Mr. Winter's popular success, whereby a man says to a presumed lady: 'What a bloody-minded woman you are!' and the lady is made to reply: 'I think you're bloody, too!'?

I shall make no bones about the acting and say straight out that as a mosaic it is in a different class from anything else to be seen in London. As the centre jewel of the pattern, Miss Watson is blazingly good; the riot is always just below the surface of that libidinous old eye. Miss Boucicault is old age, fussy and silvered. Miss Terry-Lewis conveys with a certain acerbity the tender grace of a day that is dead; she has that air of perfect breeding which the vulgar mistake for looking down one's nose. Miss Holmes-Gore has the enormously difficult task of keeping our sympathy for a wanderwit, elderly and grotesque; what she has of mind is, like her dress, younger than her sisters, and it is very clever of the actress to perceive this. Miss Drake rakes with the eye of a searchlight the repressions of that venomous duck, Miss Vulliamy. Miss Hunt gives a bravura display of luxury of mind, body, and estate. Miss Turleigh is like some spiritual tureen whose soup has grown as cold as chastity. Miss Renee de Vaux, as Mrs. Dawe in whose car Sir Lothar travels, bubbles like some vulgar organizer of charity balls. And last, my soul's delight, Miss O'Doherty, squats in that garden as though Heaven had planted her there with the cedar.

Perhaps the men are not quite so perfect. The two bores of Messrs. Lathbury and Edwards are a little too much like the real thing. But as the young artist Sir Basil Bartlett is at least a gentleman; we thank him for holding the breach against some other players who would have over-conveyed this impression. I admired the imperturbability of Mr. Douglas Payne's butler, while feeling certain that the footmen, Mr. Colin Gordon as James and Mr. Ian Aylmer as Charles, dead-heated in a race to tell the second chauffeur what they had seen in the tower. This brings me to Mr. Warmington, who is the hub of the play's intrigue, and must stay as motionless. Having nothing to do or say, he must just be, and I don't know anybody who is better at just being. He stands in the background, the pink of polite attention, and attending. A lesser artist would, we feel, have given only the appearance of heeding, dividing his character's mind between the shoals of past solecisms and the snags of the impending peerage. But Sir Lothar has accepted hospitality, and during his stay belongs to Pagnell Bois.

The production by Mr. John Wyse is exquisite, and we may attribute some over-elaboration to the ardours of a first essay. The changes of scene are marvellously contrived, as the scene-shifters must have operated half in the wings of this tiny theatre and half in the street. To conclude, this is a piece for all those highbrows who pretended to despise *Cavalcade*, and I hereby challenge them to keep it going for a fiftieth part of that play's run!

March 17, 1935

AFTER OCTOBER

BY RODNEY ACKLAND

(Arts)

MARY CLARE

IT would be interesting to see this play performed by Russian actors before a Russian audience. It would be still more interesting to read the Russian dramatic critics next morning and find out whether they would say the same kind things about Mr. Ackland that we say about Tchehov. *After October* has not the momentum or drive of the great Russian playwright, and it does not anywhere pretend to beauty. But it is all extraordinarily like that scene which occurs in every Tchehov play when everybody is talking nineteen to the dozen and nothing in particular is being said. There is the same atmosphere of melancholy, in the English case more apparent than actual, and the resemblance is stressed by the fact that everybody is a failure. Mr. Ackland's theme is gloom, his orchestration is as sparkling as Rossini's at his gayest, and Mr. A. R. Whatmore has produced in the spirit in which Sir Thomas Beecham conducts. In fact, were the score a musical one I should mark it *Adagio ma con Brio*. This may possibly be dog-Italian, but it comes from one dog-tired with laughing at this play. The story, such as it is, concerns the household of Mrs. Rhoda Monkhams (Miss Mary Clare), a lady bereft of both husband and profession, since in palmier days she was an understudy at the Gaiety. Ill-luck has always pursued her. The principal having influenza, Rhoda had a chance of running her pagoda. But the principal was well enough to attend the dress rehearsal and on seeing Rhoda's performance screamed out: 'I shall play to-morrow if I catch my death!' And, as Rhoda says: 'She did appear — and died of double pneumonia!' Rhoda lives in these and other succulent memories not unmixed with dressing-room tittle-tattle on which the dust of ages lies thick. She remains a trouper at heart and, with the valour of her kind, is battling when the curtain goes up with a carpet-sweeper, an unbreakfasted family, reiterative duns, communications from owners of plain vans, and the laundry shrieking down the telephone. Her son Clive (Mr. Griffith Jones) is a playwright with a passion equally divided between the theatre and Frances (Miss Iris Baker), who is a manicurist, neurotic, and lodger or, as she would prefer to put it, Mrs. Monkhams's paying guest. Though Frances loves Clive she is accepting the roses and attentions of Brian (Mr. Whatmore), epitome of semi-public school, would-be pukka sahib, and sports addict, all of them hearty, good-natured, moneyed, and frantically boring to anybody outside their kind.

There is a younger daughter, Joan (Miss Ursula Marx), who is vaguely secretary to Alec (Mr. Geoffrey Denys), who is vaguely dipsomaniac. 'Is Arabella Mr. Winkle's mistress?' asked Mr. Beerbohm in his parody of George Moore on Dickens, and returned the answer: 'If she is not, she has been, or at any rate she will be.' The same applies to Joan and Alec. An older daughter of Mrs. Monkhams is Lou (Miss Leonora Corbett). Lou has been in the dancing business at Toulon, Toulouse, *que sais-je?* and has married Armand (Mr. Godfrey Kenton), who is alluded to in the family as 'Almond' and is now helping in a shop in Soho. Armand confesses that, outside his love for Lou, he is as much *désorienté* as if he were living among the Chinese. And with good reason, since in no country but this could he meet the Betty of Miss Merle Tottenham, a little drudge among whose forbears must have been Dick Swiveller's Marchioness. It would take a Dickens to tell us what the Marchioness would have thought of Greta Garbo's Anna Karenina, but Mr. Ackland does very well, and Miss Tottenham does even better. Two more characters remain. One is Marigold (Miss Gwladys Evan Morris), fat, forty, and frowsty as only

Bloomsbury tea-parties know how. This is a Miss Mowcher with an over-developed mothering instinct thrown away on a scapegrace nephew who is continually in gaol. 'Holidaying', is Marigold's euphemism for this state, and when asked how long it is to last she has fallen into the habit of replying: 'Three months!' Last in the sad, eventless category — for nothing happens to any of them — is Oliver (Mr. Peter Godfrey), who is our old friend Ulric Brendel all over again, existing on the crumbs of charity and the cud of a long, unpublished dramatic poem. It is typical of this play — and how like Tchehov! — that though the flat is Rhoda's it is frequently empty except for people unwelcome to Rhoda who have no business to be in it at all.

Rhoda has a contempt for Marigold because she has been seen to eat peanuts in Bond Street, and dislikes Oliver still more because he insists upon turning up at meal-times. Oliver and Marigold have only to meet to take an intense dislike to one another, and here is a passage which shows how, when the dialogue is good enough in the theatre, Time can stand still and Space go 'round and around until the talkers have had their say:

OLIVER Do I inflict myself? One day they'll be proud to say that Oliver Nashwick came into their house. Look at it! This bourgeois pretentiousness! They've put on evening dresses. They've bought two bottles of wine. They're celebrating. Like a wedding of proletarians. Or a funeral. You think I'm rude, don't you? Rude, because I don't say 'How do you do? I'm delighted to meet you. Will you have two lumps or three, and was it the Monday or the Tuesday?' D'you ever say what you mean? D'you ever *know* what you mean? D'you ever think? Have you ever, for one moment, been honest with yourself?

MARIGOLD I knew you'd go on like this, directly I saw that beard!

OLIVER Why is your gown such a phantasie? (*walking round her*).

MARIGOLD (*sternly*) It's a very beautiful dress.

OLIVER Don't you mean to be ridiculous? Please tell me. What were your parents? Shopkeepers? Bourgeois?

MARIGOLD No, indeed, they were not. They were the Ivenses of Buxton! What were yours?

OLIVER My father was a buyer in a draper's shop and my mother an assistant who 'lived in'. She seduced him, and afterwards, I've heard, he entered the merchant service, where he saw a great deal of the world. I've never met him, but I often think of my father. I believe I should have liked him because he had an adventurous spirit. When my mother was left alone she became a servant. My life has been spent in kitchens listening to servants' gossip . . . I've a finer brain than anyone living, and I dwell among servants. I am bitter, but I am not full of hatred. Perhaps one day I shall be. And that would be a pity because I have a great capacity for being gay.

It is possible that this does not read wittily, the reply to which is that if it did I should fear for it on the stage. Oliver's lines are written for an actor who can act, and Mr. Godfrey delivers them superbly. Marigold has little to say, but there is a world of meaning in Miss Morris's: 'They were the Ivenses of Buxton!' For it is the folds of Marigold's cheeks and the flounces of her preposterous dress which make you realize that the Ivenses, whether of Buxton or not, were never, in point of fact, anybody. Now and again, Mr. Ackland permits himself to be a little serious, and Clive has this excellent passage:

Why is looking forward such a necessary thing? I'll tell you why. It's a law of nature so that one shan't look too far forward. 'Something to look forward to' is something for one's mind to stop at, like a wall in time, between oneself and death and the rest of the unpleasant things lying in wait. When the wall is reached, one passes through it. And then quickly — so as to shut out any glimpse of the journey's end — up goes another wall. And I think one continues putting them up until one's dying day. Even very old people, I'm sure, erect little walls between themselves and death, even if the walls are merely to-morrow's dinner or the visit of a grandchild.

But — says the reader — can I be certain of enjoying a play, however well written, in which nothing happens? The answer is that it entirely depends upon what kind of playgoer the reader is. If he is the kind which refrains from visiting a play until he is bidden by the Board of Agriculture and Fisheries or the Port of London Authority, I should think that he may spend a very dull evening. If he has one grain of playgoing sense to rub against another, he will, I venture to think, be entranced. I was spellbound throughout by a piece which it is nevertheless important not to rate too highly; I should place it exactly half way between *Call It A Day* and *Uncle Vanya*. It is dazzlingly acted; and flibbertigibbet though Rhoda has been and still is, it is Miss Clare who plays luminous centre to the galaxy.

February 21, 1936

THE FLASHING STREAM

BY CHARLES MORGAN

(Lyric)

GODFREY TEARLE, MARGARET RAWLINGS

Her passions are made of nothing but the finest part of pure love.—*Antony and Cleopatra*

CAN a man embrace pure love as he embraces pure mathematics or pure poetry? I think the answer is to be found in Stevenson's remarks on the Permanent Possibility of Sensation. As it is within the area of conjecture that here and there a reader may be a little vague about those remarks, I permit myself to jog his memory. Philosophy's definition of life, says Stevenson, 'is a Permanent Possibility of Sensation'. He goes on: 'Truly a fine result! A man may very well love beef, or hunting, or a woman; but surely, not a Permanent Possibility of Sensation!' How the author of our play must have shuddered at the trist anastomosis! Then again: 'As for caring about the Permanence of the Possibility, a man's head is

332

generally very bald, and his senses very dull, before he comes to that.'

But some of us have said much the same thing about the age a man must be to accept the definition of love as set forth in Mr. Morgan's novels. Not to shift the blame on other shoulders, I remember a certain uneasiness with regard to that letter in *The Fountain*:

> I do not believe that the bodily delight of love is sin, but that it becomes a deadly betrayal wherever a human relationship is obsessed by the acceptance, or by the desire of it. Either you and I were by our discovery of each other made gods with power to create, in our relationship, a perdurable essence, higher than ourselves, independent of our delights, or we were animals caught in a trap . . . Our love was a predestined force that would create of itself a personality — a hypostasis — more beautiful and vital and lasting than ourselves, or it was a sterile pleasure, no more.

In this, his first play, Mr. Morgan has realized that whereas disembodied ecstasy is feasible on the stage, bodiless ecstatics are infeasible. Wherefore his characters are a flesh-and-blood lot, very much the people you and I might meet at dinner. Which, again, does not prevent them from talking out of full and firm minds. The hero of this play makes the first full-throated statement of the theme at which its author has often hinted: 'A man's love for a woman, though one of the expressions of it be carnal, may be the very air in which his soul grows.' Novelists, explains Edward Ferrers to Karen Selby, are wrong in their delineation of love as an arithmetical progression, passing from sentiment to sublimation through a middle stage of passion. 'Love is all things at once', declares Ferrers, 'a cake to eat and something to worship.' The theme once announced, every reed and stop is pressed into service of this grand Morgan Voluntary.

And now it is time to explain who these people are. Commander Edward Ferrers, R.N. (Mr. Godfrey Tearle), is in charge of a naval experimental station on an island in the Atlantic.

He and four more officers are at work on a torpedo which is to destroy enemy aircraft. Ferrers is a mathematical genius, and as much in love with his science as an artist with his art. His right-hand man, Selby, dying, it is proposed that Selby's sister Karen (Miss Margaret Rawlings), also a first-class mathematician, shall take Selby's place. Ferrers objects on the ground that an equation is one thing and a personal equation another, and that in properly conducted naval stations never the twain shall meet. In the end he consents. Which brings us to the curtain of the first act.

In the second act interest is divided between the swaying fortunes of the experiment and the gravitation towards each other of Ferrers and Karen. The reader must now be told that this play is like some river rich in tributaries, creeks, and inlets — one of which is the discussion of the pure mind in the incontinent body. Also that, since it would be impossible to deal fully with this play at shorter length than the play itself, I shall confine what follows to the main stream. Ferrers, very much the conquering male, tells Karen that he is to be her god or nothing. This noway displeases Karen, who in the matter of subjugation to her lord is a pattern for Sultanas. But by 'god' Ferrers means a mathematical god; his invention has to succeed or there will be no marriage. For, argues Ferrers, how can he remain a god who was once regarded as a mathematical genius but has been relegated by failure to the depths of schoolmastering and the heights of Swiss Cottage — a degradation known only to Viceroys declining from elephants with jewelled mahouts to a couple of housemaids in Kensington Gore? The experiment does in fact fail; there is much excitement in the tussle between an impatient Admiralty, playing into the hands of an Admiral's jealous lady, and mathematical theorists of genius denied sufficient time to perfect the practical workings of their gadgets. This brings us to the curtain of the second act.

Mr. Morgan has confessed that in order to ensure an ending which should not disappoint he wrote his third act first. And I am to suggest to our playwright that the beginning of his third act is precisely the point at which Ibsen would have begun his play. How well one knows that opening, not at Swiss Cottage, but in some worm-eaten Nordic cot. Harvard Solness Ferrers and Hilda Wrangle Selby have been married seven years; five children cluster round their four knees. Throughout three acts we learn of all that happened in the Atlantic eight or nine years before. We see the jealous, mischief-making lady, now in the guise of a nautical Thea Elvsted, turning up at Hilda's house carrying Ella Rentheim's melancholy valise. She is the senior wrangler of the two. From time to time we see Hilda going to a cupboard to take out a Vibrational Equation, pet it, and put it back as Harvard returns from the schoolhouse, takes off his goloshes, and draws from his coat that bundle of exercise books which he has brought home for correction. His impatient thrusting into the fire of some brat's discovery that two and two make five gives the clue to the 'total gesture' of Ibsen's play, which is that a hypostasis by becoming unendurable ceases to be perdurable. But that is not the play Mr. Morgan wrote, *and nothing will induce me, as a lover of pure criticism, to blame him for not having written it!*

No! Mr. Morgan's way with this piece has been the Swan of Avon's way in *Antony and Cleopatra*, whose spirit has been hanging about ever since the curtain went up. It was not for nothing that Miss Rawlings made her first appearance in a veil or cloud exactly like the traditional headgear — called, I think, a nemis — of the Queen of Egypt. Now it is a fault in human nature, though an excusable fault, to imagine that the rest of the world is *au fait* with one's particular hobbies. Shakespeare's play is a critic's play, and I doubt very much whether anybody except a critic would be able to answer offhand the question put by the First Lord of the Admiralty (Mr. Felix Aylmer) to Karen: 'What did Pompey say to Menas?' The answer, of course, is: 'In me 'tis villany; In thee't had been good service.'

Here is the point. The First Lord has said to Ferrers: 'If you will admit to an error in your mathematics I will give you time to correct it. But if you hold by your mathematics I must call off your experiment, as it just doesn't work.' To which Ferrers has replied: 'Deny my mathematics? Go back on the multiplication table? O Weederdee! The scientist's pole is fall'n; boy and girl mathematicians are level now with men; the odds is gone.' And so on and so forth, all in Shakespeare's best Egyptian manner. Whereupon Karen, who has been desperately recalling her High School lessons in English Literature, suddenly remembers the incident in Pompey's galley and starts a scene of excellent dissembling. She has been through Antony's calculations and has found a squiggly little error gnawing at the square root of one of them. 'Excellent!' says the First Lord. 'Now you can have all the time you want to put your calculations right.' And Ferrers overlooks the insult to the purity of his mathematics in the joy of getting enough time to make his gadgets work properly. After which Karen confesses her stratagem and is forgiven. Last we are to presume that the experiment is successful, that this country becomes immune from raiding aeroplanes, that Ferrers gets an earldom and a grant of cash, and that henceforth he and his Countess enjoy a hypostasis which has no reason for not being perdurable.

Well, this third act is exciting, though I confess a sneaking curiosity as to what would have happened to this pure passion if, after marriage, the couple had been unable to square the milkman's circle or box the butcher's compass. But, taking it for all in all, *The Flashing Stream* is a magnificent play, at once subtle in thought and downright in exposition, swift in action and noble in expression. It is a compactom of philosophy about passionate truth and impersonal passion. Every sentence, every word, has the thing which matters most in a man, a horse, a piece of writing, or work of any sort if it is only laying one brick on top of another — quality. Mr. Morgan has dug his play out of a marble quarry with a pickaxe of gold tipped with witty steel.

Mr. Tearle magnificently suggests the artist consumed by his own flame, the man of science to whom scientific truth is this world and the next. Miss Rawlings matches this fine performance with a lovely sweep of passion in all its manifestation — physical, spiritual, maternal; in short, the *Ewig-Weibliche* in full tide and spate. Not a word wrong, not a movement out of place. Grandly they sing and act the love-duet from *Tristan*, while poring over blue-prints of rhomboids and parallelopipeds. Grandly sine calls to cosine; passion, constant, declines to go off at a tangent. Will Mr. Morgan forgive me if I say that he will not know what he owes to this superb pair till he sees what Hollywood makes of his 'impersonal passion'? I trust his answer will be Lear's: 'Never, never, never, never, never!'

There are contributory performances of great skill and charm by Miss Marda Vanne, Mr. Aylmer — a delicate piece of acting, this — Mr. Leo Genn, Mr. Anthony Ireland, Mr. H. G. Stoker, Mr. Desmond Roberts, and Mr. Roger Maxwell. Mr. Peter Creswell's production is impeccable, and the house on the first night received the piece with so much enthusiasm that I can almost predict a Possibility of Sensational Permanence.

September 1, 1938

RHONDDA ROUNDABOUT

BY JACK JONES

(Globe)

MERVYN JOHNS

'Is it a good play?' asked Mr. Shaw's Count O'Dowda, and received the answer: 'If it's by a good author, it's a good play, naturally.' Bannel then produced the knockdown: 'What merits can a play have except the author's merits?' Therefore let us make up our minds about Mr. Jack Jones's merits before allowing merit to his original and refreshing piece. Fortunately this is easy. I happen to have read Mr. Jones's autobiography, *Unfinished Journey*. My notebook tells me that I found it 'staggeringly good — intensely vivid. One chapter of fourteen pages only gets the whole of the war into them. J. has been soldier, miner, actor, impresario, salesman, navvy, broadcaster, and novelist. Time he wrote a play.'

Well, *Rhondda Roundabout* is the play, and it is easy to see that
Mr. Jones has not found it quite so direct a matter as telling his
life-story. And why should he? If life is only, as the laughing
philosopher held, one dam thing after another, no autobiography
need be more. Heaven help the addicts of that art, science, whim,
foible, what you will, if ever it has to be more! But a play must
take a form as surely as, say, a tea-pot. It must be filled with the
author's message which, when brewed, is poured into the ears and
minds of the audience gathered to partake. The older and more
elegant way of saying this is that a play must have a 'total gesture'
— the one thing lacking in plays about adjacent bath-chairs and
contiguous bathing-vans, whose whole point is dissemination
rather than cohesion. Has Mr. Jones's play a 'total gesture', and
if so what? The answer would seem to be that life in the Rhondda
Valley, as elsewhere, is a prize-fight. Possibly without any dis-
coverable prize, but a fight all the same. It is surely significant
that it is a pugilist who brings Mr. Jones's curtain down on the
words: 'We must fight on up to the bell!'

Who are the fighters? There is a boxer squaring up to a bosomful
of unrequited love with an intensity that recalls the infighting of
Jimmy Wilde. There is his backer, a bookmaker whose compassion gets the better of his rapacity. There is the local draper
who is knocked out by death. There is the conductor of the local
choir whose life is one long bout of all-in wrestling with the scores
of *Elijah* and *Messiah*. There is the local preacher, a fledgeling
doubtfully at grips with a weak chest. There is the miner who has
brought into the world eight children on the strength of his dole
and a poor constitution. There are the Communist agitators
fighting for a cause they liberally misinterpret. Last but one,
there is the Captain, a monocled, C.3 dipsomaniac with a nervous
tic, in whose outpourings we are to hear once again that windy
indictment of war of which our abstract intellectuals never seem
to tire. Last of all is Shoni Lloyd, the miner, who has fought the
good fight against spiritual unrest, and won it. His is the dead
calm which, we are told, is at the centre of every vortex.

And that's the play! There are some women, of course; but

they are unimportant. To them are allotted the rôles of wifehood degenerating into termagancy, of innocence betrayed and moping, of maidenhood meditating on the uniquely feasible subject of maiden meditation. Yet such is Mr. Jones's sincerity that we feel we are making acquaintance for the first time with men and women whom common sense tells us we have met a hundred times before. With this difference — that hitherto we have met them in the theatre, and now we are encountering them in real life.

The plot? For indeed to goodness, look you, a play must have a plot. It is the queerest assemblage. Domesticities *à la* Stanley Houghton, mob-appeals and pit-head disasters *à la* Galsworthy, a death-bed *à la* Van Biene, world-lamentations *à la* Priestley though minus the mask and pirouette. These things are obviously intended to be impressive; actually some of them are merely gaps in the play's 'persuasiveness'. And there are other times when Mr. Jones's skill deserts him, and he mistakes the theatre for the floor of a barn. *Rhondda Roundabout* is, then, an extraordinary mixture of unforced effectiveness and forced ineffectiveness. It soars, topples, and recovers. It is too good for the West End theatre. It is provocative and interesting, full of mind, and always the work of a man deeply moved and endeavouring to render deep emotion in a form which he has not yet mastered.

The acting is a fascinating jumble. Much of it is on the level of an amateur dramatic society which has won honourable mention, but no prize, at one of those North-country competitive jamborees. A little of it — and one would instance Mr. Charles Williams's boxer — is of a vigour, sincerity, and lifelikeness which take away the breath. Mr. Williams may or may not be a good actor; in this piece he defeats criticism by giving one the impression of being the thing he pretends. Of the strictly professional players one would make first mention of Mr. Mervyn Johns's Shoni, a lovely study in withdrawal of the spirit. That good actor, Mr. Raymond Huntley, objurgates on the tops of Welsh mountains with admirable intention. That he fails is not his fault. No actor living could do more with what Vesta Tilley would have called the 'shell-shocked Johnny with the little glass eye'. The women fill in more than competently, Miss Dilys Davies contributing a study of spousedom whose painful truth half the audience must recognize. For the rest, Mesdemoiselles Pearl Evans and Kay Bannerman flit hither and thither with equal Welsh charm in both directions.

May 31, 1939

THUNDER ROCK

BY ROBERT ARDREY

(Neighbourhood)

MICHAEL REDGRAVE

SOMEWHERE or other I remember writing: 'Be simple about the abstruse, and you can afford to be abstruse about the simple.' The present play calls for one hundred per cent simplicity. In 1849 a packet called *Land o' Lakes*, out of Buffalo bound for Milwaukee, struck a reef in northern Lake Michigan. She foundered, and the captain, crew, and sixty passengers were lost. A lighthouse was subsequently erected, and it is inside the lighthouse that this play's action happens, the date being the midsummer of 1939. The lightkeeper is a man named Charleston, and the visiting inspector cannot understand why this man resents his visits, declines relief, and refuses the Government's grant of a wireless set. Accompanying the inspector is one Streeter, the pilot of the supply plane and an old crony of Charleston.

Soon the two friends are left alone, and it emerges that both are seeking escape from the world-impasse. Up till now world-problems have had their solutions; to both it seems that the day of solutions is over. Streeter is about to find escape as an airman on the Chinese side in the Sino-Japanese war; Charleston finds refuge in *défaitisme* and isolation to the extent of shooting even the lighthouse gulls. Streeter objects that his friend cannot live entirely without company, and Charleston quietly says: 'But I have company — a regular world, with people, plain, ordinary, courageous people, the kind I like.' These, if you please, are the drowned captain and six of his passengers! For Charleston has not yet acquired the imagination of a Balzac who could conceive an entire society of non-existent human beings; he has got as far as six people, not counting the captain, and he hopes to add more as he goes on. To which Streeter says in an awed whisper: 'You sound like God the day before Genesis!' Presently the inspector and Streeter depart, and, as the first-act curtain falls, the drowned Captain Joshua takes shape before us.

Up to this point the play has been exciting but three-dimensional, and in the interval one heard people eagerly debating whether the author could keep up excitement in the new dimension. We have understood that henceforward everything takes place in Charleston's brain, and at first it seems that the society he has created for himself is no better than the society he has abjured. The discouraged medical pioneer, the spinster advocate of women's rights, the improvident begetter of consumptive children — all are shown as vapid and petty creatures. (I think that this section of the play should be shortened and speeded-up, to lessen the time during which the spectator is tempted to think that the play has gone to pieces.) In the middle of this scene Captain Joshua appears and rehabilitates the author. It seems that Charleston, who after all is only a dabbler in creation and needs a confidant, has revealed to the captain that he and the others are all dead. This enables Joshua to say to Charleston: 'Stop, you are not doing my passengers justice! You are remaking them at less than their full value. Turn back the clock and try again!' The scene is then re-played, the characters now being cast in the full mould of Charleston's mind instead of merely in the *défaitiste* half of it.

What next? Their little drama played out to the end, Charleston bids his creatures vanish from his mind. They refuse, and the play then proceeds to a long argument as to the terms on which these figments will consent to a second death. The terms are these, and, of course, it is Charleston who has to put them into minds which are only his mind: The world is no darker in 1939 than it was in 1849. To the disappointed of 1849 it might have seemed that the last great genius was dead. But what did 1849 know of Lincoln, Darwin, Pasteur, Brahms? So must we argue in 1939. And the conclusion is that just as the old world conquered plagues and pestilences, so some day means will be found to eradicate the present evils of unemployment, starvation, and even war. The ghosts depart, but as Charleston takes up the business of life again one more ghost appears. It is Streeter, who has fallen to his death in China and now comes to bid his friend take heart again.

It seems to me from a single hearing that the piece is watertight, always provided that the spectators keep in mind the conditions which the playwright has formally imposed. This is made easier by the author's willingness to take us round any obstacle which he does not think we can surmount. Thus when the Viennese doctor says: 'I fought on the field of Austerlitz and saw my Fatherland vanquished. But I lived to see Napoleon fall and Europe survive!' Charleston replies: 'From the business of describing modern warfare to a man who fought at Austerlitz may I be delivered!' And there are continual reminders that the whole thing is fantasy, as when the captain, who throughout has been helping himself to Streeter's cigarettes, says to Charleston: 'Thank your friend for the smokes, and point out to him that the packet is just as he left it!'

I suggest that it is up to the playgoer to make what he can of this remarkable play. The cast at the new Neighbourhood Theatre in South Kensington makes a great deal of it. Mr. Michael Redgrave, playing Charleston with a mixture of passion and restraint, gives reality to the proceedings by very subtly absenting himself, as it were, during the second and third acts. There is, too, a highly convincing performance of Streeter by Mr. Robert Sansom, and I have only space to pick out from a very good company Mr. Percy Parsons as the captain, Mr. Frederick Valk as the Viennese doctor, and Miss Rosalind Atkinson as the emancipated woman. I congratulate this more than enterprising little theatre on breaking ground with a play infinitely superior in craftsmanship, intellectual interest, pure theatre *and entertainment value* to anything the commercial theatre can offer in these heart-searching days. That the fault lies not with that theatre but with the public is matter for another article.

June 23, 1940

AMERICAN PLAYS

THE ADDING MACHINE
BY ELMER RICE
(Stage Society)

BREMBER WILLS, LOUISE HAMPTON

WHY do the big men in the theatre imitate the little man's passion for big words? 'Expressionism' — what fearful wildfowl is that to set before a man hungry for an evening's entertainment? Cannot you imagine a conversation in the tube: 'What's on at the Exemplary Theatre to-night?' '*The Adding Machine*, an expressionistic drama.' 'Oh, is it? Well, let's see if we can get into the Pantechnicon. There's no blooming what-d'you-call-it about *Felix Keeps on Walking*!'

Perhaps it is our fault for being skeered of these long words. But, then, those who use them are, on the whole, scarifying people. Says Goldberg, summing up Manfred Schneider in *Der Expressionismus in Drama*:

> Expressionism designs for the stage a musicality of word, a broad sweep, a vast simplicity, a preference for types rather than well-characterized individuality, the whole to be infused with, or suffused in, an atmosphere of exaltation. The expressionists favour intuition rather than artifice, even in the acting. They would fill their pieces with ideas yet shun the thesis play. They would produce the impression of deep feeling, yet without what we are accustomed to term psychology in drama. Most of all they would abandon the ivory tower and seek social, universal significance.

Mr. Ashley Dukes expands this. In a note on the Stage Society's programme he tells us that Expressionism has very much in common with Melodrama. The latter sacrifices character and plausibility, the former renounces the individual, and the particular act. Melodrama is the drama of outward situation, expressionism represents the drama of mental situation 'from which outlines of character are derived and essentials of action "expressed"'. Well, nothing is ever quite as bad as it looks at first sight except, perhaps, the accounts of absconding financiers. The expressionism of *The Adding Machine* boiled down, so far as the first four scenes were concerned, amounted simply to this — that the characters spoke their thoughts instead of the polite nothings without which society would come to an end. Thus Mrs. Jones would say to her caller, Mrs. Smith, not 'Delighted to see you, won't you come in?' but 'Drat the woman! Just as I wanted to do a bit of washing!' And Mrs. Smith would smile sweetly and say not 'How lucky to find you in!' but 'I wouldn't have come, only I felt sure you'd be out.'

In the first scene Mr. and Mrs. Zero — which name means that they are any husband and any wife in the wage-earning class — are preparing for bed. He says nothing; she talks, and pours out the whole of her commonplace, sentimental mind. You can hardly call it talk; the woman 'runs on', as Mrs. Nickleby or Flora Finching might do, upon such matters as the inefficiency of her man, the dullness of her existence, the films she has seen, the jealousies she has experienced. The second scene shows the husband at his office desk sitting opposite a woman clerk. He exposes his dull, unimaginative, sneakingly dirty little mind; she exhibits a dingy romanticism; and the duet sounds like bowdlerized James Joyce. At the end of this scene the clerk is sacked in favour of a mechanical reckoner. The third scene shows the clerk, his wife, and a party of friends seated in the parlour, all voluble and all damned. At the end of this the clerk is arrested for having murdered his employer. The fourth scene shows his feelings expressionistically — that wretched word is getting longer — in the dock as the lawyers make their footling little moves and counter-moves. The clerk is executed.

Up to this point the whole thing was intensely interesting, and, if you believed in the pessimistic view of the working classes, extremely moving. Personally, I don't at all agree that the existence of the Zeros is tragic. I don't believe that the life of the store-worker is a 'wale'. Are there no street bookies in America? Is there no baseball, no evening recreation? We know there is no beer, but is there not chewing gum? But, given that life over there is wholly Gummidgean, then the presentation was as wholly moving as if it had been expressionless, or, as we should say, realistic. There was a cheering absence of all that toying with hat and gloves, handing round of teacups, quipful butlering — the minuscule traffic of the stage. Whether Mr. Rice has anything new to say in his new medium is doubtful.

His last three scenes, showing Heaven and Hell, in which he seeks to prove that man was once a perfectly good monkey and has degenerated ever since, are highbrow drivel of the most preten-tious kind. We must not confuse matter with manner, and though it may be good fun to exhibit humanity, as some modern painters do, in the form of parallelopipeds and gas tubing, there remains the obligation to do something with the ironmongery. And this particular dramatist does little. It would be nonsense to compare this minor play with any of the major Galsworthys.

It was well produced, though in the trial scene Mr. Brember Wills forgot about expressionism, and harangued the jury to their faces. He should have intoned and monotoned, without gesture, like a man thinking aloud. The women in this play were in more obviously pitiful case. Miss Louise Hampton, as Mrs. Zero, gave one more proof of her great artistry. Was Miss Edith Evans, as the storewoman, a little less good than usual? Perhaps not, but I will hint that she was, and so make show of non-slavish admira-tion. The great thing about this play is that it was produced and enjoyed, at least as to four-sevenths of it. Expressionism turns out to be no fearsome bogey after all, and playgoers should not be deterred because of what German professors and Mr. Dukes may say. After all, it may be only their fun.

March 23, 1924

ANNA CHRISTIE

BY EUGENE O'NEILL

(Strand)

PAULINE LORD

THIS American play turns out, on reflection, to be a mighty queer jumble — Conrad and Synge and Dumas *fils* and Huysmans, and whoever writes the scenarios for little Lillian Gish. But the whole business of the playwright is to banish reflection, or at least to keep us unreflecting till we get home. 'Story first' is his motto, or should be. *Anna Christie* is a fine play because of its inherent quality of simple emotion. If Anna had not been taken to her lover's arms at the end, I believe that every member of the crowded audience would have left the theatre in genuine distress. Happy endings are not necessarily bad art. This play called for a happy ending, though perhaps not in the particular manner devised by Mr. O'Neill. Consent to tragedy is only rightly wrung from us when the tragedy is inevitable and serves as a warning. There is nothing tragic in a street accident, there is only horror; and for little Anna to have ended miserably would have been horrific.

The theme of *Anna Christie* is an inversion of that old French thing, the repentant courtesan. Every modern playwright since Augier and Dumas *fils* has had his whack at it, so that it comes into twentieth-century drama like a tin can kicked down the street by a parcel of vigorous schoolboys, and bearing the dints made by individual boots. Indeed, the earliest form of this type of play has been likened to a watering-can with which that good husbandman, the dramatist, douses those Colorado beetles, the adventuresses, pours upon them the caustic solution of morality, 'and so keeps them away from the crops'. Augier and Dumas pointed out that if beetles would insist upon being beetles, they must learn what to expect; their most lenient punishment was to

347

be allowed to crawl on to a Louis Seize sofa and curl up in a romantic atmosphere of repentance and consumption. Two or more generations have played the gardener, diluting the solution now with comprehension, now with pity. Lastly, Mr. O'Neill turns up with a story, not of green-fly, but of some pathetic rose. He uses a new *milieu*, a new setting, and something that looks like a new technique to tell us an old and moving tale.

When Anna was a child she was sent by her father—a drunken sailor obsessed with the fear of the sea, a Conrad will-o'-the-wisp, this — to earn her living on a farm inland, out of the sea's way. Enslaved and seduced, she fled to the town, and of necessity took to the streets. The brothel, prison, and hospital followed; and when the play opens Anna returns to the old sailor who for fifteen years has trusted to her bogus accounts of well-being. At her first entry we know Anna's past; we know her life of want, misery, and simulated gaiety, of lies and pretended passion. Every big town knows the type. As she sits drinking at the inn-table she might be the younger of Huysmans's Sœurs Vatard. But we know from the actress's face that Anna is no essential prostitute; we do not need her off-hand remark to another drab — 'Gee, I hate them, every mother's son; don't you?' — to make us aware of her essential disgust at her way of life. Probably there was not a father in the audience who would not at sight have entrusted his daughter to Anna's care. She was, you felt, as innocent of that outrage at the farm, and all that followed, as the heroine of *Way Down East* was innocent of her misfortunes. Anna fills you with the same simple emotion that you know when Lillian Gish turns away from the farmstead and begins to trudge up that long, dreary road. There is no question of the Immortals treating these poor women badly, either for their punishment or our purgation. When Anna meets her honest sailor-lover she refuses him in the self-sacrificing Dumasian way. Her lips tremble, and frame themselves to yet another version of the old: 'Ainsi, quoi qu'elle fasse, la créature tombée ne se relèvera jamais. Dieu lui pardonnera peut-être, mais le monde sera inflexible,' etc., etc. In her father's presence Anna blurts out the truth; the lover calls her a strumpet and threatens to beat her brains out with a chair; Anna defies him and reels off the age-long indictment of man's lust. For some time the ghosts of other dramatists have seemed to beckon from the wings. First Pinero, proposing that. Anna shall marry the sailor and then that some common crony shall cross their path. Then Mr. Galsworthy, suggesting that the chair must be brought down, that the father must shoot the lover, and the President of the Immortals, in the person of a kindly, white-haired old judge, end his sport with all three. What actually does happen is that both men go off to get drunk, the lover casting Anna back upon the streets, the father promising to shelter her in spite of the past. And, of course, within two days the lover creeps back. Mr. O'Neill's difficulty was to decide upon the exact method of his happy ending. The girl's purity and innocence are so fully established, our sympathies have been so acutely aroused in circumstances which defy avoidance by circumspection, that tragedy can have no useful meaning. On a plane with the rest of the play would have been a frank facing and acceptance of the facts. Instead, the lovers agree to pretend that the new Anna is no longer the old Anna. Whereas, of course, she has not changed. Of course, if the girl had been a courtesan at heart, then the real play begins where this one ends, and tragedy sets in. But that way Ibsen lies. It appears that in America Mr. O'Neill despaired of persuading his public that soilure of the body is not necessarily impurity of the mind, and that he had to insist upon a new Anna. Over here the applause after the first three acts was tremendous, and slight after the fourth, although the happy ending had been conceded. The audience had become inured to the truth about this particular case, and seemed to resent the concluding falsity. All the more because the play, which had boomed with quite irrelevant echoes of Conrad, now tailed off into some perverted Synge. But three-fourths of it had been immensely fine.

Before hailing Miss Pauline Lord as a definitely great actress, I want to see her in some other part or parts. Her Anna is certainly an exquisite performance. Only a highly accomplished artist could have given that suggestion of childlikeness and *canaillerie*, of maiden virtue rudely strumpeted, of a loving heart, and the stare of the streets. Plain, if you like, slight, undistinguished, the actress gave you at her first entrance that indefinable sense of trouble which marks the great players; and she has the gift of melancholy. Her face, in repose, can show the ravages of past storms. When Duse played Marguerite Gautier she received Armand's love, Lemaître tells us, with a gesture of religious ecstasy quite outside Dumas's imagining. Whether Mr. O'Neill intended it or not, this Anna made a sacrificial offering of the sailor's wooing. Her hard yet frightened assurance, her vehemence when in her scene of passion she allowed the street to come to the surface, her pathos and even her queer fun were alike admirable. And the gesture of humility with which, at the end, she abased her head before her lover was one of the most beautiful I have ever seen. Mr. George Marion as the father was magnificent, and Mr. Frank Shannon only a little less good.

April 21, 1923

STRANGE INTERLUDE

BY EUGENE O'NEILL

(Lyric)

RALPH MORGAN, BASIL SYDNEY, MARY ELLIS

'MEANTERSAYING' plays a double rôle in this piece. It is its gist and the reason for its extraordinary length. As all the world knows by now, Mr. O'Neill makes his characters interlard everything they say with asides containing what they are really thinking. 'Having no hearts, partner?' has queried many a polite bridge-player when his mind was really saying: 'Why doesn't the silly fellow play a heart? I know he's got a fistful of 'em!' This illustration, though homely, is a good one if it serves to show Mr. O'Neill's new way with the aside. New, because it is claimed that our author is only doing elaborately what others have done sketchily. Shakespeare uses the soliloquy, so why shouldn't O'Neill? — is the argument. To which there is this answer, that they use it with a profound difference. Here and there in Shakespeare there may be a melodramatic villain who says one thing and goes on to explain that he means the exact opposite, whereas this is nearly the whole of Mr. O'Neill's method. We are to note that where the earlier dramatist is really in earnest he entirely abandons the aside at the very point where Mr. O'Neill would have most use for it. When Lady Macbeth welcomes Duncan to the castle she says: 'We rest your hermits!' and leaves it at that, whereas Mr. O'Neill would have made her add: 'And if my husband and I remain anything of the sort, our name isn't Cawdor!' In the great third act of *Othello* Shakespeare is content to let Iago's lies speak for themselves, just as he leaves it to his audience to find out for itself the truth about Lear's daughters. Briefly, Shakespeare uses the aside as an amplification, a foreshadowing, or a hint, whereas Mr. O'Neill uses it almost entirely in contradiction, a use which another good dramatist, Ibsen, utterly scorned.

Take that moment when Tesman returns home and Hedda asks him whether he enjoyed himself at Judge Brack's. Tesman says: 'Have you been anxious about me, eh?' and Hedda replies: 'No, I should never think of being anxious. But I asked if you had enjoyed yourself.' Whereby we see that Ibsen, being a dramatist to his finger-tips, has no need of an aside to explain Hedda's complete contempt for her husband. Mr. O'Neill cannot, or will not, do this by the *oratio recta* method, so to speak, and when in this play he wants to express Nina's contempt for her husband he must first plump Sam down on the sofa with some fatuously marital remark, in reply to which Nina has to voice to the audience her unspoken thought: 'God, give me the chance one day to tell this fool the truth!' As far as this part of the method is concerned it seems to me to show Mr. O'Neill not as a better, but as a much less good dramatist than his forerunners, any one of whom upon reading his script would probably have said: 'Capital notion, my boy. Why not make a play of it?'

The method is still further extended to tip the audience the wink as to matters which could not possibly be conveyed in stage dialogue. Thus one character will say about another: 'What about exploding a bomb under him and seeing if that will make him talk? But not too big a bomb or I shall frighten the speech out of him altogether!' Here, surely, Mr. O'Neill confounds the function of the playwright with that of the novelist, and indeed large portions of the play are like a novel read aloud, first the characters talking and then the author talking about his characters.

So much for the manner. What now of the matter to which it is applied? Here one must argue that a play which has been called a great tragedy must contain matter of universal interest, so that the normal audience can be subject to the familiar pity and terror. But this play's interest is particular even to the point of being 'curious', in the second-hand bookseller's sense of that word. Consider the theme. Nina loses her fiancé in the war, and, in despair at not having given herself to him, becomes the mistress of whoever cares to take her. To cure her of this, Darrell, a doctor, recommends marriage with Sam, an able-bodied simpleton. At this point the play completely breaks its back, because it can only be continued by the forced addition of a new theme which does not grow out of what has gone before. *It so happens* that Sam has a grandfather, a father, and even an aunt, who have all become insane, and Sam's mother informs Nina that she must not allow Sam's child to be born and that she must later bear him a child by some healthy father. Nina consents to both sacrifices, which is astonishing in a woman who nowhere exhibits fortitude, will, or any trait whatever except an overwhelming and predatory egotism. The rest of the play is a discussion as to whether Nina loves her dead fiancé, her husband, Darrell, who is her child's father, or the family friend who, in a part longer than Hamlet, has meandered introspectively throughout the play.

'It so happens', which was the strength of Greek drama dependent upon the whims of unreasonable gods, is a weakness in post-Shakespearean tragedy dependent upon human failings. There is no reason why Nina, recovering from her first emotional mischance, should have stumbled upon a husband with this medical history, though this does not mean more than that Mr. O'Neill has tried to make a whole out of one odd and one end. A more grievous fault is that this play has no discernible tragic implication. A tragedy, to be worth the name, must contain a moving and skilfully told story, profound analysis of human character, vitality, philosophical significance, beauty. The story of *Strange Interlude* is held together by the safety-pin of accident, and the technique of its telling is pretentious and wearisome. The characters are not human beings, but entries in a neuropath's case-book; few members of an audience will identify themselves with the sex-harassed virago who dominates this play, with her complex-ridden and unwholesome father, with the highly unprofessional doctor, or with the poor introspective fish. The play is morbid and rotten with decay; there is no vitality, vigour, or anything approaching life in it, and no character has any preoccupation except sex. The essence of tragedy is fallen nobility; there is nothing in this play's characters to lay low.

On the other side of the account must be put the fact that Mr. O'Neill has a mind, however much one may dislike its present texture. He has some of Strindberg's power of regarding the world as an asylum and peopling it appropriately, and the same uncanny gift of creating and holding you with his unpleasant situations. There can be no doubt about the reality of the characters who fascinate without arousing sympathy, and there is even the risk that an actress of genius will wheedle some sort of maudlin sympathy for Nina, continually yapping after happiness and doing nothing to deserve it. There is this to be said, too, that out of nothing nothing can be made, and that this company of very remarkable players could not have achieved its prodigies without some sufficient material. Miss Mary Ellis is a very good actress, and Mr. Erskine Sanford as the father, Mr. Basil Sydney as the doctor, Mr. Donald Macdonald as the husband, and Mr. Ralph Morgan as the poor fish all gave displays of acting founded on sheer brainwork, which compelled attention to the last of their far too many words. The audience was impressed by, in this order, the acting, the wilfully shabby scenery, the penumbral lighting, and the play's air of being the intellectual goods. But were I pressed for a summarized opinion as to whether *Strange Interlude* is a great play, I should reply in the words of Joe Gargery: 'Pip, which I meantersay that were not a question requiring a answer betwixt yourself and me, and which you know the answer to be full well No.'

February 3, 1931

MOURNING BECOMES ELECTRA
BY EUGENE O'NEILL
(Westminster)

MARK DIGNAM, ROBERT HARRIS, REGINALD TATE, BEATRIX LEHMANN, LAURIE COWIE

A POLICEMAN in one of Mr. Maugham's stories says: 'I don't believe remorse for a crime ever sits very heavily on a man when he's absolutely sure he will never be found out!' The essence of Greek tragedy, and this play is Greek tragedy, is that you can never be sure of not being found out, if it's only by your sin. The Ancients couldn't call it conscience, since Man, being the plaything of the gods, was not responsible as we moderns know responsibility. But even so there was something inside a man which was policeman, judge, jury, and conscience all rolled into one.

Professor Gilbert Murray pretends that Sophocles, that determined classicist, made Electra the pivot of a drama of matricide and high spirits. Euripides took a soberer view, and there is no doubt in my mind that Shakespeare would have taken the soberest of all if he had pursued the Gertrude-Clytemnestra issue instead of losing himself in the maze of Hamlet's mind. By the

354

way, would Mr. Shaw like to write us a sixth act of *Hamlet* in which the poison on the rapiers has lost its efficacy, and Hamlet is left alive to examine his conscience in the matter of his step-father's murder and his mother-complex? Like his predecessors, Mr. O'Neill is absolute for remorse, and, to conclude this part of the argument, if Mr. Maugham is in step a fair number of august people have been out of it!

Mourning Becomes Electra is about souls in hell. Black and spotted souls sporting on Hamlet's 'couch for luxury and damn'd incest'. No glimmer of hope pierces the blanket of this dark, which is thickened by pessimism and has all possible holes metaphysically stopped. Death has ceased to be the gateway to life; we are in a limbo in which all life opens the door to universal death. In the meantime there is existence here, and by the same token we are to bethink ourselves that this is an evening at the theatre, with readers expecting to be told whether they will enjoy the play or not! Let us inform them in our grandest style that we rate the evening among the six highest of our life, but that if they are searchers after pure diversion we recommend them to stay at home, draw up their chairs to an empty grate, and by some farthing dip discover in the pages of Emily Brontë entertainment less shiversome.

We warn such, however, that they would be missing tremendous theatre. Also that they would — and if I know anything about London playgoers they will! — miss some of the finest acting seen in our theatre since the War. Miss Beatrix Lehmann has for some time been knocking at the door marked 'Great Acting Only', and with this performance she gets in one foot and one shoulder — an awkward image, but one which, I venture to think, suits the strained intensity of this performance. Whole scenes of it demand that Electra shall be as silent as the Hungarian gentleman at another theatre; it is the actress who takes care that her silence shall shout the house down. Or you might write of this performance in terms of banked-up fires, crust over lava. The author has enjoined immobility upon his character; it is the actress who expresses that immobility in terms of a jaw slewed round. Miss Lehmann in her magnificent playing brings to mind two images. One of these, which is not too happy, will disappear when she is more practised in a part the mere apprehension of which would have struck most actresses stone dead. In the earlier acts she is, be it confessed, a little too poker-stiff, a little too much like Judy Smallweed as 'Phiz' saw that redoubtable young woman. But in the later scenes she replaces Smallweed by the great flower of French acting, Rachel, to whom she bears a remarkable physical resemblance. And on this is superimposed something else, something which is not Rachel acting, but Charlotte Brontë, who watched Rachel and realized with every fibre of her brain and body that Vashti was in hell.

Has Miss Laura Cowie quite enough guns for Clytemnestra? The point is that Clytemnestra carries enough guns to sink a whole battleship, or any actress unprovided with extraordinary genius; what this part demands is Mrs. Campbell at her greatest. Miss Cowie gives the very best of her very considerable means. There is no suggestion of failure, and perhaps the result might be described as a brilliant draw. Mr. Mark Dignam's Agamemnon in its stiff obstinacy and Mr. Robert Harris's Orestes in its slow awakening to lively horror are very fine performances. Mr. Reginald Tate's Ægisthus is a good study in the breezy-ominous, and the whole tragedy is knit together by the superb Chorus of Mr. John Abbott. Mr. Michael MacOwan has produced most admirably. I congratulate him on giving Mr. Brian Easdale his head with the music, and Mr. Easdale on using it. But what stroke of luck or imagination was it which suggested to Mr. MacOwan to make the houses of both Agamemnon and Ezra Mannon exactly like Ken Wood? Are we to gather that the tragic spirit is the same yesterday, to-day, and for ever?

November 19, 1937

DESIRE UNDER THE ELMS
BY EUGENE O'NEILL
(Westminster)

STEPHEN MURRAY, BEATRIX LEHMANN

THIS play seems to me to have been written backwards. The drama being elemental—for if Mr. O'Neill is not that he is nothing — let us look at some of the elementary differences between men and women. Would a man for love of a woman shave his beard, or grow one of those, when not obnoxious, foolish appendages? One conceives that this is possible. Would a man for a woman's sake exhibit himself in the clothes worn by, say, a member of the Hon. Ivo Bligh's Australian cricket team? At a pinch, yes. But not for ten thousand of Phoebus's amorous pinches would any woman shave her head or wear the tippets of yesteryear. Does the reader suspect flippancy? I have never been more serious in my life.

'I might give my life for my friend, but he had better not ask me to do up a parcel', says Mr. Logan Pearsall Smith. Mr. O'Neill's play asks us to believe that for the love of a man a woman will sacrifice something infinitely more important to her even than her personal appearance. To wit, her new-born child. Now women, I submit, don't do this thing for Mr. O'Neill's reason. Poor wretches do it out of fear, or shame, or starvation; but never to please the baby's father.

And now we must go back a little. Herr Hitler has laid it down that if you want to deceive a whole nation a little lie is of no use: it must be a whopper. Similarly, a playwright might argue that whereas a plain improbability will not take in an audience, a blazing one will do so for the time that that audience is in the theatre. No woman is going to kill an ordinary baby. But what about an extraordinary one? Which sets us asking: What could

357

there be about a baby to make it extraordinary? Might it not, for example, bring wealth in its train? Mr. O'Neill may very well have bethought him of Maupassant's long-short story *L'Héritage*, in which the *ménage* Lesable, unable to produce a child within the time specified in a capricious will, invite to dinner a certain M. Maze. This is a clerk in M. Lesable's bureau, concerning whom Mme. Lesable's father, equally teased by the itch for inheritance, says: 'Tu verras, c'est un rude gars, et un beau garçon. Il est haut comme un carabinier, il ne ressemble pas à ton mari, celui-là!'

And this is exactly Mr. O'Neill's situation, since Ephraim Cabot is seventy-six and his youngest son, Eben, is, like Maze, 'un rude gars et un beau garçon'. And the inheritance? Nothing less than the old man's farm, which, Abbie realizes, will if she fails to produce a child pass to her stepson. 'What', says the horrified reader, 'should this play's title be *A Village Phèdre*?' Mr. O'Neill may well have been aware that there are themes with which not even a Theatre Guild can, in the cant phrase, get away. And that an American setting-forth of Racine's re-statement of Euripides might be one of them. Why not another kind of enracination? Why not give the play roots in the wholly laudable theme of land-hunger?

Here comes a point which I do not remember to have seen made before. This is the unwritten law that in an elemental play not only the plot but the relationship of everybody in it to everybody else must be intensely difficult to grasp. (I challenge any playgoer to say that at a first seeing he has ever been able to get the hang of *Œdipus Rex*.) Mr. O'Neill's play is no exception to this rule, the difficulty being to disentangle Ephraim Cabot's wives. Shakily we constate the existence of three. There was the first wife who gave him Simeon and Peter. (Since these oafs have no part in the Phaedra section of the plot, they must be got rid of. Whence their land-hunger must not be for their father's farm but for the far-away goldfields of California.) Then there was his second wife, the mother of the *rude gars* Eben, who appears, in some way which Mr. O'Neill does not make clear, to have proprietary rights in Ephraim's farm. At least her ghost is said to walk, not to be laid until . . .

Into this kettle of alarmingly Greek fish comes Abbie, the third wife, no more explained by Mr. O'Neill than the motiveless goddesses whom Euripides got to help him launch his play. Why should Abbie, still presentable at thirty-five, throw herself away on a man of seventy-six? What is there about Abbie which has prevented her from finding a husband in the whole of New England? Is it old-maidishness? Not a bit of it, as her invocation to the propagating virtues of sunshine sufficiently proves. Is it that the men who wanted her were insufficiently endowed with this world's goods? We hazard yes, since Abbie's first words proclaim her the very goddess of cupidity. And since goddesses are not susceptible of mortal explanation, the playgoer is not bothered when this elemental creature turns out to be as complicated as the heroine of any modern, ultra-sophisticated novel. Abbie wants to have a baby, first because the sun stirs the primitive mother in her, second because the baby will give her possession of the farm, and third because at first sight she has taken a liking to her stepson, which liking deepens into love so strong that it leads her to the sacrifice with which we began. And why should Abbie suppose the baby to come between her and Eben? Because old Ephraim in the first fury of cuckoldom apprised Eben of Abbie's Reason Number Two for wanting to become a mother.

Well, there is your play, and I was staggered to read in some printed matter sent out by the Westminster Theatre how I must realize 'that the fiercest passions of primitive people can be ennobled and given a new significance by an artist who believes unflinchingly in the ultimate "innocence" of human nature'. I do not understand this. Though you surround 'innocence' with a cartload of inverted commas, I do not see how the word can be applied to a woman who seduces her stepson and smothers his baby, or to a son who yields to his stepmother in order to lay his own mother's ghost! Twenty years of living among Old England farmers have convinced me that such a pair would make much of their baby, agree to smother the old man, and inherit and enjoy the farm. And I regard Mr. O'Neill's 'interpretation' of these New England animalities as merely more of the Higher Guff. Obviously in a drama about dumb cattle a tongue must be provided for them. Where I fault this play is that its characters, instead of speaking with the newly-descended tongues of cattle, blurt out what might be felt by high-powered beings astray in their byre.

Will dunderheads please note that my view of this play is my own and not intended to be anybody else's, that it may well be a masterpiece, that the first-night audience was much impressed, and that nothing hereinbefore contained is to dissuade anybody from seeing a production for which at this particular moment in our theatre's history all thinking playgoers should be profoundly grateful! As theatre it is increasingly and cumulatively effective; the play's handwriting is always that of a master. Miss Beatrix Lehmann, while not making us wholly believe in Abbie, plays like a Theatre Guild star acting her darnedest. But cannnot Mr. Stephen Murray for once in a way cast his nighted colour off? As *beau garçon* his Eben is altogether too rasping. Easily the best performance comes from Mr. Mark Dignam, who seems to me to make old Ephraim as thoroughly American as Hardy's Mayor of Casterbridge is English.

January 24, 1940

IDIOT'S DELIGHT

BY ROBERT E. SHERWOOD

(Apollo)

RAYMOND MASSEY, TAMARA GEVA

Ils virent Barnabé qui, devant l'autel de la sainte Vierge, la
tête en bas, les pieds en l'air, jonglait avec six boules de cuivre
et douze couteaux. Il faisait, en l'honneur de la sainte Mère
de Dieu, les tours qui lui avaient valu le plus de louanges.
—ANATOLE FRANCE, *Le Jongleur de Notre-Dame*

THIS is not the occasion or the place for an essay on the difference
between the average Englishman, who probably exists, and the
average American, who certainly doesn't. But any such essay
would fail if it did not stress the Englishman's view of art and
artists. In England no man is considered a serious artist who does
not take himself seriously. Not his art, mark you, but himself! Consider the esteem in which, since he composed oratorios,
Michael Costa was held, and the regard lavished upon Edwin
Long, whose 'religious' pictures, framed in black velvet, drew a
congregation rivalling Spurgeon's. Another odd thing about
your Englishman is that the more serious the matter, the more he
likes to be bored. Murder is a serious matter. The most successful serious play of modern times is undoubtedly Mr. T. S.
Eliot's *Murder in the Cathedral*. Since I have only read this play
but not seen it, I am not competent to pronounce upon its entertainment value as an acted thing, though I suspect it of not being
wholly gay. I base my suspicion on a sentence by my ever-trust-
worthy colleague Mr. Ivor Brown: 'Exposed to the holy chanting,
the smell of incense, and the sermonizing of Becket, one soon, a
trifle wearily, decides that no play in London more thoroughly
deserves to be let off entertainment duty.'

Now, modern warfare is mass murder, and your serious Englishman desires that mass murder should be treated *ex cathedra*. Therefore, he argues, a play about war should be in verse, chanted by

a chorus of flat young ladies singing slightly sharp. Is such a piece of work a feeble echo of that great war play which Euripides called *The Trojan Women*? Never mind. War is a serious subject and must receive serious treatment. And the audience, having yawned its fill of edification, goes home to uninterrupted sleep. But since bombs fall upon serious and non-serious alike, what about the frivolous-minded and their right to expression? Shall they not be permitted juggler's licence? Mr. Eliot does not write in the Sherwood manner. Why should we expect Mr. Sherwood to write in the Eliot manner? If one wanted a serious American war play, Mr. Maxwell Anderson is, as Bunthorne would say, the shop for it. Mr. Sherwood is a horse of a very different colour. He writes pungent, satirical comedies to please the hard-bitten, hard-boiled audiences of New York. His vein is lighter than Anderson's, though less light than Kaufman's. *Idiot's Delight* is true to this vein. It is that new thing — a tragic farce. In a postscript to this play Mr. Sherwood has written: 'I believe that a sufficient number of people are aware of the persistent validity of the Sermon on the Mount.' And here is his offering in support of that belief.

No! The weakness of this play is not the form in which it is cast, or its plot, which is a harum-scarum affair about the guests at an hotel in Central Europe demolished by enemy aeroplanes. (Perhaps I am not quite satisfied about the mechanics of the imbroglio, and perhaps I find the character-drawing a shade wobbly.) But the real weakness is in the polemics which are this play's kernel. Among the characters is one of those rich international thugs who, as financiers, armament-makers, or what not, pull the strings releasing the bombs. His mistress rounds on him in a tremendous tirade prophesying the end of an English boy and girl honeymooning in the hotel. She foretells that he will die as a soldier, and here is the rest of the speech as given in New York, though stupidly weakened here:

Before the moment of death he consoles himself by thinking: 'Thank God *she* is safe! She is bearing the child I gave her, and he will live to see a better world!' But I know where she is. She is lying in a cellar that has been wrecked by an air raid, and her firm young breasts are all mixed up with the bowels of a dismembered policeman . . .

Mr. Sherwood has seen that for his piece to rise above melodrama he must provide his thug with an answer. He does his best, but it is not good enough.

Readers will not have forgotten the magnificent case which Mr. Shaw made for the burning of that innocent and pious maid Joan. Some dazzling polemic would doubtless make a case for the burning of the innocent and the pious in a world war. Did not Henley write:

> In a golden fog,
> A large, full-stomached faith in kindliness
> All over the world, the nation, in a dream
> Of money and love and sport, hangs at the paps
> Of well-being, and so
> Goes fattening, mellowing, dozing, rotting down
> Into a rich deliquium of decay.

And did he not go on to argue that 'if the Gods be good, if the gods be other than mischievous', then comes the swoop of war?

> And in wild hours
> A people, roaring ripe
> With victory, rises, menaces, stands renewed,
> Sheds its old piddling aims,
> Approves its virtue, puts behind itself
> The comfortable dream, and goes,
> Armoured and militant,
> New-pithed, new-souled, new-visioned, up the steeps
> To those great altitudes, whereat the weak
> Live not. But only the strong
> Have leave to strive, and suffer, and achieve.

Henley's poem is dated 1901, and it may be that he would sing another tune to-day. But his case, weak though it is, is better than that of Mr. Sherwood's armament-maker:

Apply your intelligence, my dear. Ask yourself: why shouldn't these young people die? And who are the greater criminals — those who sell the instruments of death, or those who buy them, and use them? You know there is no logical reply to that. But all these little people — like your new friends — all of them consider me an arch-villain because I furnish them with what they want, which is the illusion of power. That is what they vote for in their frightened Governments — what they cheer for on their national holidays — what they glorify in their anthems, and their monuments, and their waving flags! Yes — they shout bravely about something they call 'national honour'. And what does it amount to? Mistrust of the motives of everyone else! Dog-in-the-manger defence of what they've got, and greed for the other fellow's possessions! Honour among thieves! I assure you, Irene — for such little people the deadliest weapons are the most merciful.

Of the play's theatrical effectiveness there can be no question; my only doubts are as to its cogency. It is not a masterpiece of argument. It is very nearly a masterpiece of light theatre with a core of thought, and, as such, a play which nobody else could have written. There is one brilliant performance. This is Mr. Raymond Massey's impersonation of a third-rate cabaret-artist travelling with six blonde dancers. This is a death's-head spouting braggadocio, chap-fallen and boasting. It catches perfectly the American note — the inferiority complex hiding behind a shield of strut and bombast. There is a fine piece of hysteria by Mr. Carl Jaffé as a professional agitator, and the honey-mooners are played with beautiful simplicity by Mr. Valentine Dyall and Miss Janet Johnson. Mr. Franklin Dyall accomplishes the feat of submerging his very strong personality in that of a German scientist, but I must be forgiven if I do not think that world-thugs have the sensitiveness which Mr. Hugh Miller inescapably suggests.

And now I come to the delicate question of Miss Tamara Geva. Delicate because the part of the armament-maker's mistress was written for Miss Lynn Fontanne, who is a practised comédienne, and because, though Miss Geva is a very intelligent young lady, she obviously lacks experience and authority, and Irene must be crammed to the teeth with both. To put it kindly, I think her art wants another ten years.

March 22, 1938

PARADISE LOST

BY CLIFFORD ODETS

(Stage Society)

NOEL HOWLETT, BARBARA COUPER

PERHAPS it will clear the ground if I say that this failure is better value for money, dramatically, emotionally, and in the scale of pure entertainment, than all of London's current successes put together, bar two plays that I have seen and one that I haven't! Watching this piece, any knowledgeable playgoer must say to himself: 'The fellow's a born dramatist!' at least once every five minutes, whereas your fashionable authors might just as well have been shopwalkers, toastmasters, or shoemakers who have wearied of their lasts. When Mr. Odets's *Golden Boy* was produced a well-known English novelist and playwright wrote to me protesting that this was a hokum play without integrity: 'Practically every scene is jazzed up, given more punch and excitement and noise than it should have, without reference to reality at all.' Now it was Ibsen's way, when told what message he ought to have preached instead of the one he actually did preach, to write his next play according to the prescription enjoined upon him, and to disgruntle his audience more than ever. I am not very clear about the dates of Mr. Odets's plays. But of this I am sure: either *Paradise Lost* was written to confound the detractors of *Golden Boy* or vice versa. And my impression is that vice versa wins. The whole atmosphere is one of complete integrity. There is not an inch of intentional hokum to be glimpsed, and every scene, and every line of every scene, has reference to reality. Indeed, there are so many references to reality that the poor thing is buried beneath them.

At this point I have to put the vulgar question — what, in this piece, is Mr. Odets getting at? The answer would appear to be — social conditions in a Capitalist state, the method used being the old one of faulty analogy. Now we know that the strength of a chain is its weakest link, the speed of an army the pace of its slowest footslogger, and so forth. But we also judge the height of a mountain-range by its peaks, and the genius of a Beethoven by his symphonies and not his Turkish Marches. Is an economic system to be judged by its successes or by its failures? I suggest that both tests are wrong, and that the test of a civilization is not its tyrants or its slaves, but the general run of happiness among its wage-earners. The cross-section of society which Mr. Odets has chosen to show us is a miasmatic welter of failure, decay, and death. Mr. Odets, an American, tells me that the home of the Gordons is what you may expect under a Capitalist régime. I, as an Englishman whose acquaintance with America is limited to a three weeks' visit to New York, tell Mr. Odets (*a*) that he cannot produce such a home, and (*b*) that if he can, the life contained therein would be equally catastrophic under Socialism, Communism, or any other 'ism'. These people are without virtue, and their faults cry to heaven. What's the good of blaming Capitalism?

Let us look briefly at the weird collection pinned by Mr. Odets to his stage as a butterfly is pinned to a showcase. Leo Gordon is a spineless, nostalgic, vapourizing manufacturer who would lose money in a tobacco kiosk. He has been for some years in partnership with a Mr. Katz without discovering that his partner has the soul of a thug and the mind of a fire-raiser. Katz would also be a hundred per cent sadist if he were not also a hundred per cent coward, and, moreover, the victim of some obscure disease. Gordon has three children. Ben is an amateur sprinter with the mind of a professional gigolo; he marries a wanton and joins in partnership with his wife's lover, who is a taxi-driver turned gangster. The second son is dying of sleeping sickness, and there is a sleepy daughter who, by giving music lessons, appears to earn the only money coming into the house. Her heart is broken because some down-at-heel young man, who ought to be behind a counter selling gloves, wants to be an orchestral conductor, but, finding competition with the Toscaninis and the Barbirollis too keen, mooches off to Chicago. Lastly, Gordon has a wife, a self-complacent, detached creature who wears delightful silk stockings and goes out to play bridge. I do not believe that any American middle-class family as unpretty as this one owes its unprettiness to Capitalism, Communism, or any other 'ism'.

Now let us be fair to Mr. Odets. It is a first-class mistake in criticism to dislike the whole of a piece because there are aspects of it with which one is unfamiliar. *This play is American,* and we must not be put off because it is not English. The set, designed by Mr. Hamish Wilson and passed by Mr. Guy Glover, the producer, suggests to the English eye the hall of some noble mansion behind whose folding doors footmen preening their calves prepare to announce the Duchess of Road and Lady Agatha Mender. The English playgoer is necessarily a little at sea when into this magnificent apartment, alleged to be the living-room of the Gordons, irrupt without waiting to be announced a boiler-stoker and a queer little piano-tuner who seems to be a mixture of Quilp and Little Nell's grandfather. The latter character, who has the biggest part in the play, is always cropping up in American comedy, one of the variants being Grandpa in *You Can't Take It With You.* He is a master of foolish saws and antique instances, all of them disconnected. When, then, the stage is cleared for this odd creature who has spent all night in gaol, a stoker in dungarees, and the dying boy who has now exchanged a dinner-jacket for a silk dressing-gown, the English playgoer may be excused if he finds that his finger is not, so to speak, on the American social pulse. This, however clearly one may recognize the fault as that not of the patient but of the pulse-feeler, does make it difficult for us.

Despite this difficulty three things emerge from this play. First, that Mr. Odets holds the attention of the spectator with every word he writes and every pause he enjoins. Second, that he is a born dramatist whom no amount of pretentious thinking can make into anything else. Third, that what he has tried to say in this play is complete nonsense. In the end the ruined manufacturer, whose furniture has been piled on the sidewalk, has a lyrical passage in which he expresses his conviction that in the failure of the individual is to be read hope for the nation as a whole. Which, of course, is bunk, and pretentious bunk. Why, then, do I say that this play is better than all London's commercial successes? Because it is brainy nonsense about things worth thinking about. Because this doesn't bore me and those do. Because I prefer sitting up in protest to lying on my neck yawning till my spectacles fall off into the lap of the stall-holder in the row behind me.

The piece was brilliantly acted by an assemblage of players relying on their talents rather than their reputations. So faithfully and sensitively acted that apologists for Mr. Odets must not try to ride off on the plea that his play was insufficiently interpreted. I shall select for special mention Messrs. Noel Howlett, Alan Wheatley, Christopher Steele, Gordon Brown, Guy Glover, Alan Keith, and George Benson, and Mesdames Barbara Couper, Nell Carter, and Ilona Ference.

December 11, 1938

OF MICE AND MEN

BY JOHN STEINBECK

(Gate)

JOHN MILLS, NIALL MACGINNIS, CLAIRE LUCE

WHEN I was in New York two years ago I called at Brentano's and asked them to give me the book most representative of what young America was thinking. Brentano's handed me not *Gone with Aurora Borealis* or other spinsterish guff running to 1072 pages, but a book the length of a long-short story by Joseph Conrad and called *Of Mice and Men.* I gave this novel immense praise in the columns of the *Sunday Times,* and then persuaded the *Daily Express* to serialize it. The next step in the book's history was its dramatization in New York, where the play ran for nearly two years. That the big film studios would studiously ignore it was obvious. For the story is what in the 'nineties we were calling a slice of life, meaning something raw and bleeding, whereas what Hollywood means by a slice of life is a cream puff drenched with Chanel No. 6.

Again, the film public would not stand for such a story without drastic alteration. For it is a law of the cinema that in a film in which a platinum cutie and a tousled husky have a broken neck between them, the neck must be that of the husky and broken while accomplishing some act of obeisance to femininity. And in Mr. Steinbeck's story it is the neck of, if you please, the cutie which gets broken, just as a mouse and a puppy-dog have already had their necks broken by the simpleton husky who does not know how strong he is.

Is this an appalling tragedy? Yes. But it is not the girl's, since we are no more concerned for her than we are for that mouse and that puppy. The tragedy is that of Lennie the husky, and even more of his friend George, who has nursed and fenced in Lennie throughout his horribly precarious existence, and must now shoot him to avoid his inevitable lynching at the hands of the cutie's husband and the other ranchers. Obviously there is not a scenario-monger living who would touch such a plot. His kind realizes that what the film-goer wants to see is a Norma or a Loretta extravagantly alive and not expensively dead. Also that in the eyes of the one-and-ninepennies the Georges and the Lennies are pure thugs, to be kept in their place, which is the edge of a picture and not the centre. However, it is early days, and I have no doubt that we shall presently be given a film entitled *Of Mice and Women* in which the batting order will be the lynching of Lennie, the discovery that the cutie's neck was only bruised, the dispensing with the cutie's husband, her marriage with George, who until then has not, as they say, spoken, the further discovery that George is not a rancher at all but the son of Mervyn T. Huggermugger, the Brooklyn Chewing-Gum King, and the revelation that the cutie is not a cutie at all but a blonde who was platinum at birth!

In the meantime the production of the play in London has been left to one of the coterie theatres. This is odd because there is nothing spruce, affected, or, as Shakespeare's Holofernes would say, peregrinate about it, depite the fact that Lennie and George are, strictly speaking, peregrinators. In other words, they are Californian hoboes or tramps, whereas by all the coterie laws they should be ghosts, or souls of mummies, or other-selves, or characters out of the lost plays of Æschylus. But George and Lennie are none of these things. They are just a pair of ordinary, dirty, unsavoury tramps, chained to the pettifoggery of three-dimensional existence. And what do the pair stand for? The poetry of earth? The prose of humanity? The redemption of capital through the sweat of labour? Aw, shucks!

Here is a passage which continually recurs like a litany, showing how far removed is the earthly paradise of George and Lennie from the signs and symbols of the metaphysical dramatist. This is what they look forward to:

Got a little win'mill. Got a little shack on it, an' a chicken run. Little fat iron stove, an' in the winter we'd keep a fire goin' in it. It ain't enough land so we'd have to work too hard. Maybe six, seven hours a day. An' we'd keep a few pigeons to go flyin' around the win'mill. An' it'd be our own, an' nobody could can us. If we don't like a guy we can say, 'Get the hell out', and by God he's got to do it. An' if a fren' come along, why we'd have an extra bunk, an' we'd say: 'Why don't you spen' the night', an' by God he would. An' if a circus or a ball game came to town we'd just go to her. We wouldn't ask nobody if we could. Jus' say: 'We'll go to her', an' we would.

This is something which has been in the mind of man since the first delver — a handspan of land on which he shall be his own master, of earth fertilized by the sweat of his brow and the rain from heaven.

The play is the oldest and most intelligible of poems, mercifully free from the newest and least intelligible of poetry. It is grandly acted. As the dumb giant Mr. Niall MacGinnis, who has hitherto been merely feeling his way as an actor, arrives at something that is very close to power; Lennie's inarticulacy is the most articulate thing this young and promising player has yet done. As George Mr. John Mills provides the most explicit and direct of foils. Here is another young actor on whose previous admirable work this performance of shrewdness, subtlety, and pathos sets a seal. I warn him, however, not to expect the highbrows to cotton to him on the strength of a commonplace young man with a penchant for pigeons flying round a windmill. A Greek reincarnation absorbed in the wheeling flight of his ancestors' spotted souls would be another matter!

Miss Claire Luce handles the cutie with all possible discretion, cleverly making us feel that the girl is neither wholly bad nor wholly good, and that it is merely a matter of circumstance that she has found her way to the barley-fields. Another turn of the wheel and she might have adorned a heavyweight champion's two-seater or a film magnate's limousine. Wholly authentic, as I judge, and well diversified performances are given by Messrs.

Sydney Benson, Edward Wallace, Nicholas Stuart, Robert Berkeley, Richard Rudi, Jefferson Searles, and Conway Palmer. It is all nonsense that this piece is not playing at a big public theatre instead of a small private one. In the meantime all honour to the little Gate Theatre.

April 12, 1939

THE WOMEN

BY CLARE BOOTHE

(Lyric)

MISS BOOTHE would have done well to take a leaf out of another book and issue as *First Aid to the English Dramatic Critics* her admirable preface to the printed version of her play. Had she done so we might have been spared a humiliating display of muddled thinking on the part of that critical fraternity which Mr. Max Beerbohm once described as 'a fine body of men, like the Metropolitan Police'.

'A crude, coarse narrative of the sexual jungle . . . beauty parlours, exercise salons, bedrooms, bathrooms, and jaded, arid dialogue by grim women about men and money and money and men', sniffs Distinguished Colleague A. This is like complaining that Ibsen's *Ghosts* is a crude, coarse play about transmitted disease, with grim, unpoetical dialogue between a hidebound pastor and a woman who didn't have the sense to leave her husband. Surely A has fallen into the old critical trap of mis-liking a play through dislike of its subject-matter?

Eminent Colleague B thinks that the play is 'pretty horrible' and goes on: 'This is a satire which in New York bites home. Here, it is not true and fails to bite.' Again I rub my eyes. Why should a play which is about a restricted New York coterie be supposed to apply to the women who do their shopping in Kensington? And what does B's second sentence mean? Will he hold that because the plays of, say, Tchehov are not true to

English character, they must fail to bite when performed over here? One might as justly complain that the remedy for African beri-beri is no cure for a whooping-cough in Bayswater.

Cherished and Revered Critic C is of the opinion that Miss Boothe's picture is 'grossly inaccurate', and for the reason that 'no capital in the world could contain in one area such a collection of tedious harridans . . . a very *common* play'. So Sheridan's Mr. Sneer on the morning after the first performance of *The School for Scandal* might be imagined as saying: 'A very common play, egad, and vastly inaccurate. Where in St. James's will you encounter these Candours, Sneerwells, Teazles? I vow they are but Mr. Sheridan's foppery!'

Now let us find out how much of all this Miss Boothe foresaw. Her preface begins with the categorical statement: '*The Women* is a satirical play about a numerically small group of ladies native to the Park Avenues of America. It was clearly so conceived and patently so executed. The title, which embraces half the human species, is therefore rather too roomy. . . . The play is a clinical study of a more or less isolated group, projected, perhaps, in bad temper, but in good faith.' From which it surely appears that the play is not to be judged as a study of women in Kensington or Kidderminster, Kenya or Kamchatka, or anywhere except a tiny, highly circumscribed area of America's capital cities.

Miss Boothe, still in her categorical vein, asks: 'Is this play "a crime against the spirit"? Does it "degrade the whole human race"?' She goes on: 'A good misogynist would quote Mr. Burke as the ungallant author of the brute statement: "A woman is an animal, and an animal not of the highest order." Strindberg, Schopenhauer, Ibsen, and a great horde of other bilious misogynists, including St. Paul, could then be called upon to uphold speciously, no doubt, but brilliantly that loutish definition. But I have no heart for the easy game of woman-baiting. . . . I truly, heartily, and thankfully echo the cry of all who have been revolted by the *specific* bitterness of *The Women* that "*All* women are not like that!" ' From which it would seem fairly obvious that Miss

Boothe does not intend *The Women* to be a portrait of all women.

Now is the play true to *any* women? Miss Boothe says: 'Whether or not this play is a good *play* is any man's business to say. But whether or not it is a portrait of *such* women is a matter which no man can adequately judge, for the good reason that all their actions and emotions are shown forth in places and times which no man has ever witnessed.' Is the behaviour of these women condoned, which would certainly make this a bad play? Or are they held to execration, which does not necessarily make it a good play, but keeps the door open? Read Miss Boothe: 'The women who inspired this play deserved to be smacked across the head with a meat-axe. And that, I flatter myself, is exactly what I smacked them with. They are vulgar and dirty-minded, and alien to grace, and I would not if I could gloss their obscenities with a wit which is foreign to them, and gild their futilities with a glamour which by birth and breeding and performance they do not possess. Everything they say and do is in deplorable taste, because everything I have ever heard such women say and do *is* in deplorable taste.'

Is the play poor considered as a piece of plot-making? Miss Boothe has her answer: 'The plot is deliberately a commonplace squirrel-cage, full of holes, getting nowhere, serving only the purpose of further emphasizing the minuscule, foolish, whirligig activities of a few cancerous little squirrels, whose little cheeks bulge with rotten little nuts, which in their civilized little cage they have neither the wit, nor the grace, to hide.' And then comes the final challenge to the playgoer: 'That the antics of these women do strike most audiences as funny, instead of dull or nauseating, is a very happy accident for me at the box-office.' And just to make assurance doubly sure Miss Boothe winds up her case by saying: 'But indeed, if one is not susceptible to these women's ludicrousness, tickled by their gargantuan absurdities, one is quite justified in being either bored or appalled by them.'

So there you have it! If you are bereft of logic and/or a sense of fun, if you hold the Coventry Patmore or 'Angel in the House' view of women, if you stamp indignantly about the foyer, as I saw one man do, barking: 'Thank heaven, our Englishwomen are not like that!'—why then, this play, which in my opinion is the wittiest in ten years, is not for you. For once in a way I range myself with the younger school of critics. With Mr. Lionel Hale, who descibed it as a play about Cressida written by Thersites. With Mr. Alan Dent, who makes no bones about calling it a 'scathing, shocking, searing, sizzling, and almost unbelievably witty play'. I have no doubt that I shall presently resume quarrelling with this Blest Pair of Sirens. But for the moment the alliance stands firm. Having seen the play in New York, where it ran for two years, I firmly decline to say anything about the way it is acted over here. My dislike of second elevens would make me unfair to a performance which anyhow is plenty good enough. All that remains for me is to thank Miss Boothe for having written my notice for me!

April 20, 1939

INDEX

INDEX

INDEX

INDEX

INDEX

INDEX